TREASON'S PEACE

HOWARD WATSON AMBRUSTER

TREASON'S PEACE

GERMAN DYES & AMERICAN DUPES

A CROSSROADS PRESS BOOK

NEW YORK: THE BEECHHURST PRESS

A NOTE OF APPRECIATION AND GRATITUDE

The material for this volume would neither have been assembled nor recorded here except for the loyalty and sacrifice of Ursula Ambruster, whose unswerving support despite years of hardship, made it possible for both of us to carry on.

The author is deeply indebted to a number of others whose assistance and support have made possible the preparation of this book. To name a few of these would be unfair to the others; to name all of those who have aided me would result in disaster to those to whom I should not, knowingly, bring disaster. But I would be lacking in candor if I did not express here my profound appreciation to Jack Morris, to whose untiring efforts its final publication is largely due, and to Jack Shuttleworth, for his collaboration in the preparation of this volume. I pay grateful tribute also to the fact that, as strangers to me, Jack Shuttleworth and Jack Morris came forward from the throng who turned away.

THE AUTHOR

Contents

DEDICATED TO

CAPTAIN WATSON AMBRUSTER II, U.S.A. AIR FORCE
AND TO HIS CHILDREN,
WATSON III AND MARGARET URSULA,
FOR WHOSE FUTURE SECURITY, WITH
THOSE OF THEIR GENERATION, THIS STORY
HAS BEEN WRITTEN.

The Pattern of Farben

THE HUGE INTERNATIONAL chemical combine and cartel leader that is known today as I. G. Farben had its beginning some seventy-five years ago, with the founding in Germany of six small coal-tar dye companies. By 1939 these six companies had grown into the ominous-sounding INTERESSEN GEMEINSCHAFT FARBENINDUSTRIE AKTIENGESELLSCHAFT, of FRANKFORT am MAIN, which translated literally, means "community of interests of the dye manufacturing companies."

I. G. Farben is usually discussed as a huge German cartel which controls chemical industries throughout the world and from which profits flow back to the headquarters in Frankfort. Farben, however, is no mere industrial enterprise conducted by Germans for the extraction of profits at home and abroad. Rather, it is and must be recognized as a cabalistic organization which, through foreign subsidiaries and by secret tie-ups, operates a far-flung and highly efficient espionage machine—the ultimate purpose being world conquest—and a world super-state directed by Farben.

Perhaps the chief distinguishing characteristic of this vast organization is the definite pattern to which it holds. From its beginning the Farben pattern—based upon intensive research wedded to applied science, plus a cynical disbelief in the existence of social, economic, or political morality—has never varied; its rhythm appears changeless.

This book is the story of the Farben pattern—as it has appeared in the United States, and a glimpse of its extent in Latin America. It is a story of the shadowy designs that repeatedly have come up through the fabric of our industrial, social, and political life.

Viewed over a long period of years it appears as an interlocking design of propaganda, espionage, sabotage, and corruption.

Fragments of this pattern have been revealed to the public from time to time in press reports of official investigations and court actions here in the United States. These detached items, however, could mean little to the public. To understand their significance—as a part of a never ending menace to world peace—the activities of Farben must be traced from the beginning, and chronicled in some kind of sequence.

The events in this story are not set forth in chronological order. Rather, they are grouped according to subject matter—to bring out the many designs of the pattern, and to make clear each phase of the menace that is Farben. Space does not permit a history of this nebulous structure, or the part it has played in German politics—in making Hitler Chancellor, and providing money and munitions for his armies.

For more than forty years the author, through business, professional and official contacts, has followed the activities of this colossal cartel structure and its predecessors, the "Big Six" dyestuff companies. He has followed the establishment of their chemical cartels in this country prior to the first World War; the partial destruction of those monopolies during that war; and the rebuilding, in the next two decades, of a far stronger and more sinister framework inside our militarily strategic industries, our agencies of public opinion, and the very fabric of government itself.

He believes that the story told here shows clearly that Farben was largely responsible for our spiritual and physical disarmament when the present war began—just as the Big Six was largely responsible for our unarmed condition at the start of the first World War.

He believes also, that the story shows what we may expect from Farben during the peace.

It is well to say now that every statement of fact in this book is supported by irrefutable evidence in the form of official documents, court records, or private papers. From these the reader may draw his own conclusions regarding the guilt or gullibility—or both—of some of those American citizens who find mention in these pages.

Be it admitted that unhappy instances of corruption, double dealing and cupidity appear and reappear in our history from the earliest days of this republic and will continue—yet a distinction must be made between ordinary violations of our criminal statutes and those committed, or secretly instigated, by an enemy which is obsessed with the lust of enslaving this nation.

This, then, is the pattern of Farben.

CHAPTER I

Graft—and America Unarmed

ON A STORMY
evening early in 1912, a raiding party armed with a search warrant
proceeded to one of the fashionable residential districts of Philadelphia, broke down the door, and ransacked the apartment of one
Alfred J. Keppelmann.

Mr. Keppelmann was the executive in charge of the Philadelphia
office of the American Bayer Company, owned and directed by
one of the leading German dyestuff manufacturers. The local office
of the Bayer company was at 9 North Water Street, but the young
attorney who led the raiding party had been tipped off that Mr.
Keppelmann kept his more important business correspondence in
his home.

The tip was a good one and resulted in a rich yield of evidences
of bribery and fraud engaged in by Mr. Keppelmann over a period
of years.

Thus was launched an exposé of commercial corruption that is
without parallel in the history of legitimate business in the United
States. But that raid was the first of a long series of ineffectual
blows at the German-controlled chemical cartels that for seventy-
five years have operated within our borders—ineffectual because

they have not yet destroyed the corrupt influence and power of these monopolies, whose purpose, since their inception, has been to stifle our military effectiveness and to strengthen the resources of the Fatherland.

The leading German chemical companies before the first World War were known throughout the world as the Big Six. Direct predecessors of the gigantic I. G. Farbenindustrie, in which they were later merged, these six companies were:

1. Badische Anilin und Sodafabrik. (known as Badische)
2. Farbenfabriken vorm. Friedr. Bayer & Co. (known as Bayer or Elberfeld)
3. Aktiengesellschaft für Anilinfabrikation. (known as the Berlin Company)
4. Farbwerke vorm. Meister Lucius und Brüning. (known as the Hoechst Co.)
5. Leopold Cassella G. m. b. H. in Frankfurt. (known as Cassella)
6. Kalle & Company. (known as Kalle)

All of these companies made dyestuffs and the intermediates from which coal-tar dyes are produced; several of them also produced pharmaceutical products from coal-tar intermediates and other chemical bases.

There were numerous other smaller German dyestuff producers but these six concerns, with several hundred million dollars in assets, united early in the century in two cartels, dominated the coal-tar industry in Germany, and controlled the world's markets for dye stuffs.

In America, where business was a strictly private affair, and all attempts at government supervision were fought tooth and nail by our rugged individualists, the Big Six found fertile ground for their "peaceful penetration." Here in America with the cooperation of the German government, they established their agencies, and pursued a ruthless policy of economic strangulation, with the result that upon our entry into World War I, America's organic chemical industry, the very lifeblood of modern warfare, consisted of little more than a series of small assembly plants.

The completeness with which we failed to develop this militarily strategic industry attests the determination of purpose and the typical German thoroughness with which the representatives of *Kultur* carried out, within our borders, their coordination of industry with the forces of war.

The early history of these six German companies takes in the birth of the commercial development of dyes made from coal tar. Three generations ago these dyes began to replace many of the natural or vegetable dyes. However, it was not a German, but a young English chemist, William H. Perkin, who discovered in 1856 that a usable purple, or mauve color, could be produced from aniline, the oil-like product distilled from coal tar, which had been produced originally in 1826.

History records that young Perkin was not attempting to make a dyestuff at the time, but was experimenting, unsuccessfully, with the aniline in an attempt to produce synthetic quinine. Some 70 years later, one of Farben's chemists succeeded in doing what Perkin had set out to do and produced the coal-tar derivative known as Atabrine which today, as a substitute for quinine, occupies such a vital place in our control of malaria.

It was the Germans, however, who most industriously followed up Perkin's discovery of an aniline dye. Intensive research was encouraged at German universities, and by subsidies from the German government. The late Congressman Nicholas Longworth told of a conversation he had with a distinguished American chemist who had graduated from the University of Heidelberg many years before, and who told Longworth that when he said goodbye to his head professor he asked why it was that so much of the German research work in chemistry was in the development of coal-tar dyes. The professors so engaged were receiving higher salaries than their colleagues, and the industries were receiving government bonuses. The German professor replied, "Young man, some day this work will save the Fatherland." In light of more recent events, that professor can hardly be considered a good prophet, but his remark indicated the early German vision of world supremacy in science—out of which the Farben pattern of world conquest was to emerge.

The objectives of the original German dye cartels in the United States were by no means confined to obstructing our development of the dye industry. It was of utmost importance to forestall the establishment of any primary phase of the coal-tar industry which might make this country independent of Germany for coal-tar intermediates, and for other chemical products used in making dyes during peace, or explosives and munitions during war. In the early development of the dye industry in Germany, the high cost of individual dyes was due to the large quantities of certain by-products which had no value but which had to be extracted from the coal tar in order to produce the dyes. And the great variety of colors was due largely to the continuous research devoted to the profitable utilization of these by-products. Despite this research, however, the stock piles reached enormous size. Then, early in this century the Germans realized the military significance of the coal-tar product, trinitrotoluol (TNT) which could readily be made from the by-products. Thereupon, research to produce certain new colors suddenly ceased, and the stock piles were allowed to accumulate for the war that was to come.

The two Big Six cartels appeared perfectly willing that the few American manufacturers who were trying to make dyes should continue their struggle to do so, providing they secured the bulk of their intermediates from Germany. They laughed at this competition, but they were systematic in their price cutting and utterly ruthless in their determination that a coal-tar industry which could quickly be turned from dyes to munitions should not exist in the United States.

Throughout this period, while our coal-tar industries languished or were still-born whenever attempts were made to start them, it is estimated that we were letting a billion dollars worth of coal gas go to waste annually through the chimneys of the old-fashioned beehive ovens in which substantially all of our coke was then made. The gas went to waste because we had no coal-tar dye industry to make it profitable.

At one time, when a group of three of the largest American manufacturers of heavy chemicals decided to start the production of aniline oil so that our feeble dye industry would not be totally at the mercy of the Germans, a special emissary of the Big Six came to the United States with the impudent demand that production of the oil be stopped, and made the equally impudent offer that the cartels would repay the Americans for such expenditures as had been incurred.

To protect the domestic producers from the price slashing on aniline that followed the refusal of the Americans to shut up shop, Congress placed a 10 percent duty on aniline oil. The Big Six, however, retaliated by dropping the price on aniline far below any possible cost of production in the United States.

Originally the German dyes were exported to the United States through houses which handled a variety of imported products. Later, exclusive selling agencies or branch houses were established here by each of the Big Six. These branches and agencies had their main office in New York City, and maintained branches in New England, Philadelphia and other centers where dyes were consumed in quantities by textile, leather, paper and printing ink manufacturers.

The author's first contact with these powerful German firms was in the early 1900s, while working on the original production of rayon, or artificial silk, as it was then known, in a plant located in the suburbs of Philadelphia. Continuous experimental work was required in order to determine which dyes were suitable for the new textile yarn, and we received much assistance and many fine samples of dyes from the local agents of the Big Six. Our interest in dyes was confined to samples and laboratory experiments. The subject of bulk purchases did not arise, and the matter of graft, of which I had heard a great deal in my visits to commercial dyeing establishments, never arose. A few years later, however, I cornered a textile mill owner, a most forthright citizen with whom I had been doing business, and asked him why he tolerated the graft which the German dyestuff companies were handing out to the boss dyers who used their products. It was common knowledge, I told this mill owner, that this bribery was what made it practically impossible for the few American makers of dyestuffs to compete with the Germans. My friend's reply was characteristic of the dejected attitude of the men who were paying the bills for German dyes. Without pretending to quote his exact words, his reply was: "I know perfectly well that my boss dyer receives bribe money on every ounce of dyestuff that goes into the products which my mill turns out. However, it happens that we are making money on the work this man is doing. Now, if I fired him, as I am justified in doing, I would have to get another boss dyer. I can't dye these fabrics myself, and the new man would also take bribes from the German companies. Competent dyers are hard to get, but good or bad, they all accept the graft. So why make the change? We mill owners all know that this thing exists, but each of us feels that he is helpless to do anything about it without risking ruin."

Not long after this conversation, I was invited to have lunch with an executive of one of the American branches of the Big Six. This man was a native born American whom I had known when he was engaged in another branch of the chemical industry. In the past, I had found him a reputable business man. During that luncheon he offered me a position with the German company he was representing, and quite casually mentioned that one of my duties would be to handle the Saturday pay-offs of bribe money to the boss dyers. He remonstrated with me when I declined. "It's customary," he protested. "Everyone in the industry does it, everyone knows it is done and no one is objecting except a few small concerns that don't count—so why be squeamish about it?"

I have recounted these personal experiences to illustrate the corruption, and the callous acquiescence to it, through which the Germans maintained their impregnable monopoly in the American dyestuff market during the two decades preceding the first World War. Along with the bribery and other dishonest practices went the legend, then accepted in America, that products derived from coal tar did not present an attractive field for exploitation because American chemical brains were inadequate to fathom the mysteries of coal-tar dyes.

However, the bribery of the boss dyers had become so notorious that the storm was bound to break. Late in 1911 the grafting was brought forcibly to the attention of the top executives of John and James Dobson, the oldest and largest of the carpet manufacturers in the Philadelphia area. The owners' investigation which followed, disclosed that an astounding annual excess cost was being paid by their firm for its supply of colors. Also, that the bribery had reached much higher up than the boss dyers of the several mills operated by the Dobsons. Criminal proceedings of various kinds were started, and a group of mill owners from Philadelphia, New York and New

England formed themselves into the Textile Alliance, Inc. This group was very bitter at the revelations of how its members were being robbed and their employees corrupted by the German dye companies.

This investigation, which began with the raid on Mr. Keppelmann's apartment, was conducted by three Philadelphia attorneys under the leadership of the late Thomas Earl White, and lasted for several years. Hundreds of witnesses were examined, and much of the sordid story of bribery, corruption and fraud came tumbling out and became a matter of court record.

It might be pointed out here that the American dyestuff market of that period was peculiarly susceptible to dishonest manipulations of both quality and price. The consumers of coal-tar dyes were numerous, and most of them operated relatively small establishments. Few textile mills or commercial dye houses had laboratories, so formulas and sample dyeings were frequently supplied by the Big Six salesmen, through their head-office laboratory. In many of the dyeing establishments, individual purchases of various colors and shades, which changed with the fashions, were small, and the constant variations made it impossible for the owners, who were not dyers, to determine which dye was best or which should cost the least. Under these conditions, the owners were compelled to depend on their boss dyers. These men were usually highly skilled, self-taught artisans, frequently of foreign birth, who carried in their heads the trade secrets of mixing colors and blending shades for the peculiar requirements of each fabric. They had neither union nor guild, each boss dyer was a rugged individualist who regarded himself as a master craftsman and held his employer in contempt.

As an illustration of the huge extent of the corruption at the time of the exposure, it was revealed that Bayer claimed an allowance of $700,000 from its colleagues in the German cartel on the allegation that this sum represented graft payment in the United States for the preceding year. Evidence in another case revealed that a mill had been paying eighty-five cents a pound for a black, the correct price of which was twenty-one cents. When the graft was stopped at another mill, its yearly bills for dyes dropped from $265,000 to $125,000.

Elaborate systems of bookkeeping and filing were maintained in the American offices of the Big Six companies to keep track of the graft without revealing more of its details than were necessary. These records identified each color or blend shipped on each order, with its correct price; the phony name it had been billed under; whether salt, which adds to the weight, but doesn't affect the quality of the dye, or any other adulterant had been added; and, finally, how much bribe money was paid the boss dyer. These records went to the New York offices, other copies to the home offices in Germany. All of the records were in code, except the one set which represented the actual billing. These last records were always available in case a customer should drop into the office to discuss a previous purchase.

Alfred J. Keppelmann, the branch-office manager who played an important part all through this exposé, was an upper class German who apparently had no inhibitions about the peacetime service he owed to the future welfare of the Fatherland. The boss dyers of Bayer's important customers were paid by Keppelmann personally, and Keppelmann's chauffeur testified to the frequent occasions when he drove his employer to call on these susceptible gentlemen. Usually the car would be parked around the corner from the dyer's home. At other times, this energetic executive would meet his beneficiaries at a saloon, or pick them up in his car at some prearranged place, for Keppelmann had had trouble with salesmen who held out on the dyers and wickedly pocketed the graft. In one instance he had lost a customer because the dyer only secured half the graft he was "entitled" to. According to this dyer's own testimony, Keppelmann finally straightened this out by a special Sunday visit to the dyer's home, where he gave the latter his promise as a gentleman that there would be no further trouble about the graft. "This promise he kept," testified the dyer. "Two or three times each month Mr. Keppelmann came to my house and paid me the graft money which was due me."

Another witness, a chemist, who had been employed by the Bayer branch, testified that Keppelmann had instructed him to experiment in the laboratory to find a compound which, when put into a dye bath, would ruin the fabric. This was to be used when Keppelmann deemed it advisable to get rid of a competitor. The compound to be planted had to be one which would not so change the dye bath as to be conspicuous, but would be strong enough to spoil or streak the material. This, the witness said was a common practice and many different compounds were devised to spoil the various types of dyes in use. Keppelmann had still another social-business side. He kept a yacht on the Delaware River near Philadelphia, and his engineer testified to luxurious yachting parties that were given for employees of the textile mills and, on occasion, for some of the mill owners themselves: "They served rare food and champagne, and ladies were frequently present to help entertain the guests."

Keppelmann also had a private stenographer, one of whose duties was to count out the bribe money and place the correct amounts in envelopes marked with the code numbers of the boss dyers. The stenographer was, of course, in the complete confidence of her boss. She even went on the yachting trips at times. After the exposé, this young lady indicated her willingness to talk freely to the investigators, and so was scheduled to become an important witness for the prosecution.

Joseph H. Choate, Jr., distinguished New York lawyer, who was one of the early attorneys for the Textile Alliance, told the following story at a Congressional hearing in discussing the bribery practices of the Big Six: "A prosecution was begun against the Philadelphia agent of the Bayer Company, and I might say that they had the goods on him. The man had a duplicate set of books which showed what he paid everybody. All the parties were gathered at the trial, which centered around the testimony of a stenographer. As the trial was about to be called, somebody burst into the office of the District Attorney and threw up his hands. 'It's no use, boys, it's all off, the defendant has married the evidence, and it is not admissible!'"

Keppelmann, the night before, had in fact made his stenographer the second Mrs. Keppelmann, having divorced his first wife after settlement on her of $100,000. The Bayer companies' Mr. Keppelmann was no piker!

Criminal prosecution of the individuals involved in the dyestuff graft was faced with innumerable difficulties, and the attorneys representing the mill owners finally decided upon another approach to the problem—by invoking provisions of the Sherman Antitrust Act against offenders.

The late Nelson Aldrich, Senator from Rhode Island, had been instrumental in having translated and printed as a Senate Document, a revealing German publication called, "The Great German Banks and Their Concentration in Connection with the Economic Development of Germany" by Professor J. Riesser of the University of Berlin, who described in detail the then recent cartel alliances of the Big Six dyestuff companies. The professor also indulged in a little prophecy—which was to come true—when he indicated that a complete consolidation of all the important aniline producers was in prospect. (In 1916 this prophecy was fulfilled when the companies comprising the Big Six were combined into the German I. G. Dyes.) The translation of this German book turned attention to the fact that Germany permitted combinations which the Sherman Act forbade. It was also discovered that the United States branches and agencies of the German companies were acting under rigid instructions from Germany in dividing the United States market on sales.

More than thirty separate actions under the Sherman Act were thereupon instituted in 1913 in the Federal Courts of Pennsylvania and New Jersey against the members of the Big Six and their agents in the United States; damages were asked not only for bribery and dishonest commercial practices, but for combinations in restraint of trade by all concerned. In these actions the Big Six was represented by a New York attorney, Charles J. Hardy (later to become president of American Car & Foundry Company), who fought so vigorously for his clients that the cases were never brought to trial. All were finally dismissed in 1916, long after the outbreak of the war. Before the dismissals, however, large cash settlements were made out of court by several of the defendants.

Twenty-five years later, after Germany had again started a war of conquest, another series of anti-trust law actions was instituted against the I. G. Farben affiliates and subsidiaries in the United States. Among them are the direct successors of the Big Six affiliates; and this time it was not just dyestuffs, but many other vital national-defense products which were involved. Again, as will be discussed in other chapters, this second series of antitrust suits

against the Farben pattern of unlawful practices were ineffectual
in providing real punishment for the culprits, and were for the most
part compromised and settled, or remain, at this writing, untried.

One member of the Big Six, the Hoechst Co., was first represented in the United States by an importing house which went
through several changes to become, in 1902, the H. A. Metz Co.,
of New York. Brooklyn-born Herman Metz, president of this company denied on numerous occasions that he or his company had
ever been involved in the bribery of boss dyers. Elected to Congress
in 1912, just before the antitrust suits were instituted, Metz said
that he knew he would be "a shining mark for attack." "So," said
Metz, "I settled, rather than fight in Court."

In one of his public statements on the subject, made before a
Senate Committee, Metz declared with some heat that "so much
is made of this bribing of dyers—this tipping business. It is not
limited to the dye industry." Metz also pointed out that with the
exception of Keppelmann, all of the dye company agents involved
were Americans. "The Germans were not doing it," said Metz, "it
was their agents here."

Metz's special pleading, characterizing the bribing of dyers as
a customary American way of doing business, constituted a rather
contemptible libel upon his fellow citizens. The author has been
active, and behind the scenes, so to speak, in a great many American industries during the last forty-five years, especially those
connected with or dependent upon chemical products of one kind
or another. Commercial dishonesty and fraud have been encountered here and there, it has existed and always will exist among
a small and shifty percentage of the human race. But with the exception of one other industry, never in my experience or in the
knowledge of any one with whom I have discussed the subject has
there existed in the United States such systematic corruption, on
a large scale and by a recognized plan, as was engaged in by the
predecessors of I. G. Farben to obstruct the development of our
domestic coal-tar industry during the two decades preceding the
first World War. The one exception mentioned is discussed in a
later chapter on patent medicines.

The late Francis P. Garvan, who more than any other prominent
American fought to destroy the German dye cartel's hold in Amer-

ica and to prevent its reentry after the war, always refused to accept the denials of Metz that his company was involved in the bribery. Garvan first delved deeply into the affairs of the Metz company, and all of the other German dye houses, when he was made Chief Investigator for the Alien Property Custodian in 1917. He based his allegations about Metz on letters which were taken from Metz's own files in the New York offices of the Hoechst Co. Metz, said Garvan, was present when these letters were produced at Congressional hearings and has never questioned their authenticity. Some of these letters, addressed to Metz by Dr. Haeuser, president of the German company, are revealing. In one of them dated July 31, 1913, Dr. Haeuser wrote Metz:

> As for what concerns the paying of dyers I inform you confidentially about the development of matters as follows: The proper assistance has been explained to the Elberfeld (Bayer) gentlemen, at the establishment of the new business over there, that they must unconditionally avoid in the future any graft, else the matter may become very bad for them. Elberfeld has then, the comprehensible endeavor, that not they alone, but also all other firms, should cease payments to dyers in future. They immediately came to an understanding with Ludwigshafen (Badische) and Berlin, and then also secured the consent of Cassella. After these four firms were agreed, there remained nothing for us to do but to agree likewise, as Kalle had also to consent. It is also to be expected that still other factories will join, and if they refuse to join this shall be used against them among the customers . . . . . Aside from the fact that we were in a forced position, we had little cause to hesitate as you wrote to me repeatedly that the payments to the dyers must unconditionally stop. We are of the opinion that it must be serious, at least for the six firms concerned, to discontinue all affairs with the dyers in the future, and we are furthermore of the opinion that the business will get along very well without the payments to the dyers, since substantially all large firms share the same point of view. A certain transition period is very likely necessary, and therefore the union should first go into effect on January 1 of next year.

It will not be feasible then any more that you set expenses in the bill; you will have to get along without the expenses.

Your independence, as far as it is concerned, will not be affected by this agreement, and at all events, no one, even in America, will wish to reproach us for an agreement whose purpose it is to further the discontinuance of the unlawful acts on the part of our customers. If you wish to come over here this year yet, which would please me very much, I would ask you not to arrive here in October, as I must go on my vacation in that month after having endured it here the whole summer long. In case Mr. George Gordon Battle should come here, I will receive him with pleasure. With best greetings, yours respectfully,

Dr. Haeuser

Dr. Haeuser was also the president of "The World Society for the Preservation of German Business." Emphatic as this letter appears to have been on the matter of stopping the bribing of dyers by January 1, 1914, a later letter dated February 6, 1914, from the German Hoechst office to Metz indicated otherwise. This letter read:

Now as far as extras are concerned, I hear with regret that according to your opinion not much will be changed. I agree with you that you will not be able with one stroke to wipe out all extras but the striving must be to abolish this unwholesome condition entirely. The propositions that you now make seem to me to indicate a practical way in this direction, and we are satisfied therewith.

Again, on March 30, 1914 Metz received another letter from Hoechst from which Garvan quoted as follows:

So far as "extras" are concerned, I am of the opinion that this practically amounts to simply a transition period and that the same will rapidly go backward. At any rate, all our endeavors must be in that direction. Your idea that the paying out of extras in future could be done through a third party, in cash, as for instance through your carpet mill at Worcester, I do not find sound. You give yourself through this into the hands of such third party, who could at any moment turn against you . . . . . Regarding the charging of your account in your letter of March 3, I have to remark that it is not entirely clear, as in the past year, besides the $100,000 you also according to your letter of October 14, 1913, have kept back a further dividend of $50,000 for extras. As you do not mention this last $50,000 it seems to me that you have already used this in the previous year for extras. Will you please confirm this?

Said Garvan, "These 'extras' meant graft, pure and simple."

Still another light upon the pattern of bribery of the Big Six, and the innocent surprise of their executives when exposed, is the report of a later convention called by members of the cartel at which a resolution was entered upon the minutes reading as follows: "Resolved, that henceforth bribery shall be abolished, except in the United States and Russia."

CHAPTER II

Congressman Metz of the Bleeding Heart

"ENGLAND KEEPS her navy intact and her soldiers at home; she will carry on the war until the last Frenchman has been killed." With these words Dr. Hugo Schweitzer closed his address to a gathering of leading textile manufacturers who, with the speakers of the evening, were guests of the Drysalters Club of New England on January 20, 1915.

The next speaker, our old friend, Congressman Herman A. Metz, began his address with this statement: "If I had any doubts about Dr. Schweitzer's neutrality before I heard him speak tonight those doubts are now removed." Thus was fabricated, and approved by a member of Congress, this still familiar-sounding canard about the British people.

America had just discovered how dependent she was on the chemical industry of Germany. With the outbreak of war in 1914, our imports from that country ceased. American manufacturers were panicky, and President Wilson was being bombarded with demands for relief in the name of the suffering consumers of German dyes and pharmaceuticals. Accordingly, the President had lodged a formal protest with the British Government—a request that the blockade be relaxed so that trade between the United States and Germany could continue.

Dr. Hugo Schweitzer's address before the Drysalters Club was entitled, "The President's Protest to Great Britain and its Justification by Perils to Our Trade and Industries." The speaker was introduced as president of the American Bayer Co., and former president of the Chemists Club of New York.

The Drysalters Club guests, already in a state of high indignation about the dye shortage were, of course, in a most receptive mood for an attack upon England. They ate it up that night and they spread it far and wide thereafter.

During that period no public suspicion had been aroused regarding the under-cover activities of Dr. Schweitzer, and it was not to be revealed until later that at the very time of his anti-British address the illustrious doctor was secretly making plans to secure control of substantially all of the phenol (carbolic acid) then manufactured in the United States, in order to prevent its use in the manufacture of munitions for England.

Thomas A. Edison had been a very large consumer of phenol as a material for making phonograph records. Prior to the outbreak of the war his supply had come from Germany—the cartels having seen to it that we had no domestic production. However, when his foreign supply was threatened, Mr. Edison, with characteristic initiative, began producing it here and did so on a scale sufficiently large to have a considerable excess supply over his own requirements. This excess would have gone into the production of war munitions for Great Britain had not the neutral Dr. Schweitzer quietly grabbed every bit of it.

Schweitzer accomplished this by secretly organizing a company called the Chemical Exchange Association which contracted with Edison for his entire excess production of phenol. The Chemical Exchange was not identified with Schweitzer nor did it become known until later that it had been financed with funds supplied by the notorious Dr. Heinrich Albert, financial adviser to the German Government. Von Bernstorff, the German Ambassador, also collaborated in this Schweitzer project. The Chemical Exchange resold all of the Edison phenol to another domestic company, also German owned, which used it to make salicylic acid for medicinal purposes.

So delighted was Dr. Albert with the success of this means of depriving England of munitions that he sent Schweitzer flamboyant congratulations:

"One should picture to himself what a military coup would be accomplished by an army leader if he should succeed in destroying three railroad trains of forty cars, containing four and one-half million pounds of explosives."

Dr. Albert's letter then went on to urge the doctor to next go after America's bromine supply, because:

"Bromine, together with chloral, is used in making nitric gases, which are of such great importance in trench warfare. Without bromine these nitric gases are of slight effect; in connection with bromine, they are of terrible effect."

When it finally came out that Dr. Schweitzer was the brains behind the Chemical Exchange-Edison contract, Schweitzer defied criticism with an attack upon what he called the "greedy explosives manufacturers who were paying fabulous prices for carbolic acid." Said Schweitzer:

"I wish emphatically to state that all carbolic acid purchased by me is now and will be converted into highly salutary medicinal remedies . . . . . It needs no imagination to realize how many men would have been killed, wounded, and maimed by the use of this enormous quantity of one of the highest explosives known. I made Mr. Edison especially happy by converting this carbolic acid into medicines, because, as he personally said to me, he would dislike very much that any of the merchandise manufactured by him should be used for killing people."

These humanitarian sentiments of Dr. Schweitzer might have been more impressive but for the fact that those same deadly chemical gases, first used by the Kaiser's army at Ypres in violation of Germany's pledge at the Hague convention, were manufactured by Dr. Carl Bosch, Schweitzer's colleague in Badische. And the formula of one of them, the dread mustard gas, had already been invented, in 1913 in a New Jersey laboratory, by a Schweitzer employe, Dr. Walter Scheele. The latter, again directed by Bayer's Schweitzer, later prepared the incendiary sabotage bombs used to destroy ships in New York harbor after World War I began.

During this period, Dr. Schweitzer's activities spread to many fields which were remote from his duties as president of a company making dyes and pharmaceuticals at Rensselaer, New York. With funds supplied by the German Government Schweitzer organized the Printers and Publishers Association, and the German Publishers Society—for the dissemination of Teutonic culture. He is also credited with being the instigator of the scheme through which the *New York Evening Mail* was purchased with German funds by Dr. Edward A. Rumely, and, for a short time, turned into an organ of German propaganda.

The good doctor's advice was, of course, relied upon by Ambassador von Bernstorff on all problems relating to chemical munitions. When Congress, to encourage the newly created domestic dyestuff industry by an embargo and very high duties, passed the Tariff Act of 1916, Schweitzer wrote von Bernstorff that it would be "child's play" to defeat the purpose of the bill. A special clause in the Act, Schweitzer pointed out, permitted the President to remove the duty on certain of the more essential dyes after five years. In the meantime, the cartels could absorb the high duties and dump dyes into the United States so far below costs that they could "apply the lever" and regain domination of the market. Dr. Schweitzer's "child's play" also was to include the election of the right kind of a President of the United States. "Party politics," said Schweitzer, will control whether the President to be elected to office "will make an honest effort to abolish the specific duty, and again let in the German dyes without restriction." His letter, however, did not explain how he proposed to bring about the election of the right kind of President. Perhaps he thought the Ambassador, or his friend, ex-Congressman Metz, could handle that minor detail.

The good doctor, of course, was confident that Germany would win the war while the United States was being persuaded by propaganda and corruption to keep out of it. However, the Farben pattern is always based on win or lose, and when Germany did lose, Farben, as will be shown later, merely moved in and under cover of American-born citizens and American corporation, regained control of many of our vital industries.

Eventually, it came out that Bayer's Dr. Schweitzer was in reality the undercover head of the German espionage and sabotage organization in the United States. When Dr. Albert had first arrived in the United States, it was Schweitzer who met him and supplied him with an automobile. And when the United States Government forced Albert's departure in 1917, it was to Dr. Schweitzer that he handed over his remaining espionage funds— some $1,800,000.

But busy as he was, Dr. Schweitzer always found time to write articles and make public addresses on scientific and business subjects. These, like his Boston speech to the Drysalters Club, were then neatly reprinted in small booklets of uniform design, and copies bearing the legend, "Compliments of the Author," were mailed to important public and college libraries, and to newspapers and other publications throughout the United States. Schweitzer always spoke and wrote as a patriotic American citizen devoted to the welfare of his country; and observed our relations with Germany and England with the detachment of a true scientist. Some of the titles of these speeches and articles are of interest: "The Present and Future Peril to our Commerce and Industry," "German Militarism and Its Influence upon the Industries," "Can Germany be Starved into Submission?" The theme was always the same, that his fellow-American citizens should learn from scientific facts that friendship with Germany was a matter of self-interest. How familiar that false slogan has become! In one of his papers entitled, "The Chemists' War," Dr. Schweitzer set forth at great length how Germany's chemists had contributed more to the success of their country's armed forces than either the Army or Navy. He would also seem to have anticipated some of Farben's future activities and tie-ups in the United States as he stated in this article that German chemists had already solved the problem of synthetic rubber, and had made the important discovery of magnesium-aluminum alloys for war purposes.

A decade later Schweitzer's successors in I. G. Farben were making their secret and illegal agreements with American industrialists to discourage or control all developments here in synthetic rubber, magnesium alloys and other war essentials. In another ten years—when Schweitzer's successors were to give the word to the German army: "We are now ready, you may start marching," the success of these efforts had contributed greatly to our pitiful state of unpreparedness. And when once again Farben's lust for world conquest has been thwarted we are now told, again, that as a matter of self-interest we should permit Farben's industries to survive.

When Congressman Herman Metz at that Boston meeting in January 1915 put his public approval on Dr. Schweitzer's vicious anti-English sentiments, he also informed his audience that he had just returned from a trip to Germany where he had talked to high officials in Berlin and to the leaders of the German dye cartels, including, of course, Dr. Schweitzer's German employers in the Bayer Company. Anyone who chooses to do so is now welcome to assume that Congressman Metz at that time had no knowledge or suspicion of the real character and purpose of Dr. Schweitzer's activities in the United States. However, in December 1917, shortly after Dr. Schweitzer's death, and after at least a part of his secretly conducted treasonable activities had become public, Metz, by then an ex-Congressman and a colonel in the U.S. Army, joined with several other American representatives of the German cartel and with other citizens who should have known better, in organizing a Hugo Schweitzer Memorial Committee to pay tribute to the sterling qualities of this late-departed German spy.

Five years later Mr. Metz was not quite so proud in public of his late colleague, for although he informed a Senate Committee in 1922 that Dr. Schweitzer had a right to buy up the phenol supply with German money in order to deprive Great Britain of munitions, he also referred to Schweitzer's activities as "unpatriotic" and objected vigorously to being compared with his former friend.

The part played by Herman Metz, however, in the German-inspired political pressure upon the U.S. Government is indicated by the following:

New York, March 6, 1915

Hon. William J. Bryan,
Secretary of State, Washington, D. C.

My dear Mr. Bryan:

Referring to my letter of yesterday regarding the dyestuff situation, I beg to say that I received the following cable this morning from Germany via Milan: 'Latest developments make further shipments dyestuffs impossible.' The cable was sent to me by Dr. Adolph Haeuser . . . . . the president of the Verein zur Wahrung der Interressen der Chemischen Industrie Deutchlands, which is composed of the various chemical and dyestuff manufacturers of Germany, with headquarters in Berlin, and shows the attitude of German manufacturers of dyestuffs in the present crisis. It is safe to assume that they will take every precaution and go to any length to prevent their products from reaching consumers of enemy countries, and unless some agreement can be reached to have the present condition modified, the manufacturers of this country will suffer as much as those of belligerent countries.

Yours very truly,
H. A. Metz.

Mr. Metz thus served official notice on his own government, in the name of the German cartel, that we must change our policy toward Great Britain or suffer the consequences. That this diplomatic pressure was inspired by the German Government was made clear by an intercepted cable which Dr. Albert sent from the United States to his home office on April 26, 1916. In this message Dr. Albert said:

The policy of withholding dyestuffs was at the beginning of the war without doubt the only possible one.

A week after Metz's letter to Secretary Bryan, Ambassador von Bernstorff contributed his advice to the home office by cabling Berlin that:

the stock of dyes in this country is so small that 4,000,000 American workmen may be thrown out of employment.

Dyes, in fact, were so scarce that the mills would pay any price for such as were available. Old warehouse stocks were overhauled and revealed priceless treasure in odds and ends of discarded German colors. In one instance a barrel of abandoned dye which originally cost 23 cents a pound sold for $7.50 a pound.

Meanwhile Congressman Metz did succeed in arranging for several cargoes of German dyes to be brought to the United States through the British blockade and was widely acclaimed in certain circles for his success in so doing. Then, on March 11, 1915, the British Government issued its Order of Council prohibiting all trade with Germany, which so tightened the blockade that further shipments appeared impossible.

In July 1916 the American people received a real thrill of excitement when it was announced that the German submarine *Deutschland* had arisen from beneath the surface of Chesapeake Bay and proceeded to a dock in Baltimore to discharge almost 300 tons of dyestuffs. These dyes had been concentrated to save cargo space and the shipment really represented about 1300 tons of dyes of the prewar standards. Hearst's pro-German *American* hailed this exploit "as marking a new era in the world's commercial history." Another paper termed it "Man's greatest single victory over the forces of the sea."

It was of course ridiculous to suppose that an occasional submarine could bring any real relief to the shortage of dyes and medicinals that existed in the United States, but as a propaganda stunt this first submarine voyage was a great success. So, while editorial writers were busy acclaiming German ingenuity, it remained for a well-known consulting chemist, the late Dr. F. X. Harold, to point out that the character of the undersea cargo indicated that the motive of the German dye trust was propaganda rather than profit or real friendship, since an equal amount of coal-tar medicinals would have yielded a far greater return, and would have been even more welcome. Said Dr. Harold:

It seems therefore, that Germany's object in sending dyes must be regarded as a sort of warning to American manufacturers. If she can postpone, even for a few months, the investment of further capital in the American dyestuff industry, it will facilitate greatly her efforts to regain her dye monopoly after the close of the war.

Despite the selection of the less profitable merchandise for this first cargo, almost a million dollars profit to the cartels was represented by this single trip. Four months later the *Deutschland* again turned up in an American harbor, this time at New London, Connecticut. It was said that this cargo was worth $10,000,000 and included a limited quantity of drugs, securities and diamonds in addition to dyes.

There was a romantic, Jules Verne-like aspect to the resumption of commerce between this country and the German dye concerns, that appealed to the emotions of many Americans. This was made good use of in anti-British propaganda, with jests at the futility of a blockade when the Germans could outwit the great British navy by merely sailing under it.

The next German submarine that paid us a visit shelled our coast.

The Senate hearings in 1922 at which Mr. Metz objected to being compared with the departed Dr. Schweitzer were held in compliance with a resolution introduced by Senator William H. King of Utah which called for an investigation of expenditures by American dye interests for the maintenance of a lobby at Washington. These expenditures, Senator King alleged, were being made to secure a wicked monopoly of the domestic dye markets by keeping out the Germans. Senator King stated that this was most reprehensible. He opened the proceedings with a vituperative attack upon American dye manufacturers, and elaborated on six reasons which he alleged proved that the domestic dye industry needed no embargo to protect it. Ex-Congressman Metz supported Senator King's charges, and informed the Committee that he had placed at the disposal of the Congress one of his own employes, Dr. Eugene R. Pickrell, who had been chief chemist for the U.S. Customs Department from 1912 to 1919, and who was therefore well qualified to advise the Senators on the pending legislation.

These hearings were lengthy and many witnesses for and against the embargo were heard. Late in the hearings, Mr. Metz's employe, Dr. Pickrell did testify, and, after qualifying as an expert on domestic dyes and dye imports, gave high praise to the arguments and findings of Senator King, which he termed unanswerable. Here were three American-born citizens, one a Senator from a western state, one an ex-Congressman and ex-army officer, and one an ex-government expert, all vigorously opposing the embargo, and maintaining that sufficient protection for the new domestic industry could be had by duties instead. It was only a few years back that Mr. Metz's friend, Dr. Schweitzer, had written von Bernstorff that it would be "child's play" for the cartel to break through any tariff duties, however high.

Senator King apparently stood for the highest ideals of disinterest: "The war is over," said King, "and if we can begin to think in terms of world peace and world unity it will be better for the United States." The Senator went back in history more then a century and a half, to the first treaty between the United States and Germany, to sustain his allegation that the United States should not have seized the properties and patents of the German dye cartel, and should have returned them after the war. Metz pleaded for the ultimate consumers of dyes—"for whom my heart bleeds," he said. Dr. Pickrell put into the record of these hearings page after page of complex tables to support his contention that the domestic dye industry did not need an embargo. However, Dr. Pickrell made no reply when a letter was introduced showing that he, too, had stated previously, before entering the Metz employ, that not even a 100 per cent duty on dyes would be as efficacious as an embargo. None of these three Americans appeared to be at all concerned about the danger to their country if it were again to be deprived of an essential war-munitions industry.

Eight years after these hearings another Senate Committee, which was investigating lobbies and lobbyists, drew from one Samuel Russell, the former secretary of Senator King, an admission that in 1922, in the dye-embargo fight, Mr. Metz had paid Russell $1000 in cash to be used in the Senator's campaign for reelection—and that the money had been handed to the witness in Metz's New York office by none other than Dr. Eugene R. Pickrell. An account of the relations of these three disinterested American citizens, whose hearts bled for world peace and the poor consumer, is to be found in the minority report of the 1930 Lobby Committee.

Dr. Pickrell testified that he had left the employ of the H. A. Metz Co. the year before, and had opened an office in New York as a consulting chemist. He denied repeatedly that he represented the German dye cartel, or that he knew anything about its interests in the United States. The Committee, however, drew an admission from the doctor that his income included payments of $12,000 a year, plus expenses, from four Farben-controlled companies. These four Pickrell clients were: General Dyestuff Corp., of which Herman Metz was president; Agfa Ansco Company, which, in 1929, had been taken over by American I. G. Chemical Corp.; Kuttruff-Pickhardt & Co., the old Badische agency; and Farben-owned Synthetic Nitrogen Products Co.

To accusations that he had used Senator King's office as his headquarters while representing the interests of these clients, and had prepared material for the speeches of Senators favoring his cause, Dr. Pickrell replied that he only saw Senator King a few times. The Committee's Minority report found this statement to be "decidedly at variance" with other evidence given before it; and called Frank K. Boal, a Washington newspaper correspondent, to the witness stand. Mr. Boal testified that it was known among newspaper men that when Pickrell was in Washington he could be found in Senator's King's office, and that he had seen the doctor there—with his coat off, dictating to a stenographer. Direct questioning also brought out that Dr. Pickrell was the author of material Senator King had presented to the Senate Committee of 1922. Small wonder the doctor had been so lavish with his praise.

Ex-Congressman Metz was inclined to be irascible on the witness stand, and complained bitterly at questions of Republican Senator Arthur R. Robinson, especially those which had to do with his activities as treasurer of the American I. G. Chemical Corp., and that company's relations with Farben. "Everything is inference," he protested. Metz also denied vigorously that he was a lobbyist, but he did affirm his friendship for Dr. Bosch and the German dye companies, and described them as "my friends abroad, by whom I have been standing all of these years, and they have stood by me."

Prior to the minority report of the 1930 Lobby Committee, I had made a number of efforts to awaken the Senate to the menace to our national security that was being revealed by that Committee. The report was issued May 22, 1930. One of my letters, dated March 8, 1930, was as follows:

> Hon. Guy D. Goff,
> United States Senate
> Washington, D. C.
>
> Dear Senator Goff:
>
> Noting your remarks in the Senate yesterday regarding the activities of Dr. Pickrell, the paid agent of the German I. G., it occurs to me to send you herewith copy of a letter addressed some time since to the chairman of the Senate Lobby Committee. The information contained therein, so far as I can learn, has not been utilized as yet for the purpose of developing the extent of the activities, the background, and the connections of this Dr. Pickrell.
>
> Without attempting to discuss the merits of a high or low tariff with relation to any domestic product, I would point out that the so-called German I. G. is the one group which has attempted to influence pending tariff legislation which, by no stretch of imagination, may be said to have any proper motive relating to the social well-being or prosperity of our working class, our agricultural groups, or the industrial and commercial developments of the American people.
>
> It is also obvious that control of our chemical manufacturing industries means control of the munition plants of the next war . . . . . that control of our pharmaceutical industry . . . . . means control of an important factor in the public health.
>
> It is also obvious that secret control of an enormous group of the most profitable patent medicines in the United States means secret control of the expenditures of unlimited funds for advertising . . . . . with its secret influence on news and editorial expression on all subjects.
>
> I am not an alarmist trying to wave a bloody shirt, but I say to you without fear of contradiction that the uncovering

of the tentacles of the so-called German I. G., in every element of our social order in the United States at this time, will astound and shock the American people.

Please use the letter which I have inclosed herewith as you see fit.

Respectfully yours,
H. W. Ambruster

Senator Goff acknowledged receipt of this letter with his thanks, and the comment that he would use the material in it to advantage if the opportunity arose. Apparently that opportunity did not arise.

A similar letter, sent to Senator Joseph R. Grundy, of Pennsylvania, received a more forthright reply. "I am quite sure," he wrote, "that not only what you stated in your letter but the apprehension contained in your closing paragraph are correct, and the American people have comparatively little knowledge of what is going on in this country to undermine their material wellbeing." Senator Grundy, a high-tariff Republican, was also a Quaker and appears to have had sufficient insight to be fearful of the dangers to our future peace. Be that as it may, the Senate took no action.

Twelve long years after my letters to Senators Goff and Grundy, the "shock to the American people" that I then prophesied was echoed when Senator Harry S Truman, in another Senate hearing, shouted "treason" at revelations of some of the agreements entered into by the Standard Oil Co. of New Jersey which had enabled Farben to obtain such control of our chemical-manufacturing industries that the production of synthetic rubber in the United States had been obstructed to the grave injury of our war economy. As will be shown in a later chapter, these Standard Oil-Farben agreements were actually being arranged and consummated at the time of Pickrell's activities [and prior to the date of my letter to the Senators].

After the 1930 exposure Mr. Pickrell dropped out of sight as a disinterested dye expert before Congressional Committees. Later, he was listed as a director of H. A. Metz Co., and as an attorney at 10 East 40th Street, across the hall from the notorious German-American Board of Trade—which was organized by Herman Metz in 1924 and operated as Farben's high level propaganda machine by one Dr. Albert Degener until that gentleman was interned after the outbreak of the present war. According to the published statements of the *Bulletin* of the German-American Board of Trade, Attorney Pickrell was listed as one of its directors in 1940; and as appearing before Secretary of State Hull in protest at the British blockade after the war started and before the Treasury Department in customs matters in 1941.

Senator William H. King retired from the Senate in 1940 and opened a law office in Washington. As for Herman Metz, it seems that while he was still vehemently proclaiming sole ownership of his two companies, his loyalty to the German cartel was rewarded by the round sum of $1,750,000—the purchase price of his General Drug Company and the Metz Laboratories. While Winthrop Chemical Company was ostensibly the buyer of these profitable enterprises, it was our old friend I. G. Farben that put up $875,000, or half the purchase price.

Ex-Congressman Metz, the Democrat, turned Republican to support Harding because his old party was mean to his German friends, the American consumer's friend with the bleeding heart who had so bitterly denounced the American dye manufacturers as an iniquitous monopoly in 1922, and who claimed that he did not represent the cartel, in 1925 helped to organize, and became president of, the General Dyestuff Corp., a concern that was to become the exclusive U.S. sales agency for Farben's dyes. At the very time his company was being sued for damages in American courts by Farben's Hoechst, Metz was being paid huge sums by Farben to turn over his drug and dye interests to Farben's new American hideouts. In 1929 Metz helped Hermann Schmitz, chairman of I. G. Farben, organize the American I. G. Chemical Corp. which took over the General Aniline Works and the Agfa Ansco Corp. Metz became vice-president and treasurer of American I. G., and shortly afterward issued a public statement denying that the company was a branch of I. G. Farben. In 1934, while still head of his German-American Trade Board, after a visit to his friends in Farben and in Hitler's new government, Herman Metz died and was buried with military honors.

In 1939, shortly after Germany started the present war, Farben caused the American I. G. Chemical Corp. to change its name to General Aniline & Film Corp. In 1941 and '42 multiple indictments were filed in U.S. District Courts accusing General Aniline & Film, and several other corporations and individuals, of conspiring with Hermann Schmitz, and with I. G. Farben to restrict the production of dyes and chemicals in the United States, to prevent domestic exports from the United States, and to control competition with imports from Germany. Among those indicted on these charges were the E. I. duPont De Nemours & Co., Inc., and the Allied Chemical & Dye Corp. It was also set forth in these indictments that systematic efforts had been made from the beginning to conceal the ownership by I. G. Farben of the American companies with which Metz had been associated.

In December 1941, the Treasury Department seized General Aniline & Film Corp., and prior to the seizure, Winthrop, owned jointly by General Aniline & Film and Sterling Products, Inc., had already been prosecuted for illegal relations with Farben. After the seizure, the Treasury removed several of Winthrop's employes and officers as objectionable enemy aliens, and a complete removal of every trace of the Farben influence was announced. Then, in October 1942, the Winthrop management announced in the press that as a master stroke of this housecleaning, it had appointed as its director of research one Dr. Chester M. Suter, professor of chemistry at Northwestern University. One fact, however, that the announcements neglected to mention was that Dr. Suter had completed his chemical education at Yale University on what was known as the Metz Fellowship. This fellowship was established at Yale in 1925 by Farben's Herman A. Metz and was financed thereafter by Metz and his Farben-controlled companies.

Herman Metz had four sons, one of whom was to carry on with Farben as a banker and an aid to its Central Finance Administration at Berlin (the polite name for the Farben foreign espionage and propaganda bureau) and who was also to marry into royalty, not of the ersatz Farben variety but that of the ancient 14th century duchy of Schleswig-Holstein, subject of many disputes between Denmark and Prussia before it became finally an integral part of Bismarck's German Empire.

So, when Richard, son of Herman, in 1941, married Marie Luise, daughter of the 14th Duke of this Danish-German principality, who came from war torn Europe to wed in New York, the family of Metz, of humble Brooklyn origin, became linked with the Royal families both of Germany and Denmark, and, by those same ties, with England's Kings and Queens, and even with Carol of Roumania. And young Metz also became related, through his princess, with the millionaire American Leishman family, the duke's first wife having been Nancy Louise Leishman, daughter of our Ambassador to the Kaiser's court when William Howard Taft was President.

As some of the readers of this story may recall in news dispatches at the end of the war, it was Princess Valerie-Marie, sister of Marie Louise, who was so indignant with a squad of American doughboys on their way to Berlin when they bivouacked on her 16,000-acre estate and permitted her to retain as living quarters only 14 rooms of her 300 room palace.

Richard Metz, according to a report of the American Military Government of Germany (O.M.G.U.S.), as submitted to a Senate Committee in 1945, was in Belgium in 1940 in some connection with Farben's espionage bureau, and, returning to the United States in October of that year, was requested to deliver a message to one of Farben's most notorious agents in Latin America, Alfredo Moll (see Chapter XIII) instructing the latter how to get his confidential reports out of Peru, Brazil or Mexico.

So Herman's son, as a private banker living on Park Avenue, New York, carried on the traditions of the name.

It would appear to the author that nothing could better reveal the threads and texture of the Farben pattern than a study of the life and activities of Herman A. Metz, Brooklyn-born American. Back in March 1914 in one of the letters written to Metz by Dr. Haeuser—from which excerpts on bribery of the boss dyers have already been cited—the head of the German Hoechst Co. wrote these significant words: "So far as our other agreements are concerned I have no objection to having you send these back; *our entire relationship is really a confidential relationship, and it will be and must without agreements, so continue in the future as in the past.*" When Dr. Haeuser wrote that all-inclusive phrase "in the future as in the past" he must have anticipated what was to happen within the five months following, when Germany was to make "scraps of paper" of written agreements, and begin its march through Belgium.

Should Germany have won the first World War, it is interesting to speculate on the influence and power which might have come to Colonel Herman Metz through his "confidential relationship" with Dr. Haeuser and other German cartel leaders. Metz's pre-war written agreements with Hoechst might not carry over, but the record shows that the confidential relationship was all that the cartel required to hold the Metz loyalty. We have had similar revelations of carry-over relationships and post-war understandings reached by other American industrialists with Farben's leaders during the early period of World War II. Metz's career gives at least some indication of what Farben's leaders have prepared for, and, unhappily, have a right to expect, in the peace to come, as will appear in chapters to follow.

Herman Metz was self-made. Starting as an office boy he became a successful business man, manufacturer, politician, Congressman, Army Officer, philanthropist, and leader in many walks of American life. Always a rough-and-tumble fighter, he stormed through all accusations of impropriety with assertions of patriotic motive and vindictive slander of his opponent. As a table thumper Metz was in a class by himself.

My personal acquaintance with Metz started just after the first World War, when the chemical company of which I was the general manager was supplying the Metz Laboratories with arsenic acid. At an official reception at Washington in 1926 I asked Metz if he would care to meet my good friend, the late Dr. Charles Herty, distinguished engineer and adviser to Francis Garvan in many of the latter's battles with Farben and Farben's agents. "Sure" shouted Metz at the top of his lungs. "Where is that old son-of-a-bitch? I'll meet him any time, any place, and tell him what's what about that gang of goddamned horse thieves he runs with." So Mr. Metz started with me to look for the mild and gentle doctor, and I was much relieved that we did not succeed in finding him in the crowded hall.

In 1932, several years after I had first publicly denounced Farben and its activities in the United States, I had my last encounter with Herman Metz, and received the high distinction of having him call me a lunatic. This was in reply to a letter in which I denounced as criminal the advertising slogan of Bayer aspirin: "It does not harm the heart." I did not respond in kind to Metz's description of my mentality.

Instead I sent him a form of affidavit to fill out and sign in which, if he chose, he could swear to his approval, as an authority, of that advertising claim. This letter also requested Metz to present to his friend "Doctor" Weiss, of Sterling, my comments relative to the advertising. Metz declined to take advantage of the opportunity to give his personal seal of approval to the therapeutic qualities of one of Farben's most celebrated products. That he was wise in refraining came out some two years later when these claims were admitted to be dangerously false—in actions brought by the Federal Trade Commission as a result of my complaint.

CHAPTER III

The Lost Provinces Regained

ON SEPTEMBER 1, 1939 when the mechanized armies of Adolph Hitler thundered into Poland and began a war which was to spread across the face of the earth, most of the people of America were smug in the fancied security of their geographical position, entirely unaware that a gigantic industrial pincers movement had again rendered them very nearly helpless.

These pincers were the result of a grandiose plan initiated by the leaders of the German chemical cartel a few short months after the gunfire of World War I had ceased—while the exile of Kaiser Wilhelm and the feeble pretense of a German Republic were being hailed as the birth of a new day for the innocent people of the Fatherland.

In this post-war period of delusion and muddled thinking, Farben's predecessors proceeded quietly to reconstruct their international framework of industrial and political domination. During the war many of their properties in America had been confiscated, and a number of their key men deported or interned. For these Teutonic tycoons the struggle for world conquest had not ended when the German army had quit. The armistice and the paper peace merely signalled a change in pattern that had been determined long before. This time the plan was to be made possible by corruption on a scale which would make another failure in combat war impossible. Industrial encirclement was to be accompanied with peace propaganda, social espionage and sabotage of law enforcement. Compared with these plans the earlier pattern of activities of the "Big Six" was insignificant.

In the last months of 1918 and thereafter, when Germany's military leaders were in disgrace, the big boys of I. G. Dyes had become the strongest cohesive force in Germany, despite their apparently hapless economic plight at the mercy of the Allied Reparations Commission. They could say, with some appearance of logic, that it was not their fault that the war was lost, and that Germany, to be restored, must depend upon their world-wide resources and industrial leadership. Their prestige had increased by the failure of the military war for which they had been so largely responsible. Chemistry had so advanced through the individual efforts of these men that it was now recognized as the keystone of modern warfare. The tremendous increase in the quantity and destructiveness of gunfire, due to the use of coal-tar explosives, had lifted these Big Six leaders to positions of far greater importance in German military circles than had been accorded them prior to 1914. The use of poison gas was wholly their plan, and the supply of gases had come wholly from their dye factories. The process of extracting nitrogen from the air had been invented by Dr. Fritz Haber, of the Kaiser Wilhelm Institute, and the nitrogen production of the Badische plants, directed by Dr. Carl Bosch, had been on such a vast scale that for the first time Germany had become independent of the great nitrate beds of Chile.

The one great lesson which the I. G. leaders learned from the first World War was that their original pattern of industrial conquest had not been sufficiently broad to prevent the twofold disaster of the armistice and of the loss of most of their branches and properties in the United States. The seizure of thousands of their United States patents covering dyes, pharmaceuticals and other chemical products had been an especially hard blow, and it was of the utmost importance that control over these products be regained as quickly as possible. And it was apparent that better methods must be devised to disguise the American fronts to which titles to new patents and processes might safely be transferred. Some of the earlier disguises had been too crude and their wearers too obvious. The German industrialists had learned their lessons from the war, but as events were so tragically to prove, the people of the United States had not.

To some readers, the record which follows of a few of the many agreements and tie-ups consummated by Farben in the United States may prove a tiresome list of industries, companies and dates. However, it is impossible to understand the framework which the men of Farben erected in order to destroy our national security, unless their activities in this country are pictured in some kind of chronological grouping of the more important products and companies involved. These industrial tie-ups, the start of the German pincers movement in America, included agreements, partnerships and subsidiary controls of every conceivable kind for sharing processes, patents, profits and markets. Where specific control was not secured by Farben, a sharing of management gave Farben great influence; where both were lacking, Farben held negative control through its power to withdraw its participation and thus destroy the share of profits by which its American associates were induced to serve its purposes. Behind and above written documents and formal legal contracts were verbal understandings and "pledges of gentlemen" which bound certain of our American patriots to their Farben associates with personal ties and obligations that neither court proceedings nor war itself might obliterate.

The list of American corporations involved in the Farben pattern reads like a roster of big business, high finance and bi-partisan politics in the United States. A roll of the names of the men who consummated these tie-ups, and without whose active participation the Farben framework would have remained a lifeless skeleton, achieves its greatest significance when it is realized that these individuals were not the broken-English, German-Americans of the Bunds and singing societies. They were and are native born Americans, many of them nationally known industrialists to whom thousands of their fellow citizens look for leadership.

In those early post-war years there was a strong feeling of resentment at what the "Big Six" had done, and an equally strong and bitter conviction that our new organic-chemical industries must be protected against competition from the Germans. This latter belief was tempered somewhat by distrust of the two largest American companies making dyes, E. I. duPont de Nemours & Company, and the National Aniline & Chemical Corp., the latter having been absorbed into the huge Allied Chemical & Dye Corp. in 1920 by Eugene Meyer, and the late Orlando Weber.

M. R. Poucher of duPont was a former Badische agent in the United States, and William J. Matheson of National Aniline the former Cassella agent. Years later it was to be revealed that this early distrust of duPont and Allied had some substance of fact to support it. As early as 1919 and 1920, while duPont and Allied were leading the cry for protection against imported dyes, representatives of both companies were meeting the leaders of I. G. Dyes in Germany and France to negotiate for process and marketing agreements on dyestuffs and atmospheric nitrogen.

It was in this early postwar period that Attorney General A. Mitchell Palmer, former Alien Property Custodian, made the prediction that: "The next war, if it ever does happen, will be a chemists' war, and the country which has the best-developed dye and chemical industry is the country which is going to come out on top." Mr. Palmer said that, "of all the important industries developed during the recent war, none stands out more conspicuously, or is of more vital importance to the health, the commercial life and the preservation of American institutions than the dye and chemical industry." There was of course complete agreement among patriotic Americans with Mr. Palmer's conclusion that the new organic chemical industries should be developed; unfortunately, his forebodings of a future war went unheeded by all but a few.

Throughout this period the author occupied what might be called a front-row seat at the fight between friends of the "Big Six" and the advocates of a strong American-owned chemical industry. Early in 1918 I had become associated with the late Frank Hemingway, chemical manufacturer of New York City and Bound Brook, N. J., later becoming general manager of his company; Hemingway was one of the organizers of the American Dyes Institute, started in 1918 to bring together all of the American manufacturers in the fight to protect the new industry. Later, I opened my own office in New York City as a consultant, and, although active in other branches of the chemical industry, I was brought in contact with many of the principals in the fight for and against American-made dyes and drugs.

It was not long after the armistice that I. G. Dyes resumed open business relations with the firm of Kuttroff, Pickhardt & Co., which had escaped seizure on the specious plea that it was not a Badische branch or subsidiary. However, that firm did not hesitate to re-cross the lines into the green pastures of I. G. Dyes as soon as the government lifted the ban on communications with Germany. William Paul Pickhardt, son of one of the founders, and an officer of the company, cabled Badische for prices on dyes, and then left for Germany to begin a vigorous campaign to import German dyes through his firm—dyes which the U. S. Government had decreed could come into this country only on license through the Textile Alliance, and then only when they were dyes that the new domestic producers could not supply. As a result of Pickhardt's activities, the State Department cabled its representative at Paris in December 1919 that Kuttroff, Pickhardt & Co. had attempted to induce the German cartel to refuse to ship dyes to America through the Textile Alliance, in order to force all importations to come through their own company.

As the German I. G. got under way in their new activities in the United States a mass of rumor, conjecture and, in some instance, fact, was broadcast as each step was taken. It so happened, however, that the first of the new I. G. tie-ups, which was in the drug industry, attracted no attention at all. The principal on this side was Sterling Products, Inc. (now Sterling Drug, Inc.), a comparative newcomer and relatively unimportant at the time. The Sterling executives had a good reason for keeping this first tie-up secret, as it was made in direct violation of a pledge they had made to the Alien Property Custodian.

One of the war-time seizures of German property which caused great public interest had been that of the American Bayer Co., and its subsidiary, Synthetic Patents Corp., and the partial disclosure of the subversive activities of Dr. Schweitzer and some of his colleagues in Bayer. This company, with the Bayer aspirin trademark as its most valuable asset, was the first to be offered at public sale in 1918 by the Alien Property Custodian. Sterling Products was the buyer for $5,310,000. Details of the sale were arranged by Earl I. McClintock, an attorney on the staff of the Custodian, and one of the first acts of the new owners was to hire this public servant at more than triple his government salary.

Before the sale was consummated, Francis P. Garvan, then Alien Property Custodian, attempted to make sure that the executives of the new company were native-born Americans, and demanded their solemn pledge that there would be no renewals of the contacts with German interests.

The rules adopted by the Alien Property Custodian of World War I (unlike those of World War II) provided that deception by a purchaser of enemy property sold, if acting for an undisclosed principal or for resale to, or for the benefit of, a person not a United States citizen, should be subject to a fine of $10,000, or 10 years imprisonment, or both; and the property thus purchased should be forfeited to the United States.

Perhaps as this story unfolds, the reader may ponder on the possible relation of this rule to some of the incidents which occurred after Warren Harding became president of the United States.

The original contact between the Sterling management and the German cartels is a matter still shrouded in mystery. In the fall of 1919, however, and only a few months after he had given his pledge to the U. S. Government, William E. Weiss, president of Sterling, was in Baden Baden, Germany, in conference with Dr. Karl Duisberg and Rudolph Mann. At these meetings an informal understanding was reached in which the German and American Bayer companies would work in harmony in marketing Bayer aspirin in South America. Within a year Sterling had signed a formal, fifty-year agreement on this with the Germans.

In view of subsequent tie-ups with many of the largest corporations in America, through which the cartel extended its pattern in dyestuffs and in other chemical industries related to our national defense, it is significant that this first new tie-up by the Germans was with a relatively small patent-medicine group. Also, that the agreement provided, among other things, that expenses for "propaganda, advertising and legal costs," were to be shared, and that the Americans were to consult with their German partners on their advertising. So far as is known, not one of the many agreements which Farben had with other American industries mentioned propaganda, advertising and legal costs.

Sterling, originally known as the Neuralgyline Company, was started in Wheeling, West Virginia, in 1901 by two retail druggists, William E. Weiss and Albert H. Diebold. In 1917, these two nostrum vendors purchased the original Sterling Remedies, which was marketing a fake, lost-manhood cure called No-Tobac, and the candy cathartic, Cascarets, which had as its slogan, "They Work While You Sleep." Sterling Remedies was founded in 1887 in Attica, Indiana, and is said to have made its early profits from the tasty candy Cascarets rather than from the bad tasting No-Tobac.

Soon after the purchase of Bayer, Sterling organized the Winthrop Chemical Company, Inc., to handle Bayer's ethical preparations; a name being needed to which none of the odium of Sterling's patent-medicine advertising was attached. Winthrop was made the vehicle of the second important formal agreement with the cartel in 1923. On the basis of a fifty-fifty division of all profits, the cartel agreed to assign to Winthrop all of its new medicinal patents in the United States. The agreement was perpetual, and Sterling also bound itself to keep hands off the trademarks and patents of its subsidiaries so as not to interfere with the cartel's profit-sharing in Winthrop.

Weiss had written to a German Bayer executive the day the 1920 agreement was signed, that some parts of that document were not altogether clear and "would have to be worked out in the spirit in which it is entered into as forming a copartnership in a joint enterprise." When the 1923 Winthrop agreement was signed a clause was included by the German Bayer company declaring that it was not "a partnership or a joint venture" between the companies. The Weiss theory of partnership implied an equality which, apparently, the Germans did not relish. If Weiss and Diebold were to be partners they must be made to understand that they were the inferiors in the association.

In 1925 and 1926 the I. G. Farbenindustrie succeeded I. G. Dyes, adding to the original "Big Six" and their earlier associates another group of five of the larger chemical companies of Germany. It was then that Farben, with its world-wide affiliates, became the largest corporate structure in the world's chemical and allied industries. A new agreement was then consummated between Farben and Sterling by which the Germans' share of Winthrop profits was exchanged for assignment of fifty per cent of Winthrop's stock.

In the course of these corporate changes the Metz pharmaceutical interests were transferred (as revealed in Chapter II) to the now jointly-owned Sterling-Farben-Winthrop Company. Following the Metz deal, Farben also contributed another million dollars as half of its share of the purchase by Winthrop of the Cook Laboratories, and the Antidolor Company. So a total of something less than $2,000,000 was all the cash that Farben ever paid to recover a firm hold on its pharmaceutical interests in the United States,—interests which we had been told were wrested from Germany for all time during World War I.

While the details of the agreements with Farben remained a secret so far as the public was concerned, in 1926 the fact that Sterling-Bayer-Winthrop had close ties with the great German cartel began to receive frequent mention in the press. "We now have the Metz representation, and the I. G. representation," boasted Weiss, "conditions are now different." Yes, conditions were, in truth, different. Sterling had become a real power in drugs, and Weiss, even then, had visions of the financial and political power which his alliance with Farben was to bring him.

Sterling had also acquired all of Farben's U. S. patent interests and marketing rights in cosmetics, perfumery, agricultural insecticides and disinfectants, and all materials used in these products. As a result of these additions, the Sterling-Winthrop management was able to bring the duPont Company into a Farben tie-up and, in 1928, the Bayer-Semesan Company was formed with Weiss as president. This company, which was owned coequally by duPont and Winthrop, was organized for the development of all inventions by either party relating to insecticides. (In 1943 Sterling sold its 50 per cent share of Bayer-Semesan to duPont.)

Meanwhile, Sterling had purchased a number of the most profitable patent-medicine concerns in the United States. These included the makers of Fletcher's Castoria, Phillips' Milk of Magnesia, and other nationally advertised remedies. Then, in 1928 Weiss started to gather the entire American drug industry into one huge cartel; and, with Louis K. Liggett, put together Drug, Inc.—a holding company for all the Sterling-Bayer-Winthrop properties, the United Drug Co. and the Liggett chain of retail drug stores. Farben's new affiliate, Drug, Inc., then absorbed Bristol Myers Co., owned by the Bristol family—makers of Sal Hepatica and other so-called home remedies; Vick Chemical Co., owned by the Richardson family—makers of Vick's Vapo-Rub; and Life Savers, Inc., controlled by Edward J. Noble—maker of the well-known package candies. Each of these companies added to the already huge structure of Drug, Inc., and greatly increased the far reaching influences of its enormous volume of national advertising. Its stores and distributors were found in every city in America, its salesmen in every hamlet, its advertising slogans and products in every home.

It was at this time that another influential American citizen whose name was Musica, but who was known as Donald Coster, attempted to induce his good friend, Bill Weiss, to absorb the McKesson & Robbins wholesale drug company into the new pharmaceutical cartel. It was reported in financial circles that Coster worked hard to convince Weiss that it would be a splendid arrangement to have under his control not only the thousands of Rexall-Liggett retail drug stores, but also the hundred or more wholesale drug distributors which Coster already had or was preparing to absorb in the McKesson & Robbins chain.

Everyone who was at all active in the drug industry, however, had heard rumors that Coster was a common criminal, that McKesson & Robbins was based on fraud of some sort, and that Coster was planning to unload the securities on the public as soon as a financial statement could be put together which would enable him to list the securities on the New York Stock Exchange.

Weiss and his associates, although pressed by some bankers to do so, would have none of Coster's fake securities in their Drug, Inc., but they did encourage Coster to expand, and thus provide a more unified distribution for Sterling's increasing lines of drugs and patent medicines.

Any one who chooses to believe that no leader of the drug industry knew that Coster was a crook, and his financial empire a stack of phony bookkeeping entries, is welcome to that opinion. The fact remains, and the record proves, that I knew these things, and made repeated attempts to induce Washington to do something about them. And if I knew them, so did others. Incidentally, the famous accounting firm of Price, Waterhouse & Co., which so conveniently overlooked the nonexistence of the McKesson & Robbins Canadian warehouse inventories—and received more than half a million dollars for audits which included examination of many of these fraudulent book entries—was the same firm which has been certifying and approving the books and accounts of two of the leading American affiliates of Farben: Sterling, and Standard Oil Co. of New Jersey.

When Drug, Inc., was formed in 1928 Louis K. Liggett made the statement that the tie-up of the United Drug Co. with the Sterling group had the approval of the Department of Justice. Liggett was Republican National Committeeman from Massachusetts, and the Department of Justice, under Coolidge, quite evidently was not interested in the existing Sterling-Farben agreements—every one of which, thirteen years later, was admitted in court to have been illegal from the day it was signed. The blessings of Washington, however, were not proof against the coming depression and the ousting of the Republicans which followed. In 1933 after Herbert Hoover's oblivion, Drug, Inc., was dissolved, and the Sterling group returned to its original status as Farben's principal affiliate in the American drug industry.

In 1928 Sterling became involved in a cartel agreement in the vitamin D field through patent rights which Farben had assigned to Winthrop in the United States, and around which a tie-up was arranged with Wisconsin Alumni, Inc. (This has no connection with the University of Wisconsin.)

Conflicting patents relating to the activating of ergosterol, the product so useful in fortifying milk, bread and other food products to combat rickets, were thus pooled and restricted. Winthrop, duPont, and numerous other leading pharmaceutical, dairy and prepared food manufacturers were then licensed under these patents by Wisconsin Alumni.

Meanwhile we observe two figures which appear to be new in the Sterling-Farben post-war orbit, in the persons of the notorious Dr. Edward A. Rumely, who had been let out of jail by President Coolidge after conviction for pro-German activities during the first world war (in which Bayer's Dr. Schweitzer was involved), and one Robert McDowell Allen, president of the Vitamin Food Co., of which Dr. Rumely was organizer and director.

Under Sterling auspices a new company was organized in 1928 called Vegex, Inc., with Dr. Weiss, Earl McClintock and Farben's Winthrop director, William Hiemenz, as officers, and the Rumely-Allen team as directors. Judging by their lavish advertising in the *Journal of the American Medical Association,* and in *Hygeia,* Vegex and Vitamin Food Co. specialized in pepping up soups and gravies with Vitamin B, but this advertising was repudiated later by Dr. Fishbein's Council on Foods and Nutrition.

Dr. Weiss soon lost his enthusiasm for these tasty soup and gravy flavors, or for the lack of profits so derived; and Sterling turned Vegex over to Mr. Allen who became president of Vegex as well as of Vitamin Food, with Dr. Rumely still on their directorates.

However the Sterling-Winthrop-Farben interest in the Wisconsin Alumni licenses for ergosterol continued unabated, and in 1937 we find Dr. Weiss and his colleagues again discussing Farben vitamin matters with Dr. Rumely. (The latter, by that time was engaged in a new variety of educational propaganda, as will be revealed later.)

In 1935 another new Sterling-Farben subsidiary called Alba Pharmaceutical Co., was organized with capital supplied jointly by Farben and Winthrop, and with Weiss's son William E. Weiss, Jr., as president. This company received the processes and American patents of two of Farben's German subsidiaries. Meanwhile all of the Sterling-Farben tie-ups relating to Bayer or affecting property and patents originally purchased at the auction of 1918, were in direct violation of the pledge given to the Alien Property Custodian. In a little over a decade, Weiss and his associates had built up Sterling with German aid into a corporate structure which dominated the entire pharmaceutical industry in America.

Weiss and McClintock dominated the small group directing Sterling, and participated in the constant exchange German-American visits which the ramifications of the mutual interests of Sterling and Farben made necessary. Albert H. Diebold, more conservative, was the financial wheel horse, and James Hill, Jr., a former Internal Revenue official, the controller and treasurer. Another member of this select little band was Edward S. Rogers, the Weiss legal adviser, whose connection with the company dates back almost half a century. Rogers, like McClintock, had been associated with the Alien Property Custodian during World War I. He signed the 1926 Winthrop contract with Farben as witness for the signature of Weiss, and later represented the Sterling interests before government officials in tariff controversies. He attained prominence after 1929 as the American delegate to several inter-American conferences held in South America on trademarks and industrial properties. The importance of these conferences was made clear some ten years later, when Thurman Arnold stated that, "German control of drug outlets in South America has been one of the most effective instruments of propaganda and German influence in this hemisphere."

The late Frank A. Blair, president of Sterling's Centaur Company, and of the Proprietary Association, which Sterling dominated, was one of this group until he died in 1939. Blair, as will be shown later (in Chapter XI), was also a power behind the scenes at Washington.

In 1941 Weiss and Diebold were forced out of Sterling because of their personal relations and contacts with Farben. The others remained; McClintock as president of Sterling International in charge of foreign sales, Rogers as chairman of the board, and Hill as president. Weiss died after an automobile collision in Wisconsin in 1942. His death was as sudden and as unexpected as had been the mysterious demise in 1917 of Dr. Hugo Schweitzer, his predecessor as head of the American Bayer Company.

Once the cartel had regained a foothold in the United States through the friendly offices of our patent-medicine patriots, they lost no time in initiating the next step of their pincers strategy. Embargo and high tariff could keep out most of the German-made dyes, but there was nothing to prevent the "Big Six" from engaging in the production of dyes within the United States, always providing that American companies and American citizens could be induced to make these dyes inside the new tariff walls. Certain of our citizens not only did not object, they actually welcomed the Germans with open arms—sold them their holdings, took them in as partners or entered into agreements and iron-clad contracts to share patents, profits and markets.

In 1919 the Grasselli Chemical Company had established itself firmly as a domestic dye producer by purchasing from Sterling all of the dyestuff interests, including patents which Sterling acquired with the American Bayer Co. In 1924 Grasselli made an agreement with German Bayer to pool their respective United States interests in dyes in a new company known as Grasselli Dyestuff. Profits were to be divided equally and the initial German stock interest, forty-nine per cent, was to equal that of the Americans as soon as certain financial obligations were met. The control of foreign markets remained with the I. G., but the latter bound itself to turn over all of its United States patents on dyestuffs to the new company. It was also agreed that the production of heavy chemicals by Grasselli should be restricted.

Then, in 1926 when the huge I. G. Farbenindustrie cartel was formed in Germany, another new company known as General Dyestuff Corp., became the sales agent for all of the dyes made by Farben's affiliates in this country. And the Germans were back in American dyes, in the one industry that can be converted overnight to poison gas and munitions production.

Dr. Carl Bosch, head of I. G. Farbenindustrie, was not impressed when the League of Nations outlawed the use of chemical gas in warfare. The League had also abolished the use of force as an international policy, and the United States had taken the lead in disarmament. These peace moves fitted splendidly into the Farben pattern, and Bosch was all the more determined upon a complete penetration into every phase of the American dye industry. In 1928 Grasselli was taken over by duPont, and the latter thereupon was induced to hand over to Farben the entire Grasselli interests in the dyestuff industry. The transfer of title of the Grasselli dye interests to the Farben-owned General Aniline Works passed first through the hands of Farben's handy man, Herman Metz, and gave the Germans another good-sized chunk of the new American dye industry. Farben's strategy was crabwise, when a direct approach was repulsed.

Later Allied Chemical & Dye joined with duPont in agreements with Farben's Continental dye cartel covering certain foreign dye markets; these agreements were extended several times to cover different countries. Other agreements between duPont and Farben covered license or assignment of dye patents in the United States and Germany. These various interests required many meetings and understandings, the final outcome of which (according to allegations in several indictments handed down in 1941 and 1942 by Federal Grand Juries), was to enable Farben, acting through General Aniline & Film and other American companies, to restrict production of dyes and intermediates in the United States, and to eliminate competition through market-sharing in foreign countries.

When World War II began, Farben was not in such complete control of the coal-tar dye industry in the United States as its predecessors had been in 1914, but in 1939 Farben's American drug and dyestuff affiliates were much more powerful than those "Big Six" agents who had so effectively prevented the establishment of our munitions industry prior to the first World War. Drugs and dyes were Farben's "lost provinces" in industrial America. Deprived of the whole loaf, Farben had crept back through side doors and cellar windows and seized a good half, meanwhile adding its own Nazi flavor to the entire composition.

CHAPTER IV

New Conquests of America's Industry

THE OIL INDUSTRY
came next on Farben's agenda. There were several reasons for
this, the main one being that Standard Oil Co. of New Jersey, the
largest industrial corporation in the world, was reported to be
interested in new chemical developments which were related to,
or based on, the petroleum and natural-gas industries. The Germans knew that these new chemical products promised to be
among the most important munitions of the next war. So Farben,
within a few brief years, had induced the leaders of the all-power-
ful Standard Oil to pay them over $30,000,000 for an oil refining
process that turned out to be a commercial fizzle in the United
States. They also bamboozled the New Jersey executives into turning over to them technical details of the new chemical processes
which Standard Oil's research men might discover; and were given
control of the exploitation of such processes as well. Thus the
Farben overtures turned into an industrial strip poker game, the
results of which would have been highly amusing had not so

47

much of the Standard Oil raiment which passed over to Farben been processes and products vital to our national security.

The first understanding between Farben and Standard was in 1925, according to statements made subsequently to stockholders by Walter C. Teagle, then president of Standard. This informal understanding developed into negotiations of a comprehensive character and, in 1926, an agreement was drafted covering exploitation by Standard of Farben's new refining process for the hydrogenation of oil through the use of tremendous pressures. This process was the bait which brought about the strange union between Farben and Standard—a union which ultimately went far afield from petroleum, and led Senator Truman to cry "treason" at a Senate hearing after Germany had declared war upon the United States.

In 1927 a formal contract was consummated between Farben and Standard by which Farben agreed to supply the details of its new refining process to Standard, and Standard agreed to erect a commercial plant in the United States to demonstrate the process. Others were to be licensed to use the processes on a royalty basis in which Farben would share. Standard paid Farben with more than a half-million shares of its stock, worth approximately $30,-000,000, as consideration for this contract. In addition to the stock transfer, Standard expended a great many more millions erecting hydrogenation plants in the United States and demonstrating that the process did not come up to the rosy expectations of its young technical expert, Robert T. Haslam, who had inspected the Farben plant in Germany, and had recommended the purchase. Apparently Standard missed one point about this new high-pressure cracking method—its cost. Farben used it to produce gasoline from coal. Germany had plenty of coal, and to the Germans, the excessive cost of the gasoline over that produced from oil was not important. They knew that the time was coming when Germany would again begin war and probably be cut off from the most of its crude oil supplies by another British blockade.

Dr. Bosch and Hermann Schmitz played the leading parts for Farben in negotiating the 1927 contract; Teagle and Frank A. Howard, who was later made head of Standard Oil Development Company, looked after the interests of Standard and its stockholders. To Farben this tie-up was of vast importance, because it not only established a close working alliance with the world's largest industrial company, but it was also to lead to tie-ups with other American companies on important chemical developments related to the petroleum industry. Some of these new processes have little real relation to oil, but they did very directly relate to Farben's preparation—and our own lack of preparation—for World War II.

Other aspects of Standard Oil which made it an ally of great potential value in Farben's eyes included the fact that its distribution system of filling stations reached into the intimate life of so many communities. Unlike Sterling, prior to the latter's expansion, Standard already had a nation-wide army of employes. Also, Standard's organization was world-wide—in South America and the Far East as well as in Europe. This army could feel the pulse, and possibly even change the beat, of countless bloodstreams. Standard's political power and influence with many governments were not the least of its attractions to Farben.

That Farben had long contemplated and sought such an arrangement was indicated by a statement made early in 1926 to William Weiss by one of the Farben leaders that they had to be careful in negotiating with Sterling for any products other than pharmaceuticals, because Farben was already negotiating with Standard Oil, and did not want to give Sterling any of the products that should go to the other company. Standard was big game, even for Farben, and had to be stalked with great care. Personal friendships between the negotiators sometimes count much in affairs of this sort, and personal ties were made use of in this instance. Agreements are entered into by corporations acting as legal entities but they are negotiated, wrangled about, drawn up and signed by corporation officials who are real persons, not legal fictions. Mr. Teagle, in a public statement quoted in the *New York Times* in November 1929, referred to his "close and pleasant personal relationship of some years standing with the leaders of the I. G.," which, said Teagle, was the reason why he had consented to serve as a director of the newly organized American I. G. Chemical Corp., in which he denied Standard had any financial interest.

Dr. Bosch of Farben reciprocated these expressions of Teagle's friendship in 1930, after Teagle had interceded between Farben and duPont in a controversy relating to the manufacture of synthetic ammonia. Bosch wrote his friend Teagle to thank him for arranging the meeting with Lammot duPont, and concluded his letter with:

"I believe that as a result of this intervention, the deadlock in the negotiations between duPont and I. G. has now been overcome, and that thereby our desire will be realized to reach a cooperation with this very energetic and cleverly proceeding firm, which we have endeavored to bring about for years. The reason for the failure of our former negotiations may be the lack of the right personal contact which has now been established, *thanks to your personal interest.*"

Farben was the largest corporation in Germany and the greatest chemical cartel in the world; Standard was the largest industrial corporation in the world; duPont was not much smaller and, with its multiplicity of products and its stock control of General Motors, U. S. Rubber, Remington Arms and others, it ranked with Farben and Standard in importance. When it came to drawing up written contracts, however, or even arriving at gentlemen's agreements, it was the conclusion of Dr. Bosch that the earlier refusal of the huge duPont Corporation to play ball was due mainly to the aloofness of Mr. duPont—an aloofness which Mr. Teagle, as mutual friend, had changed into the right personal contact. On the other hand it is quite possible that recollections of the part played by Bosch and his associates in World War I lingered longer in the memory of Lammot duPont than they did in that of Walter Teagle.

After the 1927 contract Farben and the Standard leaders continued their meetings, Farben constantly pressing Standard with the advantages of a more comprehensive tie-up between the two companies. At one of these meetings, early in 1929, Dr. Bosch stated that it appeared certain Standard would be compelled to expand its activities far beyond oil refining, into the chemical field, and naïvely suggested that as Farben was already supreme in the chemical industry, it should of course have a dominant position in any such arrangement. This sounded plausible, and Teagle signified his willingness to let Standard become the junior partner provided the minority interest was sufficiently large. Mr. Teagle, it would seem, had little confidence in the ability of Standard's research men to forge ahead in those new chemical developments which were already being discussed in the technical journals as certain to arise from the petroleum industry. DuPont and other American corporations had already demonstrated that American chemical research was amply qualified to compete with the Germans. The prewar legend of the supremacy of German chemical brains had been punctured. But the Standard leaders seemed to ignore this fact.

Thus, Dr. Bosch cozened his friend Teagle into handing over to Farben what amounted to the direction and control of the chemical-munitions affairs of the largest industrial organization in America. If Mr. Teagle and his colleagues realized what power they were giving away they didn't care. If they did not realize it, then they were among the few in the chemical industry who were not aware of it.

The result of these negotiations was four new agreements, entered into in November 1929 between Standard and Farben, which provided for exchange of chemical patents and processes. They also covered the commercial exploitation of new products, payment of royalties, and the division of world markets. The more important of these agreements expressed the intention of the parties to cooperate with each other and avoid overlapping and competition through a recognition by Standard that Farben had a preferred position in chemical products, and a recognition by Farben that Standard had a preferred position in oil and natural gas. The joker in the agreement provided that such new chemical processes contributed by either party, which were not directly related to the refining of oil or natural gas, should be controlled by Farben. Dr. Bosch thus extended the Farben pattern to a dominant position in the group of chemical developments which were on the way, and which he knew would have a vital bearing on the rearming of Germany, and on the national defense of the United States.

The relationship established by the 1929 agreements was aptly summarized several years later by Mr. Howard in a letter to one of his colleagues in which he stated:

> The I. G. may be said to be our general partner in the chemical business as to developments arising during the period beginning in 1929 and expiring in 1947. The desire and intention of both parties is to avoid competing with one another . . . . . The general theory of the agreement is that chemical developments more closely related to the oil business than to the outside chemical business remain in control of Standard, with I. G. participating . . . . . whereas developments more nearly akin to the outside chemical industry than to the then existing business of Standard pass to the control of I. G. with suitable participation by Standard . . . . . One additional fact might be pointed out: for a variety of reasons it seems quite probable that if we desire to make any additional important affiliations in the oil-chemical field, such affiliations will be with the duPonts, the Shell Company or both. The I. G. relationship is in no respect a handicap but on the contrary, a definite asset to us in considering the possibility of any such affiliations.

Standard was courting duPont, as was Farben, but for different reasons. Standard's great power lay mainly in one industry—oil, and the Standard Oil executives were dazzled by the audacity of the duPonts, who were then entering one new field after another with such brilliant success.

In 1930 another Standard-Farben agreement was consummated which provided for the organization of a jointly owned development company, later established as Jasco Inc., at Baton Rouge, La. The name Jasco stood for Joint American Study Company, but might well have meant Jackass Americans Surrender a Continent. In Jasco, under Standard management, but acting under Farben instructions, a group of technicians were to develop new chemical processes outside of oil and gas refining. Jasco appeared to be an American corporation operated by Americans, and was not identified in the public mind with Farben. Actually it became the medium through which Farben secured the results of chemical research done by Standard. Farben in return, furnished Standard with a bare minimum of its own research.

When pressed for more data by Standard, Farben at first procrastinated with the excuse that its research was incomplete, then bluntly stated that the Hitler government would not permit the information to leave Germany. In one instance it was revealed later than Standard had even supplied data relating to the production of high-test aviation gasoline which Standard research had not developed, but which had been secured through an association with other large oil-refining concerns, including the Anglo-Iranian Oil Company, which is controlled by the British Government. Standard was accused of continuing to send these developments on aviation gasoline to Farben until November 1939, two months after the war between Germany and England had started.

Synthetic rubber was one of the new products which should have been turned over by Farben to Jasco. This development was, in fact, the choicest bit of the limburger with which Farben had baited its trap.

Back in 1927 Standard learned that Farben had developed commercial production of synthetic rubber. Standard also knew that duPont was working on synthetic rubber and, in April 1930, before the Jasco agreement was signed, a Standard vice-president, E. M. Clark, wrote Farben warning them to review their patent situation on artificial rubber so that duPont could not get ahead of them.

Farben, in Germany, developed a type of synthetic rubber called Buna. Standard, later at Jasco, developed one called Butyl. Buna was considered better than Butyl for some purposes, especially for tires. Butyl was cheaper to produce and better for other purposes, particularly inner tubes. What happened in the jug-handled one-way pot called Jasco? Standard, as rapidly as it made progress in its Butyl research, supplied all pertinent data to Farben, whereas Farben not only delayed supplying the data on Buna but, for a period, actually attempted to discourage Standard about its new synthetic. "It's not so hot," indicated Farben. "Why bother with it? Let's wait until we develop something really worth while."

At this time, duPont was making rapid strides in the commercial production of its own synthetic rubber, Neoprene, which had excellent qualities but under normal conditions was too expensive to compete with natural rubber for making tires. Farben had already succeeded in making a number of agreements with duPont on exchange of other patents, but duPont was still gun shy; and Farben wanted Neoprene very badly indeed. So, in 1935 Farben notified Standard that they had a proposal from duPont for a tie-up on the latter's synthetic rubber. Accordingly, suggested Farben, it might be well if a new development company should be organized to take care of synthetic rubber research and exploitation for all three. One third of the proposed new company was to go to Standard, duPont and Farben respectively, and each was to put all of its synthetic rubber patents and processes into this new pot. Thus Farben tried to play Standard against duPont, and duPont against Standard. By suggesting a minority part for itself and leaving a two-third interest to the Americans, Farben was sugar-coating the syphon through which it hoped to extract the desired technical information on this vital synthetic. This proposal did not go through, possibly because the Messrs. Irenée, Lammot and Pierre duPont had a more acute sense of smell than had their friends, Messrs. Teagle, Howard and Haslam.

Farben, however, does not become discouraged easily, and some three years later succeeded in getting duPont to grant it certain patent licenses to make a Neoprene type of rubber in Germany. Meanwhile Farben was building synthetic rubber plants for the Hitler Government large enough to supply Germany's requirements and supplement the reserve stock pile of natural rubber which was being imported in anticipation of the blockade which would again cut off her outside supply.

Reports of the success of Germany's synthetic rubber production were discounted by many when Austria was invaded in 1938, and stories strangely leaked out of Germany that its motorized troops were delayed in getting to Vienna because the new ersatz tires blew out. Eventually, a few individuals in our government became mildly alarmed at the possibility of losing our natural rubber supply, and Standard, responding to pressure, renewed its efforts to induce Farben to put the Buna developments into Jasco where, under the 1930 agreement, they belonged.

In 1938 Howard reported to his Executive Committee that Farben continued to decline to supply its data on Buna rubber, since, because of military expediency, the German Government refused to allow the information to leave Germany. Thus the Farben-Hitler military machine clearly showed its teeth.

As late as October 19, 1939, after the war had started, Howard again reported sorrowfully to his Standard colleagues that Buna rubber had never been made at Jasco because Farben had not supplied the necessary information. A week later Howard explained in writing:

> We haven't complete technical information on Buna, and cannot get any more information from Germany. The only thing we can do is to continue to press for authority to act, but in the meantime loyally preserve the restrictions they have put on us.

So, until December 1940, after our Lend-Lease program was under way, and Hitler's intentions were clearly defined for the whole world to see, Standard loyally continued to preserve the restrictions of the Germans and to transmit to Farben its latest research data on this strategic material of national defense.

Synthetic rubber was by no means the only new research development which came within the provisions of the lopsided mésalliance between Farben and Standard. Farben had discovered a process for making acetic acid from natural or cracked gas by means of an electric arc. This process tied into synthetic rubber research, and also produced an acetic acid of superior purity and at what promised to be lower cost than resulted from the methods then in use.

Acetic acid, widely used in the industries of peace, is invaluable in the manufacture of various chemical munitions in war. (In World War I its price advanced in this country from a few cents to more than a dollar a pound.) This acid was being made by various American companies, but the market was expanding, and Standard had ample supplies of both natural and cracked gas. So the new Farben method fitted splendidly into the Jasco program of joint research and exploitation.

A pilot plant was erected at Baton Rouge, and the excellence of the process demonstrated. The plant produced acid beyond the normal requirements of Standard, and it was proposed to sell the surplus to various large consumers. Farben, however, was very definitely opposed to the commercial production of acetic acid, or of any other acetylene products from the electric arc process. Some strange reasons were given: Farben had other commitments in America which might be interfered with; a disagreeable price war might result in Europe; the acetic acid market offered no incentive to take up the manufacture of this product, etc, etc.

When Standard persisted in its desire to enter the acetic-acid field, Farben came up with the suggestion that the acid sales be handled, not by Jasco or Standard, but through Advance Solvents & Chemical Corp., with which Farben had other ties. This plan fell through, however, as did a later effort to interest the Shell Oil Co., the American subsidiary of the Dutch Shell interests. Farben then informed Standard that it was developing improvements in the original acetylene process but that the German Government would have to approve any contracts relating to it. Finally, Farben threw all pretense aside and requested that the Jasco acetic acid plant be abandoned. This was done. Standard dismantled the plant. In 1940 the patents covering the acetic acid process were transferred by Farben to its own subsidiary General Aniline & Film Corp., which at the time was engaged in a furious campaign to convince the American public and the U. S. Government that it was not controlled by Farben.

Another product which was turned in to Jasco for development was a laboratory curiosity called Oppanol. Oppanol had not been considered previously as a basis for compounding lubricants, but through Jasco research it was found to have great value in the production of a superior lubricating oil for planes, tanks and naval vessels. These developments, invaluable in war, and wholly the result of research by Standard technicians, were promptly handed over to Farben and thus became available for the German war machine. Other processes and products which were worked on by Jasco, became the mediums through which numerous American companies were brought within the Farben orbit. Through the kindly offices of Standard Oil, the intelligence department of Farben was thus enabled to peek into technical minds, and enter doorways that would not otherwise have been open to it.

When the present war started, Standard and Farben entered into a new series of agreements, some of which, by their wording, were undoubtedly intended for carry-over understandings, effective for the duration and until such time as the old agreements could be reinstated and "business as usual" resumed. While Hitler's army was on its way to Warsaw, Standard's Mr. Howard was on his way to Europe to meet a Farben representative. This meeting resulted in what came to be known as the Hague Agreement—a most interesting document which was signed by Mr. Howard for Standard, and by Dr. Fritz Ringer for Farben, on Sept. 25, 1939, two days after the German Army announced its victorious destruction of Poland's resistance. Messrs Howard and Ringer, however, dated the document back a few weeks to September first, feeling perhaps, that it would read a bit better as a peacetime understanding.

By the Hague Agreement Farben purported to transfer to Standard all of its rights in Jasco in consideration of a small cash payment which was to be paid to a Farben designee. A division of market rights on the products was also included. Standard to have the United States, the British and French Empires and Iraq, Farben to retain the rest of the world. Then came carry-over provisions which obligated Standard and Farben to report to each other on all future business in their respective territories, with the understanding that if there should be inequities in the monetary returns, adjustments would be made on the basis of the original agreements of 1930. War or no war, the Standard-Farben alliance was to go on.

Mr. Howard reported to his colleagues that this agreement was a *modus vivendi* which would operate for the duration—"whether or not the U.S. came in." The report continued with:

> It is hoped that enough has been done to permit closing the most important uncompleted points by cable. It is difficult to visualize as yet just how successful we shall be in maintaining our relations through this period without personal contacts.

In making this report, Mr. Howard may have had in mind the

fact that the Trading with the Enemy Act, passed during the first World War, had never been repealed.

Despite Mr. Howard's anticipated suspension of communications, in June 1940, Standard asked Chemnyco, Inc., Farben's New York headquarters, for a license and transfer of title on a patent on an asphalt process, with a provision for retransfer of title under suitable conditions. And, six months later, Farben suggested an understanding through which it would sell on a royalty basis certain products for Standard in countries the latter could not reach. Meanwhile on Sept. 4, 1940, Standard's executive committee ratified a brand-new arrangement, covering payment of royalties on hydrogenation patents with Farben, which was dated back to January 1, and in which some provision of the original 1929 agreements were either reaffirmed or modified.

After the fall of France, Farben kept in touch with Standard by meeting the latter's representative in Paris. And, in February 1941, a message from the French capital informed Mr. Howard that his friend Dr. Ringer wished to reply to a question raised by a cable with the advice that:

> Jasco cable will be difficult but one underlying point is that Jasco contract has not been wiped out as agreed whatever done the final financial outcome original intention of old Jasco agreement should govern.

The exchange of information continued until a few weeks before Germany declared war upon the United States. On Oct. 22, 1941 a cable went to Farben advising that Jasco had filed suit against the B. F. Goodrich Rubber Co. for alleged infringements of patents covering Buna. The cable also asked Farben to send copies of the German patent applications which should be duly certified by a United States Consul. Again, war or no war—business as usual.

In addition to Messrs. Teagle, Howard, Haslam and Clark, among those most actively concerned in the later negotiations with Farben was the late W. S. Farish, who came into the Standard organization in 1919 when that company purchased control of the Humble Oil Co., of Houston, Texas. Farish had organized the Humble Co. a few years previously with several men who were high in Texas political affairs. In 1933 Farish became chairman of Standard, and in 1937 he succeeded Teagle as president. Another Standard stalwart was Dr. Per K. Frolich, director of their chemical laboratories. Dr. Frolich, in 1942, was elected president of the American Chemical Society.

Mention has already been made of the kindly intercession of Mr. Teagle in bringing about a friendly conference between Dr. Bosch and Lammot duPont. Previous meetings had not run too smoothly, as indicated by the 1929 conference at which Lammot duPont challenged Dr. Bosch about the report that Farben and Standard Oil planned a joint synthetic nitrogen plant in Louisiana. Dr. Bosch replied that the report was true and that a company had already been formed in which Farben held fifty-one percent of the stock. This, of course, was entirely untrue. The 1929 agreements between Farben and Standard had not been signed at that time, and the stock interest of which Bosch bragged was not in those agreements. Apparently Farben was bluffing and had no intention of building a synthetic plant here in its own name or at its own financial risk. Why invest in a horse and buggy if someone else could be induced to furnish a free ride? What Farben was after was to hold the reins, no matter who owned the steed.

Synthetic nitrogen was the personal baby of Dr. Bosch, and Farben's annual production of 600,000 tons was one-third of the world's consumption. So the good doctor was fully aware how great had been the loss to Farben when, in 1918, the Haber-Bosch patents for the production of the synthetic nitrogen were seized by the Alien Property Custodian. Prior to the war, an unsuccessful attempt had been made in the United States to produce nitrogen commercially by atmospheric fixation, and while the war was in progress a huge nitrogen plant was started with government aid at Muscle Shoals, Alabama—too late for the war effort.

However in the postwar decade atmospheric fixation had begun in the United States and with this background and the prospect of a large American production of synthetic nitrogen and ammonia, Farben did not relish the thought of new American plants which might serve as munition factories in the next war. As always, Farben was looking to the future, and the importance with which its leaders regarded a participation in the production of these synthetics in the United States has been amply justified by the tremendously increased use of high explosives in the present war. Their use has dwarfed all earlier needs for nitrates and ammonia; an example were the huge two and four-ton "Block Busters" charged with amatol, a new high explosive which is made by compounding TNT with ammonium nitrate. Yes, Farben knew what was coming.

Eight years after the friendly conference arranged by Mr. Teagle, Farben caused the formation of the International Nitrogen Association, a world cartel, which brought into unity of action the producers of both natural and synthetic nitrogen and ammonia. Ostensibly this cartel was to rule the markets for fertilizer materials. Actually, the far more important objective was to limit the capacity of synthetic nitrogen plants outside of Germany.

Farben went far around Robin Hood's barn to secure some sort of nitrogen and ammonia tie-ups in this country, and to bring duPont within its sphere of influence on these important synthetic war munitions. DuPont's main interest in synthetic nitrogen and ammonia in the decade after World War I was for the explosives department of its business. Fundamentally duPont has been a producer of gun-cotton rather than fertilizer.

In January 1926 duPont entered into a rather illusive agreement on explosive patents and processes with Dynamit A.G., which later became a Farben subsidiary in that field. The agreement that was drawn up was not signed, but was held as a gentlemen's understanding. It covered ammunition of various sorts, industrial explosives, and the countries in which licenses under the patents should be granted. It did not however, mention military explosives as such. Dynamit A.G. was also a manufacturer of celluloid, which is made from nitro-cellulose, and another informal agreement was reached by which duPont and D.A.G. would exchange information and give each other the first option on rights to patents and processes. These two casual understandings are significant because, apparently, they were the first through which duPont became allied with Farben.

A later tie-up which was to have wartime repercussions was made in 1929 between Dynamit A.G. and the duPont-owned Remington Arms Co., by which information was exchanged and royalties paid by Remington on a patented chemical product of

German invention known as Tetrazine, a substance of great value as a priming charge for ammunition. This agreement stipulated that Remington could not sell military ammunition containing Tetrazine in any of the countries comprising the British Empire. When war began in 1939, Remington received huge orders for ammunition from the British Government, but because of the clause in the contract with the Farben subsidiary, it had to supply the British with cartridges containing an inferior priming agent. This restriction continued in 1941. Later it was rescinded. Only a tiny speck of the primer is required in each cartridge, but the efficacy of that small particle might well mean the life or death of a soldier.

Returning for a moment to the period immediately following the Armistice, we find that the great chemical plants that had mushroomed up in the United States during the war presented a big reconstruction problem. Clearly, it was up to the industry to evolve new peace-time products, and in this effort the duPont chemists outstripped all other American research workers. The war plants which gave the impetus to this research were largely in the organic chemical field—based upon the conversion of coal tar or other once-living organisms as distinguished from inorganic materials such as sulphur, sodium and other metallic elements.

Among the most important developments of this post-war research were various types of synthetic resins or plastics made by what is known as polymerization. This may be described briefly as a method of changing liquids into solids through application of heat, light or the use of catalysts. Chemically, polymerization is the combination of a number of molecules to form a single new and larger molecule. The number of new materials in which these rearranged molecules may be formed is endless. It might almost be said that the chemist, having unscrambled matter down to what seemed to be its smallest particles, the physicist then stepped in to rebuild it into heretofore unsuspected forms. Thus such elements as oxygen, hydrogen, nitrogen, carbon and chlorine, all obtained from inexpensive raw materials, are formed into solids of surpassing beauty that for many constructive uses are unequalled in nature. Unhappily, however, these new substances supply some of the most important implements of war.

Among these postwar products in which duPont research kept so far ahead of its competitors in the United States and at least abreast of Farben's technicians were Neoprene, Nylon and the glass-like product called Lucite. This last was an evolution of the laminated safety glass, designed primarily for automobile windshields. Lucite proved to be a most superior product. It was far stronger than glass, was practically shatterproof, and provided equally good visibility.

DuPont's commercial production of Lucite began in 1935. It had been preceded by the production of a somewhat similar plastic known as Plexiglass produced in Germany by the firm of Röhm & Haas A. G., Darmstadt; and in the United States by a company of a very similar name, Röhm & Haas Co., Inc., of Philadelphia. Years before, when the firm was founded, Dr. Röhm was the German and Mr. Haas the American partner. During World War I the American Röhm & Haas had been seized by the Alien Property Custodian because of an alleged sixty per cent enemy interest. The enemy interest was sold by the Custodian to a Chicago concern which promptly sold it back to the American Röhm & Haas company. A forty per cent interest in the American company was then trusteed so that the dividends would go to Dr. Röhm and his family in Germany. Thus the partners lost no time in circumventing the seizure by the United States Government.

In 1927 there began a series of agreements between the American and the German Röhm & Haas companies, and between the latter and I. G. Farben. These agreements related to new developments in sheet plastics. In this same period duPont and the English Imperial Chemicals Industries were cooperating in similar plastic developments. Conflict over patents arose between these two groups. Finally, in March 1936, after protracted negotiations, duPont and the American Röhm & Haas agreed on an exchange of patents and processes, which arrangement tied in with Imperial Chemicals and the German Röhm & Haas, and thus with Farben.

Three years later, just a few months before World War II started, the two American makers of plastic glass entered into several more understandings which provided for control of prices, market sharing and restriction of production. Also, restrictions on the sale of the plastics abroad were entered into by the American Röhm & Haas with its German namesake and with Farben.

By this time the use of plastics for airplane enclosures and gunners' screens had become of vital importance. And a result of the limitation of production was said to be a shortage of these sheets of plastic for the construction of military airplanes and other military equipment scheduled for the Lend-Lease program, and the long-delayed United States national defense program. Farben strategy, again by the indirect approach, had succeeded.

The relationship between the American Röhm & Haas and Farben is illustrated by correspondence between them after the war had started. Farben, in December 1939, wrote to the Philadelphia company releasing it from restrictions on the exportation of certain of its products, and requesting it to take care of Farben's customers in Latin America—orders from whom would be referred to Röhm & Haas through another of Farben's allies in the United States, Advance Solvents & Chemical Co. Mr. Haas replied on January 22, 1940, that his firm would of course comply with Farben's request, also that:

> No matter who is doing the shipping we shall revert to the *status quo antem* as soon as normal conditions have been restored. The thought uppermost in my mind is to serve you in the most faithful and most efficient way possible in this emergency.

Otto Haas, an American citizen for many years, was not only faithful to Farben in the emergency of war, but appeared confident that when the war should end he and his supposedly American firm would be permitted to resume their relations with Farben—and that Farben would again rule the roost as before.

In October, 1935, two of Farben's leading officials; Georg von Schnitzler and Dr. Fritz ter Meer, came to Wilmington and attended a meeting at the home of Lammot duPont. At this meeting Farben's representatives pointed out how friendly Farben's attitude had been in cooperating with duPont on the amicable settlement of patent disputes and foreign market problems and that Farben had invited duPont participation in the synthetic rubber developments. Yet duPont, according to the Farben report of this meeting, remained apprehensive that Standard Oil, by reason of its Farben tie-ups, might break into duPont's field in the chemical industry.

DuPont's ideas on the subject of its relations with Farben are recorded in a memorandum dated March 18, 1936, in which was stated:

"The duPont-I. G. relationships have notably improved, due partly to the personalities of individuals entrusted with negotiations, and partly to an officially more friendly attitude from higher up in the I. G. organization."

This memorandum also indicated that patent disputes were being settled very satisfactorily, especially those handled by Dr. George Lutz, an expert employed by duPont, who formerly had been associated with I. G. Dyes. The memorandum further suggested that the relations with Farben which did not seem to stand so well were on artificial silk and cellophane. However, on May 23rd, 1939, Farben finally induced duPont to sign an agreement which covered Nylon.

Artificial silk has had its place in the list of chemical-munition products since the first World War, when its value was demonstrated for powder bags, electric insulation, and other military requirements. More recently the use of different types of rayon as a substitute for cotton in heavy-duty airplane and auto tires, and to replace silk for parachutes, had placed these synthetic textile fibers definitely among the more important chemical munitions. These qualities, plus the adaptability of some of the chemical processes involved in rayon production to other war materials and the rapid advance of technical developments, made it important to the Farben strategy to add this industry to the list of those in the United States to be penetrated, and handicapped for war.

Farben first reached into the United States photographic field in 1926, shortly after it succeeded I. G. Dyes. At that time William E. Weiss of Sterling Products wanted Farben to turn over to him the American development of the photographic interests of Kalle, which owned the German Agfa, and was already in a strong position in Germany. Farben refused Weiss's request, and proceeded to purchase complete control of the Ansco Photo Products, Inc., of Binghamton, N. Y., the oldest maker of photo supplies in America. Farben also organized Agfa Raw Film Corp., and Agfa Photo Products, of New York City. Then, in 1928, it combined all these interests in the Agfa Ansco Corp. Ten years later Agfa Ansco had become the second largest concern of its kind in the United States. Its importance as a supplier of materials for war requirements, especially for aerial photographic maps and for blueprinting war plants and equipment, made this Farben-owned company a potential menace to the national defense of this country.

We now come to a phase of Farben's strategy which reached out into metallurgy rather than chemistry, although its inception came from the chemical process by which metallic magnesium is recovered from solutions of brine. Farben's early development of large-scale magnesium production and the light metal alloys into which this metal is combined, constituted a most important contribution to the German war machine—incendiary bombs and airplane metals.

As already mentioned (in Chapter II), Dr. Schweitzer, World War spy and head of the American Bayer Company, had boasted of the day when his colleagues' development of magnesium alloys would be of great value to the Fatherland. It was. Germany made great strides in the first postwar decade in producing the metal and its alloys, and in making castings of the latter.

In this same period the Dow Chemical Co., and the American Magnesium Co., began to produce metallic magnesium in the United States. The Aluminum Co. of America (Alcoa) then took over the American Magnesium Corp., and shut off its production of the metal, leaving Dow the sole American producer. In 1927 Alcoa made a cross-licensing arrangement on alloys owned respectively by Dow and American Magnesium, and also secured licenses to United States patents on magnesium owned by British Aluminium Co.

Farben had been biding its time. It had taken out various United States patents which were of no great value on the production of the metal, but which did have some advantages in its fabrication. Then, in 1929 Farben made advances to both Dow and Alcoa for partnership arrangements covering the entire magnesium field— production, alloys and fabrication. Dow repulsed these advances and refused even to discuss any partnership with the Germans.

Possibly they recalled an experience twenty-five years earlier, when a visitor from Germany came to Midland, Michigan, and warned the senior Dow that if his firm did not discontinue exporting bromine, the Germans would retaliate by dumping two pounds of bromine in the United States for every one that Dow exported.

Dow had defied those early threats, and the Germans dumped their bromine in this country at less than the cost of transportation and duty. This vicious commercial blackjacking continued to handicap Dow's business until war broke out in 1914, but Dow had not yielded to the Germans then, and did not intend to do so on magnesium.

However, Dow failed to reckon with the power of the new Farben strategy which tied up Alcoa as its partner in 1931, and a year later organized the Magnesium Development Co. Under joint ownership, but with Farben's Dr. Walter H. Duisberg as president, the new company pooled all the magnesium patents and developments of Farben and Alcoa, and notice was served on Dow to play ball—or else.

Dow held what appeared to be trump cards in development of processes, valuable patents and contracts with Ford and other automobile companies. But the heat was on, and threats of patent litigation were made. One suit was actually started.

A gentler approach was through a series of luncheons at which one Edward L. Cheyney, suave Alcoa sales executive, entertained an aged director of the Dow company at the gloomy Union Club in Cleveland and, between courses, pictured the doleful things that could happen to a company that persisted in bucking the Farben-Alcoa combine. No threats were made but the deep regret of Alcoa was expressed at the unfortunate obstinacy of the Dow management. The luncheons were held on direct instructions from Farben, but Mr. Cheyney soft-pedaled the Germans' place in the setup, and emphasized the probity of Alcoa. Dow finally decided that further resistance was useless, gave up the unequal contest and, in 1933, signed up with the Farben-Alcoa magnesium team.

During this triumph of the Farben strategy in breaking into another American industry on the traditional German shoestring, its emissaries were negotiating with the Ford Motor Company on the fabrication of magnesium alloys for piston heads and other automotive parts where light weight was an advantage. Quite possibly these negotiations traced back to the Ford Motor Company's plant in Germany, and may also have had bearing on the willingness of Mr. Edsel Ford to act as one of the directors of the American I. G. Chemical Corp. to which Farben's fifty per cent interest in the Magnesium Development Corp. was assigned.

However, once Dow was securely tied into the Farben-Alcoa combine, Farben's next step was to make sure that the production of magnesium metal in the United States be restricted, and its fabrication in alloys be developed as slowly as possible. This was important, because magnesium, in its natural form, is one of the most plentiful of the elements, and so many new methods of extracting it had been experimented with, and so many new uses were in sight that there were good prospects of lower costs for the metal and the consequent rapid expansion of its production.

In its first 1931 agreement with Farben, Alcoa had accepted a restriction on initial production of the metal should a new United States plant be built by the partners. When Dow signed up, the plans for a new plant were at once abandoned, and competition in the domestic magnesium industry was at an end. Farben meanwhile had greatly expanded its own production of magnesium and magnesium alloys in Germany. With one hand Farben prepared Germany for war by creating a sufficient supply of light metal for its huge fleet of warplanes; with the other it throttled the growth of the industry in America, and saw to it that a good part of the limited United States production was shipped out of the country.

Thus Farben inoculated our magnesium producers with industrial sleeping-sickness, which the larger of its partners, interested mainly in aluminum, did not resent, and which the other partner, shanghaied into a shotgun Farben marriage, was unable to prevent. When the United States started its schedule of expanded airplane production, one of the greatest, and seemingly insurmountable barriers which confronted the Army and Navy was the acute shortage of magnesium alloys.

Other metals of vital importance to national defense which are found in restrictive agreements involving American producers with Farben, directly or indirectly, included aluminum, nickel and molybdenum.

Contrary to opinion so frequently expressed elsewhere, it was merely incidental to the Farben strategy (as illustrated in this chapter and that preceding it) that the cartel mechanism lent itself to Farben's purpose in tying into some of the great industrial corporations of this country. The almost complete abandonment of anti-trust law enforcement had made many of these American combinations inevitable and likewise made Farben's technic possible. This technic would have been ineffective and Farben's task much more difficult if the anti-trust laws had been enforced. Farben's part in procuring two decades of lax enforcement of federal statutes may best be understood after reading other chapters of this story.

When the war started in 1939 Farben's tie-ups in the United States were by no means confined to the particular products and companies which have been mentioned thus far. The thousands of United States patents taken out during the preceding seventeen years by Farben and its affiliates in Germany had been utilized to effect an almost countless number of agreements with corporations and individuals in the United States. These agreements ranged from royalty payments on products of relative unimportance to complete control of militarily-strategic industries. The greatest number of these patents related to coal-tar dyes and pharmaceuticals; others involved a wide range of chemical and metallurgical products.

It is proper to state that the mere fact that each of those many companies had relations of some sort with Farben or its affiliates, does not necessarily imply any degree of illegality on the part of each such American company. Farben's broad purpose was to accomplish so complete a saturation of our industrial structure, by fair means or foul, that our progress at all times would be under observation, and, when advisable, might be restricted.

As we have seen, some of its contracts were viciously illegal. Other arrangements however were not tainted with illegality.

An indication of the extent and diversification of this penetration is a partial list, in the appendix, of some of the better-known American corporations, including those already mentioned, which are officially reported to have made agreements with Farben or to have been involved in some of Farben's direct tie-ups with other companies. This list reads like a directory of American industry. Because of the character of these agreements and relationships, at least some degree of Farben's influence or espionage may have resulted in each instance.

CHAPTER V

Farben's Royal Family

LIKE MOST great industrial corporations, I. G. Farben has a royal family— the original members of which created its pattern and formed its corporate policy.

Leading members of the Farben royalty are Dr. Hermann Schmitz, perhaps the most dangerous of Germany's living war criminals, and the late Doctors Karl Duisberg and Karl Bosch.

These three gentlemen, their relatives, and their associates appear from time to time in other chapters of this story. But the plan to plant their offspring in our midst plays so important a part in the Farben pattern that the individual profiles gathered here may appear of value.

Dr. Hermann Schmitz, by sheer brain power and complete ruthlessness, came up the hard way from his boyhood commercial school in the iron city of Essen and a bank clerk's training. Then World War I shoved him into the Dye Trust Badische nitrogen affairs as a staff member of the Kaiser's war machine.

Entering the Badische management in 1919 Dr. Schmitz was an Executive Committee Managing Director of Farben from its beginning in 1926—became chairman in 1938, and also was Farben's director on the board of Fritz Thyssen's Vereinigte Stahlwerke from the time the Steel Trust was tied in with Farben in 1926. Active in politics from the early days of the Weimar Republic, Schmitz made personal contributions to the Nazis, was a member of Hitler's puppet Reichstag, and War Economy Chief before and during World War II.

This elder statesman of the Schmitz family did not emigrate to America to become a citizen but he commuted regularly during the years when, as shown elsewhere, he personally directed Farben's American subsidiaries and consummated many of Farben's most important partnerships and illegal tie-ups in this country. He enjoyed intimate friendships with top men in American industry and finance. Dr. Schmitz created the Swiss I. G. Chemie as a hideout for Farben's false fronts abroad and installed his brother-in-law, Albert Gadow, as its resident manager, with instructions to acquire Swiss citizenship.

Dr. Schmitz was also a Director of the great Deutsche Reichsbank and of the Bank of International Settlements, that financial catch-all for cartel members at war, with its headquarters in Switzerland where Schmitz throughout the war was able to maintain direct contact with its American president, Thomas H. McKittrick, and with various cartel associates, to put out peace feelers after his criminal gang finally decided that Farben should call for an intermission before another war.

In his various capacities in finance, industry and government, corruptionist in each, and as chairman of the American I. G., the Swiss I. G., and the German I. G., Schmitz appears as a triple threat, one of the most vicious and dangerous of Germany's war criminals. Frequently addressed as Geheimrat (Privy-Councillor), the doctor was also entitled to be called Justizrat as a doctor of laws (honoris causa).

On his many visits to this country Dr. Schmitz personally took an active part in directing Farben's American subsidiaries—as a result of which activities he won top honors in having been indicted on three separate occasions as Farben leader and organizer or head of General Aniline. The Justizrat was also named as co-conspirator in two other criminal cases. His three indictments remain untried as this is written, also one of those in which he was

called a co-conspirator, and the other was abandoned by a complacent Attorney General.

In July 1945, while being examined at Frankfurt by the United
States Army, Schmitz admitted that he had tried to persuade Hitler
to use a new and very deadly Farben war gas on the Allied Armies.
Then, a few weeks later, the good doctor publicly proclaimed his
ambition to become Germany's representative on the Security
Council of the United Nations. This from the man who is credited
with having developed the plan of making I. G. Farben a vast
international espionage machine cloaked under cover of industrial and commercial activities—and the most important part of
this vicious design was the Schmitz proposal that trustworthy
members of the Farben families emigrate to other countries, especially to the United States, to serve the Fatherland's Farben in
peace and in war.

Dr. Karl Duisberg, who died in 1935, was known, and deserv-
edly, as the father of German industrial chemistry. Holding high
office in the first World War, it was he, as founder of the American
Bayer Company, who sent Hugo Schweitzer to this country to
become Bayer's chief chemist in public, and Germany's espionage
and pay-off man in private. Dr. Duisberg was also leader of the
I. G. Dyes plan of postwar strategy, and personally negotiated
the first of its new tie-ups with Sterling by which control over
American Bayer was reasserted. His secretary, one H. Gattineau,
like his son-in-law, Max Ilgner, is said to have been a main Farben
connecting link with the Hitler Government after the Nazis came
to full power in 1933.

Duisberg probably more than any of his colleagues epitomizes
the vicious union of applied science and industrial productive
brains—which in itself is the core of Farben's potential for world
conquest.

A young relative of Karl Duisberg (through his wife, who was
Johanna Seebohm) appears in the notorious Hermann C. A.
Seebohm, who had come to America before World War I and
gotten kicked out. He was a director and Secretary of the American Bayer Company, involved in the World War I espionage and
crooked business of this Dye Trust false front by which sabotage

in North and South America was financed and the company was milked of its assets. So Mr. Seebohm was arrested and interned in 1918, later to be shipped back where he came from, to turn up as a Managing Director of Farben, and after the rape of Austria, as chairman of one of the Farben subsidiaries in that unhappy country.

Dr. Duisberg had two sons, Karl Ludwig and Walter H. He kept Karl at home to serve on the Farben boards, and Walter H. was sent overseas to join the Farben colony in America. Another Duisberg, of uncertain relationship, turned up in Frankfurt in 1945 after the American Army seized Farben's headquarters there, and was quoted in news dispatches as saying that "German industry can make a quick recovery after the war if the Allies will be so kind as to permit it so to do."

Dr. Karl Bosch, winner of the Nobel Prize, with Fritz Haber, for invention of the first synthetic ammonia nitrogen process by which Badische made it possible for the Kaiser to launch his war; and inventor of war gases introduced by the Kaiser's armies, became the first chairman of Farben's board of managing directors. After the death of Duisberg, Dr. Bosch shifted to chairman of its supervising board until he died in 1940.

Bosch, like Duisberg, sought only one thing—world conquest through perverting science. This criminal of two world wars had a son, Dr. Karl Bosch, Jr., whom he trained with great care and affection to carry on for Farben. He also had a brother, Robert, of Bosch Magneto fame—who also appears elsewhere in this story and whose American subsidiary, like several of those of brother Karl, had the dubious distinction of being seized by the Alien Property Custodian, during both world wars.

This criminal of two World Wars had a magnificent estate near Heidelberg, where he royally entertained his American partners on their frequent visits to Germany. In his gentler moments of relaxation when not planning treachery, aggressive war, or mass murder, Dr. Bosch enjoyed displaying his collections of crystal and of beetles and butterflies, said to be the best in Germany.

Another royal family of Farben, from the earlier days of the

I. G. Dyes cartel, was headed by two Frankfurt aristocrats and Junkers, Dr. Walther vom Rath and Dr. Wilhelm von Meister, who prior to the formation of Farben in 1926, had been controlling and interrelated figures in Farbwerke vorm. Meister Lucius & Brüning, the great Hoechst firm in which members of the Meister family, from its foundation, had played important parts. So they sent their sons to America.

The senior vom Rath had a nephew, Georg von Schnitzler, who stayed at the royal court to rise high in the Farben dynasty. Von Schnitzler was a brother-in-law of the famous, or notorious, General Fedor von Bock who led the Nazi armies to defeat in Russia, got back with a whole skin, to be shot down by the British near Hamburg as the war was ending in 1945.

Georg von Schnitzler, as a managing director of Farben, became one of its most powerful rulers, he was a heavy financial contributor to Hitler's rise from the gutter, and in his handling of Farben's foreign tie-ups, camouflage and espionage, he appears as among a half dozen of the most dangerous of Germany's war criminals.

In 1943 von Schnitzler, knowing the war was lost, established a residence in Madrid—a veritable castle in Spain—where he could keep and renew his close friendships and carry over alliances with leading American cartelists, to begin the repair of Farben's war-damaged foreign empire and preparations for World War III. So in 1945 this Farben Junker was back in Germany for the finish, and became the most notable and possibly the most informative of the Farben family in giving up secrets and conclusions about Farben's war activities.

Among the statements in his voluminous "true confessions" one ended with: "Thus I conclude that I. G. Farben is largely responsible for Hitler's policy."

Georg von Schnitzler's daughter Lilo, celebrated as a beauty and an early friend of Adolf Hitler when the latter was emerging, was married to one Herbert Scholz, an erstwhile friend of the lamented Ernst Röhm before that degenerate pal of Hitler was bumped off by his ungrateful boss. So Mr. and Mrs. Herbert Scholz, as an effective team were shipped off to American to help along Farben's cause of world conquest.

Not to a Farben hideout, but to Washington came Georg von Schnitzler's Lilo and her Albert; sinister beauty teamed with vicious brain, that historic combination for diplomatic intrigue. Mr. Scholz, as secretary to the German Ambassador, dominated his official master, while Lilo played her dazzling part among influential members of high society in the nation's capital.

As she had charmed and helped to train to Farben's social graces the unspeakable Adolf, so were those charms displayed and used to beguile democracy's chosen rulers to do those things that Farben's royalty desired. Lilo and Albert then moved on to conquer Boston, Massachusetts, where that precious scion of Farben, officially the German Consul, carried on in secret as a No. 1 Gestapo pay-off man, until June 1941, when he was grabbed by the F.B.I., to be kicked out of the country with the rest of the official Nazi brood. The full story of what Lilo and her Albert did in Washington and in Boston in the period after the war had begun in Europe must remain untold, still concealed in official files—for some strange reason.

So now we come to a few highlights in the activities of some of the younger members of the Farben dynasty—relatives who were sent over here, not as visitors but as permanent residents. Usually they became American citizens without delay, they married, established homes in suburban districts where social ties could readily be formed, and they made the right kind of professional and political contacts.

As reputable, well-to-do business men these Teutonic termites added strength and respectability to Farben's new American fronts, and, in anticipation of the war that was to come, their cloak of citizenship was designed to prevent such unhappy incidents of the past as internment and property seizure. They composed the field staff of Farben's industrial pincers in America; they received and carried out orders from headquarters, and directed the accumulation of funds and information, much of which somehow found its way back to Germany.

Among the Farben delegates to this country were William H. vom Rath and F. Wilhelm von Meister. Here they held important positions in Farben's American subsidiary, General Aniline & Film Corporation.

William H. vom Rath, son of Walther, and cousin of Georg von Schnitzler, was also a cousin of Ernst vom Rath, Secretary of the Germany Embassy in Paris, who was assassinated in 1938 by the young Pole, Herschel Grynszpan. During World War I, Wilhelm was involved in the direction of the German Secret Service at Geneva, Switzerland.

Wilhelm came to the United States in the early 20s and after a few years was naturalized as William H. vom Rath. The "Wilhelm" was no more. In 1929, he received his first real Farben responsibility, he was elected Secretary and made a director of the newly organized American I. G. Chemical Corp.

Young vom Rath bought a fine home at Glen Cove, Long Island, and made many influential friends. Some of his activities in Farben's interest will be mentioned later on in this story. It is sufficient here to relate that in December 1941, William H. vom Rath, was indicted for conspiracy to violate the anti-trust laws, along with other Farben agents and corporate subsidiaries. As this is written the indictment has not been tried, nor is there apparently any prospect of its being tried. Until Germany threw up the sponge the official excuse was given that to try Mr. vom Rath (and some of his royal pals) would interfere with our prosecution of the war.

F. Wilhelm von Meister, son of Wilhelm, Sr., and also cousin of Georg von Schnitzler, came to this country to become vice-president of Farben's photo paper subsidiary, Ozalid Corporation, when it was ostensibly owned by Chemnyco. In 1940, when Ozalid became a part of General Aniline, von Meister was made manager, where he remained until kicked out by the Treasury Department after being indicted in December 1941 along with vom Rath and other members of the royal family.

American citizen von Meister is as yet among those sons and brothers of Farben accused of criminal acts who remain untried.

Dietrich A. Schmitz, brother of the regal Hermann, did many odd jobs for Farben in this country and in Latin America, but two incidents stand out. One occurred when Dietrich, as president of American I. G. Chemical Corporation, brazenly and falsely denied under oath before the Securities and Exchange Commission that he had any knowledge of who was the beneficial owner of the controlling shares of that company.

Nothing being done to him for this offense, he may have felt immune, but three years later was indicted in three separate (and still untried) conspiracy actions. Then in 1945 Dietrich was summoned before a Federal Grand Jury and questioned without waiving immunity; as result of which a Federal Judge, with consent and approval of United States Attorney General Francis Biddle promptly dismissed all three indictments against this brother of war criminal Hermann Schmitz.

It is perhaps needless to say that efforts to induce the Department of Justice to explain this chain of events have been unavailing. Neither has elucidation been forthcoming as to why the indictments against Hermann Schmitz himself—which were not tried during the war because we couldn't catch him—have not now been tried; nor has this distinguished gentleman paid us a courtesy visit to plead not guilty and have the indictments dismissed.

Geheimrat Hermann Schmitz also has two promising nephews, Max and Rudolph W. Ilgner; Rudolph was shipped off to America in the 1920's. Max, the more brilliant, remained with Uncle Hermann, married Karl Duisberg's daughter, and rose to high rank as a Managing Director and head of Farben's Central Finance Bureau, which polite name cloaked Max's activities as chief of espionage, sabotage, and propaganda. In that capacity, Max was directly responsible for carrying out the financial details of Farben's cartel and patent agreements and for placing and using secret funds and secret agents in foreign countries. Max Ilgner has admitted that these activities were tremendous in scope and corrupt in character in the United States.

Strongly attracted to the vicious doctrines of Nazism as offering the appropriate vehicle for Farben's pattern of world conquest, Max Ilgner was Farben's main representative in the inner councils of the Nazi party.

Nephew Rudolph won the undying gratitude of his kinfolk, in Germany and in this country, by destroying by fire not long before Hitler invaded Poland certain secret files which a Grand Jury had demanded. These were the files of Chemnyco, Inc., the New York firm through which Rudolph had been publicly arranging patent licenses, and secretly directing espionage, propaganda, and other subversive activities.

Instead of being jailed and heavily fined for conspiracy and arson, Mr. Ilgner, on a change of plea to guilty, was let off with a thousand dollar fine and precisely no.years in jail. Whereupon he left the country club pleasures and social contacts of Greenwich, for a rural chicken farm in Connecticut, where he is today.

Among Rudolph's many propaganda jobs was running the German American Board of Trade, and his best known feat was the grand banquet he threw in New York in March 1939 to welcome Fritz Wiedemann, Hitler's old commanding officer, who after successfully conducting Herbert Hoover about Europe on an educational tour, had arrived in this country to take up his duties as a Farben gumshoe in the Consul General's office at San Francisco.

Walter H. Duisberg, son of Karl, arrived in the promised land in 1927; settled first at Quogue, Long Island, and later in a fine home in Englewood, New Jersey; registered as a consultant on United States patents; and within the next decade engaged himself in multitudinous activities both here and in South America. He was a stockholder, director or executive of every one of Farben's important corporate hideouts in this country and several in Latin America as well.

This son of America's vindictive enemy won honors approximating those of Hermann Schmitz in the various conspiracy indictments which broke out like a rash after the war began; Mr. Duisberg was named by various Grand Juries in no less than five different criminal cases involving charges of restricting the production of nitrogen and ammonia, fertilizer materials, magnesium alloys, dyes, chemicals, and photo materials. Only the magnesium cases have ever come to issue in court, but Walter Duisberg had no cause to worry about any of them because, strangely enough, he was named merely as co-conspirator. (A co-conspirator designation in a criminal indictment is like a mild case of chickenpox—a little rash, but no possibility of serious consequences, provided the patient has competent doctors.)

In such a favorable atmosphere it may not appear strange that Mr. Walter Duisberg should have decided to press his luck and try to regain possession of a large block of stock in the Farben-owned General Dyestuff Corporation, of which he was registered as the owner when the United States Government rudely seized it as enemy-owned after we entered the war.

At any rate, Mr. Duisberg brazenly went into court with a complaint that the Alien Property Custodian had stolen his property, and would the judge please make the thief give it back to him. The Court, to its credit, threw out this complaint.

Later, however, an appeal was filed on this decision and lost, so it appears that the Duisberg claim is no go; in which respect, as will be seen later, he has not been as fortunate as some of his pals.

Brief pictures belong here of other men of Farben, not rulers nor kin of rulers, who also came inside our lines in the prewar invasion. Also of some who, although born in America, appeared to regard this great privilege as a grant of right to serve the German Dye Trust first and always.

A Farben employe in South America who proved most useful in softening up that continent for the recent war was Kurt Wojahn, brother of Max Wojahn, manager of Sterling's Export Department. It was Kurt's duty to place Farben's patent-medicine advertising in those Latin American newspapers which published news and editorials friendly to the Nazi government. Max seems to have had similar duties with regard to Sterling's advertising and, as will be shown later, this brotherly relation was of considerable value in harmonizing the advertising policy of Sterling with that of Farben.

Another close relationship in Farben's American family was the Hutz father-and-son combination. Rudolph Hutz, the father, was head of General Aniline Works and vice-president and director of General Aniline & Film on that day in January 1942 when the Treasury Department requested him and a number of his colleagues to take their hats and go. His son, W. H. Hutz, was a member of Farben's New York patent law firm of Hutz & Joslin, until some time in 1942, when he also received his marching orders from the United States Government.

The story of Rudolph Hutz goes back far into the history of the Big Six. Born in Germany he was employed as a chemist by the German Bayer Company at Elberfeld from 1902 to 1909. He was then transferred to the American Bayer Company as Boston manager, and was there when Bayer and the other Big Six houses got into a little jam for bribing boss dyers, salting dyes and faking brand names in 1913. Hutz remained with Bayer until 1918, when he had a misunderstanding with the United States Government about espionage, and was indicted and interned at Ellis Island.

After the Armistice Rudolph was released and soon thereafter became an American citizen with the sanction of some federal court which was either grossly deceived or else had a strange concept of what kind of citizens this country has need of. Be that as it may, as a naturalized American, Mr. Hutz climbed high in the American front of Farben, his one other mishap of record being the mention of his name as a co-conspirator in one of those 1941 conspiracy indictments which are still on the stove—or rather in the icebox.

Many others, not related to Farben's leaders but trained in the Farben pattern, came to America to enter Farben's subsidiaries. Hans Aichelin, a former Farben dyestuff expert came over in the late 20's, was put to work with General Aniline, and later became vice-president and director of General Aniline & Film. Mr. Aichelin, too, was among those indicted in December 1941 and was named again in a criminal complaint in 1942. Forced out of General Aniline's board, he was finally ousted as vice-president by the Treasury in January 1942. He, too, will never be tried. He died in 1944.

Ernest Schwartz, himself a former official of Farben and one of its leading research men, transferred his domicile to this country and became a director and president of Agfa Ansco in 1934, later director and vice-president of American I. G. when that company changed its name to General Aniline & Film. Mr. Schwartz, whose duties included experiments with photographic equipment for the United States Army and Navy, did not become naturalized until late in 1939, after the war started—but when he did so he wanted everyone to know that he was a changed man. "I am now an

American citizen," he announced, "and have only sympathies with America." Two years later he, too, was indicted for conspiracy. And never tried.

Leopold Eckler, another Farben-trained chemist, came to America, was naturalized, and took his place in the management of Agfa Ansco. There he stayed until ousted by the Treasury, in January 1942.

J. Rudolph Worch was still another newcomer whose rose to be assistant vice-president of Agfa Ansco at Binghamton, N. Y., and at one time was president of the Chamber of Commerce of that city. He left Ansco at the request of the Treasury in March 1942.

The plant manager of General Aniline Works at the former Bayer dye plant at Rensselaer, N. Y., was Harry W. Grimmel, who worked in a Farben dye plant prior to 1926, and was then transferred to its American operations.

Another higher-up technician was William Henry Cotton, born in Russia, who was employed by the German Hoechst from 1905 to 1928, and then sent to General Dyestuff as chief chemist.

Dr. William Hiemenz, a pharmaceutical chemist in I. G. Dyes, was sent to Rensselaer, N. Y., in the early 20s as Farben's director on the Winthrop board, and factory manager of the Winthrop Bayer manufacturing plant. The Treasury kicked him out of Winthrop in December 1941.

Another pharmaceutical expert came to the United States from Farbenland in the early 30s, and wound up in an important position in the Winthrop plant. His name is Wolfgang Schnellbach and some of the things he took part in require special mention elsewhere in the story. However, it should be related here that something actually did happen to Mr. Schnellbach. Not having been naturalized, and appearing to be somewhat objectionable, he was interned at Ellis Island where, at last accounts, he was waiting for his family to join him through some sort of special dispensation.

Dr. Bruno Puetzer was another Farben chemist who came to this country and became a Winthrop chemist. Winthrop also inherited one of the first World War technicians of the Metz Laboratories in the person of the Swedish-born A. E. Sherndal, who later became a Bayer-Winthrop expert at the Rensselaer, N. Y., plant.

Alba Pharmaceutical, after it was organized in 1935, was assisted in its cooperative relations with Farben by the election of a German national, H. Vogel, as secretary, treasurer and director.

Dr. Karl Hochswender came to the United States and served in Chemnyco as an expert on Farben patent licenses and the collection of royalties. In 1941, at a critical time for Farben, the doctor was twice indicted as president of Magnesium Development Corp., and denied knowing his master's voice with somewhat unhappy results, when Attorney-General Robert H. Jackson impounded Farben's bank account in 1941.

There are many others who might be added to this dubious honor roll. Some are important and would be described except for the official hush-hush policy behind which, unhappily, so many of these imported Americans still remain hidden. One more sketch belongs here.

In December 1941, shortly after Germany declared war on the United States, *The New York Times* published a statement by Ernest K. Halbach in which he denied that General Dyestuff Corp. was foreign owned. *The Times,* a few days earlier had referred to an action of the United States Treasury Department in freezing the assets of General Aniline & Film Corp. and of General Dyestuff "due to foreign ownership."

Mr. Halbach, as president of General Dyestuff, thereupon wrote *The Times* that his company, "is a New York corporation; that all of its stock is owned by American citizens; and that all of its officers and directors are American citizens." "The ownership and management of General Dyestuff Corporation is exclusively in the hands of American citizens," continued Mr. Halbach, "therefore there cannot be any possible justification for your statement."

Mr. Halbach, in his dissertation on American ownership was adhering strictly to the Farben pattern, and repeating the exact words used back in 1917 by Kuttroff, Pickhardt & Co., and the New York Badische, both of which had employed Mr. Halbach, and were predecessors of General Dyestuff. The occasion in 1917, as in 1941, was the declaration of war between Germany and the United States, and the imminence of the seizure of enemy-owned property in this country.

In 1941 these protestations were of no avail. The Treasury Department disregarded them. The Department of Justice indicted both General Dyestuff and Mr. Halbach for conspiracy, and six months later they both were again indicted and the new Alien Property Custodian seized General Dyestuff as a German- or Farben-owned concern.

Now going back for a moment to the 1917 incident, a newly formed corporation called Kuttroff, Pickhardt & Co., of which Halbach was an important employe, had just become the ostensible owner of the assets of the New York Badische, the American branch of the largest of the Big Six, which it was claimed, went through voluntary liquidation. However, World War I had started a few months previously, the Trading with the Enemy Act had been passed, and the Alien Property Custodian was threatening to seize both Kuttroff, Pickhardt & Co., and Badische. "You can't do that to us," protested Mr. Halbach's employers. "All the officers, directors and stockholders of this company are citizens of the United States." That time the American-citizen stuff partially worked. The new Kuttroff, Pickhardt concern escaped but the custodian did seize about half a million dollars which was in a New York bank.

The Custodian's investigation uncovered the fact that various records and account books had mysteriously disappeared and certain entries in those available appeared unexplainable. For example, in the early years of its existence all importations from the German house were entered on its books on a consignment basis. Then, the year before the war began, they appeared as purchases; yet during the war the bulk of its profits, amounting to more than $1,500,000 were transferred to Germany.

When New York Badische secured German dyes from the two submarine cargoes in 1916, they were entered on its books as purchases. Later, when a profit of $400,000 was made on these dyes, the book entries were charged to a consignment, and the funds sent to the parent company.

Finally, an agreement was turned up by the Custodian which showed that an option was outstanding by which Messrs. Kuttroff and Pickhardt were obligated to turn back their shares in the New York Badische at par value to the Big Six house on its demand. So it was evident that this company, like all the other Farben fronts, had a string tied to it—a German string to be pulled at the proper moment in Farben's perpetual "All-American Puppet Show."

In 1919 we find the patriotic Mr. Halbach, in the interest of imported German dyes, canvassing for signatures to a petition which protested the efforts of the American Government to protect the infant domestic coal-tar dye industry then struggling to survive.

When Halbach in 1941 was proclaiming the American ownership of General Dyestuff, successor to the Kuttroff, Pickhardt dye interests, he was referring to his own alleged majority control of its stock. This alleged Halbach stock control dated back to 1939 when the company transferred to his name shares formerly held by that other American patriot, Herman Metz. Metz became majority stockholder in General Dyestuff through his holdings as an organizer of the company, plus the shares he acquired when duPont turned over to him, as Farben's agent, the Grasselli interest in General Dyestuff.

These many transfers of stock may appear complex and bewildering, but the pattern is plainly discernible—the objective always the same. The truth is that in 1941 Halbach held majority stock control of General Dyestuff, and with W. H. Duisberg, held title to nearly all of the shares. However, an option on all of the Halbach-Duisberg stock was held by Chemnyco, Inc. The latter's stock was owned nominally by American citizens, but these were also Farben agents, and Chemnyco was incorporated and functioned exclusively as a Farben agency.

Kuttroff, Pickhardt & Co., as a name, disappeared from the scene in 1931 when its various Farben interests in the United States were segregated into new companies. This name had served its purpose long and well, the original members of the firm were gone and Farben was now entrenched in several brand-new American subsidiaries. However, William Paul Pickhardt, American-born son of one of the early partners, along with Halbach, continued to play an important part for Farben. Mr. Pickhardt during the next ten years held many offices in Farben subsidiaries, including chairman of the board of Synthetic Nitrogen Products, and of Agfa Ansco; president of Chemnyco; vice-president of General Aniline & Film; and director of American Magnesium; Gen-

eral Dyestuff; Ozalid Corp.; Jasco; and Plaskon Co. The latter
was a manufacturer of waterproof glue and plastics, seldom recognized as a Farben subsidiary.

William Paul Pickhardt was indicted on Sept. 1, 1939, along
with Synthetic Nitrogen Products and others in the synthetic
nitrogen-ammonia conspiracy. He died in January, 1941, while
the indictment was still pending.

Now let us go back for another moment—a long way back—to
1871 when Adolph Kuttroff and William Pickhardt, two young
German nationals, organized a firm called William Pickhardt &
Kuttroff to import coal-tar dyes and chemicals from the Father-
land. In 1906 this firm changed its name to Continental Color and
Chemical Co. Then, in 1917, the good old American names of
Kuttroff and Pickhardt again appeared on its letterheads.

Ernest K. Halbach entered the employ of Pickhardt & Kuttroff
in 1899 and from that day on, for more than half a century, this
native-born American was to shuttle back and forth in the long
razzle-dazzle of changes of name and concealment of ownership
through which first Badische, and then Farben as the actual employers of Mr. Halbach, attempted to hide their identity.

By 1920 Halbach had risen to be a director of Kuttroff, Pickhardt and was directly involved in the firm's efforts to bamboozle
the State Department into turning over to it the importation of
German dyes. In 1926, when Kuttroff, Pickhardt transferred its
dye business to General Dyestuff, Mr. Halbach went along with
the business.

And in 1942 Mr. Halbach, living luxuriously in ultra-fashionable
Short Hills, New Jersey, environment with a summer home at
Nantucket, was presumably unhappy because he, an American-
born citizen whose country was at war, had two criminal indictments chalked up against him which involved him with the enemy; also because the 4,725 shares of stock registered in his name
or that of his wife and trustees, which carried alleged ownership
control of General Dyestuff Corporation, were now locked up in
the strongbox of the Alien Property Custodian.

So, Mr. Halbach consulted counsel—and it will appear that he
chose his legal advisers wisely, in that old and well-known Wall

Street law firm which is still addressed as Sullivan & Cromwell (although its founders of those names have long since been gathered to their fathers).

Ornamenting this law firm is that celebrated attorney, public spirited citizen, religious leader and adviser on affairs of state, John Foster Dulles.

It was perhaps a coincidence that Mr. Halbach should have selected as his counsel the law firm of Mr. Dulles during the period when the latter, in addition to his many other commendable public activities, was the chief adviser of Republican Governor and candidate for President Thomas E. Dewey; was about to become adviser to our Secretaries of State on problems of war and peace; and was a member of the consulting committee established by the Alien Property Custodian to assist in formulating the basic policies of that office on the methods of controlling foreign property. As a sidelight on such activities it might be appropriate to mention here that Mr. Dulles is also listed, as recently as 1945, as one of the directors of the International Nickel Co., of Canada, which company, and several of its officers also have been among the unfortunate corporations and individuals like Mr. Halbach, to be accused of conspiracy with I. G. Farben and others.

As to the two indictments in which Mr. Halbach was so unhappily accused, one, that of December, 1941, was postponed as has been mentioned before; and the other, of May, 1942, after a long succession of legal technicalities and behind-the-scenes wire pulling came finally to an issue in 1946, when eight of the corporate defendants, including General Dyestuff, and General Aniline & Film, along with seven of the individuals named, were found guilty on pleas of *nolo contendere*, and fined from $2,000 to $15,000 each. Mr. Halbach, along with twelve of the other individuals indicted, was cleared of all culpability by having the charges dismissed. So the Halbach indictment score now stands at one down and one to go.

Meanwhile the new management of General Dyestuff appointed by Mr. Leo T. Crowley, as Alien Property Custodian, decided that it would be sadly handicapped in its efforts to drive the Farben dyestuffs—and the Gestapo secret agents who distributed them—

out of the Latin American countries unless they should retain
the services of Mr. Halbach, who according to the indictments
pending, had enjoyed such intimate conspiratorial relations with
those very same agents of the German Dye Trust both before and
after the war started, his company having been grabbed by Uncle
Sam for trading with the enemy.

So Mr. Halbach was re-engaged as an adviser to General Dyestuffs at an annual salary reported to have been $36,000 a year,
plus bonuses which increased his annual take to some $82,000,
quite a bit more than the president of the company received and,
strictly speaking, this cash all came out of the United States Treasury via the office of the Alien Property Custodian and the staff
appointed by the latter to run this enemy property.

Then, on March 18, 1944, in the United States District Court
at Newark, New Jersey, Elisabeth S. Halbach and Franklin H.
Stafford, as Trustees for Ernest K. Halbach, followed the example
set by Walter Duisberg in 1943, and filed suit against the Alien
Property Custodian, demanding the return of the 4,725 shares of
stock in General Dyestuff which had stood in Mr. Halbach's name.
(Mrs. Halbach was not working for Uncle Sam or the Alien Property Custodian. Why shouldn't she sue them if she felt so inclined?)

At the same time seven other stockholders, allegedly owners of
a total of 1,178 more shares in this Farben subsidiary, also filed
suits against Mr. Crowley in the New Jersey and New York courts.
All of these gentry were American-born citizens who, while employed by General Dyestuff, had not only taken title to certain
holdings in its stock by paying various sums in cash for same, but
each had also signed an agreement which, among other things,
gave the company an exclusive option to repurchase these holdings. Same old stuff of the first World War—American owned, with
a Farben string attached.

In these eight lawsuits, as in the Duisberg case, the Alien
Property Custodian very properly began to defend the seizure
of these holdings. In an affidavit filed in December, 1944, by James
E. Markham, who had succeeded his friend Mr. Crowley as Alien
Property Custodian, the seizure was justified by affirmations, in
rather blunt language that

General Dyestuff Corporation and the record owners of the stock were acting in behalf and for the benefit of I. G. Farbenindustrie, a national of an enemy country, Germany.

and that the Government case would be proved

by bringing together the complicated threads of a conspiracy extending over many years and involving persons in many different countries.

(which was a pretty good brief description of I. G. Farben's worldwide conspiracy against peace).

This Custodian affidavit contains some other good points touching on the activities of Mr. Halbach and these employes of General Dyestuffs and, in plain language, called the titles to the stock fraudulent and a camouflage to cloak Farben's actual ownership. For all of such reasons the Custodian demanded a trial in open court of the factual issues involved in these cases.

The Halbach claim being by far the largest, it was decided that this case should be tried first, so that decision on the others could be more readily adjudicated.

Among the other claimants were one Rudolph Lenz who, prior to its seizure, had been a vice-president of General Dyestuff, H. W. Martin, and A. T. Wingender, also executives. All three were kept on the job under Mr. Crowley. Lenz was indicted along with Mr. Halbach, in the May, 1942 criminal action but unlike Halbach his indictment was not dismissed when fifteen of the defendants were fined.

Mr. Lenz was also fortunate in having Mr. John Foster Dulles' law firm, Sullivan & Cromwell, represent him against the Alien Property Custodian; as did Mr. Percy Kuttroff another of the claimants, of the old family concern out of which General Dyestuff was created.

What happened then may appear strange unless we could get behind the scenes and listen in at the secret agreement secretly arrived at—instead of the public trial in open court as demanded in the Custodian's affidavit.

As of February 2, 1945, the settlement out of court was made public, eight separate settlements, by which the claimants were paid off in cash on condition that each should withdraw and forget their claims for the General Dyestuff stock, sums totaling some $696,554, out of the United States Treasury.

The Halbach share of the booty was the tidy sum of $557,550. Attorney General Francis Biddle, and the Custodian, announced through the press that the settlement "cleared the way" for the sale of General Dyestuff to some one else. We may agree that this settlement might have cleared the way, but it hardly cleared the air.

One characteristic may appear to stand out in these sketches—the arrogant defiance of law, and the gentle treatment that has been accorded the royal family of Farben when these gentlemen have been caught with the goods.

CHAPTER VI

"Tarnung" The Magic Hood which renders the wearer invisible

"AFTER THE FIRST war we came more and more to the decision to 'tarn' (hood or camouflage) our foreign companies . . . . . in such a way that the participation of I.G. in these firms was not shown. In the course of time the system became more and more perfect.

"If the shares or similar interests are actually held by a neutral who resides in a neutral country, enemy economic warfare measures are ineffectual; even an option in favor of I.G. will remain unaffected.

"Protective measures to be taken by I.G. for the eventuality of war should not substantially interfere with the conduct of business in normal times. For a variety of reasons it is of the utmost importance . . . . . that the officials heading the agent firms which are particularly well qualified to serve as cloaks should be citizens of the countries where they reside.

"In practice . . . . . a foreign patent holding company could conduct its business only by maintaining the closest possible relations with I.G., with regard to applications, processing and exploitation of patents—it is sufficient to refer to our numerous agreements providing for exchange of patents or experience.

"The adoption of these measures would offer protection against seizure in the event of war."

The above excerpts, taken from original pre-war records of Farben's legal department, describe in vivid language the purpose of Farben's American hideouts and the instructions by which Farben's American agents were guided.

Also included in these pre-war memoirs was anticipation of the victory which at that time Farben contemplated, when disguises would no longer be in order, as follows:

In the case of winning this war the mightful situation of the Reich will make it necessary to re-examine the system of 'Tarnung.' Politically seen, it will often be wished that the German character of our foreign companies is openly shown.

After the war began Farben's legal solons continued their discussions and reports on *tarnung*. Some of these also may appear appropriate here—as follows:

"These camouflaged companies . . . . . proved very useful.

"Only about 1937 when . . . . . a new conflict became . . . . . apparent did we take pains to improve our camouflage in the endangered countries in a way that they should . . . . . even under wartime difficulties, at least prevent immediate seizure.

"Camouflage measures taken by us have stood us in good stead, and in numerous cases have even exceeded our expectations."

Reference in these reports to Farben American hideouts permits no doubt as to the importance attributed to the use of *tarnung's* magic in this country.

The firm of Kuttroff, Pickhardt & Co. was always meticulous in the handling of its commercial affairs. It held itself aloof from the rough stuff indulged in by other Farben agents and conducted its business dealing with the American public with a dignity and courtesy which was in marked contrast to the loud-mouthed bull-dozing and slapstick with which Herman Metz displayed his Farben wares in the American marketplace. But both, in their respective fields, were of similar value to Farben. They were "Americans."

My own contacts with Kuttroff, Pickhardt & Co., originated in the early 1920's through a request for advice regarding the production of arsenical insecticide products which that company had made to the Crop Protection Institute of the National Research Council in behalf of the German Badische. The Institute referred the inquiry to me, and I am happy to relate that as a result of my advice, Badische and Farben did not enter the field. That was one of the few branches of the chemical industries in the United States which Farben decided to keep out of; possibly they considered it wiser to save up Germany's arsenic as a reserve for making the deadly arsine war gas.

It may appear uncertain whether the earlier creation of the illusion of American ownership of Kuttroff, Pickhardt was due to the threat of anti-trust proceedings or was in anticipation of the first World War. On the record, however, the concealment of ownership of both Kuttroff, Pickhardt in 1914, and of General Dyestuff in 1941, directly preceded our two wars with Germany. And in both instances Yankee Halbach was in there pitching for Farben.

In 1919 Francis P. Garvan denounced the conduct of Kuttroff, Pickhardt with the statement that:

> "If they were American citizens their conduct was such as would not entitle them to much consideration, because Mr. Kuttroff endeavored to send as much property as possible to Europe after Bernstorff had gotten his papers, and when war with Germany was certain he collected every bit of cash possible and resorted to every possible subterfuge in the manipulation of books etc., to transfer those assets to our enemy a

few days before we actually went into the war, and long after relations had been severed and Bernstorff had gone back."

When he said this Mr. Garvan might well have been foreseeing some of the same kind of transfers of American funds which in 1941 were passing into the invisible hands of Farben from successors of Kuttroff, Pickhardt.

Nor did Mr. Garvan hesitate to express his convictions about the relations between these native-born American citizens and their German I.G. masters. In 1922, after years of searching investigation of the Badische and Hoechst American companies, he announced his conclusion that the German owners had never really parted with control of these branches. Said Garvan:

> "The truth is that neither Metz nor Kuttroff, Pickhardt & Co. —it is my contention—ever owned a dollar's worth of their companies here . . . . . They never have been and never will be anything but clerks of the German I.G."

Mr. Garvan deeply resented the fact that after he had seized the Hoechst-Metz company as Alien Property Custodian, Metz claimed that he had already "bought" back the assets of the company in an absurd jack-in-the-box transaction by which not one cent of money was passed, and in which Metz signed an irrevocable power of attorney transferring back to Hoechst the shares he had pretended to purchase. This transfer was attached to the stock certificate, deposited in a safety deposit box outside the United States, and held at the sole disposition of the German company.

In 1919, over Metz's violent protests, Garvan seized the Hoechst New York bank account and attached the Hoechst shares in the name of the United States Government as enemy owned. Then started a protracted court battle in which Metz exhausted his vocabulary on the witness stand and in the courthouse corridors in expressing his opinion of Garvan.

There followed, in 1921, one of the most notable triumphs ever scored by Metz in his long career as the I.G. hatchet man in the United States. On June 2nd, Judge Julius M. Mayer in the Federal Court in New York City, handed down a verbose decision which awarded the title of the Hoechst shares to Herman Metz. Judge Mayer predicated his decision upon several rather naïve pronouncements:

> "As a seizure by the Alien Property Custodian is likely to carry the suggestion to those not informed in respect of the controversy, that the demandee (Metz) in some manner may have been improperly associated with the enemy, it is desirable at the outset to state that no such situation exists here . . . . . The transactions here took place long before our entry into the war and, indeed, before the European war started and had no relations to either."

The court's decision conceded that some of the correspondence between Metz and Hoechst bearing on the transaction was missing, and that the testimony of Metz contained what the Judge politely described as "inaccuracies." "However," held the court, "that Metz should deliberately by his testimony falsify the true transaction is not to be thought of." Finally the court came to the conclusion that although the:

> "Stock ownership would not affect the apportionment of profits (between the Metz Hoechst and the German Hoechst) . . . . . this testimony of Haeuser can only be rejected upon the theory that both Haeuser and Metz have willfully deceived the court by false testimony."

Judge Mayer rejected the Garvan proofs that Messrs. Haeuser and Metz had for years been willfully deceiving the American people as well as the court. So Metz got back the Hoechst stock and the Hoechst New York bank account of more than $500,000— a sum which came in very handy in the development of the dye and pharmaceutical factories which, a few years later, Metz was to turn over to Farben's new American fronts.

Shortly after this decision was handed down, the Harding-Daugherty administration recognized the keen legal mind of Judge Mayer and elevated him to the Federal circuit court.

Two of the more prominent of the Metz employes during this period were his brother, the late Gustave P. Metz, and Alfred E. Sherndal, both of whom were educated in Germany. Gustave was also vice-president of Farbwerke Hoechst during the fight about its seizure, and in that official capacity served notice on the Alien Property Custodian in 1919 that he would be held responsible for all loss or damage for having swiped brother Herman's property. Later, both of these men were to have important positions on the staff of the Winthrop Chemical Company.

Winthrop, it will be recalled, was started so that Sterling could have an outlet for so-called ethical medicinals. Having progressed from the status of patent-medicine pitch artists by the acquisition of the Bayer Company, the Sterling management decided that a Dr. Jekyll was needed to sell prescription medicines to physicians, while the Mr. Hydes of Sterling peddled the nostrums.

One fact stands out in the history of Bayer, from the time it first became prominent as the Farben Fabriken of Elberfeld, up to the recent war: its pattern of hidden control, unlawful activities and subservience to Farben has varied only in the type of treachery employed and the identity of the individuals involved. On the record, if any one of the Farben names should be selected to head the roll of dishonor, that name is Bayer.

The name Bayer Company was first used in the United States in 1906; the plant of the Hudson River Aniline Works at Albany was acquired, and the manufacture of aspirin and a limited number of dyes was started. It was recognized as the American branch of the German company, but after the war started in 1914 the entire stock of the American company stood in the name of H. E. Seebohm, one of its German-born officers. Seebohm held this stock as trustee for three of the major stockholders of the German company, Dr. Karl Duisberg, Rudolph Mann and Christian Hess.

Thereafter a subsidiary was set up called Synthetic Patents Co., the stock of which was also trusteed for Duisberg, Mann and Hess. An elaborate bookkeeping system was devised by which almost all of the profits of the parent company were siphoned off to Synthetic Patents on the pretext of patent royalties and rentals. Seventy-five percent of the Synthetic profits then went to Duisberg and his colleagues for the pay-off men of German espionage and sabotage in the United States.

After the United States entered the war, Bayer resorted to the old shell game; they organized a new company, the Williams &

Crowell Color Co., and quietly slid the cash drawer under this third shell.

The Alien Property Custodian was gratified and surprised when the Bayer executives stated frankly, "We are enemy owned," and permitted seizure without protest. It was not until some time afterward that Mr. Garvan's bookkeeping bloodhounds uncovered the dodge by which everything of value was being transferred out of Bayer's custody to their newly organized and nominally American-owned subsidiary.

Charles J. Hardy, the New York attorney who had represented the Big Six houses in the pre-war anti-trust cases, was attorney for Bayer when it was seized, and he was retained by the Custodian to continue to act in that capacity while the property was in the hands of the Government. However, according to Mr. Garvan, it was discovered that Hardy was still representing the German interests, and that they were conspiring to establish an underlying company. So Mr. Garvan bounced Mr. Hardy and hired a new attorney.

After months of painstaking investigation, Mr. Garvan's sleuths uncovered the whole sorry Bayer mess, and proved that German nationals and American-born citizens had worked together for a long period of years under the directions of German Bayer and the German government to set up and operate an espionage, sabotage and propaganda machine in the guise of an American manufacturing plant producing dyes and pharmaceuticals.

In the final report of the Alien Property Custodian, relative to Bayer, there was summarized the utterly treasonable character of its hidden control and secret activities, in part as follows:

"The Bayer Co., of New York, was the largest and most powerful German-owned dye and drug manufacturing concern in America at the outbreak of the war. Carl Duisberg, the chief of the War Trade Board of Germany, was the owner of one third of the stock, and the company was largely used for the distribution of German propaganda funds in America. The higher officials of the Bayer Co. were nearly all unnaturalized German citizens, and the entire capital stock was voluntarily reported as enemy property within two or three months after the passage of the Trading with the Enemy Act. It became apparent, however, that this voluntary surrender was simply in line with German cunning."

"Examination of depreciation charges, profit-sharing payments, and royalties, resulted in uncovering and paying to the United States Treasury over $1,000,000 income taxes running back to 1913 which had been systematically concealed."

Ten years later I was publicly accusing the new owners of that same Bayer Company of doing many of the same things their predecessors had done. My reward was a kick in the pants—many kicks. Another ten years passed, and the proofs that I was right about Bayer and all the rest of Farben's evil brood began to come out. I say these proofs began to come out because that coming out was stopped ruthlessly in federal administrative offices, in courts of law and in the Senate and House of Representatives of the United States, as will be shown in detail before this story is concluded.

The Sterling agreements have been described in Chapter III. Messrs. Weiss, McClintock, Rogers and the others never had any illusions about the Germans with whom they were dealing. Weiss, bumptious and arrogant by nature, did at times attempt to outbrazen the I.G. leaders; as when Duisberg and Mann demanded that Sterling permit them to buy openly into the capital structure of the Sterling-Bayer Company.

During the early negotiations for the I.G. comeback, Weiss frequently harked back to his promise to the Alien Property Custodian, and in one letter stated:

The advice of our counsel is that, this sale having been made by the United States Government, and this country still being technically at war with Germany, the Peace Treaty not being signed, we would run a grave risk of destroying the business, and of incurring the charge of bad faith in our dealings with the Government, if we entered into any contract affecting the property acquired by us at the Government sale of any part thereof.

In later years, when Sterling, Winthrop and Bayer had become in effect an integral part of the Farben Empire, and the 1919 pledge had been violated repeatedly both in letter and spirit, Weiss again referred to his probity as a reason why Farben should not assume any technical ownership in the Bayer plant at Rensselaer, N. Y. In this instance Weiss stated his position in these words:

> I had always stressed to Dr. Mann and Justizrat Doermer the undertaking which we had to give to the United States Government at the time of the purchase of the Bayer Company, Inc., from the Alien Property Custodian, that under no circumstances would the property purchased at that sale be otherwise owned, in whole or in part, than by interests one hundred percent American. The grounds and the building at Rensselaer are part of the property purchased and are therefore covered by the undertaking given by us.

So Sterling then put entries on its books by which Bayer appeared to rent part of the Bayer land and factory to Winthrop—which was not one hundred percent American owned—and also sold to Winthrop machinery and equipment in the Bayer factory. This was done in order that Winthrop might claim to be a manufacturer of the medicinals it was getting from Farben and packaging as "Made in America." The manufacturing consisted mainly in diluting or tableting imported Farben products and putting them in Winthrop bottles. The celebrated Winthrop Research Laboratories were in Leverkusen, Germany, where most of its products were made.

An early and flagrant instance of breach of faith was the turning over to Winthrop of patents and trademarks on so-called ethical medicinals which were involved in the purchase of the Bayer Co. Veronal and Luminal were two of the better known Bayer trademarks transferred to Winthrop in violation of the pledge.

However, the I. G. people were persistent. During the negotiations one of them wrote: "I quite understand that in its final form the agreement will have to leave room to read between the lines." Later, another letter expressed their abiding determination in the following:

If you should still hesitate because of Washington, it should be taken into consideration, that for a certain provisional time, say, for instance, five years, another way could be found to get together so that no relation between our firm of Leverkusen and your firm of New York would be apparent to the outside world . . . . . We are sure that if the will exists, a way can be found to attain the purpose we have in mind.

Weiss and his usual associate in the dickering, McClintock, stepped back gradually from critical opposition to most of the proposals put forward by Dr. Duisberg and Rudolph Mann. A possible explanation of this more compliant attitude is found in a letter written by Mann to Weiss during the 1926 negotiations. This letter contained what may appear to have been the tender of very personal advantages to Weiss. One paragraph read:

As a personal remark, we would like to add that the friendly relations between you and ourselves through such a new organization become only still more intimate . . . . . You can be convinced that in the long end the new situation will be more advantageous to you.

Whatever these personal advantages may have been they were evidently effective, and for many years Sterling worked hand in glove with Farben in concealing Winthrop's German ownership.

And the United States was not the only country with which Sterling broke faith. Pledges or understandings were made to the British and French Governments when Sterling purchased the English Bayer Co., and the French Bayer trademarks respectively. In each instance it was specifically understood that Sterling was buying these foreign property rights as Americans for American ownership; instead Messrs. Weiss, Diebold and McClintock were acting, in effect, as agents of the German I.G., to whom partial or total ownership in these properties eventually passed.

Another instance of flagrant deception resulted because of a requirement by the Chemical Foundation that all licenses granted by it under former I.G. patents should go to companies owned at least seventy-five percent by Americans. The Metz company, after one half interest in it had been "purchased" for Winthrop with Farben funds, needed a Chemical Foundation license. So the license was applied for, obtained and signed for on the basis of utterly false statements which denied a fifty percent foreign interest.

In August 1928, word came to the leaders of Sterling that that ancient institution of learning, the University of Cologne, had conferred upon Weiss the degree of *Doctor Philosophia honoris causa*.

Then, shortly after the election of President Hoover, three of the University's directors came to the United States, and at a banquet at the Biltmore Hotel, made the formal presentation to Herr Wilhelm Weiss, their beloved brother in intellectual attainment.

The three directors, Justizrat Otto Doermer, Dr. Rudolph Mann and Dr. O. von Hoeffer of Farben, were, on this auspicious occasion, tactfully announced as *die direktoren* of the University of Cologne.

Dr. Fritz ter Meer was present, also Walter Duisberg. Dr. Wilhelm Hiemenz, Colonel Metz, and Dr. E. von Salis of the original Bayer organization. Leader of the American cheering section was the great Republican potentate, the late Louis K. Liggett, who, of course, shared in the congratulations with Weiss for the recent triumph at the polls of his candidate, that eminent student of business and international affairs, Herbert Hoover. As Sterling window dressing came H. F. Behrens, Stanley P. Jadwin, John F. Murray, George C. Haigh, C. A. Aul and Otto Schenk; along with Earl I. McClintock, A. H. Diebold, Frank A. Blair, Raymond Foster and brother Fred E. Weiss. It was a happy occasion for all concerned.

The Farben academicians who were present must have laughed up their sleeves at the notable success of such inexpensive soothing syrup for the rambunctious Weiss. A piece of parchment with a wax seal and a bit of ribbon attached was a small price to pay for a more docile obedience on the part of the wild west patent-medicine man who had already demonstrated his abilities to bully the American press and seduce the learned professions of this country. When it included a tie-string to the Hoover Republican, Louis Liggett, the doctorate became a rare bargain indeed. As a matter of fact those slick Farben scholars should have made it an earned degree, rather than an *honoris causa*. His acquaintances said at the time that Wild Bill Weiss had surely earned everything that Farben gave him.

So the ceremony of robing the learned Weiss, the delivery by Justizrat Doermer of the *Rektor's* address in high Latin; and the candidate's humble response (in drug store Latin) came to a glorious end with buckets of champagne and the haunting strains of *"Nach die Heimat Wieder"* stirring the potted palms and guests of the decorous Biltmore. A waiter who understood neither German nor Latin decided that it must be some kind of Ku Klux enrobing event. It was just that.

According to the announcements the degree was awarded Mr. Weiss, in recognition of the arduous labors of the recipient in promoting more cordial industrial and scientific relations between German and American pharmaceutical companies. Thereafter it was always "Doctor" Weiss. The pharmacist who had left his prescription counter to peddle patent medicines could now point with pride to a title which gave rise to a belief in the minds of many that he was a member of the profession of medicine. Even real physicians were fooled by that title.

It was just at this time that I was appealing in vain to Senator David I. Walsh of Massachusetts to demand a Senate investigation of Drug, Inc.

On Nov. 8, 1928, I wrote Senator Walsh a forecast which missed the Hoover 1929 Stock Market debacle by six months. In part, that letter read as follows:

> Many of these who gave the mandate on Tuesday will be sick of their work inside of eighteen months, unless I miss my guess.

> I would like very much to be permitted to call to your personal attention a situation which I am convinced warrants your official scrutiny, and which later, after investigation, you may be inclined to bring to the attention of those of your colleagues in the Senate who appreciate the real significance of what happened on Tuesday.

A few days later I talked to Senator Walsh at some length about the situation as I saw it and received his assurances of great interest. On Nov. 19, 1928 I wrote him the following:

Dear Senator Walsh:

To further illustrate the point I made, when I saw you last week, about the power behind the National Republican Committeeman from Massachusetts, I enclose herewith a collection of advertisements clipped from a limited number of daily papers purchased at random in different parts of the United States.

I also enclose a list of the companies which are alleged to be now all under one control, and which include these national advertisers and many others.

If you think it would be helpful or informative to you I will undertake to have a file prepared which will include:

1. The advertisements under one control appearing on the same day in at least one daily paper in every state in the Union.

2. The advertisements under one control appearing on the same day or week in every paper published in one or more states. East or West, which you may designate.

3. The advertisements under one control appearing in the same week or month in the weekly or monthly journals of the U.S., popular and professional.

I do believe that if this exhibit were made available to you you would have a picture of the background or twilight zone of the Republican Party as now constituted that would make the Trade Commission investigation of the Power Trust look like small potatoes indeed.

Hoping this may interest you and thanking you indeed for the courtesy you showed me, I remain

Respectfully yours,

Howard W. Ambruster

Enclosed with this letter was a list of thirty odd American drug and patent-medicine companies and national advertisers which, according to published reports and trade rumors, had been brought into direct or indirect affiliation with the German I. G. Farben as part of the German-American relations promoted by "Doctor" Weiss and the Liggett Republican machine.

That was the end of the interest of Senator Walsh in this subject, as regards any expression to me, or to the public, so far as I have heard.

It was never a secret that Bayer's Dr. Karl Duisberg, as former chief of the German War Trade Board, and Cassella's Dr. Karl Weinberg, as first president of the I.G. Dyes, were among the strongest early supporters of the Weimar Republic. As cabinet ministers, Reichstag members and Councillors, a succession of dye trust leaders served and directed the Reich; and through ownership of leading German newspapers, helped to make and break its ministries.

It was also a matter of official record in the United States that, in 1926, when I.G. Farben was put together, under Dr. Duisberg as its first chairman, to become the largest industrial combination in Germany, it promptly tied in to an indissoluble union with the Hugo Stinnes and Fritz Thyssen steel interests which, as the Vereinigte Stahlwerke, had become the second largest cartel in Germany.

United through their jointly owned coal mining combine, the Rheinische Stahlwerke, and through interlocking directorates and mutual stock ownership, Farben and the Thyssen Steel trust from then on were the dominant force behind the scenes, of a succession of German governments which finally descended to the gutters of Munich for Hitler's Nazis.

And it was Dr. Duisberg, for the industrialists, who joined with the Junkers or Reichs-Landbund (landed agricultural gentry) in 1927, to make the gift of the Neudeck Castle and huge estate to the senile Hindenburg, thus securing a stranglehold on the aged soldier and inducing scandals which, when the time came, served as a pretext for the downfall of the republic and the elevation of a Hitler, also financed, armed, and implemented for conquest, by the combined Farben-Thyssen interests.

While the elder Duisberg was thus occupied with the Fatherland's puppet show, his son Walter, as an American citizen by choice, was becoming a chief connecting link with substantially all of Farben's false fronts in the United States and Latin America. Weiss, McClintock, and other Sterling leaders were continually in Germany and they were advised from the inside how political and governmental affairs were developing. In the early 30s

Farben's leaders began bringing the Nazi government into the picture as a reason, or pretext, for the restrictions and conditions which they insisted upon in their dealings with Sterling. Time and again Sterling yielded to Farben demands that were predicated on an alleged government requirement. However the Sterling people were told that the Hitler Reich was right down Sterling's alley for sound money and safe international trade.

Rudolph Mann communicated the complacent viewpoint of Farben towards the Nazi government in a letter to his good friend Doctor Weiss in 1933:

> With regard to Germany we undoubtedly are . . . . . in a clearly noticeable change for the better, as the present National government has within their rows prominent, moderate elements so that all of us confidently believe that—irrespective of the maintenance of the strong, psychologically valuable, national feeling—they will desist from making commercial experiments.
>
> I lay special stress on telling you and all my friends in America that the ghastly fictions on the activity of the National Socialists, which have appeared in some American papers, do not correspond to real facts whatsoever. We actually have behind us a revolution which will entail a complete remodeling of our spiritual and commercial life in the positive direction. That such a revolution will not go by without some single cases which have been dealt with in a somewhat unfortunate way, is not worth the while being mentioned. In German this is called: 'Where one planes, there will fall shavings' . . . . .
>
> Today's Germany is the safest country you can find in Europe, free from Communism, strongly conducted, with their currency in good order, and with men who not only have the desire but also the force and capability of changing the important commercial problems for the better in the interest of Germany and of international trade.

Mann was making Farben's support of Hitler attractive in the kind of language which Weiss and his pals could comprehend.

Some writers who have discussed this matter appear to believe that Farben was helpless to control the actions of Hitler's officials.

But there is abundant evidence that the Nazis were financed by Farben, that Farben leaders occupied high places in the Nazi government from its beginning, and that Hitler's armies would have been helpless without the years of preparation and continued support of Farben. History will tell which end of the dog was Farben.

However in considering the subservience of Sterling's leaders to the restrictions and continued deceptions insisted upon by Farben, it makes no difference whether the latter was in fact compelled to so instruct Sterling or whether Farben itself was really responsible for the alleged official instructions which it passed out on alleged compulsion. Either way the result was that Sterling, and all of the others in the United States who yielded to any such instructions and deceptions were in plain fact acting as agents for the Farben-Hitler government, and helped conduct its economic industrial warfare and subversive activities.

The "government" instructions insisted upon by Farben and with which Sterling complied covered every important aspect of the relationship between them. Farben compelled Sterling to pay large sums of money over and above the contract provisions on the plea that these funds were required by order of the Hitler government; Sterling was denied technical information relative to patents and processes to which, under the contracts Sterling was entitled, on the plea that the Nazi officials would not permit that data to leave Germany; Sterling was required to conceal various phases of its relationship with Farben on the plea that the government might not approve of them; and finally, Sterling's officials were compelled, or instructed, to assist in the Nazi underground work in the American Hemisphere.

What all this amounted to was that Farben was conveying to the Sterling leaders orders from the Nazi government, and Sterling's officials obeyed them. Their absolute loyalty was to Farben and to Farben's government, to the complete exclusion of all other considerations.

In 1934 after Farben's interest in Winthrop had been transferred to the American I.G. it was gently intimated to Sterling that it might not look right if the German government discovered all that Farben was doing for Winthrop without getting paid for it. (American I.G. was meanwhile getting the dividends on fifty per cent of the Winthrop stock but the German government, as well as that of the United States, was not *supposed* to know that Farben owned American I.G.) Therefore, suggested Farben, a "service fee of $50,000 a year" over and above all existing contract arrangements, should be forthcoming. So Sterling, or Winthrop, came across with the extra $50,000 a year.

In 1938 another squeeze play was worked, this time it was actually claimed that the German government had just discovered Farben's agreement with Winthrop and was upset because Farben apparently was not getting anything out of Winthrop on the Winthrop-Sterling contract. A hurried call was sent out for a conference at Basle, Switzerland. Several of the highest Farben leaders, headed by Dr. Hermann Schmitz, attended, and Earl I. McClintock was sent to represent Sterling and Winthrop. Walter Duisberg, D. A. Schmitz and Hugh Williamson were present, presumably to represent the interest of American I.G.

McClintock, according to his account of the meeting, was taken for a ride around the city of Basle while the delegates conferred. Then he was led into the meeting and taken for another, and different, ride. They told him that the German government had decreed that somebody, Sterling or Winthrop, would have to come across again with another good, fat annual sum. It was all very pleasant and just too bad that the Nazis were so nosey but what could poor Farben do but to tell Sterling to tell Winthrop to pay up—or else? So Winthrop began paying a new "service fee" of $100,000 a year. As a pre-war gangster's squeeze play it was perfect.

However, the Sterling leaders knew they were trapped long before this; if they refused to play ball Farben could cut off their supplies of Winthrop's "American made" products. The patents under which these products were sold in the United States exclusively by Winthrop were of little use to Sterling except to protect the monopoly, because Farben had not told Winthrop how to make them and accordingly, Winthrop did not know how to do so.

Weiss and his colleagues also had ample warning that war was coming, and then they began to squirm in earnest. When one of the Alba contracts was being entered into between Sterling and Farben in 1937, Nazi government restrictions were the reason given for refusal to assign Farben United States patents to Alba unless a re-transfer clause was included. At this time the possibility of war between the United States and Germany was definitely indicated in correspondence between Alba and Sterling officials, both of whom, it appears, were former Farben employes. In a letter dated July 29, 1937 which passed between these two American companies about the Farben Alba patents it was stated:

> It is to be considered, however, that the patents, if assigned to an American firm, cannot be seized, say in the case of international complications.

The only kind of international complications which could possibly result in seizure of Farben's United States patents was war between Germany and the United States. Despite the warning, Sterling officials went right along expanding and even tried to get Farben to join them in further relations. The latter replied that they could not spare the funds just then.

Some futile efforts were made to get data from Farben in order that products which were being imported could be made at the Rensselaer plant, "in case manufacture should become necessary." Atabrine, the antimalaria substitute for quinine, was one of these products. Winthrop had never made Atabrine and did not know how to make it when the threat of losing our supply of quinine from Dutch East Indies gradually began to dawn upon our super-statesmen at Washington.

The Farben pincers through Sterling on Atabrine worked in conjunction with that applied by the Japs in the Dutch East Indies on quinine; just as the Farben pincers through Standard Oil, on synthetic rubber worked in conjunction with the Japs on natural rubber. There is evidence also that Farben intended to work its pincers on synthetic nitrogen in conjunction with a friendly Chile staying with the Axis and cutting off our supply of natural nitrates.

However, that Atabrine story belongs in another chapter, as do the details of deception and downright sabotage that involved Sterling's agents in South America.

CHAPTER VII

False Fronts Become Bold

ON APRIL 20, 1929, Dr. Carl Bosch and a coterie of his Farben associates waved triumphant farewells to the Statue of Liberty and marched into the bar of the Hamburg-American liner *New York,* to celebrate the success of their mission to America.

The Germans were returning to the Fatherland with all that they could have hoped for. Their understandings with our myopic industrialists had been most satisfactory, their arrangements with our avaricious financiers most profitable. And less than a week after their departure the American I.G. Chemical Corp. was launched suddenly and with a great blare of Wall Street publicity. According to reports on the Street that afternoon, its entire issue of $30,000,000 of 5½ percent convertible debentures was oversubscribed in an hour.

The formation of American I.G. had been a closely guarded secret, but after its announcement on April 26th no attempt was made to conceal Farben's part in the achievement. Both the prospectus and the half-page advertisements announcing the underwriting contained a letter addressed to the National City Bank and signed by Geheimrat Dr. Hermann Schmitz and Dr. Wilfrid

Greif, as managing directors of Farben, which recited the huge size of Farben and stated that:

> As a result of the development of its worldwide activities, I.G. Dyes (Farben) has found it desirable to cause a corporation to be organized in the United States, under the name of American I.G. Chemical Corp. . . . . . with broad corporate powers to foster and finance the development of chemical and allied industries in the United States and elsewhere.

The prospectus then went on to state that all of the common stock to be presently outstanding would be issued against cash, or to acquire stocks of Agfa Ansco Corp., and General Aniline Works. Both of these companies were known to be controlled by Farben. The prospectus also announced that the principal, interest and premium upon redemption of the 5½% debentures were unconditionally guaranteed by I.G. Farben and were payable at the National City Bank of New York in gold, with approximately $450,000,000 in Farben assets back of the guarantee.

It was thus evident that the American I.G. was to be a Farben holding company for its manufacturing subsidiaries in the United States. The Farben guarantee of the interest on the debentures, plus the big names of the financial houses which underwrote the issue, and the big names of the American industrial and financial leaders on the board of the new company were sufficient incentive to cause unthinking American investors to fall over themselves in the rush to get in on a good thing.

It should have been apparent by the most casual reading of the prospectus that control of American I.G. would remain not with the owners of the debentures but with the Farben promoters. Approximately ten percent of the voting stock was all that the American investors could possibly secure.

Just before Farben organized this new company and thereby financed its American industrial pincers with thirty million good American dollars on a prospectus signed by its Geheimrat Schmitz, that astute gentleman had also organized another dummy company in Switzerland with the imposing name of Internationale Gesellschaft für Chemische Unternehmungen A. G. of Switzerland. Known as the I.G. Chemie, this Swiss concern was a holding company for Farben's properties in foreign countries, and a part of its stock was offered to Farben's stockholders with Farben's guarantee of payment of dividends.

When American I.G. was organized, I.G. Chemie did not appear as the recorded holder of majority control of its voting stock. But by 1940, after the war was started, this "neutral" Swiss concern, with one of its Swiss subsidiaries, held title to over 85 percent of the outstanding shares of General Aniline & Film, successor of American I.G. At one time in the history of these two Farben fronts, the Swiss company was the recorded holder of something over 10 percent of the stock of the American company, while the latter was also the owner of some 9 percent of the outstanding stock of the Swiss company. This exhibition of two Farben snakes swallowing each other by the tail undoubtedly afforded much amusement at the home office.

However, back in April 1929, I.G. Chemie was a dark secret. Farben's ballyhoo centered around the names of the American financiers and industrialists who participated in the underwriting of American I.G., and much was made of the fact that the banking syndicate that floated the debentures was headed by National City and included such houses as International Manhattan Co., Lee Higginson & Co., Harris Forbes & Co., Brown Bros. & Co., and the Continental Illinois Co.

Still greater acclaim was accorded the prominent Americans whose names appeared on the board of directors of this new symbol of Germany's friendship for the United States. Listed in the prospectus and in the newspaper advertising were Walter C. Teagle, Charles E. Mitchell, Edsel B. Ford, Paul M. Warburg, William E. Weiss, Adolph Kuttroff, and Herman A. Metz.

The three other directors were Carl Bosch, listed under the imposing title of "Professor Doctor," Dr. Hermann Schmitz; and Dr. Wilfrid Greif.

Dr. Hermann Schmitz, president of the unheralded I.G. Chemie, was also the first president of the widely publicized American I.G., and soon after its successful financing the campaign to conceal the ownership of American I.G. began in earnest. In October 1929 (as already related in Chapter II) Herman Metz started the ball rolling by his public statement that although Farben was a stockholder in American I.G., the latter should not be referred to as the American branch of the German I.G., because that was just not so. Some three months later, while testifying before the Senate Lobby Committee, Metz again denied the Farben ownership:

> The Germans haven't got a dollar's worth of stock in the American I.G., of record; nor the Swiss, either.

Finally Metz gave the whole thing away when Senator Robinson stated:

> Now, it is pretty clear that the American I.G. was organized by the German I.G., and that they both are officered by the same people, and therefore are practically the same concern.

> Mr. Metz replied:

> Well, that can be so construed, but the reason for it was to take over what the Germans had or were trying to do in this country, and get the industry established, which I always preached to them, to come over here and manufacture over here.

The Geheimrat Dr. Hermann Schmitz, along with Prof. Dr. Carl Bosch and the other Farben executives, did everything in his power to hide Farben's control of the new holding company in the United States. The Geheimrat even tried to pull the wool over the eyes of the two duPont representatives who visited him in Berlin in July, 1933, to discuss the possibility of exchanging some duPont investments in Farben for shares in either I.G. Chemie or in the American I.G. The growth of nationalism, the Wilmington executives naïvely explained, made it advisable for their company to get rid of its interests in Farben.

Dr. Schmitz opined that such a horse trade was impossible and solemnly stated that I.G. Chemie was strictly a Swiss company, and that Farben owned not a single share.

The duPont officials were not impressed with the truthfulness of Dr. Schmitz's statements and reported to the home office that they presumed Farben had a dummy Swiss director in I.G. Chemie.

They also reported that in London an official of Imperial Chemical Industries told them definitely that the Geheimrat had lied to them.

In 1934, Mr. Teagle decided that he had better resign as director of American I.G. Chemical Corp., but, instead of exercising his own discretion and resigning, he cabled his subordinate, Frank Howard, who was in Paris, to find out whether he should take up the matter with Dr. Bosch, or whether Howard would ask Mr. Schmitz about it.

Howard cabled back on November 29th, that Teagle take a firm stand with Dr. Bosch, and stated that the resignation was

. . . . . certainly wise under present conditions since it will tend minimize chauvinistic comments in both countries should there be any public interest aroused in the relations of the two companies.

However, Mr. Teagle did not resign as director of American I. G. Both Bosch and Schmitz refused their permission, despite a rather pathetic letter dated June 6, 1935, in which Mr. Teagle begged Dr. Schmitz "to permit Mr. Clark (a Standard vice-president) to replace me on the board."

The Hitler régime in Germany had aroused some official interest at Washington in American companies with German ties, and, in 1938, the Securities and Exchange Commission decided to go through the motions of investigating the ownership of American I.G.

In its preliminary exploration of the records, the S.E.C. discovered that although Farben was never to be a record shareholder, a resolution was adopted at the first board meeting of this "American" company, before the public had bought its stock, by which the officers were authorized to loan any part of its funds to either Farben or to I.G. Chemie.

At that same meeting, the sum of $10,000,000—ostensibly transferred to the United States by Edward Greutert & Cie., Farben's Swiss bankers, for the purchase of voting shares in the new company, was adroitly switched back to Farben as a loan from the new American I.G. That ten-million-dollar silver spoon from Grandpa Farben never entered the new infant's mouth—it got only a book entry on its birth certificate.

This ingenious method of tapping Wall Street was worked overtime and, within a few weeks after the public had planked down its cash, nearly $20,000,000 of American I.G.'s capital funds had been transferred, by vote of its directors, to Switzerland or Germany as loans to Farben.

The S.E.C. accountants also uncovered data which established nominal stock control of American I.G. by Swiss I.G. Chemie from the date of organization. This condition had never changed and, at the time of the investigation, I.G. Chemie held nominal control of more than 85 percent of the shares of American I.G.

With these facts established, Mr. Teagle was called to the witness stand and sworn to tell the truth, the whole truth and nothing but the truth. Unhappily, however, he did not know who owned control of American I.G.—the company of which he was a director. More, he had never known, from the day the company was organized. He did not know who owned the little block of 500,000 shares of the company stock that had been issued in his name—stock worth at least half a million dollars. He did not know how many shares I.G. Chemie owned, or who owned I.G. Chemie.

It was just too bad, but Mr. Teagle really could not tell to the S.E.C. things about the company which no one had ever told him.

Mr. David Schenker, chief attorney for the S.E.C., was exquisitely polite in his questioning. After some discussion of the snake-swallowing act by which American I.G. and Swiss I.G. Chemie purchased each other's shares, the question was asked:

> SCHENKER: So that you have a situation where the American
>   I.G. Corporation, the control of which is unknown to us,
>   is buying over a period of one year approximately $21,-
>   000,000 of the stock of this I.G. Chemie Corp., the control
>   of which is unknown to us and to you; is that not so?
> TEAGLE: That is correct.
> SCHENKER: So far as you know, you do not know the exact
>   extent of the control of the I.G. Chemie in American I.G.
>   Corporation; is that true?
> TEAGLE: That is correct.

SCHENKER: And you do not know at the present time who controls that corporation?

TEAGLE: That is correct; yes.

The examiner's queries continued to be approved by Mr. Teagle.

SCHENKER: Throughout your entire tenure of directorship you say you did not know who the controlling owners of American I.G. Chemical Corp. were?

TEAGLE: That is correct.

On the little matter of 500,000 shares.

SCHENKER: Now, the record discloses that 500,000 common shares were issued to you. Were you the beneficial owner of those shares?

TEAGLE: I was not.

SCHENKER: Do you know how it was that those shares got into your name?

TEAGLE: No, I do not.

When asked whether he thought that his colleague on the board, Mr. Edsel Ford, might be better posted than he was, Mr. Teagle expressed the opinion that Mr. Ford did not know any more about it than he did. Teagle also stated that he did not know who was voting for him at the stockholders' meetings.

When asked to express an opinion as to whether all this was a healthy condition, Mr. Teagle begged to be excused from answering.

One thing Mr. Teagle could explain. He recalled distinctly that he went on the Board at the request of his friend Dr. Bosch:

My connection with the American I.G. came about through an explanation made to me by Dr. Bosch of the German I.G. of his plans, and my interest was prompted by the fact that I hoped to secure for the Standard Oil Co. of New Jersey a supply of the raw product for the fertilizer plant.

Just how his American I.G. directorship was to help supply Standard Oil's proposed fertilizer plant with raw products, while he was voting for loans to Farben, Teagle did not explain, neither did he mention the efforts he had made to resign from the board.

Another matter which Mr. Teagle neglected to mention was a letter which he had received back in 1932 from Dr. Wilfrid Greif, the managing director of Farben. Written on the letterhead of the American I.G. Chemical Corp., 521 Fifth Avenue, New York City, and dated May 6, 1932, the letter read, in part:

> I.G. Chemie is, as you know, a subsidiary of I.G. Farben, organized in 1928 . . . . . As officially stated in the annual report of the I.G. Farben for 1931, the net income of I.G. Chemie for 1931 is sufficient to pay on its stock the same dividend which will be paid by I.G. Farben.

Another item of possible pertinency to the S.E.C. inquiry which was not brought out in the Teagle examination, was the fact that Standard Oil had decided not to be identified publicly as a stockholder in American I.G. This had been the subject of a cable sent to Teagle by Mr. Howard on May 27, 1930, when the former was in London:

> In view of fact that we have repeatedly denied any financial interest in American I.G. it seems to me to be unwise for us to now permit them to include us as stockholders in their original listing which is object of present transaction. It would serve their purpose to issue this stock to you personally . . . . . Will this be agreeable to you as a temporary measure?

Mr. Teagle, or the S. E. C. investigators, might also have dug up correspondence which passed between Teagle and Mitchell back in 1932, when those two American I. G. directors for a time opposed the action of the board in swapping Farben securities for those of the I.G. Chemie.

One of these letters, dated May 27, revealed the existence of a contract, or option through which Farben might completely absorb I.G. Chemie by exchanging its own shares for those of the Swiss company. Mr. Mitchell's letter to his friend Teagle went on to say that:

> Professor Bosch and Dr. Schmitz should thoroughly understand how anxious we are to be of assistance to them in

bringing about a development of the chemical industry along most approved lines in the United States, but they should realize just as fully the fact that you and I are in a very embarrassing situation whenever transactions are proposed as between the German I.G. and the American I.G.

Finally, there was the letter which Mr. Teagle wrote to Mr. Mitchell on May 26, 1932, enclosing a memorandum which he stated had been prepared at his direction to be used in discussions with Dr. Bosch about the exchange by American I.G. Farben securities for those of I.G. Chemie.

It might appear from two statements of fact in the memorandum that Mr. Teagle had already reached a very definite conclusion regarding the ownership of both American I. G. and I. G. Chemie. The statements were:

> The transaction between American I.G. and the I.G. parent company involving the exchange of I.G. bonds against the I.G. Chemie shares . . . . .
>
> Transaction between parent and subsidiary company like that of the exchange of I.G. bonds against the I.G. Chemie shares . . . . .

It may be assumed that if Mr. Teagle's testimony before the S. E. C. had been more informative, Mr. Schenker might not have felt it necessary to also summon Messrs. W. H. Duisberg and D. A. Schmitz.

Mr. Duisberg qualified as director, first vice-president and treasurer of American I.G. and stated solemnly that he didn't know who owned it. He then produced correspondence which he had conducted with Farben and with Edward Greutert & Cie., bankers of I.G. Chemie, at the request of S.E.C., requesting them for information about who was which and which controlled whom? Farben's reply dated August 13, 1937, was brief and to the point:

> We have no direct or indirect participation either in the American I.G. Chemical Corp., nor in the other corporations mentioned in your letter (I.G. Chemie and other stockholders of record).

This letter added that it was not Farben's custom to give such information, so no precedent was to be established in making the exception; also that the letter was to be treated as confidential.

Greutert's response was a rebuke for making so unethical a request of a banker about its clients. On August 18, 1937, Greutert wrote:

> We regret not to be in a position for reasons of principle, to give you the requested information. Such a disclosure by us would be entirely irreconcilable with the bank secret, particularly strictly observed in our country by the banking community, and with the duties and practices resulting therefrom.

(It is of interest here that the so ethical Greutert & Co., and Edward W. Greutert, head of this Swiss banking firm, were among those named as co-conspirators, along with various officers, subsidiaries and affiliates of Farben, in the indictment of September 1, 1939, for conspiracy with Farben's international nitrogen cartel which restricted production of nitrogen and ammonia. This distinction did not cause either co-conspirator Greutert or any of those indicted any real trouble because this multiple indictment was one of those *nolle prossed* by a complacent Department of Justice.)

Also called to testify by the S.E.C. was D. A. Schmitz, brother of Dr. Hermann (the Geheimrat) Schmitz, who added his bit to this fantastic, corporate merry-go-round. After qualifying as a director of American I.G. since 1933, and its president since 1936, he was asked by Mr. Schenker:

> Do you know who was the beneficial stockholders . . . . . of the class A and class B stock of American I. G. Chemical Corp.?
>
> SCHMITZ: No, no more than the records we have here.
>
> SCHENKER: So the only thing you know is who the record holders are and whether they are the beneficial owners or not you do not know?
>
> SCHMITZ: No.

Perhaps the crowning gem of the hearing was the tribute paid to the witnesses at its close. Said Mr. Schenker:

> I would like the record to indicate we are appreciative of the full cooperation that was given to us in connection with our study of the American I.G. Chemical Corp. and that they have made available to us all of the information we asked.

Some mention having been made in the press of the acarpous nature of the public hearing, I wrote to the S.E.C., offered my services, and enclosed various papers, one of which was a copy of the diagrammatic chart I had prepared in 1931 for Congress. This chart, or flow sheet, set forth in detail what Farben was doing and proposed to do in this country through its control of American I.G. Chemical Corp., and other United States companies.

My letter to the S.E.C., dated Feb. 5, 1938, and addressed to the Chairman, Hon. William O. Douglas (made Supreme Court Justice in 1939), stated in part:

> Having noted in the press that you are having difficulty in uncovering the identity of those interests which control the American I. G. Chemical Corp., due to the unfortunate lapse of memory indicated by some of your witnesses, I am enclosing herewith copies of some papers and documents which may assist your investigators . . . . . my own diagrammatic chart or flow sheet was worked out in 1931 with the hope that Congressional investigation might be induced into one of the most sinister groups which has ever been assembled in industry, finance, and politics in this country.
>
> Considerable water has gone over the dam since I put this chart together, but in its essential aspects of objective, the ramifications and offshoots of this grouping of interests still persist. It would be a very valuable public service if your investigators should uncover some of its present connections and agencies—but I suggest you will have to arm them with brass knuckles and a sublime indifference to their own future welfare if they really dig into it.
>
> If you feel that I can be of assistance let me know.

I doubt whether the S.E.C. Chairman ever saw this letter. It was acknowledged, however, by Mr. David Schenker, S.E.C. counsel, who expressed appreciation for my cooperation, but did not indicate a desire for any more of it.

As an immediate aftermath of the S.E.C. public hearing Mr. Teagle's earlier desire to resign as an American I.G. director was seconded vigorously by his colleagues, and considerable indignation was expressed at the embarrassment to which both Mr. Teagle and Standard Oil of New Jersey had been subjected. Standard Oil was not amused! And a memorandum by one of the Standard Oil staff, uncovered later in Mr. Teagle's files, contained these statements:

> The commission wants to know the true foreign ownership since American I.G. is a chemical company. In case of any war anywhere this ownership would be wanted by the United States Government.

> Mr. Wellman (Standard Oil attorney) explained to Mr. Schenker that any conclusion by the Commission that American I.G. is, or is possibly, owned by I.G. Farben or allied interests may well result in an ownership by the German Government with all the attendant risks to the American owners of the twenty-five million of American I.G. debentures.

> It is a real possibility that if, in another war, Germany and U. S. A. should again be enemies the non-German financial interest in American I.G. shares would have to be shown to the satisfaction of the U. S. Government to escape seizure as German-owned property.

> Mr. Teagle as a director was placed in a most embarrassing position at the hearing and also in press releases because he did not know the beneficial ownership of any of the large blocks of American I.G. shares. To the public, at any rate, it seems impossible that a man in his position would not know something as to who owns the company.

> "For Duisberg and Schmitz to say in effect that they knew nothing about the holdings of this company, and that they

had made the investment entirely on the recommendation of Dr. Schmitz, is just a plain dereliction of their duty as directors.

It seems to us also that the best thing Mr. Teagle can do is to resign from the American I.G., for, while the present inquiry, I believe, is closed, we have certainly not heard the last of it. It may be contended that the S.E.C. is poking into things that are none of its business, but after all, they take the attitude that the company raised $30,000,000 from the American public and they have a right to know what has been done with this money.

The pithy comment on various aspects of the S.E.C. hearings was unsigned, but some of the writer's forebodings about war and the seizure of American I.G. as German owned were to come true. He was correct also in his forecasts that the S.E.C. inquiry was closed, but that Standard had not heard the last of it.

Mr. Howard wrote Standard's European representative on Feb. 19, 1938, that "a very unfavorable impression" had been created by newspaper reports of Mr. Teagle's apparent lack of any real knowledge of the ownership or business of the company of which he was a director, and in which the records indicated he had 500,000 shares.

"I am afraid," the letter continued, "that one of us or both of us will have to have some pretty straight talk with Geheimrat Schmitz about this American I.G. Chemical business."

Apparently, however, it was the Geheimrat who did the straight talking, when Howard rushed to Berlin to see him. For, in a letter dated March 11, 1938, Mr. Howard reported to Teagle that he was doubtful that Dr. Schmitz would consent to the resignation, and went on to say that Dr. Schmitz appeared to see no advantage in further talk about the matter. Wrote Howard:

He knows what happened in Washington, and despite everything he still believes that his course has been the best course that could be taken and he wishes to continue it. He has pointed out to me, however, reasons why he believes there will be no recurrence of any of the past troubles in connection with the American I.G. Company. Unfortunately, these are matters which I can only talk about when I see you—this at Dr. Schmitz's specific request.

The occult powers which Dr. Schmitz indicated relating to the non-recurrence at Washington of the troubles of American I.G. were never revealed publicly by Mr. Howard, and it is worthy of note here that subsequent to the inclusion of this particular letter in the record of the hearings of the United States Senate Committee investigating the National Defense Program (Truman Committee) in 1942, Mr. Howard, who had appeared as a witness before the committee, was not asked to disclose those statements of Geheimrat Schmitz which he had not dared to put in his confidential report to Mr. Teagle. Mr. Howard also appeared later as a witness before the Senate Committee on Patents (Bone Committee) but again failed to relate just what the Geheimrat had said that he could "only talk about" when he saw Teagle.

Mr. Teagle was not called as a witness before either of those Senate hearings. He did, however. finally succeed in his long cherished desire to resign from the board of the Farben subsidiary, about which, as a witness, he knew so little. On April 4, 1939, seven long years after he had first requested permission to resign and just a few months before the start of the war, D. A. Schmitz wrote Mr. Teagle that his resignation as director had been accepted "with regret."

Brother Hermann the Geheimrat, and Carl Bosch the Professor Doctor apparently had instructed D. A. Schmitz to be nice about it, and that they could now spare from the board of Farben's American I.G. the august name of the chairman of the board of Standard Oil of New Jersey. That name had served its purpose in the Farben pattern for ten vital pre-war years.

Apropos of the non-recurrence of troubles for American I.G., as foreseen by Dr. Schmitz. the S.E.C. held no more public hearings on the subject, and issued no public statement about it until June 9, 1941. This was a few days after the discerning Lowell L. Leake in newspaper *PM* had published the first informative article which ever appeared in the press about my earlier protests at Farben's activities in the chemical industries of this country.

The S.E.C. statement took the form of a report to Congress. In this report of its four years of lethargic efforts to uncover the ownership of American I.G., the S.E.C. included the following:

> All attempts to ascertain the beneficial ownership of the controlling shares have been unsuccessful . . . . . As a consequence the American investors, mainly bondholders, are in the peculiar position of being creditors of a corporation under an unknown control.

A few days later I prepared an analysis of that report for the Non-Sectarian Anti-Nazi League which in part was as follows:

> The monkey in the box and circus merry-go-round of concealed stock ownership fools only those individuals who want to be fooled, or who are willing for some reason to play a part in the attempted deception. Unhappily an agency of the United States Government has now issued an official report or presentation, which, when we finally get to the point of seizing enemy property, as we must, will provide a document to be utilized as a pretext to permit the German I.G. Farben to continue its operations in this country, under the present management, and in the interest of the German Reich.

A year later I made one more attempt to induce the S.E.C. to reopen its inquiry into other ramifications of the activities of I.G. Farben and its agents and affiliates in the United States. In a communication dated August 8, 1942, I called attention to the fact that during the earlier period of its American I.G. investigation it had been rumored that Earle I. McClintock, high official of Sterling Products, was being considered to succeed Messrs. Joseph P. Kennedy and William O. Douglas as chairman of S.E.C. when those two gentlemen resigned that office in 1937 and 1938 respectively. I pointed out that regardless of the fact that Mr. McClintock was not made chairman, any attempt to secure his appointment became a matter which the S.E.C. might properly inquire into—in view of the Sterling and Farben secret agreements. Again the S.E.C. declined to follow my suggestion.

The S.E.C. report on the lily-white purity of American I.G., as submitted to Congress, was prepared under the supervision of Commissioner Robert E. Healy, assisted by the gentle Mr. Schenker, as counsel.

In the past I had made other appeals to agencies advised by these two distinguished public servants. In 1929, when Mr. Healy was chief counsel for the Federal Trade Commission, I requested an investigation of the German affiliations of American I.G., Drug, Inc., and the American Medical Association. And two years later, I again asked that agency to dig into the McKesson & Robbins mess. Mr. Schenker's first job in Washington was assistant to Ferdinand Pecora, counsel for the Senate Committee on Banking and Currency, which drafted the S.E.C. legislation. And it was this committee that ignored my appeals to explain the New York Stock Exchange listing of the fraudulent McKesson & Robbins securities, and also to investigate what I described as "a reign of terrorism . . . . . utilized by our so-called financial leaders to cow into submission any one who protested against the prostitution of our governmental machinery at Washington."

Messrs. Pecora and Healy became members of the S.E.C. when it was organized in 1934, and Mr. Schenker became its counsel.

On June 11, 1941, just two days after the S.E.C. report on Farben's American front was filed with the Congress, Mr. Schenker retired as its counsel and returned to the private practice of law in New York City.

When the war started in Europe, Farben decided that it might be wise to do a little face lifting on its American offspring. So, on October 30, 1939, the directors of the American I.G. Chemical Corp. announced that there was no longer an American I.G. because one of its subsidiaries, General Aniline Works, had first absorbed it and then had changed its own name to General Aniline & Film Corporation. Just like that. How could it be related to German I.G. when the I.G. had vanished from its name. There would be no change, it was announced, in the management but the offices were to move from Fifth Ave. to Park Ave. Careful in small details, Farben was moving its renamed child from the too close environment of other Farben subsidiaries, which still occupied offices at the old Fifth Ave. address.

Despite the unhappy experiences of Mr. Teagle as an American

I.G. director, Standard continued its intimate relations with Farben and permitted its vice-president, E. M. Clark, to remain as a director of American I.G., or General Aniline & Film, until 1940. Standard also took part in several sizeable financial negotiations with Farben, one of which, in 1940, involved a Standard proposal that Farben exchange its interest in General Aniline & Film for Standard's oil-refining properties in Germany. In reply General Aniline's New York management solemnly informed Standard that Farben had no interest in it or in any other American properties; and then, by way of proof, arranged a conference in Switzerland at which representatives of the three companies met.

The real purpose of this conference came out when Farben and its American front both suggested that Standard purchase control of General Aniline & Film from its Swiss "owners." This would make everybody happy and prevent any possibility of General Aniline & Film getting into a jam with the United States Government. Standard, for some reason, did not bite on that one.

Some months later Mr. Hugh S. Williamson (prominent member of the New York law firm of Breed, Abbott and Morgan, also vice-president and treasurer of General Aniline & Film), was in Europe discussing matters with the home office. Possibly Mr. Williamson feared that the S.E.C. whitewash might not stand exposure to the stormy weather in prospect, and that the Farben name might show through on the General Aniline signboard. In any event, late in October, 1940, Mr. Williamson put in a New York call from Switzerland for his friend Mr. Orville Harden then vice-president of Standard and, as a representative of Farben, asked whether Standard would not like to sell Farben its very valuable Hungarian oil properties.

Standard by then was more than willing to get some of its assets out of Europe and suggested a price of $30,000,000 as about right. Farben declined with thanks and, after protracted negotiations, came back with a counter offer of $24,000,000, mostly in cash but including a note for $5,000,000, which was to be secured by collateral in the form of a lien on Farben's American properties (which it had just denied owning) and was to be payable "three months after the end of the war."

Standard's directors bit at this last offer; took it to Washington and secured the approval of the State Department (so they said) but the chief counsel for the Treasury, and Vice President Henry A. Wallace, as chairman of the Board of Economic Warfare, refused official permission. This was in August, 1941; by this time Farben's tie-ups with American war industries were beginning to receive some rather critical public attention, and the atmosphere in official circles was a bit thick when anything relating to Farben came up.

While the S.E.C. staff was still fabricating its conclusion that American I.G. was *nullius filius*, several other branches of the Government refused to accept the theory of illegitimate Swiss parentage, and concluded that American I.G. actually meant German I.G. Among those who discredited the woods-colt story were members of the Antitrust staff of Assistant Attorney General Thurman Arnold, who had uncovered evidence of the Farben pattern in investigations of some of its tie-ups in the synthetic nitrogen-ammonia field, and in the magnesium industry and had instituted actions accordingly.

And, on April 10, 1941, the Antitrust Division issued subpoenas calling for the complete records of General Aniline, Winthrop Chemical, and Sterling Products. Then began the sort of dragnet investigation into the ramifications of Farben's affiliates and personal agents in this country that I had first asked the Department of Justice to make thirteen years previously, in 1928.

There was consternation in the ranks of Farben's New York and Berlin offices when word of those subpoenas reached them. The management of General Aniline at first declined to comment publicly; later a press statement was issued which read:

> The officers of General Aniline & Film Corporation stated that the report it was among the companies whose books and records had been subpoenaed in connection with the Government's investigation of the drug and pharmaceutical trade was an error.

It was an error all right, a very bad error on the part of Dr. Schmitz who had assured Standard Oil's Frank Howard that there would be no recurrence at Washington of the past troubles of American I.G.

Three weeks later came another blow for Farben's "American" citizens. On May 1, 1941, the British Minister of Economic Warfare, Dr. Hugh Dalton, threw some very pointed comments about conditions in the Western hemisphere into an informal statement which he made to American correspondents in London. The gist of these remarks was cabled to the United States and received considerable publicity in the press. They reflected a very natural feeling of irritation in the British Cabinet at the fact that Farben's affiliates in the United States were helping effectively to nullify the British Navy's blockade of Germany's export trade by shipping American-made dyes, drugs, and chemicals to Farben's agents in Latin America, and thus helping Farben to hold its trade and to finance German propaganda and espionage in those countries.

Dr. Dalton suggested that the United States, for its own protection and security, might well follow Britain's example by freezing the assets of Axis countries and by blacklisting all concerns whose profits were being utilized to finance Nazi activities in the Western Hemisphere.

The Minister named some of the German-controlled companies in the United States that had been carefully organized before the war to supply the requirements of German agencies in South America—when Britain should shut off their supply of products from Germany.

Among the most important of these companies was General Aniline & Film, which was supplying Farben's Latin American agents with dyes, photographic materials and other products, shipping them through General Dyestuff or other companies acting for it. Sterling Products was also branded and Messrs. Weiss and McClintock were named in person by Mr. Dalton for similar offenses.

There were immediate repercussions of this blast at Farben's American front. The American patriots who sat in the New York office of General Aniline promptly issued another chapter of the bedtime story of their firm's parentage. They denied emphatically the allegation of the British Ministry that it was owned or controlled by I.G. Farben, which has "no interest, direct or indirect. in or control over the affairs of General Aniline & Film Corporation." "They were not acting for Farben or in its interest in exporting merchandise," etc., etc.

One of its officers was interviewed by *The New York Times* at his home in Englewood, N. J. This was Dr. Rudolph Hutz, General Aniline's vice-president who, in World War I, was an official of the Bayer Company and had been arrested and interned in 1918. When asked about this incident by the *Times* he treated it lightly and described the arrest as "a so-called Presidential warrant—a purely formal charge of the Alien Property Custodian."

Dr. Hutz also stated that he knew nothing about any relations between General Aniline and Farben. However, that gentleman's peculiar lack of knowledge about such things did not save him, seven months later, from being named as a co-conspirator in an indictment against General Aniline, Farben, and his earlier employer, Bayer.

The United States Government was prompt to take the hint from the British Minister's blunt remarks, and things started to happen. On May 9, 1941, Attorney General Robert H. Jackson attached about $250,000, which was on deposit in the account of I.G. Farben in the National City Bank of New York. An order was secured from Federal Judge John C. Knox directing the bank to hold all funds or credits owing to Farben pending disposition of antitrust suits in which Farben, as a defendant, had refused to put in an appearance.

Two weeks later the Justice Department tied up some additional funds which were about to be paid to Farben's account by General Dyestuff and, following the usual Farben procedure, were informed by that company's president, E. K. Halbach, that General Dyestuff was completely independent, as it was owned 100 percent by American citizens.

On June 14, another real blow was dealt Farben when President Roosevelt issued an order freezing all funds belonging to Axis nationals.

Mr. Henry Morgenthau, Jr., Secretary of the Treasury, to whom enforcement of the freezing was delegated, had long been urging that step but, according to press dispatches from Washington, had been blocked by the unwillingness of Secretary of State Cordell Hull to give the Axis a pretext for reprisals. Our distinguished

Secretary of State apparently did not appreciate the important part which Farben played in any decision as to reprisals.

Secretary Morgenthau, however, was better advised and had already expressed the opinion that the delayed freezing action would be a matter of locking the stable after the horse was gone; but the White House statement indicated that it was also intended to curb subversive activities in this country.

The Treasury regulations included one clause calculated to give Farben's American agents a headache; it read that on or before July 14 a report should be filed setting forth all information relative to property in the United States in which any foreign country or national had any interest, direct or indirect. This meant Farben patents as well as other Farben property. It also meant that it mattered not a bit whether I.G. Chemie was Farben owned or not; Switzerland was a foreign country and the General Aniline shares were, therefore, to be frozen by the Treasury. Mr. Dalton's brutal frankness had turned the tide. The foundations of Farben's framework in the United States were beginning to crumble.

On July 17, the President issued another proclamation that hit Farben in another highly vulnerable spot. This time the Secretary of State was instructed to publish a blacklist of companies in Latin America and elsewhere which were affiliated with Axis powers. This list included the names of every known agent, affiliate or branch house of I.G. Farben in all of the Latin American countries.

While these storm clouds were gathering about Farben's American fronts, there came to the rescue one Dr. Werner Karl Gabler, who had moved to Washington some years previously as an advocate of the social and economic policies of the New Deal. Dr. Gabler now appeared as an accredited representative of the Swiss I.G. Chemie, and approached various government officials with impressive looking documents to support his arguments that I.G. Chemie was a wholly independent Swiss company.

According to *Time*, Dr. Gabler had become well known in Washington as an "economist lobbyist" for the American Retail Federation and had also done work for the late Edward A. Filene, Boston capitalist and department store operator. Be that as it may, Dr. Gabler certainly blossomed out in his new role at Washington. He had secured his assignment through the Swiss Minister at Washington, the Hon. Charles Bruggmann. And the fact that the Swiss Minister's wife, the former Mary O. Wallace, was a sister of Henry A. Wallace, then Vice President, did not detract from the prestige and dignity with which Dr. Gabler conducted his efforts to checkmate those who were saying, "Why argue any more, seize General Aniline and get it over with." Needless to say neither the Vice President nor his sister was involved in aiding the Gabler efforts.

In its article about Dr. Gabler, *Time* included this comment:

> Some of Dr. Gabler's fellow New Dealers though no more anti-Nazi than he, believe he was hired because he had an "in" with the New Deal. If that was a Nazi plan, it could be an example of the super-ingenuity of Nazi infiltration tactics.

Economist-negotiator Gabler, to give him a more polite title than "lobbyist," went about his task with great circumspection, he always notified the authorities before he put in telephone calls for Switzerland (undoubtedly they were all listened in on anyhow) and a stage battle of noisy name calling went on between him and some of General Aniline's German-born directors.

Finally, after it appeared fruitless for even a Doctor Gabler to gabble any more about I.G. Chemie's being a safe and neutral guardian of the General Aniline shares, this New Deal economist proposed a new deal for General Aniline—an American voting trust was to be set up to control the I.G. Chemie shares on which a United States Government official and an I.G. Chemie nominee should have equal voice. This was rather far fetched as the Government already had frozen the stock and was about to take over the property.

About this time one Ernest W. Flender, German born shareholder in General Aniline, and a member of the private-banking house, C. B. Richard & Co., dealt himself into the situation by starting a mysterious equity suit in a Delaware Court to secure an order compelling a stockholder's meeting. However, the U. S. Treasury intervened and the suit was dismissed after Mrs. Dorothy Pickhardt Kahle, another stockholder, had been substituted for Mr. Flender as the complainant.

The General Aniline directors made many moves on the Washington chessboard to strengthen their position. One of these was to retain the services (at an annual retainer reported to be $100,000) of former Attorney General Homer S. Cummings, who had opened an office for the practice of law in the nation's capital a few months before the outbreak of the war. More will appear about this later.

As the date of the declaration of war between Germany and the United States drew near, the board of General Aniline was in a state of wild confusion. A number of the old German-born directors resigned and were replaced by several well known Americans who had no prior connection with the company. Finally, D. A. Schmitz was asked to resign as president and, when he refused, the board voted to remove him. For several weeks the company had no president. Then, on October 30, 1941, the directors elected as president former Judge John E. Mack, of Poughkeepsie. The name of Judge Mack, known to be an intimate friend and neighbor of President Roosevelt, was calculated to lend such an aura of American respectability to General Aniline that this, in itself, might prevent actual seizure of the company as enemy owned. Judge Mack had had no previous experience as head of an $86,000,000 corporation with 6,000 employees. Nevertheless, his salary was reported to be fixed at $90,000 a year. Not long afterward, on December 5, 1941, another, even bigger, name was added to the General Aniline board, through the election of William C. Bullitt. Mr. Bullitt, however, never actually served, as he left that same day for Africa and the Far East, on a personal mission for the President.

This frantic Americanization of Farben's offspring might at least have stalled off the seizure had not the Japanese time-table decreed otherwise. With the attack on Pearl Harbor the energetic and able Assistant Counsel of the Treasury Department, J. J. O'Connell, Jr., (later to become its chief counsel) moved in on General Aniline with a commando squad of seventeen supervisors and took over in earnest. Evidently he was not content with previous housecleaning which had consisted in taking a few offensive I.G. pictures off the wall and hiding some of the hired help in the cellar.

Within a week a New York Grand Jury had returned the three indictments already mentioned charging conspiracy by General Aniline, Farben, General Dyestuff and several of its officers and directors with numerous acts of conspiracy in restricting production of dyes, photographic materials and chemicals, along with other violations of the criminal statutes of the United States.

Two months passed during which Mr. O'Connell and his supervisors did some checking up, and then ousted five of the principal operating executives of General Aniline, all naturalized Americans who were accused of obvious Farben affiliations.

Meanwhile, Mr. Leo T. Crowley, head of the government-owned Federal Deposit Insurance Corporation, and also high-salaried president of a public utility company, was offered by the President the additional position of Alien Property Custodian. However, Mr. Crowley appeared none too anxious to accept this responsibility unless complete freedom of action was assured him. So Treasury, for a time, remained supreme in General Aniline affairs.

On February 16, 1942, Secretary Morgenthau addressed an official notice to General Aniline that he had vested in his own name, title to all of the shares of the company listed in the names of Geheimrat Professor Dr. Carl Bosch of Ludwigshafen, Geheimrat Dr. Hermann Schmitz of Berlin, and of the Swiss I.G. Chemie or its nominees in Switzerland and the Netherlands.

Prior to this final seizure of the controlling shares of General Aniline, that company, as one of Farben's American dummy fronts had controlled not only its own immense war material manufacturing plants, but had also owned huge blocks of stock worth some $11,500,000 in the following American Corporations: Standard Oil Co., of New Jersey; Standard Oil Co., of California; Standard Oil Co. of Indiana; E. I. duPont de Nemours & Co., Sterling Products, Inc., Plaskon Co., American Magnesium Corp., Alba Pharmaceutical Co., and Winthrop Chemical Co.

What came after February 16, will appear in a later chapter, but it was this date which marked the end of the long fabric of lies and subterfuge behind which Farben had almost succeeded in veiling its identity. Perhaps, more important, it exposed officially the use which these Teutonic builders of a secret world empire had made of some of our esteemed citizens and, to quote from a later U. S. Treasury Department report, how Farben had:

> . . . . . been plotting the downfall of the free peoples who gave them an opportunity to prosper and grow rich by honest trade . . . . . by control of corporations, by accumulating stocks of raw materials, by carefully directed but unlimited bribery, by the use of force and threats of force, and by any other methods which came to hand.

Which is a pretty good description of the Farben pattern.

CHAPTER VIII

Republicans — Open The Door

ON OCTOBER 20, 1942, *The New York Times* published a sensational story about a "sealed" gift to the Library of Congress of some nine thousand letters comprising the files of the late Edward T. Clark, private secretary to President Calvin Coolidge. The story attracted interest because it stated that these files had been advertised to be sold at public auction on Oct. 28 at the Parke-Bernet Galleries in New York City, but instead were suddenly withdrawn from sale and presented to the nation by one Charles Kohen, proprietor of the Hobby Shop of Washington, D. C., who had secured the files from Clark's widow.

The *Times* article stated that the correspondence covered ten years, from 1923 to 1933, which period included part of the time Clark spent with President Coolidge at the White House. It was also stated that the catalog listing of the letters classed some of them as sensational.

What the *Times* article did not reveal, however, was that Edward Terry Clark, or Ted Clark as he was known in Washington until his sudden death in 1935, was not only personal secretary to President Coolidge until March 4, 1929, but that immediately after that date he became Washington representative of Drug, Inc. Clark, with the title of vice-president, was in charge of "government relations" from then until 1933 when Drug, Inc. was unscrambled, and Sterling returned to its earlier status as the Farben partner in the patent medicine industry. Drug, Inc., it will be recalled, was the tie-up of Sterling and the Louis K. Liggett group in 1928 which later took in Bristol Myers, Vick, Life Savers and other large national advertisers.

Ted Clark was, in plain English, a Washington lobbyist, maintained at the national capital in the interest of Farben's original postwar tie-ups in the drug industry, which tie-ups ten years later were admitted by all concerned (except Farben) to have been illegal from the day on which they were first entered into. After Clark left the President of the United States his boss was William E. Weiss, senior vice-president and general manager of Drug, Inc., who, some twelve years later, was to be prosecuted and fined under a federal criminal statute, and forced out of Sterling because of what the United States Treasury termed his "undesirable" relations with I.G. Farben in the latter's "plotting of the downfall of the United States."

The *Times* story also neglected to mention that in August, 1932, when Herbert Hoover was running for reelection as President against Franklin D. Roosevelt, his White House secretary, the late Thomas G. Joslin, went off on a vacation and Mr. Hoover "borrowed" Ted Clark from Farben's Drug, Inc. Thus Mr. Clark became the official secretary to the President of the United States, while Drug, Inc., agent of Farben, continued to pay his salary as though no interruption had occurred in his services as its Washington representative. (And perhaps none had.)

At the time, this incident created something of a stir. It was too much for the New York *World-Telegram's* usually sweet-tempered Raymond Clapper, who described the temporary secretary to Mr. Hoover, as a "lobbyist whose salary was paid by Drug, Inc." Editorially the *World-Telegram* commented that, "the President must be very insensitive" . . . . . "Much more than the vagary of Hooverian taste is involved."

The day after the *Times* first published the story of the sudden decision to get these Clark files under lock and key, the New York

Herald Tribune still further whetted the curiosity of those who knew of Clark's activities by quoting Mr. Kohen as having said that the files included correspondence with Col. William J. Donovan, who was Assistant Attorney General during the Coolidge Administration; Charles D. Hilles, member and former chairman of the Republican National Committee; and others. Also that there were letters pertaining to South and Central American countries, and that it would be a terrible thing if German agents got hold of them.

The description of these files printed in the Parke-Bernet catalog is intriguing in its implications. Whoever wrote it would seem to have examined the files carefully and to have had a deft sense of the value of spicy historical documents:

> They provide an insight into the political workings of official Washington . . . . . and much important information of a private nature on various public and political matters . . . . . The correspondents are persons of note, including members of Congress, governors of states, government officials, business men, financiers, personal friends, politicians, and others in various walks of life. The letters pertain to matters of government, public works, political matters, etc. Some of the letters may be classed as sensational; they reveal the workings of a political machine. The writers seek legislation in favor of their business, seek appointments to positions for friends of the Republican party . . . . . Another folder contains correspondence between Mr. Clark and the holder of an important office during the Coolidge Administration, and who has been appointed by President Roosevelt to a high government office since the outbreak of the present war . . . . . on political and private matters.

With regard to those letters referred to in the catalog as having been written by seekers of official favors, it should be recalled here that in the case of such "favors" as may have related to the affairs of Sterling, Bayer, and Winthrop, these companies had clauses in their contracts which stipulated that Farben would share in their expenses. The possibility of Farben thus having been charged its proportionate share of Clark's salary while he was

"Acting Secretary" of the President of the United States, is not edifying.

However, to return to the story of the aborted auction of the files. Several months after they had gone to their Congressional guardians, I had the pleasure of meeting Mr. Kohen. His little Hobby Shop is just around the corner from the White House, on 17th St. near Pennsylvania Avenue; its windows and the counters and cases inside display autographed letters, historic documents, stamps, coins and medals. Its proprietor told me a dramatic story.

As soon as the story of the Clark files was published, fantastic things began to happen. In one instance an imposing-looking individual came into the shop, while two other men stationed themselves outside the door. His visitor, who gave no name, was brief and to the point. He merely announced that he had come to get the Clark files, and had brought with him $100,000 in cash as purchase money. When Mr. Kohen refused this bizarre sum, his mysterious customer denounced him as a fool, and departed with his little black bag.

Mr. Kohen had another visitor, this one a gorgeous young lady —"and I mean gorgeous," he assured me—who came into the shop and wanted to know whether a certain gentleman had written any of those letters to Mr. Clark. On being told that he had, the young lady informed Mr. Kohen that she would take those particular letters at his, Mr. Kohen's price. Again the offer was rejected.

The high point in Mr. Kohen's story was the reason he gave for donating the files to his country. "As a veteran of the last war," he said, "I feared that if I let the auction go through, a German agent might get the files, destroy those which were objectional to the Nazi cause, and make use of other letters to embarrass our present war effort."

After I first heard the story, but before I met Mr. Kohen, I suggested to government authorities that in view of my own knowledge of Clark's activities, an official examination should be made of this correspondence. So far as I can learn this was not done.

That suggestion was by no means my first effort to induce official Washington to look into the lobbying activities of Mr. Clark. In December, 1929, I had written to the late Thaddeus H. Caraway, asking that his lobby committee question Mr. Clark about the connection between Drug, Inc., and I.G. Farben. I also called the Senator's attention to the fact that a few years back, Secretary of Commerce Herbert Hoover had appointed what he called a Chemical Advisory Committee to help him decide what to do about the encroachments of I.G. Farben; and that some of the individuals who had been appointed to that committee were under the influence of that same German combine.

With that letter I enclosed a reprint of an editorial from the publication *Chemicals* of May 13, 1929, entitled "Does the American Chemical Industry Need Guts." Senator Caraway never acknowledged either the letter or the editorial. The editorial was written by my good friend Sidney W. Dean, Sr., one of the few writers in the chemical industry who did not hesitate to express publicly, what was said privately by substantially all of his less robust colleagues when the subject of Farben came up.

That reads in part as follows:

> Several weeks ago. through the financial pages of the metropolitan press, it was announced that a banking group, headed by the National City Bank of New York, was offering $30,000,000 in guaranteed $5\frac{1}{2}\%$ debentures of what—the American I.G. Chemical Corporation. This American (?) annex to the German dye and chemical cartel—the Interessen Gemeinschaft Farbenindustrie Aktiengesellschaft of Frankfort-on-the-Main in Germany—proposes to manufacture in America . . . . . such chemical and dye products as synthetic gasoline and motor fuels, products from the hydrogenation of coal, dyestuffs, synthetic fertilizers, artificial silks, and solvents and lacquers. While not so stated, this new colossus with a German accent will also manufacture and vend medicinals, pharmaceuticals, photographic chemicals, biological stains, etc. . . . . .
>
> It is an amazing program—yet the most amazing thing about it is the roster of American business men announced as affiliated with it as executives and as directors . . . . .
>
> Now, what is this $30,000,000 for? Simple enough when you stop to think it over—for the acquisition of stocks of certain prominent American chemical companies . . . . . already deeply

attached to the I.G. by agreement or friendship or relationship, or patent agreement, or what have you, by filaments so
fine as to be almost invisible to the general public and chemical buyer of this country, and yet as strong as steel . . . . .

Is there to be repetition of the cut-throat tactics existing
before the War in the battle for dye and chemical markets,
not only in the United States but in Central and South America? . . . . .

Are we to again see the source of our explosives (for every
dye laboratory is a potential arsenal) under the dexterous
thumb of gentlemen wearing honorary degrees from Cologne
or Heidelberg or Berlin?

Shall our recent discoveries in the realms of film and photographic chemistry; in serums and stains, in pharmaceuticals,
synthetics, lacquers and solvents, be gathered into a mighty
merger under the shadow of the world's most grasping and
most powerful cartel?

Dare we, realizing that mergers and trusts cannot be operated legally in this country with foreign control, insist that
the actual ownership and direction of such new mergers as
shall appear from now on in the field of chemistry and allied
industries be probed to the last proxy in the safe deposit
vaults of Wall Street or the depositaries of the I.G.?

Have the American chemists and chemical producers and
dye makers and distributors the guts, as we have so expressed
it, to fight this new battle to a finish so that we may know
now and in the future into just what pockets and just what
coalitions the products of American plants and laboratories
are descending?

Have the American chemists forgotten just how and where
many of the formulae were obtained for products which have
now entered world trade in competition with Germany? No?
Well, you may be assured that Germany has not.

Is it not the proper moment to erect a few tank-proof ob-
stacles in the way of such international merger-colossi instead
of greasing their path with tears of sorrow at our own help-
lessness, while decking the oncoming monopolies with the

coupons of bonds sold to American purchasers by American banking houses?

In God's name! Has the American chemical industry no guts?

Full credit for that editorial challenge to the power of Farben belongs to Sidney Dean, but I had some small part in its inspiration and I also secured a large number of reprints with which for some time afterward, I belabored official Washington in a vain attempt to arouse a realization of what Farben had already done, and proposed to do, to our national security.

As part of the story of this editorial it should be added that the publication *Chemicals* no longer exists. It met with the sad fate that so frequently has been visited upon those who rushed in, in print, where the Farben brand of angels fear to tread.

The story of Secretary of Commerce Herbert Hoover's Chemical Advisory Committee goes back to 1925, when Mr. Hoover announced that he had appointed a group of nine men, each prominent in some branch of the chemical industry, to act as a liaison body between the industry and the Department of Commerce.

One member of that original committee was Henry Howard, vice-president of the Grasselli Chemical Co. Later Mr. Howard's name on the committee was to assume a very definite significance.

In December, 1926, several hundred men more or less prominent in the chemical industry received invitations signed by Mr. Hoover which stated that he was calling a conference in Washington at the suggestion of the Chemical Advisory Committee in order to inform the Department as to the needs of the industry.

Being one of the elect I attended the conference and the banquet which followed. By that time I.G. Farben had been formed. Its gigantic proportions were realized and the character of its early tie-ups in the American drug and dye industries had become public. For this reason the main subject of private discussion on the floor of the conference was Farben. And the one great question in the minds of all present was where Mr. Hoover stood on the issue. The answer, as far as the conference was concerned, was zero.

Mr. Hoover spoke feelingly of the wonderful service to business the reorganized and enlarged Commerce Department was prepared to render, and of his own determination to assist the chemical industry. However, when some of the diners asked questions which approached the Farben issue, it was impossible to determine from the replies what, if anything, the Federal Government intended to do to put a stop to foreign encroachments upon the industry.

A year later it was announced that a second conference of executives of the chemical industry was to be called by Secretary Hoover, and this time the engraved invitation tacitly recognized the Farben issue by stating that its purpose was "to consider present world conditions as they affect the American chemical industry." Meanwhile, and as a preliminary to this second conference, it was announced that Secretary Hoover had decided to increase the membership of his Chemical Advisory Committee with eight additional executives, three of whom were Walter Teagle, president of Standard Oil of New Jersey, Lammot duPont of the duPont Company and Frank A. Blair, president of the Sterling subsidiary, Centaur Co. It had already been announced publicly that Standard, under Teagle's leadership, had entered into the first of its tie-ups with Farben. The duPont relationship was recognized. And Sterling was boasting openly of its newly gained power as Farben's American partner in the drug industry. Blair was recognized as the most active of the lobbyists who represented Sterling's interests at Washington, especially in legislative matters.

So, here were four men, Teagle, duPont, Blair and Howard, serving on the Secretary's Chemical Advisory Committee to tell him what the chemical industry wanted done about Farben. And the companies of all of them may appear to have been on the Farben side of the fence.

About this time, many articles were being published about the tremendous strides the Germans were making in their attempt to draw the chemical industries of the entire world into their sphere of influence. And not a few of the articles had to do with Farben's new ventures in the United States.

In the New York *Journal of Commerce* of January 12, 1928, Department of Commerce officials were quoted as having stated that they had no confirmation from their representatives abroad regarding the proposed entry of I.G. Farben into the American chemical industry, and refused to comment upon the report that Farben was seeking to purchase American companies. The correspondent of the *Journal* then went on to state that there was some agitation in Washington for legislation to combat the encroachments of the Germans, but that Secretary of Commerce Herbert Hoover had expressed the opinion that "lengthy study of the situation would be necessary before steps could be taken to amend the law, and that hasty action should not be countenanced."

As events were to prove, neither hasty action nor any other kind of action was taken, save to unlock all the legal doors and throw away the keys.

Many of us who made the trip to Washington for the second conference expected some enlightenment, and possible encouragement, on the Government's attitude towards Farben. We got the enlightenment—but not the encouragement.

Among the speakers announced were Colonel William J. Donovan, Acting Attorney General; William T. Daugherty, Trade Commissioner of the Commerce Department at Berlin; and Daniel J. Reagan, Commercial Attaché at Paris.

Some pointed questions had been prepared to be put to Colonel Donovan regarding enforcement of the antitrust laws. However, that was not to be. The open forum, which had been scheduled, was turned into a closed shop by the opening remarks of the chairman who announced that it had been decided to dispense with questions from the floor because they would not be as beneficial as questions that had been coordinated by the Advisory Committee.

Mr. Daugherty, the Secretary's ace investigator of the German cartel, made some interesting observations. "The cartel," said Mr. Daugherty, "when it combines producers of varying production costs, protects the weak against the strong" (a beautiful thought but hardly an accurate one). Mr. Daugherty went on to say:

> German dye trust officials have been considerably exercised of late by press reports that their chemical industry calculated to consolidate for the particular purpose of opposing the best interests of the American chemical industry. While

it is not the purpose of this discussion to reach any definite conclusion on this controversial issue . . . . . I can quote certain leading figures of the German dye trust who deny first that they are out to fight the American chemical industry, and secondly that the dye trust has bought heavily into shares of the American chemical industry.

They emphasize on the other hand that it is their wish to frame agreements with elements in the American chemical industry . . . . . and cite as proof of this at least three German-American agreements arrived at in the past year. They indicate also that further special agreements with American chemical and related companies are in sight . . . . .

Before leaving Berlin last month, I was told substantially the same thing by Dr. Bueb, the dye trust's leading figure in that city, that if accurate information were wanted concerning the dye trusts' plans in connection with international tie-ups, either he or Dr. Bosch would welcome questions from any reasonable American firm, association, or individual.

The dye trust's argument is of course that rationalization, begun after the inflation period in Germany, is now being sought internationally in the interest of lowering costs by combatting over-production, by allocating markets, and it follows that such arrangements involve price fixing. This effort is only in its beginning now and the future may bring forth many significant international associations.

When Mr. Daugherty finished his address I found myself standing at the elbow of Mr. H. Hill of Kuttroff, Pickhardt & Co. I asked him how he liked the speech. "Very good, splendid" replied that member of Farben's American front.

Mr. Reagan's speech, in light of later events, contained some food for thought. He quoted the head of the French dyestuff industry as saying that he considered it the policy of the French chemical industry to promote peace by effecting international ententes.

Colonel Donovan was the most important speaker at the conference, and his subject, as announced, "Foreign Cartels and American Industry" gave promise of a clear-cut statement of the attitude of the Justice Department towards I.G. Farben and the latter's American tie-ups. Stated the Colonel:

> It is the belief of the Department of Justice, that when a foreign monopoly, though legal in its place of origin, comes into this country, and, by collusion with our citizens enters into agreements here for the restraint of trade and the enhancement of prices, those agreements are just as illegal, and just as much subject to our laws, as they would be if the corporations and individuals involved were creatures of our government.

This part of the talk sounded as though the Colonel was clearing the decks for action. Thurman Arnold could not have put it stronger. A bit later, however, he said:

> So far as it presently appears, the so-called chemical entente and the Franco-German dyestuffs agreement appear to involve no attempt to exploit this market. In fact, we have authentic assurances that these arrangements are not directed against this market.

Two days before the conference those of us who had accepted the invitation received a wire stating that Mr. Hoover would be unable to attend. His apologies, read to the conference, expressed his regret at not being present, and complimented the industry for having solved some of its difficulties. "The Department of Commerce," said the absent Secretary, "is created for service . . . . . We can serve only by direction of the leaders of the industry. Therefore the industry is asked to express its needs to the Advisory Council."

It was a happy thought, we could write to Mr. Teagle or to Mr. Blair. In my own case all doubts were removed. I declared an all-out war.

Mr. Hoover became Secretary of Commerce in 1920, when the original postwar Republican Cabinet was installed by Warren G. Harding. His official activities in Europe during the war, and as an adviser at the Peace Conference, had given him much firsthand knowledge of the backstage connections of Kaiser Wilhelm's

war machine. As Secretary of Commerce for eight years, he was
to be supplied with much additional data which pictured the pattern of I. G. Farben in all of its many manifestations in other
countries and inside the United States.

In January, 1924, Dr. Julius Klein, Director of the Bureau of Foreign and Domestic Commerce, transmitted to Secretary Hoover
a report prepared by Thomas W. Dalahanty, of the Chemical
Division, which contained a very excellent historical sketch and
chart of the German dye companies. The report referred to the
part played by the German government in the success of the cartel; to the cartel's practice of taking out basic patents in all countries in order to stifle others in its field; and to the dishonest practices of dumping, bribery, deceptive labeling, and false propaganda; and the setting up of, or control of factories in this and
other countries in order to assist the mother industry.

No one reading that report could have any doubt as to precisely what the Germans proposed to do and would accomplish,
if permitted, in the establishment of new tie-ups, partnerships and
subsidiaries, inside the United States.

In 1927 Dr. Klein and Mr. A. Cressy Morrison, Union Carbide &
Chemical Corp., executive, and chairman of Hoover's Chemical
Advisory Committee, attended the Economic Conference of the
League of Nations as unofficial observers for the United States.
Mr. Morrison's widely published accounts of the conference discussed at some length the so-called "Rationalization of Industry"
by which I.G. Farben, as a cartel, was alleged to reduce costs
and therefore lower prices to the consumer. Mr. Morrison was
somewhat skeptical about the usefulness of the cartel theory, and
stated quite plainly that its strength lay in its centralized control
and ability to dump its products or utilize other competitive devices to strangle its competitors. He recited one illustration, discussed at Geneva, of the prewar activities of the German dye cartel
in a South American country, which made this vicious part of
the Farben pattern stand out in such high relief that it should
have been sufficient warning to all concerned that Farben was
again erecting an espionage machine. As Mr. Morrison described
it:

In Brazil, for illustration, representatives of the German Government were everywhere, in banks and other clerical positions, acquiring information regarding contracts and trade relations with other countries, so that the information might be transmitted to Germany and there acted upon by the cartel for the benefit of German commerce.

Then, in February 1928, at the time of the Chemical Executives' conference, the Commerce Department published a lengthy analysis of the progress of I.G. Farben, which referred to the 1927 tie-up with Standard Oil; to its ties on rayon with the English Courtaulds, owners of American Viscose; and with Metz, Grasselli, and Sterling-Bayer.

Thus the record of this entire period proves conclusively that during what Thurman Arnold later called "the era of non-enforcement of the antitrust laws," the Government of the United States knew in ample detail what Farben was doing in Europe and in precise detail how illegal its tie-ups were inside the United States.

Colonel Donovan made another noteworthy contribution to the picture on May 9, 1929, after Mr. Hoover had become President and Donovan had resigned from the Justice Department. Although then in private practice, his views were regarded as indicating what action might be expected from the Hoover administration with regard to the financing of Farben's American I. G. Chemical Corporation with thirty million good American dollars, which operation, successfully consummated within a few weeks of Mr. Hoover's inauguration as President, had incited the outspoken wrath of many men in the industry.

The Colonel's address to a large gathering of members of some fifteen technical associations at the annual chemical industries banquet said little about the Farben issue, but that little was to the point. He stated that if the United States could build plants in France and in Germany for the production of American automobiles and machinery, then the Germans had an equal right under the law to erect chemical plants in this country.

The loaning of American money to Farben to enable it to erect plants in the United States, and the illegal character of the tie-ups by which Farben was tightening its grip upon our munition industries, did not enter into the argument.

In March 1930, Representative Wright Patman of Texas made a bitter attack upon both the Justice Department and the Federal Trade Commission for not enforcing the antitrust laws, and gave special mention to the Standard Oil group, to which he accused the new Attorney General, William D. Mitchell, of turning over his office. "This" said Patman, "is because he is following directly in the footsteps of Harry Daugherty." Patman's reference to former Attorney General Daugherty takes us back to some of the notorious instances of criminal malfeasance and official degradation of the Harding Administration.

Among these shameful incidents were the indictment and trials of Daugherty and Thomas W. Miller, former Alien Property Custodian, for conspiracy in receiving bribes from German and Swiss interests in consideration for the return of some $7,000,000 of German property which had been seized by A. Mitchell Palmer and Francis Garvan. Others indicted were John T. King, former Republican National Committeeman from Connecticut; and Jesse W. Smith, this friend of Daugherty, who lived in the "little house with the green shutters" had an appointment to "talk" one morning but never kept it—he was found quite dead with a revolver in his hand and a hole in his head. King died before the first trial of Daugherty and Miller, at which a hung jury resulted. In the second trial Miller was convicted, but the jury failed by a single vote to convict the former Republican Attorney General.

Regardless of the extent to which I.G. Dyes was directly involved with the German and Swiss individuals named in these indictments, the purpose of those who supplied the $400,000 bribe was the development of the Farben pattern.

In 1929 Francis P. Garvan brilliantly summed up, on a court record, some of the official infamies which accompanied the beginnings of Farben's comeback in the United States. Garvan was the most conspicuous defendant in a case which was instituted during the Coolidge administration against A. Mitchell Palmer, Garvan, and a number of others in the federal court at Boston, Mass., for alleged improper handling of the sale of Bosch Magneto

Co., headed by Robert Bosch, brother and close associate of Carl Bosch head of I.G. Dyes and I.G. Farben.

The charges were made and publicized continuously from the time Palmer and Garvan first seized and then sold the Bosch property for over $4,000,000, under authority and instructions of President Woodrow Wilson. They constituted the high point in the propaganda to discredit the seizure of the properties and patents of the Germans, and to justify their return by the Republican postwar administrations.

Among those involved was Merton E. Lewis, a lawyer who was first retained by the Bosch interests in 1919 to attack Mr. Palmer before a Senate Committee. Later, Mr. Lewis was made an assistant to the Attorney General to prosecute Garvan and Palmer, and, fantastic as it may appear, his pay for this official service again came out of Bosch funds.

Among others named by Garvan in scathing language were John Crim, former counsel for the German Embassy who was appointed by the Justice Department to secure Garvan's indictment; along with former Attorney General Daugherty and his notorious pals, Jesse Smith, Gaston B. Means, Thomas B. Felder, John T. King, Thomas W. Miller and a long list of others identified by Garvan as German agents.

Republican Senator George H. Moses was pictured as instigating Gaston Means to "get" Garvan by fair means or foul, and as appointing Otto Kahn, partner of Paul M. Warburg, of American I.G., as treasurer of the Republican Committee to raise funds with which to elect Senators who would vote favorably to Farben's interests.

Mr. Garvan's testimony, with citations from official records, was couched in language without precedent in denouncing high government officials in a court proceeding. Garvan, waiting for years for the opportunity, forced into one concise record the assembly of facts which not only cleared him and the others of wrong doing, but proved the infamy which had indicted them. He let loose with both barrels and the result was devastating.

While Mr. Garvan was testifying relative to the Bosch Magneto case one of the government attorneys asked:

Has anything occurred since Jan. 1, 1919, which had been the occasion of your having a rather accurate memory with respect to the details of the Bosch transaction?

Garvan in reply let loose a barrage of fact which completely destroyed the case against him, and which pictured the pattern of Farben and its allies in all of its vicious ramifications. For stark indecency there is no page in the history of this republic which approaches the recital of shameless bribery, brazen corruption and foul pollution of official power which Garvan, on Dec. 11, 1929, hurled into the faces of his accusers, and burned into the records, of the case.

Incriminating his persecutors with one sordid fact after another Garvan traced each link in the chain of official degradation straight back to Robert and Carl Bosch, and to the latter's plan to destroy the military security of this nation.

It is imperative to quote Garvan's testimony at some length in order that the reader may perceive, in its full significance, how the sinister facts from the record fit together to form the pattern of what has already happened—and the prospect of what was yet to come. In part, Mr. Garvan's testimony was as follows:

In answer to your question as to the refreshing of my recollection . . . . . I think it is probably better to state it this way: that the overpowering fact that has illuminated my memory, has made me search every possible record and has made me ceaselessly work night and day to ascertain the truth of the facts in this case, was the charge in the complaint here, signed and sworn to by Merton E. Lewis, to the effect that when our country's darkest hour, in April 1918, was at hand, when, as President Wilson said, we were with our backs to the wall, that I betrayed my country and entered into a con spiracy . . . . . to turn over this company . . . . . for less than its value. That is a charge of treason and there has not been one word of testimony, and furthermore there never can be one word of testimony adduced as to the truth of that charge . . . . . and then I found . . . . . the following facts: that in our files (Alien Property Custodian) on the payroll of the Hamburg American line for three years before the war was a man by the name of John T. King, receiving a salary of $15,000 a year for mysterious services; that on that payroll was Gaston B. Means; that Means had been a German spy in this country for years and years . . . . . and then this man John T. King shows up in my office and says he is to be appointed Alien Property Custodian . . . . . John King told me his appointment had been obtained by himself from Senator Moses, and next we find . . . . . that he and Senator Moses had obtained the appointment of Thomas W. Miller of Wilmington, Delaware.

Then, the day after Miller is appointed . . . . . I find Senator Moses in Tom Miller's office . . . . . asking about the Bosch case . . . . . next, in May 1921, two months after I left the office, we find Gaston Means is put in on the investigation of the Bosch Magneto case. I refer now to Gaston Means' testimony in which he admits he had been a German spy for six years; that he got $1,000 a week from Boy-ed; that he had been tried for murder in Carolina . . . . . and he himself says that Senator Moses put him in charge of the Bosch case . . . . . then we find that they must have a lawyer to take charge of this case, and whom do they select but John Crim, spelled in English C-r-i-m but in German K-r-i-m . . . . . Who is John Crim? During the war he was counsel for Hays, Kaufman and Lindheim, the counsel for the German Embassy, two members of which firm I sent to State's Prison. He was counsel for Hans Tauscher, who tried to blow up the Welland Canal, and he was counsel for the German who tried to put bombs on ships in our harbor, and his entire war service was that of serving German malefactors . . . . . When the war is over he . . . . . is put down in Washington in charge of the prosecution of the officers of the United States Government who seized German property during the war. Thus it goes on; from that time on we find Means and Crim and Burns in charge of the proceedings; we find Means reporting to Jesse Smith of Attorney General Daugherty's staff; we find Bosch now hiring another man, Thomas Felder, who is Daugherty's ward man, who since was convicted and is dead; Means since convicted of defrauding the United States Government and

bribing its officers . . . . . Later we find Miller convicted and
sent to Atlanta Prison for being an employe of the Germans
in this country. Poor Tom Miller, a decent clean boy . . . . .
a beautiful clean record in the war, and then this bunch
picked him, because he was a weakling, and then corrupted
him with German funds—for what? For getting behind their
movement to recover not only the Bosch Magneto but to
recover the whole six hundred millions of German property.

Always remember that this case is only the bellwether
of German propaganda. This case was really over in 1928 . . . . .
when they had befogged the mind of Congress, and befogged
the issue as the bill was passed which returned every dollar
of German property that had been seized during the war . . . . .

Next they concocted the scheme of indicting me in the
Chemical Foundation case . . . . . I went down there and Mr.
Crim, this counsel for the German Embassy, counsel for Hans
Tauscher, counsel for explosive bombs, counsel for members
of the bar convicted for defrauding the Government during
the war, and German spies, opened the door of the United
States Grand Jury room and said, 'Please give me your books,'
and I said, 'No sir, I will walk in with them' and . . . . . when
I got in I offered to waive all immunity and I asked Mr. Crim
to turn right around and explain to the Grand Jury who he
was and what he was doing there and what his former record
was, and how this was not a case of the United States against
Garvan, but that it was a case of Germany against the
United States, and I asked the Grand Jury . . . . . to make Mr.
Crim tell them who he was and what he was doing there.
And that was the last of Crim in the Chemical Foundation
case or in the Bosch case . . . . .

Another thing that has made this thing burn into my
mind . . . . . is the fact that the man who sat in at the beginning of these charges in 1919 (M. E. Lewis) now is able to
make this charge in this complaint under a salary of $1,000
per month drawn from the German funds in direct violation of the Penal Law of the United States . . . . .

America is entitled to know that the propaganda for the

return of German property which seemed to necessitate be-
spattering public officials . . . . . was founded upon misstatement of facts and false charges, and I want to ask that at the
conclusion of this hearing Mr. Lewis stand on his feet and
say what he had in his heart and mind when he made those
charges, and to ask me any questions under the sun, because
now, at last I see him face to face . . . . .

I wanted to prove this whole historical picture. I wanted to
call Senator Moses before you and Merton E. Lewis and Otto
Heins and Robert Bosch . . . . . and I wanted to show you how
the two Bosch brothers in Germany, Robert, the head of this
concern, with his powers of attorney from twenty or fifty
other big concerns in Germany, and Carl . . . . . the head of
the chemical cartel of the world, joined forces . . . . . and
show you the whole historical picture which came to a close
with the successful return of German property . . . . .

I would like to insert in the record from Means' own testimony the fact that he admits that Senator Moses obtained
his appointment on the Bosch case; . . . . . they published
across the country that a conspiracy had been established
. . . . . and then came the tie-up with Hearst . . . . . and the
great publications in his office where you will find all the
private papers of the Attorney General's office and the Alien
Property Custodian's office . . . . .

The pressure of the government of Germany which had
bought Attorney General Daugherty and Tom Miller . . . . .
those are the things that burn this case into my mind . . . . .
they obtained the appointment of Mr. Lewis as Attorney
General . . . . . I particularly want to put into the record letters from Senator Moses, from his office rather, Mrs. Gold to
Mr. Bennett, showing his control of the Bosch Magneto case
and showing the linking of it together with the fight against
our building up the chemical industry . . . . .

All that time the Attorney General of the United States,
Daugherty, and the Alien Property Custodian, Thomas Miller,
were in the employ and pay of German people and had $50,000
worth of U. S. Government bonds handed them and put in

their pockets by whom—Go back, go back, go back—by John T. King, the $15,000 representative who died three days before he could be tried . . . . .

Some of you saw the other day that Senator Moses had appointed Otto Kahn as treasurer for the election of new Senators. You did not associate the fact that his friend and partner, Warburg, is the head and front of the American interest in the American Interessen Gemeinschaft, in its attempt to destroy our chemical industry, and that there is a tariff pending in the U. S. Senate, and that the same question is left open, and that the same Pickrell and the same agents that worked in this case, are working around the corridors of the Senate today. The endeavor was that Kahn would furnish the money for the election of the Senators who would vote upon the question of American valuation or foreign valuation. German propaganda again eating into the vital problem of the life or death of the second greatest industry of the country today, the chemical industry. It is never a dead issue. Peace? There is no Peace. Always the fight goes on for the supremacy in the chemical industry because it is the keystone to the safety of the United States or of any country in the world today. Your rules, your statutes, your Bosch case are only appendages, they are only part of a great, great, struggle of Germany to recover the position of throttling chemical development and of domniating over the entire world the development of the chemical industry, which is the secret of industrial prosperity and the secret of military prosperity, and the secret of the peace and happiness and health of the nation, that is why I put into this record a bit of the historical picture because you will find the same bunch down in Washington, you will find Bennett in Washington, you will find Herman Metz, you will find Pickrell, you will find the same bunch working from the same offices, with the same sources of money, using every contention possible to befog the minds of Congress, which is charged with the protection of this country in its industries and in its military equipment. That is about all I think of.

Merton E. Lewis, after an unsuccessful effort to have Garvan's entire statement stricken from the record, began a rambling discourse on the circumstances which he said led to his original association with the Bosch interest, and to his later appointment as a special assistant at $10,000, a year to prosecute the case against Garvan and Palmer. Garvan continued to torment Lewis during the latter's attempt to explain away the charges; at one point Garvan demanded that Lewis cross-examine him on the alleged conspiracy:

> Now is the opportunity, if there is any question lurking in any man's mind, why for God's sake, let him speak up and ask me questions . . . . . I don't care how far astray or how personal or how anything else the questions are, but ask them of me now.

Mr. Lewis apparently did not choose to ask Garvan a single question. He did not care for the way Garvan answered questions. So Mr. Garvan, the defendant, finally asked Mr. Lewis the prosecutor:

> I understand you said that neither Attorney General Sargent, nor his assistant. Mr. Letts, ever told you you were being paid by the Germans?
>
> Mr. Lewis: I don't think they did at that time. I learned of it of course, when a check came to me . . . . .

Mr. Garvan later put into the record a letter describing how the plans for recovering German properties were progressing. This was written by Harvey T. Andrews, agent of the Bosch interests, in July 1922 to one of his employers in Germany. It stated, in part:

> The work entailed on my office in the disentangling of the German property proposition has entailed profound and constant attention. Sundays, nights, holidays and every day have been all alike since you left . . . . .
>
> It appears at the present time as if I was among the few who really had the right angle on this matter . . . . . The recognition on the part of the Administration of the fundamental principles is due largely to my efforts as well as to my con-

nections, and it would be futile for me to attempt to explain how, where and through what agencies I succeeded in getting it done . . . . . I have done all that my thirty-five years of practical knowledge of political affairs in this country induced me to do in order to win . . . . . Have a little patience and everything will be much better than you anticipated.

This astounding document was sworn to by Mr. Garvan on Jan. 22, 1930, and was then made a part of the record of the federal court at Boston, whereupon Attorney General Mitchell promptly announced that the suit was dismissed because no wrongdoing had been shown on the part of Mr. Palmer or Mr. Garvan or any of the other officials accused in the complaint of conspiracy in the seizure and sale of the Bosch property. If the government had won this suit the chief beneficiaries would have been Robert Bosch and his associates. Yet to this day, mud continues to be thrown at the memory of Francis P. Garvan on the basis of those fake charges first made and broadcast by some of Harding's gang.

Inevitably as the pattern is unfolded the story now goes back still further—it goes back to the letter written in 1916 by the Bayer Company's Dr. Hugo Schweitzer to Ambassador von Bernstorff, in which that celebrated head of German espionage spoke of electing a President of the United States whose party politics were more in harmony with the cause of the German dye trust. The story goes back also to Herman A. Metz, the dyed-in-the-wool Tammany leader and life-long Democrat who suddenly switched his allegiance to the Republican Party.

In 1930, while Metz was explaining to the Senate Lobby his campaign contributions to Senator King, he also gave his reasons for having deserted the Democrats in 1919. Senator Caraway developed this in the following testimony:

SENATOR CARAWAY: You came to Congress as a Democrat?
MR. METZ: Yes Sir.
SENATOR CARAWAY: I believe you were one of the Harding Democrats? A Democrat that supported Mr. Harding?
MR. METZ: Well, I contributed to the Harding campaign fund afterward; yes, sir. I did not like the treatment some of the Democrats gave me.

(Metz' dislike for the treatment that some of the Democrats gave him and his I.G. friends is understandable. So it is permissible to conclude that he bolted the Democrats for a more sympathetic party.)

However, according to Metz his "people abroad" did not altogether approve of his holding public office because they thought that it interfered with his business activities; or at least so he once informed a Senate Committee. Possibly the I.G. considered Metz more useful from the less conspicuous vantage point as a business man and philanthropist who would be free to contribute campaign gifts where they would do the most good.

Toward the close of the postwar decade President Herbert Hoover wrote to his good friend, Dr. William O. Thompson, president emeritus of Ohio State University, a plaintive discourse upon the problems confronting a chief executive of the nation. In that letter, dated Jan. 10, 1930, President Hoover said in part:

> We can and must, however, greatly increase the production of truth, and we must know the truth, before the grave interest of 120,000,000 people is involved in government policies.

The author has had Mr. Hoover's quaintly expressed goal constantly in mind for many years; he believes it to be particularly applicable to this chapter.

CHAPTER IX

Democrats—Facing Both Ways

EARLY IN MARCH 1942 six distinguished-looking gentlemen were seated around a conference table in one of the high-ceilinged rooms of that architectural monstrosity, the Treasury Building. One of those present was contending earnestly that the Americanization of General Aniline & Film Corp. had been assured, first, by the election of Judge Mack as president, and later by the appointment of other well-known Americans as directors. The speaker droned on and on. Finally, he was interrupted by Leo T. Crowley, long time head of the Federal Deposit Insurance Corporation, who said, "See here, Homer, we're all grown up—you know, and everyone else knows that John Mack, splendid citizen that he is, is not the man to head General Aniline."

Thus rebuffed, Homer S. Cummings, counsel for General Aniline, cut short his argument for inaction, and the meeting proceeded with its business of approving the new four-man board of directors for General Aniline which the Treasury had agreed upon.

Mr. Cummings had good reason to plead for a *status quo*. The new Treasury-appointed board could not be expected to continue his retainer as Washington attorney (rumored to be $100,000 a year) which had been arranged by the old Farben board.

In this connection, and as another example of how precisely the Farben pattern repeats, it is interesting to look back to the time when the I. G. Dyes crowd hired John King, former national committeeman from Connecticut to help Attorney General Harry Daugherty give back the German properties that had been seized during World War I. Then, some two decades later, when it again became advisable to take on some additional help in Washington—this time to prevent another seizure of similar properties—Farben's General Aniline hired Homer S. Cummings, who was not only a former national committeeman from Connecticut, but a former chairman of the Democratic National Committee itself, and who had just completed a six-year term as Attorney General of the United States.

While Farben always plays both ends against the middle, politically it strings along with the party in power and so, with the passing of the old "Ohio gang," Farben's American fronts suddenly became Democratic strongholds, at least as far as the nation's capital was concerned.

In 1932, James A. Farley, chairman of the Democratic National Committee, had solicited my support for his candidate, and asked me to discuss with Mr. Charles Michelson, publicity director of the Committee, such issues as I thought should be brought into the campaign. The result was what is known as the brush-off. To keep the record straight, I confirmed the meeting in a letter to Mr. Michelson, in which a high point of our disagreement was recorded as follows:

> When you assert that Eddie Clark, Louis K. Liggett's lobbyist is a 'nice chap,' and that you don't blame Mr. Hoover for securing the support of Drug, Inc., who pay for Clark's lobbying, you are really admitting the very point I allege, i.e., that Hoover's connection with this outfit of patent-medicine fakirs is so clearly defined that Governor Roosevelt could find no more powerful illustration of the hypocrisy of the present occupant of the White House.

On the same day I wrote to Mr. Farley, enclosed a copy of my letter to Michelson, and restated the Clark-Drug, Inc. issue:

Mr. Hoover's recent performance in taking into the White House as his secretary, Mr. Liggett's lobbyist, is in itself, without trimmings, a major issue.

Diplomatically, I had referred to Clark as Liggett's lobbyist rather than Farben's. Mr. Farley acknowledged this letter with assurances of appreciation for my suggestions, and with a nice word of thanks for my cooperation. However, he did not bring the Clark-Drug, Inc. issue into the campaign.

After the election of Mr. Roosevelt, the announcement that Senator Thomas Walsh, of Montana, was to be the new Attorney General gave a tremendous boost to the hopes of those of us who had been working for some such strong arm and keen mind to direct the affairs of the Justice Department—for someone who would start delving into the whys and wherefores of the inaction against the flagrant violations of our antitrust laws, and other federal statutes, that had stigmatized the three preceding administrations.

These hopes expired, however, when Tom Walsh died suddenly in a Pullman sleeper not long before he was scheduled to take over the direction of the Department from W. D. Mitchell. Who can say how or why the hand of Fate which led Tom Walsh to his untimely end, at a moment of triumph, should also have induced the selection of Homer S. Cummings to occupy the high office thus left open to some deserving Democrat.

The official pronouncements during Mr. Cummings' régime as Attorney General are of interest in their relation to the phrase, "the era of non-enforcement of the antitrust laws" coined by Mr. Thurman Arnold. One was a broadcast by the new Attorney General on June 10, 1933, in which he referred feelingly to the Vicar of Wakefield's complaint that "the laws govern the poor and the rich governs the law," and then announced that a vigorous campaign against racketeers was to be started. It was a beautiful address. Everybody is against racketeers.

The other announcement came from Mr. John Dickinson when

that gentleman was appointed by Mr. Cummings to take charge of antitrust law enforcement. Mr. Dickinson stated that those laws would be enforced to the hilt only when someone was getting hurt, and explained that the Antitrust Division was not a "detective agency." So far as Farben was concerned, no detective agency was needed to reveal the illegality of their contracts; but this was in 1935, no one was being hurt—then.

Later, millions were to die.

My own relations with Mr. Cummings began at arms length in 1933, when he became Attorney General, and later developed to sword's point. Finally, in a letter not intended for my eyes, the Attorney General warned a member of the Senate that it was considered "dangerous to correspond with Ambruster." Indicating an official state of mind which perhaps Mr. Cummings may share with other figures in the story of I. G. Farben.

The real gem of Homer Cummings' official writings, was the naïve allegation which appeared in his 1937 Annual Report to Congress, of his administration as Attorney General, that:

"The antitrust laws . . . . . have saved us from any cartel system."

Perhaps, though, we are going too fast with the Democratic part of the story. Away back in September 1918, when Francis Garvan house-cleaned the American Bayer Company, he installed a new set of officers to take the places of those he had jailed or put in internment camps. Unquestionably Mr. Garvan's intentions were just what he stated them to be—to create an all-American concern by putting native-born Americans in charge of the company; Americans, who so far as was known, had no connections with the former German owners.

As stated in Chapter III, among these new Bayer executives, was a young Democratic attorney named Earl I. McClintock. He had been just added to the staff of the Alien Property Custodian to become secretary of the seized Bayer Company, and retained that position all through the sale of the company and the transfer of its title to Sterling Products, Inc. When the latter took title, McClintock went along with the plant and goodwill of the business. He tossed aside his salary of $3,000 a year and opportunities for advancement in Government service for $13,000 a year as an executive for the new owners. This modest sum was, of course, to increase as McClintock rose to become the right-hand man of Doctor William E. Weiss in those deals which were to return the "Americanized" Bayer to the not too remote control of its former German owners.

As an executive of Sterling, Mr. McClintock climbed steadily while the Republicans held sway at Washington. Politically, however, he remained in a state of suspended animation until after that fateful period when the sun of Herbert Hoover slid over the horizon, leaving neither chickens nor pots; only a sheriff's notice on the empty garage.

When the Democrats got back in the saddle, however, Mr. McClintock began to go to town, and it was not long before he was reputed to have become a figure of importance among the group that had put the New Deal into power.

One of the claims to fame, boasted of by Mr. McClintock's friends, was his membership in, and some said his chairmanship of, the Finance Committee of the Democratic National Committee. Later, in 1941, after various official investigations had started some of the Government's keen young bloodhounds on the trail of the illegal Sterling-Farben tie-up, I heard more about Mr. McClintock's association with the Democratic National Committee. Usually the comment was highly critical, as the relationship was regarded as a definite obstacle to further investigation. So, on November 22, 1941, I wrote to Senator Guy M. Gillette, Chairman of the Senate Committee to Investigate Campaign expenditures, asking for:

> A searching investigation to determine the size and number of contributions which have been made, directly and indirectly, to the Republican and Democratic National Committees, and to the campaign funds of individual candidates for the Senate and House of Representatives, during the last ten years, by the German I.G. Farben and its American corporate allies; especially those included in the Sterling Products, Inc., group of patent-medicine manufacturers . . . . .

Senator Gillette's reply was not encouraging. I was a bit too late; the committee had been appointed for the 1940 campaign only, and had been dissolved, "So it has no authority or existence at the present time."

It appeared that there is an open and a closed season for investigating campaign funds. So, I put that correspondence in my "await events" file. Then, nearly a year later, on September 12, 1942, I tried again. This time I wrote to the Hon. Ernest W. McFarland, the new chairman of the Senate Campaign Contributions Committee, suggesting

> The urgent necessity for an inquiry into past and current contributions by allies, affiliates, and agents of the German I.G. Farben.
>
> Such contributions coming directly or indirectly from ..... this vicious German cartel played a tragic part in the past in influencing, or controlling, legislative and administrative acts in these United States. There is an abundance of evidence available to prove this.
>
> Largely, as a result of not stopping this kind of thing heretofore, we found ourselves in the relatively unarmed condition when the combat war which these people planned for so long finally began. It is unthinkable that repetition should be permitted, or that we should ignore it now that we are paying the price, in blood, for our neglect.
>
> If we are to win the war, if our democracy is to survive it has got to be stopped. And the only way to stop it is by a drastic investigation of all who have been, and all who still are, involved in any phase of it .....
>
> Should you request further details, names, dates, amounts, etc., I shall consider it my duty as a citizen to supply them to you.

Receiving no reply I called upon the Senator on Oct. 9, 1942, and was received by the energetic young counsel for the committee, James A. Walsh, who appeared to be intrigued by my visit, and undertook to find out the date when Mr. McClintock had retired as chairman, or as a member of the finance committee of the Democratic party. Some time later Mr. Walsh wrote me the result of his inquiry:

Following your call at the office, I contacted the Democratic National Committee and was advised that Mr. McClintock is not presently a member of the Finance Committee of that organization.

That information not being as complete as it might be, I wrote Mr. Walsh again on Dec. 24, 1942:

Many thanks for your letter of the 14th. Can you advise me of the date when Mr. McClintock was first appointed to the Finance Committee of the Democratic National Committee by the Hon. Jas. A. Farley. Also, whether he was asked to resign, or did so without being so requested after his Farben affiliations became more or less public property.

I am assuming, of course, that by use of the word "presently" your informant on the National Committee meant to imply that McClintock was just getting out or had just announced his intention so to do. I think that you would be performing a very useful public service if you would check and record . . . . . all contributions which McClintock secured from I.G. Farben and its American affiliates; also his relations with the Hague machine in New Jersey. Such facts are all matters of record, though more or less concealed and disguised, and should be brought out into the sun-light. . . .

You will understand, I hope, that I do not imply for a moment that Farben money went only to the Democrats, or to those who call themselves Democrats. Far from that! I happen to know that the record of those labeled Republicans is every bit as bad, especially when they were in power.

One thing I am very sure of; these matters must not be kept under cover now. If the Senate continues to ignore them while lives are being lost, then there is something very rotten indeed.

I am sure that you feel the same way about it. Otherwise I would not write you with such brutal frankness.

In his response, Mr. Walsh indicated that I was again trying to shoot at campaign contributors out of season, which was

positively not permitted by the Senate. As Mr. Walsh put it in a
letter dated Jan. 14, 1943:

> . . . . . with reference to possible campaign contributions
> by I.G. Farben and its American affiliates:
> I should perhaps explain that the information I obtained
> concerning Mr. McClintock did not indicate the recency of
> his separation from the Finance Committee, but was limited
> to the statement that he is not a member of the Committee.
> While an inquiry into this phase of campaign contributions
> in years past might be very revealing and informative, you
> will remember that the present Campaign Investigation Com-
> mittee is limited, by the terms of the resolution creating it,
> to matters occurring in the 1942 campaigns.

The season must have been closed early that year, for no further
word came from the Senate Campaign Expenditures Committee
or its counsel. However, I determined to continue my official inquiries into the mystery of when Mr. McClintock started and
stopped being a member of the Democratic Finance Committee.
So, I applied to the Democratic National Committee itself, and,
diplomatically, merely asked to be advised the names of the
members of its finance committee for the years 1936 and 1940.
In order to maintain my amateur, or nonpartisan status, I also
made the same request to the Republican National Committee.
The responses disclosed a deplorable lapse of memory on the
part of many well-known personages.

Under date of Feb. 13, 1943 I received the following reply
from the Democratic National Committee, signed by its distinguished Chairman:

> Dear Mr. Ambruster:
> I sincerely regret that we are unable to comply with your
> request for a list of the Finance Committee of the Democratic
> National Committee for the years 1936 and 1940. Our Audi-
> tor, who has made a search informs me that no such lists
> are available. We have recently consolidated our quarters
> and in making the change the campaign lists of former years
> were disposed of. You will, probably, find these lists pub-

lished in the metropolitan press of the years during the campaigns to which you refer.

Sincerely yours,

Frank C. Walker

Not being able to find the information in the metropolitan press, I called at the committee headquarters in the Mayflower Hotel in Washington, and explained to a most gracious young lady that if they could not recall the names of all the members of the finance committee they might at least be able to tell me when Mr. McClintock started and stopped being a member. She assured me that she would ask someone who would know, and that I would then be advised. Apparently no one knew, as no further word was received.

I also called at the Republican National Committee headquarters and was told by Mr. Spangler himself that they had their records for at least ten years back, and that he would send me the lists very shortly. Apparently, however, they got lost, too.

Meanwhile, not being too easily discouraged, I had written to Mr. James A. Farley at his New York address to see what he might remember. Mr. Farley's reply, dated March 3, 1943, was very discouraging except that it did not deny that Mr. McClintock had been a member of the committee.

Dear Mr. Ambruster:

I have your letter of March 1st, and am very sorry that I cannot give you the information you desire concerning Earl I. McClintock.

For your information, a finance committee is appointed for the duration of a campaign. They exist until the campaign is over and then pass out of existence. We have no records here of the campaign committees for the years 1932 and 1936. I resigned as National Chairman the last of July and Ed. Flynn was not appointed until August 17th of 1940, and, as you know, I had nothing to do with appointing committees for that campaign. The list serves no purpose after election and there is no reason for keeping any records. It would appear that you are out of luck unless you can run across one of the old letterheads showing the names of the committee.

Very frankly, I did not know that Mr. McClintock ever served as chairman of the finance committee. I regret my inability to give you the information you desire, but know you will understand that it just isn't possible.

Sincerely yours,
J. A. Farley

I next decided to try the New York Public Library document room but the only thing which bore on the subject was a copy of that celebrated 1936 Democratic Convention Souvenir book from which the party treasury received several hundred thousand dollars for advertising placed by numerous large corporations. Incidentally, most of the advertisers described or pictured their products. One full-page ad, however, was what is known in the program agency business as a complimentary card, and just said, "Sterling Products, Inc." The editors of the book, or Sterling, either did not want the readers to know what Sterling Products was, or else they thought that everybody already knew, and that it was unnecessary to go into details.

In this splendidly bound memorial volume of the convention at Philadelphia, there was a handsome photograph of James Aloysius Farley, chairman of the Democratic Party. Under and around the picture was a sketch written by the late J. Fred Essary.

In view of my correspondence with Mr. Farley I was intrigued to read Mr. Essary's eulogistic description of him as the man who, "carried in his prodigious memory the names and identity of thousands of the faithful." This description recalled other things I had heard about Big Jim's card-index memory, so I wrote him again on March 11, 1943, saying:

> I guess I must have been misled by the many statements which I have heard and seen about the wonderful system of names and deeds kept by Big Jim, and the infallible memory, which gives up instantly . . . . . every name . . . . . which has contributed to the Party since he quit boxfights for the big show.

TREASON'S PEACE 165

As you say, I am just out of luck—unless I can dig up an old letterhead or something.

By a quite natural error my secretary addressed this letter to Washington instead of New York. And again a deplorable lapse of memory was recorded—this time by the post office—for some one had stamped the envelope, in big red letters, right over the name of James A. Farley, "No Such. Return to Sender." So, I forwarded the letter to Mr. Farley's correct address in New York with the notation, "What awful memories everybody is getting." Mr. Farley apparently did not see the joke; his reply indicated that he had nothing further to say about Mr. McClintock. (A few months later Mr. Farley was saying plenty about the war, "which," he was quoted as declaring "wasn't our war.")

I also tried another prominent Democrat who had been Chairman of the Party's Finance Committee in 1936, Mr. James W. Gerard. No luck there either, save another suggestion to seek the information from the Democratic National Committee.

During the period which Mr. Farley now forgets, Mr. McClintock's achievements as a Sterling executive included engaging the services of Mr. David Corcoran as an officer of the Sidney Ross Co., a Sterling subsidiary that distributes patent medicines in Latin America. Mr. David Corcoran was an automobile salesman. He switched to patent medicines in the period when his brother, Mr. Thomas G. Corcoran, as a lawyer on the staff of the Reconstruction Finance Corp., was reputed to telephone Senators and bureau chiefs with, "This is White House, Corcoran speaking."

Disregarding for the moment the extent to which Mr. Corcoran, or Tommy the Cork, was ever authorized to speak for the White House, his welcome there was well known. Under the circumstances, the addition of brother David to the payroll of Sterling was recognized as a master stroke on the part of Earl McClintock.

As the decade preceding the fateful year 1939 progressed, Mr. McClintock spent more and more time in Washington. His status grew with his recognition as a factor in Democratic Party finances, and gained additional lustre from the new ties formed through brother David with that spoiled darling of the New Deal, Tommy the Cork. Many of McClintock's activities appear in other chapters. He intrudes here merely as a political angel—the Democratic angel whom Farley can't remember.

Thomas G. Corcoran originally was employed by the New York law firm of the late Joseph P. Cotton, President Hoover's Under Secretary of State who approved the huge loan made to Germany when the Nazis' rise to power began. He became counsel on the staff of the Reconstruction Finance Corporation in 1932 during the sad, dark days of the close of the Hoover administration. Corcoran held onto the job when the Democrats came into power and became an important figure among the inside New Dealers.

His fame rested upon a versatility which, as the legends grew, was said to include playing a piano with one hand, while writing New Deal legislation with the other.

With due allowance for exaggeration the fact remains that Mr. Corcoran was a much more influential figure in Washington than his official responsibilities in the R.F.C. could have caused. He was too light in weight, and too young, to play on the varsity, but he was a big shot on the Washington campus. That he was a young man of great personal charm and nimbleness of mind was conceded by all who came in contact with him.

Many of Corcoran's activities had no apparent relation to the R. F. C. This was especially true with regard to lobbying activities for legislation favored by the Administration. In 1935, in one such legislative battle, Corcoran was accused by Representative (now Senator) Ralph Brewster of Maine with having used improper influence and threats to induce Brewster to change his vote. Mr. Corcoran denied this charge and a Congressional Committee that investigated the row spanked both Corcoran and the Congressman by expressing its disapproval of their actions, then absolved each from any suspicion of improper motives.

Mr. Corcoran resigned his government job on Sept. 22, 1940 to direct what was called the Independent Voters Committee for Roosevelt and Wallace. His subsequent occupation in Washington raised a storm of criticism when reports began to circulate that Tommy the Cork was getting sizeable fees for using his New Deal influence to get war defense contracts and other official favors for his clients.

Among the official favors was one that bore directly upon national defense. This was the arrangement whereby the investigation of Sterling's tie-ups with I.G. Farben were concluded with the filing of "informations" and "consent decrees"—instead of Grand Jury indictments which were contemplated by those members of the Justice Department who had started the dragnet investigation of Sterling in April, 1941. In the Sterling case rumor had it that the Corcoran fee reached huge proportions.

This scandal finally reached such proportions that in Dec., 1941, the Senate Committee to Investigate the National Defense Program (Truman Committee) began an inquiry and public hearings on lobbying. Corcoran appeared as a witness before this Committee on Dec. 16, 1941. "There are five stories," he testified, "which have been whispered about me as a symbol in connection with defense industries." In each of the stories thus defined by Mr. Corcoran, he testified that his services were strictly those of an attorney: in one instance he received no fee; in the others, a total of $100,000. (Which did not by any means represent his total business for the year.) They concerned a shipyard (organized by a gentleman with a past), an engine contract, a magnesium plant, an oil well in Alaska (that was never drilled) and Lend Lease supplies for China. Mr. Corcoran was emphatic in asserting that in none of these cases had he acted as a broker. He added to his denial, "And I don't know what a broker is, either."

Senator Brewster, of Maine, then put the following statement, quoted from the public papers of Franklin D. Roosevelt, into the record:

> I have felt all along that it is not quite in accord with the spirit of the administration that any individual who holds a high party position should earn a livelihood by practicing law, because, in a sense, he holds himself out as having access to the backdoor of the administration. It just "is not done."

Finally, Senator Joseph H. Ball of Minnesota, another member of the committee, attempted to question Mr. Corcoran about his relations with Sterling Products and the consent decrees. Mr. Corcoran objected to discussing Sterling.

Senator, that isn't a defense matter. I have certain confidential relations with my clients. Very frankly, if this isn't a matter of the kind that the committee generally is looking into, I would prefer not to go into that matter. I have always made it very clear that I was willing to talk about this with the Judiciary Committee or anyone else, but my own relationships with my clients are such that I would rather not discuss them in connection with Empire Ordnance, Savannah Shipyards, and a lot of other things, because the public might get the impression that there was defense brokerage in Sterling Products.

Unconvinced that the relations between Sterling and Farben did not relate to the national defense program, Senator Ball said:

It seems to me that it ties in with this all-out war we are in, and also it certainly ties in with this question we have been discussing quite a bit here, of practicing before Government departments. If we are to believe the newspaper stories, you had quite a bit to do with the appointment of Mr. Biddle (the Attorney General) originally, and then had quite a bit to do with him in developing this consent decree.

Far from denying this last statement Mr. Corcoran indulged in a little modest self-praise regarding his part in arranging the Sterling consent decrees:

I am being perfectly frank with you, Senator. I have always been perfectly willing to discuss the Sterling case, because, if you don't mind my saying so, I think it was a very farsighted job. And as I told you before, when I last talked to the chairman of the Committee, I had just come back from the completion of the Sterling reorganization, which I think is one of the most brilliant things—not from my point, but from the point of view of the action of the board of directors themselves—that has been done in the defense effort . . . . . The only objection I am making is I don't want the Sterling business bracketed with an inquiry about defense brokerage . . . . . I am concerned that the name of Sterling shall not be bracketed in press reports and the rest of it with Charles West and Empire Ordnance and the rest of it . . . . .

The reader should keep in mind Mr. Corcoran's use of the phrase, "far-sighted job," in describing the Sterling Consent Decrees. The chairman of the Committee then ruled that:

> The committee will proceed with the program as outlined, and when that is finished, we will ask you to come back and discuss this under another heading.

There followed some further discussion of Mr. Corcoran's keen desire to not testify about the Sterling case at that particular time. The chairman, Senator Harry S Truman finally recessed the Committee, and thanked the witness with the advice that: "at a future date we will expect you to appear, Mr. Corcoran." However, Mr. Corcoran did not again appear before the Truman Committee to be questioned about the Sterling case or any other matter.

The date of the first intercession in behalf of Sterling by Thomas Corcoran is a matter still shrouded in mystery. Requests made to various governmental departments to investigate this have been ignored or rebuffed. Yet he did so intercede even though his name does not appear in the list of attorneys who signed the consent decrees and other court papers for Sterling. That list includes the firm of Rogers, Hoge and Hills, the regular Sterling attorneys; and John T. Cahill, a former associate of Corcoran in the New York law firm of Cotton and Franklin who, with Corcoran's backing, had been United States Attorney at New York City from March, 1939, to March, 1941, during the period of the investigation, trial, and acquittal of the only two directors of the McKesson & Robbins swindle who were ever brought even within speaking distance of the bar of justice. At that trial Howard Corcoran, another brother of Thomas, was in charge of the prosecution as assistant to United States Attorney Cahill.

The two acquitted directors testified that they had never suspected Coster of wrongdoing. And it might be mentioned here that Howard Corcoran refused the testimony and the proofs which I offered to present to the jury at that trial, that it had long been well known to the drug trade that Coster was a common criminal, and that after the Hoover depression started, McKesson & Robbins was concealing its financial difficulties with fraud.

Sterling Products and its chief executives were named on the list which I had already supplied those investigating the McKesson & Robbins mess as being among those who had knowledge of Coster's criminal activities. This list also included executives of the trade associations and trade papers which Sterling dominated.

Mr. Cahill resumed the practice of law at about the time the Justice Department was beginning its dragnet inquiry into the Sterling-Farben relations. Robert H. Jackson was Attorney General and in official circles he was regarded as "tough." Certainly he was not soft when he slapped court orders on Farben's huge deposits in the National City Bank, and instructed Thurman Arnold, head of the Antitrust Division, to turn the Farben mess inside out, no matter who was hurt.

Then, on June 2, 1941, a long-expected vacancy on the Supreme Court occurred with the resignation of Chief Justice Charles Evans Hughes. Attorney General Robert Jackson was nominated to fill the Supreme Court vacancy, and according to Washington reports, one of the most active supporters for his promotion was Mr. Thomas Corcoran. Francis Biddle, then Solicitor General, was named to succeed Mr. Jackson as Acting Attorney General but was not actually nominated until some two months later.

Meanwhile, rumors of pressure in connection with the Sterling investigation abounded. In July, Messrs. Corcoran and Cahill held several long conferences at the Department of Justice, at which consent decrees were proposed as an alternative to criminal indictment of Sterling and its executives. And, strange as it may seem, the conferences were not held with those members of the antitrust staff who were conducting the investigation.

As a result of these discussions there was submitted to the Justice Department a paper dated Aug. 15, 1941, and entitled, "The Sterling Representations to the Interdepartmental Committee of the Departments of State, Treasury and Justice." In this document Sterling, over the signature of its chairman, William E. Weiss, graciously promised to cancel its illegal contracts with Farben, and to obey all criminal statutes and war regulations of the United States Government. The crowning gem of the sixteen paragraphs in this promise to "go straight," was the agreement to remove any director, officer or employee of Sterling or its subsidiaries who was deemed by the Government to be engaged in any activities for the benefit of Axis powers or otherwise engaged in activities contrary to the national interest.

This fantastic piece of impudence was the birth of Sterling's alleged repentance, reform and reorganization. It was the document which Mr. Corcoran later acclaimed as, "very far-sighted" and "one of the most brilliant things that has been done in the defense effort."

Thurman Arnold's little band of determined investigators, however, did not feel that it was either far-sighted or brilliant insofar as the national security was involved. Some of them refused to abandon their investigation, or to withhold from the grand jury evidence already gathered which involved Sterling's executives in subversive relations with Farben leaders. And resignations, to be accompanied by public statements, were threatened.

Just about this time items began to appear in the press that all was not well inside the Department of Justice with regard to the Sterling case. The Washington *Times Herald* published a full-page Sunday feature story about the "young man who practices law out of his hat," which quoted Mr. Corcoran as saying that he wanted to make a million dollars in a year practicing law, and then re-enter official life and spend the rest of his days improving the Government.

Referring to the Sterling investigation, the article stated that Tommy's brother David did not want to be bothered by the Department of Justice about those who had been holding up the price and keeping down the production of drugs and chemicals essential to the prosecution of the war, and went on to say:

> Dave Corcoran is an officer of Sidney Ross & Co. . . . . . of Sterling Products . . . . . somehow Sterling Products has got itself tangled up in a Department of Justice investigation . . . . . Tommy, with Cahill and brother Dave is defending Sterling's interests. The temperature in the air-conditioned Department of Justice is said to have risen on occasion to

something more than blood heat. "Tommy can't get it through his head," reports one observer, "that he is not in the Government any more."

Pearson and Allen in their Sunday night broadcast on Aug. 17, 1941, announced that a big explosion was due inside the Department of Justice if criminal prosecution was not pressed of American firms for their cooperation with Germany on restraint of trade. "A high departmental official" stated the broadcasters, "is holding back the prosecutions."

On Aug. 25, 1941, Mr. Biddle was finally nominated to the office of Attorney General. On Sept. 4, the Senate confirmed the nomination, and the next day the Sterling consent decrees were made a matter of record in the District Court of New York. In just one particular Messrs. Corcoran and Cahill had been compelled to yield ground. Thurman Arnold and his staff insisted that the proceedings must have some relation to the criminal provisions of the law, so an information was filed in the criminal court against Sterling and its three subsidiaries: Bayer, Winthrop and Alba, and two of its officers: Messrs. Weiss and Diebold. All pleaded *Nolo contendere*, and were fined a total of $26,000. This sum represented an infinitessimal fraction of the illegal profits made by Sterling as result of the unlawful Farben agreements. The subversive activities of the Sterling executives could not be even considered for the good and sufficient reason that they were not mentioned in the information.

The consent decrees purported to abrogate the formal agreements with Farben, seven of which were recited at length. However, it is doubtful whether Farben will recognize the abrogation of its agreements with Sterling any more than its predecessors recognized the seizure of Bayer during World War I. For one thing these Farben agreements contained clauses requiring Sterling to settle any questions relating to them in a German court, for another, it has been admitted by a representative of Sterling that William E. Weiss sent a message to his Farben friends in Germany not to worry about what was going on in the United States because Sterling would find ways of continuing its relations with its Farben associates.

It should also be pointed out that the Treasury's freezing of foreign funds and property and the black lists of foreign nationals issued by the Secretary of State already effectually restrained all relations between Sterling and Farben. So the alleged concessions by Sterling, as stipulated in the consent decrees, were an empty gesture by which Sterling gave up nothing that was not already forbidden or impossible. In reality the decrees had just two positive effects, they served to prevent indictment and prosecution of Sterling's executives, and they put a stop to the Justice Department investigation of subversive activities by some of the Sterling people that was then in progress.

An official statement issued in the name of Attorney General Biddle, at the time the consent decrees were recorded, contained allegations and conclusions which were so at variance with facts known to exist that a wave of caustic criticism arose immediately. Stories appeared in the press about the open rebellion which existed inside the Justice Department, due to Corcoran's brazen actions, and also because evidence prepared for submission to the grand jury was being pigeonholed. Mr. Biddle's statement of Sept. 5, it was said, was actually prepared by Corcoran, and read like a Sterling patent-medicine advertisement.

On September 25, another official press release was issued about the Sterling case (this time in the name of Thurman Arnold) which also contained statements completely the reverse of facts apparent on the record. Men who knew Mr. Arnold and were familiar with the vigorous language of his privately expressed opinions, were confident that he had not prepared this second apology for the consent decrees, and that it must have been issued over his protest.

Among the more absurd allegations in the Arnold press release was the statement that:

> The illegal contracts (with Farben) were entered into in 1926 . . . . . long before the Hitler revolution.

On the record, the consent decrees listed seven illegal contracts of which three were entered into in 1936, 1937 and 1938, long after Hitler seized power in Germany. Another statement in the release argued that:

The Sterling organization must not be destroyed, nor its efficiency hampered, in the present emergency, because of the necessity for American outlets for drugs in this hemisphere.

The falsity of this argument was self-evident. The Sterling-Farben branches in Latin America had to be abolished, and the purpose of the decrees was not to preserve the existing Sterling organization, but to destroy those outlets for all time. Whoever prepared that statement for Mr. Arnold's official rubber stamp had small regard for the lustre of Mr. Arnold's name.

While this press release was issued in the name of Assistant Attorney General Arnold, copies of it were mailed out over the signature of one James Allen as "Special Executive Assistant to the Attorney General." Mr. Allen, according to press reports, was one of the numerous young men originally brought into the government service by Thomas Corcoran. Mr. Allen turned up later in the Office of War Information where, in April, 1942, he was one of the higher-ups said to be responsible for the resignation of a group of writers who issued a statement that they were getting out of the O.W.I. because it was impossible to tell the full truth when those in control were turning the O.W.I. into an office of war ballyhoo. Later it was reported that Mr. Allen was again Mr. Biddle's assistant, this time at the Nuremberg trials of Nazi war criminals.

One of the most notable aspects of the Corcoran, Trojan-horse trade with the United States Government, was the fact that only two of the executives and directors of Sterling were named in the criminal informations as in any way involved in the unlawful agreements with Farben.

Mr. McClintock, chief aide to Mr. Weiss in the Farben relations, was not named, nor was Mr. Rogers whose active legal mind worked on the details of some of those illegal agreements and whose signature actually appears on one of them.

Others whose names were conspicuously missing in the informations are James Hill, Jr., director and treasurer of Sterling and of Sterling subsidiaries; William E. Weiss, Jr., president of Alba; and Dr. William Hiemenz, Farben's director and plant manager of Winthrop. All of these obviously had something to do with carrying out the contracts with Farben as covered by the information, and the pleas of *nolo contendere*. Dr. Hiemenz stayed right on as manager of Winthrop until O'Connell's Treasury squad showed him the door several months after the consent decrees had, by negative action, coated him with nice fresh Corcoran whitewash.

Another notable who had retained his seat at the Sterling board as one of the consent decree "unmentionables" is one George C. Haigh, whose contact with Sterling goes back to September, 1918, when A. Mitchell Palmer, as Alien Property Custodian, made him a director of the Bayer Co.

In 1919, after Sterling took over and pledged to keep Bayer inviolate from any return of German influence, Mr. Haigh was made a director of Sterling. He continued as a director all through the negotiations of the long string of illegal contracts and agreements which violated in spirit and in letter the pledge and the purpose of the Americanization of Bayer.

Others were involved, but the above-mentioned principals are sufficient to indicate the fine legal work done by Mr. Corcoran in consummating his far-sighted and brilliant contribution to our national defense.

It may be relevant at this point to cite from the Canons of Professional Ethics of the American Bar Association, with which Mr. Corcoran, no doubt, is familiar.

> The responsibility for advising questionable transactions . . . . . for urging questionable defenses, is the lawyer's responsibility. He cannot escape it by urging as an excuse that he is only following his clients instructions "When a lawyer discovers that some fraud or deception had been practiced, which has unjustly imposed upon the court or a party, he should endeavor to rectify it." The canons of the American Bar Association apply to all branches of the legal profession; specialists in particular branches are not considered as exempt from the application of these principles.

Many of the American newspapers accepted Mr. Biddle's statement on the consent decrees as conclusive and final, some even commended the outcome. *Time,* on Sept. 15, exclaimed exultingly:

The Justice announcement last week gave Sterling a clean bill of health as far as further Nazi influence is concerned. This, it hoped, might undo some of the damage done by Arnold's previous blasts . . . . . The Sterling deal was Tommy Corcoran's fourth big job since he left the R.F.C. last year.

In view of the amount of advertising with which *Time* and *Life* have been favored by American affiliates of Farben this rather crude bombast in one of the Henry Luce publications may warrant calling attention to an accusation published by columnist Leonard Lyons in the New York *Post* that *Time* had slanted a story in favor of a Luce advertiser, and that its managing editor, T. S. Matthews, had confessed that his stories definitely were slanted.

The admission made publicly by the *Time* Editor was that:

Facts are the raw material . . . . . common to the whole press, but the products are as different . . . . . as the men who run the papers . . . . . a sane journalist cannot be completely impartial . . . . . the stuff he writes will be definitely slanted . . . . .

Leading trade papers also were jubilant. *Drug Trade News*, companion publication to *Drug Topics*, which admittedly is subsidized by the drug manufacturers, came out with an editorial rejoicing that "there was no evidence of willful wrong-doing on the part of Sterling and its subsidiaries."

Other press comment, however, was decidedly critical. *PM*, Marshall Field's New York daily paper, had already published several informative articles regarding the Sterling-Farben tie-ups and its comments on the consent decrees and on the Biddle and Arnold press statements were numerous and caustic.

The most devastating criticism, however, appeared in a long series of articles by Thomas Lunsford Stokes, Jr., Scripps-Howard feature writer, and probably the most feared of those Washington correspondents who consider it their function to seek out and write the truth, regardless of the high places or the immaculate shirt fronts of the personages involved. Mr. Stokes, winner of the Pulitzer Prize in 1938 for exposing political monkey business in the W.P.A., performed a notable public service in writing a detailed running story of the lobbying activities of Corcoran in connection with the Sterling case.

On Sept. 15, Mr. Stokes' comments included:

> Consent decrees . . . . . have left a sour aftermath in the Antitrust Division of the Justice Department . . . . . The dissatisfaction attributed to: (1) The pressure and pull exerted by Thomas G. Corcoran, one time New Deal brain truster and now a lawyer-lobbyist who represented Sterling. (2) Failure of the government to take the evidence before a grand jury . . . . . and the terms of the consent decrees, which, in the opinion of some are not as strong as they might be and might become unhinged after the war. (3) The fact that settlement was imposed from the top by Attorney General Biddle . . . . . Mr. Corcoran is an old friend of Mr. Biddle. He was influential in bringing Mr. Biddle into the administration and was active on behalf of Mr. Biddle's recent promotion from Solicitor General to Attorney General.

> Mr. Corcoran practically camped in Mr. Biddle's offices . . . . . was given access to secret information of the department . . . . . and contributed to the writing of the statement for the press which is described by those who know the facts as whitewash, with misleading inferences and actual misstatements . . . . . Investigators were still at work when the settlement was reached and the consent decrees taken into the court . . . . . They were called from their inquiry, which was turning up some evidence which does not appear in the 'information' . . . . . nor in the consent decrees, and is now a closed book . . . . . unless it is called for by Congress.

On Sept. 17, Mr. Stokes' column contributed the following:

> A federal grand jury never got to hear the evidence dug up by the Department investigators . . . . . It can be stated authoritatively that they were turning up some rather sensational evidence about operations of subsidiary companies of Sterling Products, Inc. in South America, evidence which leaves a question mark as to the efficacy of the consent decrees designed to drive the Germans out of that market . . . . . Who

stopped the investigation? Who stopped submission of the evidence to a Grand Jury?

From December, 1939, to April, 1941, Bayer shipped aspirin to I.G. (Farben) agencies in South America . . . . . made in the United States but packaged just like the German product.

The income of German agents of I.G. Farben in South America was increased during the war by Sterling's payments to them for the distributing of Bayer . . . . . In at least one case, in Colombia, one of these agents, manager of a local company there, heads the Arbeitsfront in the Nazi organization . . . . . Dr. E. Wolff, arrested in Panama with a trunk containing various documents, was tried and fined. He was on his way from Berlin to Buenos Aires to work in an I.G. Farben factory.

On Sept. 18, Mr. Stokes' column on Sterling and Bayer went back to the days of World War I and expressed the fear that history might repeat—that after this war the Germans might again gain a position of dominance in our chemical and allied industries. This article again castigated Corcoran as a lobbyist for Sterling, and brought Earl I. McClintock into the picture as one of those who used his official friendships during the negotiations to stop the Sterling investigation from going any further.

Another phase of the investigation revealed by Mr. Stokes was the fact that a grand jury, if it had been permitted to examine the evidence assembled in the Justice Department, might have acted upon:

> The expenditure by Sterling in the last eight years of large sums for advertising in pro-Nazi newspapers in Latin America while only negligible advertising was done in the anti-Nazi papers."

On Sept. 19, Mr. Stokes discussed Mr. Corcoran's part in the preparation of the Biddle press release saying:

> This may not be the first time that a private citizen, representing defendants in an antitrust case, has supervised the writing of a government press release but it is the first one

that anyone seems to know about; and certainly takes the prize for flagrancy.

Soft-spoken Raymond Clapper, Scripps-Howard columnist and colleague of Stokes, used very strong language about Corcoran's lobbying just as he had in 1932 about that other ex-official, Edward T. Clark. On Oct. 7, he concluded his comments with:

> What is to be the effect on these junior officials, working on moderate salaries, when they see this cynical kind of funny business going on in the very heart of the New Deal?

On November 27, 1941, *The New York Times* discussed "lobby lawyers" in an article which referred to Mr. Corcoran's activities, and quoted Mr. Biddle as stating that he planned no investigation of lobby contracts:

> Such lobbying, Mr. Biddle said, would be inquired into if the Department of Justice was so directed by some proper agency, but not otherwise.

According to the *Times*, when asked if he thought he or other government officers should make public the names of all persons visiting their offices, the Attorney General replied that he thought it would be very inappropriate to give out such names, and that the public must depend upon the honesty of its officials. (Three years later one of Mr. Biddle's chief assistants was to denounce the handling of this case in damning terms.)

I have already mentioned that I had some part in inducing the Justice Department to investigate Sterling. Also, I had been supplying the Department with historical and background data which bore upon Farben's activities in the United States, and the conspiracies and subversive activities of those involved with Farben.

In some instances, at least, my aid was of value, and on more than one occasion I was officially thanked for my assistance. In any event, I was sufficiently close to what went on both inside and outside the Department, relative to that investigation, to recognize the danger signs as they began to be visible, and to realize that regardless of the integrity and high purpose of those young men of Arnold's, the quarry would not be brought to bay unless the scope and broad purpose of the hunt was enlarged. Accordingly, immediately after the records of Sterling and Winthrop were subpoenaed, I sent Mr. Arnold a number of exhibits which brought out the fact that the Washington lobby had never been identified in the public mind as representing other than American interests. My letter, dated April 15, 1946, stated that:

> In view particularly of the refusals of the Senate Lobby Committee of 1929 and 1935 to investigate the lobby maintained in Washington by these people . . . . . I do not believe that your own efforts can ever be effective unless this lobby is included in your investigation and action. The present lobby includes some of those mentioned by me . . . . . as being paid, directly or indirectly, by the German government.

That communication was never acknowledged by Mr. Arnold. Perhaps the lobby saw to it that it never reached his eyes; certainly he never mentioned it to me afterward. However, Thurman Arnold cannot say that I did not attempt to warn him of what was going to happen to his Sterling case, and to some of his other Farben investigations, if he did not use a repeating rifle on the Farben partners—and a shotgun on the Farben lobby.

CHAPTER X

Senators and Congressmen — Who Never Knew

MENTION IS
made elsewhere of the concealed interference by the German dye
trust with tariff and patent legislation; also the strange desire
of members of the House and Senate to force through the act
of 1928 for the payment of claims and the restoration of German
property which had been seized in the First World War. One of
the Senators who joined with King and Moses to help put through
that 1928 statute, was Doctor Royal S. Copeland.

The nonpartisan broadmindedness of the German dye trust in
chosing its American friends is shown by the fact that Copeland
held office and was a candidate, from time to time, as a Republican, a New Deal Democrat and an anti-New Deal Democrat.
Farben also appeared to have no objections to the friendship of
a doctor whose medical attainments did not qualify him for membership in his own county medical society, or for the dubious
honor of belonging to the American Medical Association. Copeland once made the claim that he was a former professor in the
Medical School of the University of Michigan but, according to

the University authorities, his teaching experience was in a defunct homeopathic college which was in no way related to Michigan's famous school of medicine.

As a Senator and a doctor of medicine, Copeland's name and picture and voice were seen and heard in press advertisements and radio broadcasting for patent medicine—or home remedies, as they were politely termed. And among those advertised nostrums were preparations manufactured and sold by two of the leading American affiliates of I.G. Farben—Sterling Products and Standard Oil of New Jersey. Such arrangements for the Senator's services were presumably made at the New York offices of Copeland Service, Inc., where one Ole Salthe, his manager (of whom more later), was also prepared to arrange for the advice of the Senator on matters pertaining to the enforcement of Food and Drug Laws. These were, of course, strictly business or semiprofessional arrangements and bore no relationship to the Senator's engagements as a statesman, or his daily newspaper contributions as a literary authority on public health matters.

As to his kindly feeling towards I.G. Farben and its affiliates, our Senatorial healer made the record very clear in a speech on the Senate floor on February 21, 1928, just before the final approval of the statute to pay Farben's claims and to return Farben's properties. His address, in part, was as follows:

> Can we doubt that international business partnerships are the best preventative of international wars and conflicts that statesmen can devise? It is time to cease ringing the changes upon war hatreds and animosities, and extend the helping hand of friendship to our former enemies . . . . .
>
> Let it be remembered that some of our infant industries are predicated upon the confiscated inventions of the people of a nation originally invited into our midst by the terms of our Constitution. No compensation has ever been paid to them. I am glad they are to be paid under the terms of the bill passed yesterday . . . . .
>
> The domestic problems of farm relief, of national defense. of destruction of industry by ruinous foreign competition, would be brought nearer to solution by such commercial

alliances. The occupation of some paid Jeremiahs constantly prophesying war and woe would probably be rendered super-fluous . . . . .

Let us have done with vituperative attacks on nonexistent enemies . . . . . we have read from time to time in the chemical trade journals and in the lay press of how wicked, designing, unashamed and dangerous were those corporations whose patents we confiscated for the benefit of a privileged few . . . . .

European combinations in these industries provide additional products for farsighted Americans who have formed alliances with the possessors of the 'know how.' The question is shall we welcome alien industry and capital to our shores, in accordance with the traditional policy of our nation, or shall we lend ear to the affrighted clamor, denunciation and invective of a selfish minority? It is high time that we had an official expression of the administration's attitude in the interests of world peace and domestic prosperity.

American capital is hesitant. American industrialists are reluctant to enter into agreements with other manufacturers to obtain for this country that which we have not, and which would be of benefit to us, so long as the newspapers are filled with vituperative abuse and vague suggestions of Sherman Act prosecutions.

This address is important to this story because it records the beginning of the second postwar decade when Farben and its American stooges had decided that everything was under control, and therefore their plans for expansion could be more open, with safety to all concerned. The speech is also important because it is a condensation of substantially every false argument and sophistry of Farben propaganda. Copeland also, unwittingly, recorded officially the unheeded protests at Farben's comeback, and the unheeded demand for Sherman Act prosecutions. Copeland, in the name of the United States Senate, was bidding Farben welcome just as the Hoover subordinates, and Donovan, in the name of the executive branch of the government had extended a similar invitation a few days earlier, as related in Chapter VII.

From its earliest days, the German dye trust has utilized the patent laws of the United States to obstruct, cripple or control our dye, drug, and chemical munitions industries. The president of the American Bayer company, acting on instructions from Berlin, persuaded the State Department to send our Commissioner of Patents as a delegate to the International Patent Convention in Stockholm prior to World War I. The result was that our unsuspecting commissioner wound up as the guest of honor on Kaiser Wilhelm's yacht, and upon his return was in complete accord with the desires of his Teutonic hosts.

As a result, the United States negotiated a new treaty with Germany which complied with the dye trust's wishes that the working of a patent in either country was sufficient to protect the inventor, or his assignee, in both countries. And the president of Bayer boasted openly of his smart trick in getting the Kaiser to help soften up our patent laws.

Meanwhile Herman Metz turned up on the Congressional Committee on patents. Metz was irritated at any attempt to interfere with the rights of his German friends to do as they pleased, saying:

> Legally there could be no reason at all why the Germans should not obtain a patent in this country for which a patent could be obtained, and do with that patent what they pleased.

Again Metz declared that German patents:

> . . . . . have no value a ssuch except for the purpose of keeping out infringing products. They are simply clubs to keep out other manufacturers.

After World War I, when tariff and embargo barred German imports, the dye trust began using its patents to implement the illegal tie-ups by which it reestablished itself in the United States.

It is obvious that this reestablishment would not have been possible if our antitrust laws had been enforced. Nor would it have been possible had Congress interceded to prevent misuse of United States patents, especially those relating to the national defense.

Can anyone doubt that Congress would have been compelled to take drastic steps had Mr. Teagle, or Mr. duPont, or Dr. Weiss, or even Herman Metz, ever protested to Congress or even to the public at the illegal agreements proposed by Farben. The fact is that they did neither.

All through this second prewar period the public was largely uninformed, or greatly misinformed, about these Farben tie-ups. But the record proves that Congress had known for many years that the more important of the illegal agreements were in operation, and that others were in the making.

Members of the Senate and the House of Representatives uncovered evidence of the dye trust's plans and agreements in almost every session of Congress from the end of World War I to the beginning of World War II. They also knew the identity and the activities of the horde of lobbyists who haunted the hallways of the Capitol and the bars and club-rooms of Washington in the interests of Farben and Farben's American partners.

Despite this knowledge Congress did nothing until the 1941 and '42 exposures and prosecutions. Then loud were the lamentations of some of its members at the "surprising" revelations of what Farben had been doing to keep the United States disarmed.

In order to comprehend the breadth and scope of the Farben pattern, we might examine some of the crocodile tears shed so publicly at not knowing things that had been blazoned on the records of Congress all along. It is necessary also to observe how these facts come to be on those records, and what influences may have caused them to be ignored.

One member of the Senate who in 1942 appeared not to know anything about the Farben tie-ups in the United States was the Honorable Scott W. Lucas, Illinois Democrat, who was elected to Congress in 1934 and moved up to the Senate in 1938.

In April, 1942, Senator Lucas, as a member of the Patents Committee, made some comments about the ignorance of official Washington regarding the activities of I.G. Farben. An official of the Justice Department had just testified that some of Farben's illegal affiliations had been secret until the Attorney General's office went into their files. Said Senator Lucas:

But before the Attorney General's office went into the files to inspect these documents nobody in the government as I understand it, or in this country, knew anything about these international cartel arrangements . . . . .

I am not condemning anyone particularly for what happened in the past, but I am speaking for the future. We all learn by experience. This country ought to have a right at least to examine and ascertain whether or not a contract of this kind, if it went into effect, would affect the life and security of the United States.

Anxious as the Senator appears to have been to learn by experience, something must have caused him to conclude otherwise, because he was one of the five members of the Senate Patents Committee who later voted to prevent Senator Bone, its chairman, from continuing these hearings into Farben's agreements with Sterling, and the relations of the Sterling executives with subversive activities of their German partners.

Senator Tom Connally, Texas Democrat, started as a Congressman in 1917 and became a Senator in 1929. The Senator is reputed to be a political colleague of former Governor William P. Hobby of Texas, who, with the late W. S. Farish, organized the Humble Oil Co., and sold control of that company to Standard. Senator Connally contributed a naïve conclusion as to the innocence of all concerned about Farben's intentions. The Senator was a member of the Truman Committee which was examining Mr. Farish of Standard Oil in March 1942 at a closed hearing. When Mr. Farish appeared uncertain as to just what testimony he should give about Standard's relations with Farben, Senator Connally asked him:

> When you entered into these negotiations with Farben in Germany . . . . . did you do it with any contemplation of war or of our becoming involved in war and needing these articles in the way that we now find ourselves needing them? Or was it simply a commercial business transaction that you were contemplating?

Mr. Farish responded:

> It was always. Senator, on a commercial or business basis, and with only commercial objectives in mind . . . . .

Senator Homer T. Bone, Washington Democrat, came to the Senate in 1932, and two years later sat through the lengthy hearings of the Senate Munitions Investigating Committee which went deep into the Farben activities. In 1942 Senator Bone, as Chairman of the Senate Patents Committee, investigated the activities of Farben for several months—until the aforementioned five members ganged up on him and refused to permit the investigation to be completed.

At these 1942 hearings Senator Bone did recall that the subject was not a new one, but he also indicated an unfortunate lack of memory about the revelations before the Nye Munitions Committee and elsewhere concerning Farben. The Senator's comment was:

> I know little about I.G. Farbenindustrie in Germany because it is shrouded in mystery. I know back in 1934 and '35 when I served on the Senate Munitions Committee, we were not able to get anything definite out of Germany. There was great secrecy manifested even in some of our own departments . . . . . At that time I was fearful that what our nationals were doing might be aiding in the rearmament of Germany, thus making her a menace to the world.

Assistant Attorney General Thurman Arnold, while testifying before the Truman Committee in March, 1942, paid a peculiar tribute to his own belated investigation of the Farben tie-up arrangements, and put the entire blame for the continuance of these agreements on the lax enforcement of the anti-trust laws during the Hoover Republican administration from 1929 to 1933. For some reason he did not mention that this lax enforcement continued right on from 1933 to 1941 during the Democratic administration, Mr. Arnold's comment in part was that:

> The cost of preventing such cartel restrictions in the future is eternal vigilance and the existence of a wide-awake investigating agency to enforce the Sherman Act. Had there been such an agency operating in 1929, had this conduct been actually hazardous at that time, these arrangements would never have been contemplated. But from 1929 to 1933 business men felt safe from discovery.

In view of these and other Senatorial-Congressional expressions of ignorance about what Farben was up to, it is of interest here to refer to some of the extensive evidence available, from 1919 to 1939, to members of the House and Senate.

This consideration is warranted in order to understand the precise detail with which the Congress of the United States first explored and recorded the activities and purposes of the German dye-trust leaders, then ignored its own findings and finally, when disaster had arrived, began pitifully weeping "we didn't know." It is for the reader to decide from these facts whether the representatives of the American people were dolts or knaves—or an unhappy combination of both.

During the decade that followed the close of the first World War, the German Dye Trust was the subject of many hours of discussion and thousands of pages of testimony before committees of the Senate and House. Later hearings brought out more facts about Farben; about its lobby and campaign contributions; about its industrial tie-ups and subsidiaries; and about its propaganda and its expenditures for espionage and other subversive activities.

From 1919 to 1922 there were a number of hearings before the committees of the House and Senate which recorded the testimony of a great number of witnesses who argued whether high tariff duties or an absolute embargo would best protect the new American dye industry from the threat of German imports. At these hearings there was very little left unsaid about what Farben's predecessors in I.G. Dyes would do to this country's new chemical industry if they were given the opportunity; or of the probability of another war of conquest, if and when Germany got the chance.

When the next war did start more than a dozen members of the Senate, and several times that many members of the House, still occupied the same positions at Washington as they had during those early hearings at which the records and plans of the German dye trust were spread upon the Congressional records. A number of these legislators were members of the committees that held the hearings. Coming down to the 1934–1936 period when further hearings delved deep into Farben's consummated plans, we find that an actual majority of the members of both chambers were still representing their constituents when the last war began.

It would appear from the record, therefore, that the failure of Congress to act has not been due to lack of ample information about Farben, nor to lack of repeated warnings as to what disaster that neglect might bring about.

There were many charges and countercharges against lobbyists and German agents at those early hearings. Francis P. Garvan, among others, made definite charges that the German dye trust had attempted to influence legislation in the past and was still doing so at the very time that Senator King and his campaign-fund contributor, Herman Metz, were denouncing everyone who wished to protect America's new chemical industry. Garvan accused Metz of standing on the floor of Congress, as representative of the German I.G., shaking his fist at American manufacturers in the gallery and exclaiming, "I got you licked—I got you licked."

"And then," said Garvan, "we were like the blind beggar at the gate in Kipling's story, 'I cannot see my enemy but I can hear his footfalls.'"

In another of the Senate hearings in 1920, before the Finance Committee, Mr. Irenée duPont, president of the duPont Company, made the rather remarkable request that in addition to embargo and high tariff to keep out German dyes, Congress might well pass legislation which would authorize some government official to set aside the Sherman Act as it applied to the dye industry, if, in the opinion of the official, it became necessary for the dye manufacturers to get together on short notice to exchange information.

Congress did not then pass such a law, but Mr. duPont had little cause to complain about any enforcement of the Sherman Act until Thurman Arnold got busy after World War II had started. Then duPont and all the other leading American dyestuff makers were indicted for conspiring with I.G. Farben, and the Congress kindly did permit the Attorney General to waive or suspend prosecution of all concerned on the pretext that prosecution would interfere with the war effort. The case finally ended when duPont, among others, pleaded *nolo contendere* and took a fine. But that belongs in another part of this story.

There was much testimony in these early hearings which gave unmistakable warning of what the German dye trust might do when the next war should come. Here, again, it was Francis Garvan who put those warnings into pungent, dramatic form which, it is hoped, some members of the Senate may now recall with shame.

Time and again Garvan denounced the German dye leaders as a menace to the peace of the world—in the future as in the past. For example, in 1920 he warned the Senate Finance Committee:

> Industrial Germany waged this war; and industrial Germany was the first to see defeat, and forced the military peace in order that with her industrial equipment intact she might continue that same war by intensified and concentrated economic measures. It was Germany's chemical supremacy that gave her confidence in her avaricious dream of world empire, it was Germany's chemical supremacy that enabled her to wage four years of pitiless warfare, and it is Germany's chemical supremacy upon which she relies to maintain the war.

Another emphatic warning was sounded to members of the Senate by Dr. C. J. Thatcher, one of the smaller dye manufacturers, when he told that same Senate Committee:

> "No matter what importers or their friends of Germany may say . . . . . The ruthless war for chemical domination by Germany, started at least as early as 1880 . . . . ', was not ended by the Armistice or by the Treaty of Versailles . . . . . any treaty, law, or other provision which a German can by any means avoid in the warfare for industrial chemical supremacy is, just as in actual warfare, 'a mere scrap of paper.'"

Rear Admiral Ralph Earle, Chief of the Bureau of Ordnance of the Navy Department, also gave the Senate some words of advice at that time which were complacently forgotten. In discussing the need for encouraging and protecting our coal-tar industry as a vital measure of national defense, Admiral Earle said, in part:

> During the war we used as much toluol as could be obtained, but the production of that material was not sufficient . . . . . Time is a very important element . . . . . in

reference to war . . . . . from the standpoint of national defense we do not think we ought to be put in that position again.

The admiral also advised the committee that the production of synthetic drugs from coal tar should be encouraged through protection of the industry, as coming under the general head of preparedness.

Another unmistakable warning is to be found in the report of a Senate Finance Subcommittee in 1920, which said, in part:

> One who has read the story of the German Government in the United States just prior to the war, knows that the chemical industry in this country which was under the control of the German Government was the center of espionage, German propaganda, and direct government activities. They prevented the use of coal-tar products in the munitions industry . . . . .
>
> We know what Germany will do to regain her hold on the industry in this country. We know that she will resort to state and cartel combinations, trade export premiums, dumping, bribery, espionage and propaganda. She did this before, and she will do it again.

In 1930 the records of the Senate Lobby Committee were embellished with a detailed history of the I.G. Farbenindustrie which was presented by Senator Arthur R. Robinson of Indiana. This document had been filed by the American I.G. Chemical Corp. with the New York Stock Exchange, and it included much information regarding the enormous size and growth of Farben; its huge production of synthetic nitrogen and its other products. The 1929 agreement between Farben and Standard Oil was described, and the negotiations for later tie-ups were mentioned.

Senator Robinson's minority report, with which Senator Caraway, its chairman, and other members of the committee declined to be identified, summed up the status of the American I.G. as a subsidiary of the German I.G., and the detailed recital in these hearings that Farben had become far stronger in the United States than prior to the first World War was sufficient to warn any member of the Senate or House that the menace to American industry and to national security was already a very real one.

Additional detailed data about Farben went into the record in 1931 when the late Representative Louis T. McFadden of Pennsylvania, testifying before the Senate Committee on Banking and Currency on the nomination of Eugene Meyer to the Federal Reserve Board, inserted several lengthy documents describing the German chemical trust and its American I.G. subsidiary. McFadden commented that the "queer purpose" of the latter was to buy up American companies dealing in chemical and allied products. Mr. Meyer was not accused of participation in Farben's subsidiary, but this record made much additional data about Farben available to members of the House and Senate—had they been interested.

The Senate Special Committee to investigate the munitions industry was appointed in 1934, under the chairmanship of Gerald P. Nye, Republican isolationist and pacifist from North Dakota. The other members of that committee were Walter F. George, Georgia; Bennett C. Clark, Missouri; Homer T. Bone, Washington; James P. Pope, Idaho; Democrats, and A. H. Vandenberg, Michigan; and W. Warren Barbour, New Jersey, Republicans. Six of the seven were still members of the Senate in 1941 when Germany declared war on this country, and when revelations of the subversive activities of I.G. Farben's affiliates had attracted so much public notice that the Senate began a new series of investigations to rediscover, amid loud protestations of surprise and indignation, many of the very same facts about Farben which the Nye Committee had recorded back in 1934. In general the public has accepted those expressions of surprise as genuine and it is, therefore, necessary to go into some detail in discussing how voluminous were those revelations of 1934.

The Nye Committee delved into all kinds of munitions and implements of war. Farben's tie-ups not only were discussed generally as a menace to world peace and to the national security of the United States; they were presented in great detail in charts and lists of companies and products showing that the Farben agreements at that time in the United States covered explosives and ammunition, dyestuffs, drugs, photographic materials, rayon, magnesium alloys, synthetic oil products, miscellaneous chemicals and insecticides; also that products on which possible arrangements were contemplated included synthetic nitrogen, synthetic rubber, and plastics.

It might be remarked here that this list of chemical-munitions is almost identical to the products I had listed as under the control or influence of Farben in the diagramatic chart which I had sent to the members of the Senate and House of Representatives in 1931. Copies of that chart, like so many other documents of mine, stirred up the usual tempest in the waste baskets of Washington. However, this time, three years later, they dug out the facts themselves and put them in the record and on large elaborate charts of their own devising.

Among the most important contributions which the Nye Committee hearings recorded and which both the committee and the Senate thereupon promptly ignored, were the proofs which indicated plainly that Farben and the Hitler government were on extremely close terms, and that the rearming of Germany and preparations for war were proceeding at an alarming rate.

In one instance while Lammot duPont was testifying, Senator Clark, Missouri Democrat and isolationist, queried him on the possibility that secret and patented explosive formulas which duPont had turned over to Farben for commercial uses might be utilized for military purposes. The Senator asked the witness:

> There would be nothing to prevent them from taking those processes and using them in the manufacture of war explosives, would there?

Mr. duPont apparently had no answer to that.

Repeated warnings that Germany was rearming included advice from duPont's Paris representative in 1932 and 1933 that the Nazis were armed with American machine guns, and that a regular business had been established (not by duPont) of bootlegging weapons from this country to Germany.

From another duPont foreign relations representative came the advice in March 1932 that:

> It is a matter of common knowledge in Germany that I.G. Farben is financing Hitler . . . . . There seems to be no

doubt whatsoever that Dr. Schmitz is at least personally a large contributor to the Nazi party.

This was supplemented by a later report from the duPont London office which stated:

> Dr. Bosch . . . . . spends practically all of his time between his dwelling in Heidelberg and the government offices in Berlin, thus leaving little, if any, time for the affairs of the I.G. Farbenindustrie.

Limitations of space permits inclusion here of only these few bits of the very complete evidence assembled by the Nye Committee relative to the rearming of Germany, and Farben's part in it.

The Nye Committee charts and lists also showed many companies in Belgium, France, Holland, Italy and other countries that were tied to Farben. Thus pictured graphically, Farben was revealed as the greatest aggregation of industrial strength and military preparedness ever assembled under the direction or influence of a single small group of men. Readers of this book may wonder why the proven propensities of relatively small makers of munitions to bribe and corrupt government officials merely to sell them guns and powder did not suggest to the Senators that the greatest munition makers of all time, self-designated supermen and self-elected for world conquest, would not hesitate to utilize bribery and corruption on a huge scale to accomplish their aims among the officials of our own government. Perhaps the title of this chapter should be, "Facts of Life that a Prewar Senator Ought to Have Known."

The Nye Committee spent many days and recorded many pages with testimony about scheming lobbyists who worked against disarmament and bribed officials of foreign governments in the interest of builders of warships and war weapons; it also, unjustly, grouped with such sordid individuals various American scientists of the most distinguished character, like Dr. Charles H. Herty and Dr. Edgar Fahs Smith, beloved provost of the University of Pennsylvania and president of the American Chemical Society, whose attainments were recognized the world over and whose probity not even a Senate Committee could attack.

However, no attempt was made to record on the pages of these hearings the names and activities of the lobbyists who were haunting the capital in the interest of I.G. Farben, and who were on the payroll of certain of its American affiliates.

The committee report on chemical munitions came in 1936 after long and painful consideration of the evidence. Its recommendations were tortured and ponderous, they appeared to ignore the significance of the Farben tie-ups in the United States, but did not hesitate to condemn practices of lobbying and of bribery which "tends to rob the governments concerned of the inability to work freely for peace." The issue to these Senators was our disarmament—not Farben's rearmament.

The committee apparently was obsessed with the thought that war could be prevented by government ownership of the chemical industry. However, it finally recorded its dilemma:

> The committee recognizes the difficult problems involved in the control of the chemical industry in view of the extent of its peacetime activities.

With this profound thought, the members of the Nye Committee allowed the visible intrigues of Farben to rest in peace until after a new war had begun.

While the Nye Committee was fumbling with Farben's war chemicals, a committee on the other side of the capital was bringing to light some other Farben activities of an equally dangerous but more insidious character—propaganda. In March 1934 a special committee was appointed in the House of Representatives, to investigate foreign propaganda and other subversive activities. This was the origin of what later became famous, or perhaps only notorious, as the Dies Committee.

Its Chairman, in 1934, was the Honorable John W. McCormack, of Massachusetts. Samuel Dickstein, New York; Carl M. Weideman, Michigan; Charles Kramer, California; Thomas A. Jenkins, Ohio; J. Will Taylor, Tennessee, and U. S. Guyer, Kansas, were the original members.

Among the witnesses examined by the McCormack Committee were Mr. Ivy L. Lee, the famous public relations counsel, his partner Burnham Carter, and one Dudley Pittenger, bookkeeper for the Lee firm. The testimony of Lee and his associates revealed that the firm had been employed by the American I.G. ever since the latter was organized in 1929, and that in 1933, when Hitler became Chancellor, the German I.G. also retained Lee to give advice as to how to improve relations between Germany and the United States.

Some of Mr. Lee's testimony was confusing. For instance, his annual retainer from Farben was $25,000 paid in odd sums by the Swiss I.G. and the American I.G., yet he paid his own expenses, and these appeared to include the $33,000 a year which he paid to his son to stay in Berlin and study the German mind.

The Lee bookkeeper could throw no light on the discrepancy between the $25,000 which the firm received from Farben and the $33,000 which it paid out to keep its mind reader in Germany. Mr. Pittenger knew of no other work which young Lee was doing in Germany except on the Farben account.

Mr. Ivy Lee's testimony on his relations with the Hitler government were also confusing. At the start of the examination he stated positively that he had no contract with the German Government and that his arrangement was solely with the I.G. However, Mr. Lee did get around a bit, and found time to advise the Nazi big shots on their propaganda. Testified Mr. Lee:

> I first talked, of course, with my friends in the I.G. They all sympathized with my advice and they asked me if I would repeat that advice to different officers of the government. So, Dr. Ilgner introduced me to various ministers. He went with me to see Goebbels, the Minister of Propaganda; Von Papen, the Vice Chancellor; Von Neurath, the Foreign Minister; Schmidt, the Minister of Economics . . . . .

In explaining that his Farben contract was made within two or three months after Hitler's advent as head of the government, Mr. Lee also stated:

> At that time I did not contact any government officials except Hitler himself. They were anxious for me to meet him, just as a personal matter, to size him up.
> I had a half hour's talk with Hitler . . . . . asked him some

questions about his policies, told him I would like better to understand him if I could, and he made me quite a speech.

When asked whether it had occurred to him that because of the contract with the German I.G. he was acting at least indirectly in behalf of the German government, Mr. Lee replied in the negative.

Mr. Lee's partner, Mr. Carter, appeared to differ on the purpose of the contract. He testified that sending advice to the German firm was, in a sense, advising the German Government; and stated:

> The contract . . . . . was an advisory one whereby we were to report to them concerning American opinion in regard to Germany. The general purpose of the contract being to promote better understanding between the Germans and American people.

The reluctance of Mr. Lee to admit that he had been hired to advise the Nazi Government on how to win the friendship of the United States is understandable, especially after examining some of the recommendations which his firm sent to Farben. The following memorandum was identified by Mr. Carter as having been supplied by the Lee firm—a sort of press release which, it was recommended, should be broadcast to the world by some responsible German official:

> Questions have been raised concerning the status of Germany's so-called "storm troops." These number about 2,500,000 men between the ages of 18 and 60, physically well trained and disciplined, but not armed, not prepared for war and organized only for the purpose of preventing for all time the return of the Communistic peril. In view of the misunderstanding in regard to these civil forces, however, Germany is willing to permit an investigation into their character by such international arms control organization as is eventually established.

According to Mr. Carter the Lee advice also recommended that Joachim von Ribbentrop undertake a definite campaign to clarify the American mind on the disarmament question, first by a series of press conferences, then by radio broadcasts to the American people, and, finally, by articles in important American publications.

Mr. Lee finally conceded that his intention was that these suggestions should ultimately be considered by the officials of the German Government, and while he was not making the suggestions for dissemination in this country, they were for the benefit of the whole world, including the United States.

One point was apparently lost sight of by all concerned. The question was not asked, nor was information volunteered, as to whether or not what Mr. Lee was actually doing, as a hired Farben publicity agent, was to outline highfalutin speeches for Nazi officials to send back to America, regardless of whether or not they were truthful, in order to make the American people less suspicious of the real objective of I.G. Farben.

Mr. Lee appeared unable to agree with members of the committee as to just what kind of material came under the classification of propaganda. Asked whether he ever received any propaganda material from Germany he replied:

> It is a question of what you call propaganda. We have received an immense amount of literature . . . . . books and pamphlets and newspaper clippings and documents, world without end.

Congressman Dickstein questioned Mr. Lee about one particular lot which he described as a "tremendous quantity of propaganda, shipped from Germany on the steamship Bremen, addressed to Ivy Lee & Co., New York." Mr. Lee could not remember that particular shipment.

The committee heard many other witnesses in the course of its 1934 hearings on un-American activities, some of whom could also have been tied into the Farben propaganda machine without difficulty if the committee had been so minded. However, this testimony of Ivy Lee and his colleagues was so definitely related to Farben and Farben's part in the rearming of Germany, that it must be considered in all its sinister significance along with simi-

lar evidence uncovered during that same period by the Senate
Munitions Committee.

Appeals which I made to Chairman McCormack and other
members of his committee to unmask fully this "German I.G.
control of American affairs," and my offers of evidence pertaining to same, were brushed aside as out of order. It was also in
1934 that the Hon. James F. Byrnes, who was to go from the
Senate to the Supreme Court and then become postwar Secretary of State, ignored my offer of pertinent data relating to the
unsenatorial activities of his colleague, Dr. Copeland. And, over
the next several years similar rebuffs were received from the
Senate Lobby Investigating Committees headed by Hon. Hugo
L. Black, who was also to move on to a seat on the High Court.

In April 1935 every member of the Senate and House of Representatives of the United States received a brief, in the form of a
printed thesis prepared by Francis P. Garvan, protesting against
the extension of reciprocal trade treaties to Switzerland. This
brief had been prepared in 1934 and was submitted in behalf of
"Chemistry in the United States." Mr. Garvan's authorization to
present it came from the Chemical Foundation and several of
the other important organizations which represented the chemical industry of this country. It was also sent to Cabinet members,
officers of executive departments and others. This brief faced
all concerned with a powerful and unanswerable indictment of
the policy of governmental inaction in ignoring the dangers to
our economic security and national defense which was apparent
in the penetration of our industries by I.G. Farben, and the latter's identification with Hitler and the Nazi government.

The reciprocal trade-treaty statute, authorizing the President to
enter into foreign trade agreements, had been passed by Congress
in June 1924, and among the first countries to ask for the advantages in reduced tariff rates to be derived from such a treaty was
Switzerland, where the chemical industry was completely dominated by Farben. In his brief, Mr. Garvan paid his respects to
those who were attempting to breach the tariff walls that protected our chemical industries from a renewal of dumping by
Farben through its backdoor in Switzerland, and castigated them
with these words:

I say it with all solemnity—that this industry is as sacred
to the American people as the grave of the Unknown Soldier,
and only a traitor or a fool dare touch it.

Of Farben's ties with Hitler he said:

..... the chemical industry is under the direct supervision
and control of a Minister of Industry who in turn is subject
to the absolute will and word of Adolph Hitler, the Fuehrer.
Therefore, in all dealings with the Swiss chemical industry,
the actual partner and active member of the European dye
cartel which is dominated and controlled by the German
I.G., you are dealing with Adolph Hitler.

Garvan sketched the history of what the German dye trust,
its Herman Metz, and its spies, had done before and during World
War I; his own early fight against them, and the efforts of the
Wilson Administration to aid in the development and protection
of a coal-tar chemical industry in America. His paper made clear
the vital importance of an independent and powerful chemical
industry for the United States, in peace and in war; and he came
back time after time to what Farben had done and was still doing
with the aid of its many new industrial patents, its I.G. subsidiaries, and its literary Ivy Lees.

In one respect Garvan's brief was prophetic, although he was
mistaken in the optimism on which his forecast was predicated.
He warned of the time when our supply of natural rubber might
be cut off by Japan, but he erred in a belief that the development
of our chemical industry was a guarantee that we would have a
substitute sufficient for our needs when that time should come.

The contemptuous response of Congress to the Garvan brief
might be observed in the adoption of a reciprocal treaty with
Switzerland in 1936, and subsequent reductions in the duties on
coal tar and other chemical products from that country. In 1943,
after Congress had again "found out" about Farben and Farben's
war, a clause was actually inserted in the renewal of the Reciprocal Trade Agreement Act which purported to deprive cartels of
any benefit from such treaties.

As confirmation of his own warning, Mr. Garvan quoted in his brief from the then-scorned statesman of another nation who was also attempting, in vain, to arouse his fellow countrymen and the world to what was coming. The man who, six years later—when he was called upon almost too late, was to win immortal fame as the inspired defender of human dignity and liberty against the Nazi brutality which Farben had planned and armed. Garvan's quotation was from a debate in the English House of Commons in 1934, in which Winston Churchill had said:

> The great new fact that is riveting the attention of every country in Europe and the world is that Germany is rearming. This fact throws everything else in the background. Her factories are working under practically war conditions. Germany is rearming on land, to some extent on sea; and what concerns us most, in the air.
>
> The most dangerous attack is the incendiary bomb . . . . . Ten days of intensive bombing of London would kill or maim thirty or forty thousand people . . . . . We must face this peril where we stand; we cannot move away from it. I hope the Government will not neglect the scientific aspect of protection of the population, but pending some new discovery, the only practical measure for certain defense is being able to inflict as much damage on the enemy as he can inflict. That procedure, might, in practice, give complete immunity.

This historic premonition and warning from England's future Prime Minister went unheeded, and in America as in the British Empire, professional politicians took refuge beneath a shabby umbrella covered with the flimsy fabric of pacifism, and refused to act on the evidence under their noses of what Germany, and Farben, were again preparing to do.

CHAPTER XI

Two Drug Laws—And Two Wars

ON DECEMBER
3, 1942, the Federal Circuit Court of Appeals in New York handed
down a decision which if it had been sustained would have substantially ended all possibility of successful prosecution of corporation officials and employes for violation of the new Food,
Drug and Cosmetic Act, sometimes known as the Copeland law.

With that decision the court put its judicial interpretation on
the result of long years of effort through which Senator Royal S.
Copeland, with the assistance of the Sterling-Farben drug lobby,
and various public officials, extracted the teeth from the Harvey
Wiley Food and Drugs Act, and had enacted in its place a legalis-
tic monstrosity so full of jokers and ambiguities as to afford no
protection whatsoever against influential violators.

The case in which the decision was handed down involved
a shipment of adulterated and misbranded digitalis, and the appeal from conviction of the president of the corporation which
had shipped it. The learned appeal judges reversed the conviction, and stated that it would be "extremely harsh" to charge a
corporation official with a criminal offense—regardless of his
actions, or inaction—unless he was an officer of a very small cor-

poration. The new law was as cock-eyed as that! Or so the appeal court held. (Later the Supreme Court reversed the findings of the Appeal Court, in a close decision with four of the high court Justices upholding the appellate decision.)

Under the old Wiley law, officers of corporations could be, and were at times, prosecuted, convicted, and sent to jail. Unhappily, the old law was seldom invoked against important offenders, but it did authorize and, in fact, require such prosecutions.

It can easily be imagined how disastrous it would have been to the Farben plans had Herman Metz, or Doctor Weiss, or Earl McClintock, or Dr. Hiemenz, or any of the other Sterling-Winthrop-Bayer executives been held criminally responsible for some of the vicious violations of the Food and Drug Law practiced by their companies—some of which will be discussed in just a moment. And it has long been my contention that the frantic demands of Copeland and his clients for a new law were to prevent that very possibility.

Be that as it may, in June 1933, it was to Senator Copeland that the task of putting through the new law was entrusted.

Professor Rexford Guy Tugwell was alleged to be the author of the first bill submitted to the Senate by Dr. Copeland. This bill was bad enough—it omitted all traces of mandatory enforcement. In the second bill, drafted by Ole Salthe, the Copeland business manager, no misunderstanding was possible—a clause was inserted which actually instructed the enforcement official never to take to court any "minor violation" when he "believed" that the public interest would be served by a "suitable written notice or warning."

As the phrase minor violation is not defined anywhere in the law, it is obviously meaningless in a legal sense. In the administration of the law it means whatever the enforcement official choses to believe it means. And, in August 1935, before a subcommittee of Congress I challenged Representative Virgil Chapman, chairman, to define the word "minor" as used in the Copeland bill, saying:

> If anyone can define the word "minor" as used in this bill, I will withdraw my objection . . . . . I have been asking everyone I have been able to talk to here to define the word minor.

"Don't make me laugh," they answer. The whole purpose of
this legislation is to get rid of the mandate in Harvey Wiley's
law for criminal prosecution, and to replace it with a law
which puts in the hands of an enforcement official the power
to do absolutely as he pleases on each individual offense.

Representative Chapman refrained from accepting my challenge, and instead contented himself with constant heckling, and
demands that I discontinue my testimony.

The final version of the many Copeland bills was passed by
the House and Senate on June 13, 1938, and became law by the
President's signature two weeks later, a few days after the sudden
and unexpected death of its sponsor, Senator Copeland.

In the long and bitter struggle over this legislation, one of the
numerous protests was a brief prepared by Dr. Norman W. Burritt,
as representative of the Medical Society of New Jersey. Dr. Burritt's brief contained the following:

> Let it be thoroughly understood that the Wiley Act is a
> mandatory criminal statute on which have been based a large
> mass of district, appellate, and supreme court opinion. This
> mass of judicial interpretations would be entirely obliterated
> if the Wiley Act is repealed . . . . . This is so important in itself
> as to be the basis for summary rejection (of the Copeland
> bill).

Some of the story of the Food and Drugs law has been told
in a book* published by my wife and myself in 1935. Dr. Harry
Elmer Barnes concluded a review of that book with the comment
that his column was

> . . . . . not the place to pass any verdict upon the charges
> preferred by Mr. Ambruster, but it is evident that they can-
> not be overlooked. Either he should be prosecuted for crim-
> inal libel, or those whom he denounces should be relentlessly
> exposed and properly punished.

Being in complete agreement with Dr. Barnes, I wrote to the
three individuals who were principally denounced in my book,

* "Why Not Enforce the Laws We Already Have?"

and requested them to prosecute me for criminal libel should any of them feel that my accusations were false and unjustified. The three were Dr. Morris Fishbein, editor of the *Journal of the American Medical Association;* Walter G. Campbell, Chief of the Food and Drug Administration, and Dr. Royal S. Copeland, United States Senator.

It would take another volume as large, or larger, than this one to tell the full story of the legislative battle to repeal the Wiley law. However, it is only necessary here to outline briefly those parts of the fight which bear directly upon the immunity accorded Farben's drug and patent medicine affiliates.

When the campaign for a new law was getting under way, there was a strange unanimity in the expressed opinions of the principals involved—men whose interests should have been as far apart as the poles. Professor Tugwell, the Assistant Secretary of Agriculture, Frank Blair, Sterling's president of the Proprietary Association, and Dr. Morris Fishbein, all agreed that the poor old Wiley law was no good. Said Tugwell: "Dr. Wiley's law is obsolete." Said Mr. Blair: "It has been an effective statute . . . . . but it does not go far enough." Said Dr. Fishbein: "The Food and Drugs Act of 1906 failed largely of its purpose." Somehow they all forgot to mention that the real trouble—and the only trouble—with the Wiley law was lax enforcement.

One of the problems which confronted those directing the fight to get rid of the Wiley law, was the remarkable record which that law had made whenever it was invoked in the courts. The record showed that out of over 31,000 cases taken to court in the thirty-three years of its existence, less than 175 were lost by the Government, or a bare half of one percent. According to several informed public officials with whom I have discussed the subject, no other federal statute has ever made anything like such a record. For example, the F.B.I., with its fine record, is said to have lost a higher percentage than this of its court cases.

To justify the repeal of the Wiley law, a list of thirty-four allegations was prepared, and, believe it or not, each and every one of those allegations was either directly false or based upon a mistruth. This list made its appearance early in the fight and kept on reappearing in committee reports, and on the floor of the House and

Senate until the Copeland bill became law. Among those who issued the list as an official paper, or, at least, as officially sanctioned, was one Paul Appleby, at that time assistant to Secretary of Agriculture Henry A. Wallace. Mr. Appleby posed as an authority on the subject of both the Wiley law and the pending legislation. He was neither.

In 1936 he sent this list, as proof of the superiority of the Copeland bill, to a prominent educator who had suggested that the Department might benefit from discussing the Food and Drug law situation with me. Mr. Appleby's response to that suggestion was to say that:

> I will not join in a recommendation that more of this Department's time be wasted on Ambruster; I shall oppose it emphatically in defense of good administration and proper use of time.

One of the thirty-four alleged improvements of Copeland's bill over the Wiley law was that the new bill forbade traffic in confectionery containing metallic trinkets and other inedible substances and the old bill did not. Another, that the bill pending provided for food standards. The fact was that court cases were then on record in which the government was successful in securing the condemnation of candy-coated trinkets as adulterated under the Wiley law; while food standards covering everything edible from soup to nuts had been issued by the Food and Drug Administration for use in enforcing the Wiley law from the time it was passed.

Senator Copeland made frequent use of this list in the Senate and in public. He was especially fond of the one about the candy trinkets because it gave him an opportunity to emote on the sacredness of childhood, and the grave danger of trinket-swallowing. In an exchange with Senator A. Harry Moore, of New Jersey, when these two ornaments of our highest legislative body staged their mock debate on amendments proposed by the Medical Society of New Jersey, Senator Copeland ended his speech with:

> If we were to accept the substitute presented by the Senator from New Jersey, there would be no such prohibition

as is contemplated by the pending bill. I know that Senator's kind heart and that he would not wish this to be the case.

Both Senators seem to have been terribly anxious that day to have it appear that serious consideration was being given to the Medical Society's amendments to the Wiley act which Senator Moore had introduced. For three-quarters of an hour they staged what appears on the record to have been a valiant fight. Yet, in the entire exchange, not one of the proposals made, or the facts submitted, by the New Jersey doctors, was accurately stated or truthfully debated.

In addition to Dr. Burritt's brief, Senator Moore also inserted in the record a statement which had been prepared for him, explaining the amendments. Within an hour and of course long before the record was printed, the amendments proposed by the Medical Society were rejected by a snap vote on which the yeas and nays were not taken.

It so happens that under the rules of the Senate the bill proposed by the Medical Society should have gone directly to the committee in charge of such legislation, where it could have had a hearing and have been studied by the members of the committee before it was presented on the floor. Senator Moore, however, chose a questionable alternative when he introduced it as an amendment to the Copeland bill, then threw it into the debate at the last moment.

It was by such tactics that the stage was set for the court decision some years later which so discouraged criminal prosecutions of the executives of corporations, like Standard Oil and Sterling, which firms, it so happens, were clients of Copeland Service, Inc.

Representative Frank W. Towey, of New Jersey, made a real fight on the floor of the House of Representatives against the ambiguities and impotence of the Copeland bill as pointed out by the Medical Society of his State. Congressman Towey was partially successful in limiting the most vicious provision of the bill, the "minor violation" joker, with a restriction which forbade the enforcement official to give more than one warning to any one offender before instituting court proceedings. The House version of the Copeland bill was passed with Mr. Towey's amendment in it; the bill then went to a Conference Committee headed by Doctor Copeland where, by a very simple legislative operation the limitation on the number of warnings was quietly snipped off and deposited in the waste basket. This action thus served notice on all concerned (including any judge who may become intrigued about "minor" violations) that its administrator is instructed to continue in perpetuity to issue warnings "please not to do it again" —to the same offender for the same offense no matter how dangerous to the lives and health of the public that offense might be.

Possibly the crowning use of the false allegations about the improved protection afforded the public by the Copeland law was made by Senator Alben W. Barkley, majority leader of the Senate. On July 5, 1938, Senator Barkley indicated that Copeland's law was better than Wiley's because food standards were not amenable to control under the old law. At this distance it is difficult to judge whether Senator Barkley did not know, or did not care, what he was talking about.

No bets were overlooked, and no methods were too low for those who emasculated the food and drug law for the benefit of Farben's American drug front. In the final stages of the fight, the New Jersey Medical Society asked for a public hearing to present and discuss its objections to the Copeland bill. At the same time, the drug lobby, headed by Sterling's Frank Blair, requested a private hearing. The drug lobby got its private hearing —from Clarence Lea, chairman of the House of Representatives Committee. The Medical Society was refused any hearing whatsoever.

When the Copeland bill finally became law, the job of establishing suitable regulations for its enforcement arose. And it began to dawn on those most concerned that as no one had the slightest idea of what many of its provisions meant, and as enforcement officials were now possessed of heretofore unheard of discretionary powers, there was danger that the new law would turn out to be a boomerang. So Commissioner Campbell was persuaded to appoint, as his "technical consultant," the man who had drafted the bill for Senator Copeland, Mr. Ole Salthe; he, at least, ought to know what it meant. Mr. Salthe, by now operating his own commercial consulting business as a successor to the late Senator Copeland, took the job and then proceeded to seek clients by advertising his services as an official of the Food and Drug Administration. And please don't say he couldn't do that—he did!

Under the language of the Copeland law all new drugs would surely be safe because they would have to be inspected and approved by the Food and Drug Administration before they were put on the market.

So early in December 1940, the Farben-Sterling subsidiary, Winthrop, shipped some 400,000 tablets of a newly developed drug labeled Sulfathiazole, which at that time was the most recent modification of the original sulfa germ destroyer, Sulfanilamide.

Sulfathiazole Winthrop had been approved by the food and drug official in charge of new drugs, one Dr. J. J. Durrett, who some years previously had called on one of the foremost physicians of his generation and threatened him with dire consequences should he testify before a Senate committee about the lax enforcement of the Wiley law.

However, as it was later revealed, Dr. Durrett's approval did not mention the "inadequacy of controls" which existed in the Winthrop factory. The 400,000 tablets labeled Sulfathiazole were a mixture of the germ-destroying sulfa drug and the remedy called Luminal, which puts people to sleep. Some of these tablets contained more than five grains of Luminal, the usual safe dosage of which is one grain. So, during the next three months, numerous patients to whom the Winthrop tablets were administered did go to sleep—and never woke up!

Whether any of the Winthrop staff actually knew that the tablets were adulterated when they were shipped—or whether someone mixed the ingredients deliberately as sabotage—has never been revealed. The fact is admitted, however, that the Winthrop management knew about the adulteration very shortly after the shipments went out—when complaints came in from physicians in Louisville, Ky., and analysis revealed the admixture of Luminal.

Yet the Sterling-Winthrop executives did not issue any public warning to the pharmacists and physicians who were dispensing and administering these deadly tablets. Instead they instructed their personnel to repossess the tablets, giving as the utterly false reason that, "they do not disintegrate properly."

Then began a publicity campaign to push the sale and use of Winthrop Sulfathiazole—a campaign which had the cooperation of Dr. Morris Fishbein, in the *Journal of the American Medical Association*—a procedure completely unbelievable, if the record did not prove it. On January 25, 1941, the *Journal* announced that "Sulfathiazole-Winthrop, U. S. Patent applied for" had been accepted by its Council on Pharmacy and Chemistry for inclusion in its official volume of New and Nonofficial Remedies. (Possibly it should be stated here that a vast majority of members of the medical profession regard this "acceptance" of a new remedy as a solemn guarantee to them by the officers of their national organization that an investigation has been made and that the product could be relied upon for quality and efficacy.)

For good measure, and in that same issue of the *Journal*, there appeared a scientific treatise on Sulfathiazole, with a footnote indicating that its authors were research workers for Winthrop, and were advising the drug authorities at Washington on the subject. And finally, as though to make certain that no reader would miss the good news, the *Journal* carried a full-page advertisement: "Sulfathiazole Winthrop Now Accepted." Included was the shield of the council, and the added legend, "Winthrop Chemical Co., Pharmaceuticals of Merit for the Physician." On February 1, and March 15, this advertisement of Sulfathiazole was repeated.

In any event, it was not until April 3, 1941, that the Winthrop Chemical Co. issued its first warning to the public and the medical profession that some of its Sulfathiazole tablets were not safe to use because they were "accidentally contaminated." The return of any tablets which were still outstanding was requested and, to indicate a suitable appreciation of its public responsibility, the company also expressed its profound regret at the occurrence.

The Winthrop warning was an anticlimax. The real warning had come a week earlier, on March 28th, when state health and pharmacy departments, and local police authorities all over the United States, began sending out notices to hospitals and druggists not to dispense any more Sulfathiazole.

Meanwhile, in March, and shortly before the Sulfathiazole story broke, Dr. Durrett transferred his services to the Federal Trade Commission to become its authority on medical advertising. According to *Drug Trade News*, the industry highly approved the way he had handled new-drug applications under the Copeland law.

Dr. Durrett's work as new-drug supervisor was taken over by Dr. Theodore G. Klumpp, head of the division which inspected, sampled, and tested all drugs. Dr. Klumpp's inspectors do not appear to have done much inspection, sampling, and testing on the Winthrop shipments. Seventeen deaths were reported by physicians as apparently due to administration of these tablets during the three months of the concealment, no computation was possible of those who were injured but stayed alive.

In April, when the various official state and federal agencies completed their search of drug stores and hospitals, a hundred thousand tablets, or 25 percent of the December shipments were still missing, and unaccounted for—except by the deaths.

Food and Drug Commissioner Campbell issued a statement. He declared that the actions of the Winthrop Chemical Company, after it discovered that the tablets were in circulation, "had not been satisfactory." "The company," said Mr. Campbell, "had known of the situation in December, but the government was not informed until March 20th. The failure of the responsible officials of the Winthrop Chemical Company to notify the Food and Drug Administration immediately of this incident, has as yet not been satisfactorily explained." Apparently an explanation that satisfied Mr. Campbell was made later, because he never took any action to hold the Sterling-Winthrop executives responsible in court, either for having filed a false application for a new drug, or for having permitted adulterated tablets to be manufactured and shipped; or for conspiring among themselves and with others to conceal the adulteration while they were advertising to the medical profession the alleged guarantee of Dr. Fishbein's Council on Pharmacy and Chemistry.

However, as we have seen, the Copeland law does not require the administrator to ask for an explanation; it merely authorizes him to do what he thinks desirable. And, if he should decide that a deliberate silence which resulted in seventeen deaths was a minor violation, he might also decide, lawfully, that a letter of warning was sufficient.

Again, we have to consider that Circuit Court decision of December 1942 which held that under the Copeland law executives and employes of a corporation like Sterling could not be prosecuted, no matter what they did. Perhaps Mr. Campbell saw that decision coming, or perhaps Mr. Ole Salthe, his technical consultant, advised him that it would be useless to try those responsible. Whatever the reason, the executives were never taken to court. The Winthrop Company, however, was prosecuted for some of the shipments, and, after pleading guilty, was fined $15,800; which sum about equaled the selling price of the 400,000 tablets.

Strangely enough, at the very time when the gentle action against Winthrop was filed in December 1941, a little-known consultant for a new skin remedy was indicted in Washington on a charge of falsifying the application he had filed with the Food and Drug Administration. When this individual failed to make bail, he was arrested and lodged in jail. Evidently Mr. Campbell did not believe that that particular violation was a minor one— the remedy was said to have damaged the livers of animals used in experiments with it.

Commissioner Campbell also rejected the thought that such crimes as leaving too many cherry pits in a can of cherries should be classed as minor violations of the Copeland law. In a bulletin issued just at the time of the Sulfathiazole exposé, there were notices of successful court actions against canned cherries because they had more than one pit per 20 oz. tin; canned peas because they were not immature, canned tomatoes because the pieces were too small, and canned apricots because they were not uniform in size.

Perhaps this is an appropriate time to point out that the Copeland law is so powerful an instrument for the public health that certain of its sections also forbid, and permit severe punishment for, adulterating horseshoe nails, and misbranding ladies' brassiers; and if Mr. Campbell or his successor Dr. Paul Dunbar, really got het up about it he could prosecute a dealer in pigs nose-rings because the premises where the rings were stored were unsanitary

(Doubters please see sections 201 (h); 301 (a) (b); and 501 (a) (1) and (2), Federal Food, Drug and Cosmetic Act of 1938).

On April 22, 1941, Winthrop's license to ship Sulfathiazole was revoked. Three months later it was restored, and the company promptly reduced its prices on Sulfathiazole Winthrop, with the announcement that the tablets were again for sale as "Pharmaceuticals of Merit for the Physician."

Dr. Klumpp, by this time, had moved onward and upward. He had accepted a position awarded him by Dr. Fishbein and become Director of the A. M. A. division on food and drugs and secretary of its Council on Pharmacy and Chemistry (the same council that had "accepted" Winthrop's Sulfathiazole and approved its advertising). And Dr. Klumpp kept moving. Not long thereafter, Edward S. Rogers, chairman of the Board of Sterling Products, announced that Dr. Klumpp had been elected president of Winthrop.

One aftermath of the Sulfathiazole affair belongs in this story. The first exposé came just when the Antitrust Division of the Justice Department was starting its grand jury investigation of Sterling and Winthrop. When I mentioned the adulteration and its concealment to one of the staff he advised me to "keep my shirt on," as drastic action was on the way. This was before he and his colleagues had felt the full weight of the Corcoran big toe.

Time went on and there was no indication that the Justice Department would act, so I placed the matter squarely up to Federal Security Administrator Paul V. McNutt, to whose authority the Food and Drug Administration had been transferred in 1940. He advised me that an information had been filed against Winthrop and that he considered further discussion unnecessary, as I had already been in correspondence with the Justice Department about it. McNutt indicated full approval of Commissioner Campbell, and was just not interested in the Farben-Sterling conspiracy angle.

Later, in July 1942, a forthright member of the Justice Department staff indicated his agreement with my conclusions about the guilt of those involved in the concealment of the adulterated tablets and in my presence gave instructions that the case should be reopened on the basis of the statute which covers conspiracy against the United States. At his request, I submitted a brief outlining all the circumstances involved. The brief cited several conspiracy actions in which jail sentences had resulted for such crimes as conspiring to ship oleomargarine as butter and mixing olive oil with a cheaper product.

A few weeks later that particular member of the justice staff was no longer holding down that particular job. I was told that he had resigned. That Winthrop case was not reopened.

In February 1944, long after an alleged "housecleaning," Winthrop was again in serious trouble with the Food and Drug Administration when the latter seized and destroyed several thousand cartons of Winthrop ampules labeled as containing "Atabrine Dihydrochloride" and "Sterile Distilled Water," but which were found to be adulterated. These ampules were to be used by physicians for hypodermic injections.

Three months later Winthrop was again prosecuted criminally, charged with shipping adulterated ampules as above noted, and others containing "Neoarsphenamine" and "Dextrose" (the latter being used respectively for treatment of syphilis and as a diluent for "Pontocain," for spinal anesthesia).

When this prosecution was filed in the New York Federal Court the United States Attorney in charge announced that batches of the ampules had been picked up in navy hospitals and army bases; that more than 90,000 ampules and other packages had been recalled; that the damage apparently was due to lax control and failure at the Winthrop, Rensselaer, N. Y. plant to keep the apparatus clean, and that the situation had been uncovered when seven persons—one of whom died—showed unusual symptoms after receiving spinal anesthetics containing a Winthrop solution. Other hospital patients were adversely affected, said the prosecutor, and he concluded that the possible fines in the case could total $120,000, if the company were found guilty.

Winthrop's Dr. Klumpp immediately denied the charges in vehement public statements, then a few months later the company changed its plea to "Guilty" and took a fine—nicely marked down—of $18,000. Shipments of these adulterated ampules were found in numerous states as far west as California in 1943 and

1944. And during the period of these seizures, but before the criminal prosecution resulted in publication of the affair in the lay press, Dr. Fishbein's Journal of the A. M. A. was repeatedly publishing full page advertisements featuring Winthrop products —including "Winthrop" Atabrine Dihydrochloride, winner of the Army and Navy "E" flags; with which

> competent medical officers responsible for the health of our armed forces have seen to it that every soldier, sailor and marine will have the fullest protection against malaria that modern methods can afford.

In appraising these two Winthrop cases, as the design may appear to fit into the pattern of Farben, the reader is now asked to look back. This time the story returns to an earlier war, when the Kaiser's armies were fighting in Europe, and the German espionage and propaganda machine in the United States was under the direction of Bayer's Dr. Hugo Schweitzer. It was then, in 1915, that the United States was also faced with an immediate internal peril because imports of the supply of another important new drug, Salvarsan, had been cut off along with other medicinals and dyestuffs.

Salvarsan, the Hoechst trademark for the product arsphenamine, or arsenobenzol as it was then known, had been one of a number of important medical products imported by Herman Metz. As the only known remedy for syphilis, it was indispensable in this country for the public health and for the efficiency of our armed forces.

In June 1917, after this country had entered the war, Dr. George Walker of the Council on National Defense appeared before the Senate Patents Committee to urge that Salvarsan patents be abrogated. Metz, after threatening patent suits against new makers, was finally compelled to renounce his German friends' determination that his country should "starve to death" for vital drugs—to use his own expression—and began to produce Salvarsan himself, through the Metz Laboratories. He also was compelled to permit several other concerns to begin commercial manufacture. However, the shortage was not relieved until after the Federal Trade

Commission and the Alien Property Custodian had seized all of the Hoechst patents, and granted licenses to several concerns to manufacture arsphenamine.

While the design may vary with the times, the Farben pattern never changes and so we find that the adulterated Sulfathiazole of World War II had its counterpart in World War I—when adulterated arsphenamine made its appearance in the United States, and Metz cabled Hoechst: "Spurious and infringing products simply flooding market." At that time, too, there was no direct proof that the adulteration was deliberate.

Another important U. S. patent owned by Hoechst covered the local anesthetic, procaine, protected under the Hoechst trademark as Novocain. Other patents covered antipyrine, the first coal-tar headache cure; and phenacetin, the shortage of which for treatment of influenza had also caused much unnecessary suffering.

Two of the other Big Six German dye companies held numerous U. S. Patents on important medicinals. One of these was Kalle which controlled the remedies known as Bismon, Formicin, and Menthol Iodol. Bayer controlled Aspirin (until 1917 when the U. S. patent on acetylsalicylic acid expired) Luminal and Veronal. The last two were also made in the American Bayer plant.

When World War I broke out, all of the above and many others, were among the "accepted" new and nonofficial remedies of the A. M. A. Council on Pharmacy and Chemistry. At that time the real boss of the A. M. A., and chairman of its Council was "Doctor" George H. Simmons, the charlatan whose name remained on the masthead of the *Journal of the American Medical Association* until he died in 1937.

When Simmons withdrew from the limelight in 1924, and Dr. Fishbein took his place, the German I.G. Dyes owned the Big Six and its drug fronts here had been Americanized under the names of Sterling, Winthrop and the Bayer Co. of New York. The names, but not the pattern, had changed.

There is no implication here that some of the German dye-trust medicinals thus "accepted" by the A. M. A. Council are not useful in the relief of human sufferings. The most objectionable feature of these acceptances is that they made it possible to charge excessive prices, and that the resulting tremendous profits were used to help finance subversive activities in the United States before and during two World Wars.

Also, the A. M. A. guarantees served as a cover for violations of the food and drug laws, and the false advertising laws long before the Sulfathiazole affair. Many of these violations by Farben affiliates remain concealed in official files where they were placed by Mr. Campbell, in "permanent abeyance," and without court action. However, some did reach the light of day.

For example, in 1928, shortly after the Cook Laboratories came into the Farben-Sterling-Metz family, a prosecution was started against that company for having shipped a long list of so-called ethical and official remedies which were adulterated and misbranded under the Wiley law. For years this case was shelved, and ignored by all concerned. Then, in 1932, something slipped. Cook Laboratories pleaded guilty, and was fined $750. The penalties, under the Wiley law, could have been more than $5,000 and a good many years in jail for some of the executives. Meanwhile, Cook Laboratories' remedies remained in the New and Nonofficial list as "accepted."

In 1936, in California, a criminal prosecution was brought under the Wiley law for shipments of adulterated Amidopyrine tablets, Novocain ampules, and another medicinal by a local company which pleaded guilty and was fined. The Novocain ampules were identified as the Metz Laboratories' brand, and the charge was that the ampules contained a greater quantity of Novocain than the label stated (i.e., an overdose). Why the prosecution was brought against the shipper instead of Metz or Winthrop was not explained.

It seems preposterous that the U. S. Patent Laws could have been utilized to injure the public health and the health of our armed forces before and during World War I. Even more outrageout it is that precisely the same thing has been allowed to happen in this war—when the Farben-Sterling ownership of Winthrop used its patents on Atabrine to restrict the production of that remedy for malaria after Japan had cut off our supply of quinine from the Dutch East Indies.

The history of the drug called Atabrine goes back to the experiments of the young English chemist Perkin almost a century ago, as mentioned in Chapter I, when the attempt to make synthetic quinine from coal tar resulted in the discovery of coal-tar dyes.

It was in 1927 that Farben chemists first thought they had perfected quinine synthesis from a coal tar base. However, this product, called Plasmochin, was only partially efficient for malaria control; it did kill the germs but it did not cure the disease. So the research continued and Quinacrine Hydrochloride, now sold as Atabrine, was discovered some five years later. In the early thirties Atabrine was introduced in the United States as a Winthrop product. But it was made by Farben—all Winthrop did was to put it in ampules or to compress it into tablets and distribute the new remedy under its own label as made in America.

It should be unnecessary here to go into the history of malaria from the time when its epidemics played a part in the destruction of Athens and Rome, to its present ravages upon the health and lives of a large percentage of the world's population.

According to the National Institute of Health it is estimated that under normal, or pre-war conditions, not less than 500,000,000 persons suffer yearly from malaria. Others estimate that one-third of the population of the globe is afflicted with this disease.

As illustrative of its importance to the national defense, the annual report of the Surgeon General of the United States Army in 1941 indicates that hospitalization of enlisted men for malaria in Panama and the Philippines has been well over 100 for each 1000 stationed there. Under these conditions the grave danger to the health and efficiency of thousands of men in the Army and Navy, many of whom were never previously exposed to malaria, is obvious.

It may be added that this story is not the place to present or argue the merits of Atabrine as compared with quinine. It is necessary, however, in appraising its place in the Farben pattern, to record the fact that a wide discrepancy in medical opinion has been revealed regarding the merits of Atabrine as a malaria remedy. Possibly the highest point in the controversy is to be found in a voluminous treatise on the subject by Dr. Aubrey H. Hamilton, Lieutenant Commander in the United States Navy, who returned to Washington when the war started, after twenty years of clinical observations of the incidence and treatment of malaria in the tropics. The treatise was prepared and published under the auspices of the Board of Economic Warfare and the Department of Commerce. In it Dr. Hamilton left no doubt as to his own findings, and those of numerous other medical men, that Atabrine, as it was then made, presented no advantages over quinine in the treatment of malaria, and had certain toxic properties which had to be eliminated through change in its formula before its final acceptance as anything but an emergency substitute for the older remedy.

Back in 1935, when Atabrine was first being tried out in the United States on a large scale, medical authorities reported that mental disturbances followed its use. The public relations experts of Sterling neither conceded this fault possible nor mentioned it. They contented themselves with statements issued either directly or through sources not readily identified as friendly which enlarged upon the tremendous expansion made in Winthrop's production of Atabrine for national defense purposes, and the reduction in selling price to a figure less than one-tenth of that which was charged before the war (and before the subversive tie-up of Winthrop with Farben was officially exposed).

One notable example of this kind of publicity was a full-page Winthrop advertisement in the daily press and various lay journals in December 1942 and January 1943 proclaiming the receipt of the Army and Navy "E." One Joseph Jacobs, head of an advertising organization, then sent out full size reprints of this advertisement to professional men. Mr. Jacobs also made similar distribution of copies of a letter addressed to him by Edward S. Rogers, Sterling's Chairman of the Board, in which the latter dwelt upon the foresight of Winthrop in starting to make Atabrine in October 1940 out of domestic raw materials (when they no longer were obtainable from Farben) and in increasing the production (when the government so instructed).

The Rogers letter, nine long pages, proved the case for Winthrop by references to praises which had been heaped upon its performances by various individuals, including Dr. Morris Fishbein, who was to preside at the Army-Navy "E" ceremony and by Dr. Paul de Kruif, the author, who had just published an article in

Readers' Digest which lauded Winthrop's Atabrine as a major victory for the United Nations.

By something of a coincidence the Rogers reference to the Readers' Digest article was being circulated among anti-Farben professional men at the very time that I was in correspondence with de Kruif about that same article. I had written him on December 24, 1942, to ask whether his source of data was the Sterling-Winthrop press agent, one Mermey of the firm of Baldwin, Beech and Mermey (of whom more later). I also asked Dr. de Kruif whether he was familiar with the official record of Winthrop's lack of manufacturing integrity as illustrated by the Sulfathiazole horror; or of the relations of Dr. Fishbein with Winthrop; or of the pro-Nazi interests of the Sterling-Winthrop personnel.

To my surprise and gratification, de Kruif replied on December 31, 1942 that he had sent my serious charges to his friend Dr. T. G. Klumpp, President of Winthrop:

> I shall forward his reply to you when it comes. I am asking him to answer your charges one by one and in detail.

For the moment I thought I had drawn a bit of blood. However, something, or somebody, caused Dr. de Kruif to change his mind. In a later letter he intimated that I was being influenced by the Dutch quinine syndicate (which was a rather absurd assumption), and he resolutely declined to advise me what reply Dr. Klumpp had made to him relative to my accusations about the integrity of Winthrop, its manufacturing record, its officers and its employees.

Later it was recalled to me that Dr. de Kruif had been an early propagandist for Winthrop and Farben's Atabrine, back in 1938, when he published an article in the Saturday Evening Post which boasted of the triumph of the German dye trust in producing a new medicine so much better than quinine that it was no longer a question, "whether we can wipe malaria out of the United States," but, "will we?" (It appears that either we could not or we would not).

Meanwhile a battle in official circles to force open the Farben patent on Atabrine had resulted in bitter clashes between the administration officials of the highest rank at Washington, and efforts in the Senate and the House of Representatives to conduct an investigation of the matter had resulted in threats and other types of coercion to prevent exposing the fact that the supply of this important medicinal was not all that it should have been.

Senator Bone, Chairman of the Senate Committee on Patents, announced to the press on April 12, 1942 that the hearings which were to begin next day into restrictions on the use of Farben-owned patents would include the subject of synthetic quinine. But Senator Bone was in error. He was never permitted to open up his hearings of any feature of the Farben tie-ups with Sterling or Winthrop. His hands were tied although his committee subpoena reached into the Anti-Trust Division of the Justice Department and seized over twenty-five thousand documents from the Sterling files and elsewhere, which revealed the details relative to Atabrine, as well as other facts which had been pigeonholed in September 1941 when Mr. Thomas Corcoran succeeded in choking off the Justice proceedings against Sterling.

In August, over the vigorous protest of Senator Bone, five other members of the Patents Committee voted not to permit its Chairman, and its two-fisted incorruptible counsel, Creekmore Fath, to produce a single witness, or document, relating to Sterling and Winthrop at a public hearing.

Having been requested to assist the staff which was assembling the evidence, I watched with indignation these efforts to strangle the hearings. The five members of the committee who yielded to the persuasions of those who were determined not to have the Sterling-Winthrop situation disclosed, were Claude Pepper of Florida; D. Worth Clark of Idaho; Scott W. Lucas, of Illinois; Wallace H. White, Jr., of Maine; and John A. Danaher of Connecticut.

One of these five, Senator Pepper, prior to the vote which tied the hands of Senator Bone, received an appeal from the Non-Sectarian Anti-Nazi League to continue the hearings of the Patents Committee on the "patent and cartel connection between American concerns and Axis interests until all pertinent facts have been uncovered." Senator Pepper replied:

Appreciate your message and am sure that investigation will be all-inclusive before it is finished. Regards.

The Senator, according to Thomas L. Stokes in the *World-Telegram* of August 6, 1942, was a friend of Mr. Thomas Corcoran and the latter

..... is proudly wearing another feather in his cap as a super lobbyist. He who once started Congressional investigations has now stopped one—one that was due to produce sensational revelations about a corporation with former German connections, which he has been protecting from the government.

The Stokes article went on to describe two turbulent sessions of the committee in which Thurman Arnold, who had been so hot after other German cartel affiliates, took a very different position as regards Sterling Products, and favored dropping the investigation. Said Mr. Stokes:

So did Undersecretary of War Patterson who sat with the Committee, along with Leo Crowley, Alien Property Custodian . . . . . Suppression of the Sterling investigation climaxes one of the most amazing examples of "inside baseball" ever seen here. Suspicions were aroused that high administration officials were trying to duck the inquiry when Mr. Crowley was asked to testify about Sterling with particular reference to the synthetic quinine monopoly which one of its subsidiaries, the Winthrop Co.—still owned 50% by I.G. Farbenindustrie—possess by virtue of its control of German patents— Mr. Crowley kept postponing his appearance. Despite earlier assurances that he was going to take over the substitute quinine patents and release them generally . . . . . he never did . . . . . Questions in a public hearing might have proved embarrassing. So he never did appear.

Another short-lived effort to force out the facts about the Atabrine supply was begun by Republican Congressman Bertrand W. Gearhart of California who made a brave start to accomplish this purpose in the House of Representatives on August 13, 1942, with a ringing speech on the Atabrine production in which he criticised what he called the dark curtain of mystery which had hung over the subject. Gearhart minced no words and ended his remarks with several queries:

> Therefore, Mr. Speaker, I ask what is being done to meet this critical situation? What is our supply? Has the free flow of this indispensable medicine—quinine and its substitutes— been interfered with . . . . . ? Is it true that our soldiers, sailors and marines are today threatened with disablement because of a scarcity of this indispensable medicine? What are our war leaders doing about this all-important problem? The American people are entitled to know and to know right now.

The Congressman stated to me, and to others, that he proposed to continue the fight until an investigation should result, but the subject of Sterling and Winthrop and Atabrine was from then on definitely *verboten* in the House and Senate of the United States.

Perhaps the most inexplicable aspect of the throttling of these Sterling-Winthrop investigations was the part played by Mr. Arnold in his official capacity, as compared with his caustic remarks in private, and, on one occasion, in public. In the *Atlantic Monthly* for August 1942, Mr. Arnold published an article relative to reform of the patent law which he considered necessary and in this he discussed the control of the Atabrine patent by I.G. Farben as:

> The spectacle of the production of this essential drug, left so long to the secret manipulation of a German-American combination during a period when Germany was preparing for war against us, is too shocking to need elaboration.

Shortly after Mr. Arnold had made this vigorous statement he was himself sitting in with the hush-hush Senators in the Patents Committee.

About this time I was taken to the office of the Alien Property Custodian by a member of the Justice Department staff, and requested to give them such assistance as my knowledge of the Farben situation might permit. I was informed that the Custodian had seized 50 percent of the stock of Winthrop but had 100 per-

cent control over its Atabrine patent. Also. that a contract which
had been given to Merck to make Atabrine constituted a license
(which it did not), and that no further licenses would be given
because there was no necessity for them. Several other rather peculiar allegations were made to me on that visit.

Six months later, after rather extended and unproductive correspondence with the members of the Custodian's staff I paid another call at that office. And as the acute shortage in the supply
of Atabrine had by then reached a critical stage, I asked what
they proposed to do about it. I was informed curtly that there
was no shortage; that Winthrop was producing all the Atabrine
that was needed; and that anyone who made such a statement
was, in plain language, a liar.

However, at that time it was common knowledge in Washington
that a shortage did exist, and that allotments of this vital drug for
the Army and Navy, and for the extension of malaria control in
Latin America, had been necessarily reduced.

Several months previously then Surgeon General of the Navy,
Rear Admiral Ross T. McIntyre, issued an urgent appeal to the
pharmacists of the United States asking them to collect and do-
nate all available supplies of quinine which they might have in
reserve stocks in their dispensaries. In that appeal Admiral Mc-
Intyre made this statement:

> Although Atabrine is a very valuable antimalaria drug,
> there are many individuals in whom quinine is still the drug
> of choice and in certain cases it is life-saving and cannot be
> replaced by synthetic drugs . . . . . the need for more quinine
> is becoming increasingly urgent as the number of men fight-
> ing in malarial regions increases and the stock pile dwindles.

Under these circumstances something had to give way, even
though the most serious aspects of the shortage were given no
official publicity. Beginning in January 1943, long after the shortage had become acute, arrangements were made quietly by which
ten other manufacturers were instructed by the government to
begin at once the production of Quinacrine Hydrochloride: some
to make the base material; others to process it through the inter-

mediate steps; and others to put it into tablets for distribution to the armed forces, and as Lend-Lease supplies for Latin America.

The new Atabrine mess rescue squad now included, in addition to Merck, the following: Abbott Laboratories, American Home Products Co.; Hilton Davis Co.; Eli Lilly & Co.; William S. Merrell & Co.; National Aniline & Chemical Co.; Pharma Chemical Corp.; Sharpless Chemicals Co.; E. R. Squibb & Sons, and Frederick Stearns & Co.

None of these were given licenses permitting sale to the public. This monopoly was still reserved to Winthrop. The newcomers were merely given contracts to contribute to the huge government requirements for Atabrine which Winthrop had failed so tragically to supply. It is of interest here that among those thus invited to participate in the official Atabrine pie were concerns which allegedly have had relations with I.G. Farben or with Sterling.

Next to Sterling, American Home Products was the largest patent medicine and cosmetic combination in the country, the Weiss and the Diebold families have been among the largest stockholders. The Merrell company is owned outright by Vick Chemical, one of the Farben-Sterling affiliates in Drug Inc. Abbott and Squibb were reported to have had negotiations with Farben during the Drug, Inc., period; while National Aniline & Chemical, with its owner, Allied Chemical and Dye, were both among those indicted in 1942 for conspiracy with I.G. Farben in the dyestuff industry.

And the hush-hush continued. One F. J. Stock, a division chief of the War Production Board, who handled the Atabrine expansion program, felt the strange necessity of keeping the whole affair an official secret.

After several letters on the subject, Mr. Stock finally replied. On May 31, 1943, he wrote me that:

A number of the most reputable drug companies are producing Atabrine. We do not, however, normally make available names of producers of critical items . . . . . Supplies are sufficient to meet Army, Navy and Lend-Lease requirements, as well as export and domestic civilian use.

While the shy Mr. Stock refused to name his "most reputable drug companies," their identity was known throughout the trade; as was the undercover row which had been stirred up by the Alien Property Custodian's endeavor to protect Winthrop's monopoly on the quinnine substitute, regardless of the needs of the Army and Navy.

The War Production Board was not the only official agency which appeared reluctant to reply to queries about the Atabrine mess. Among others who declined to comment were the Federal Security Administration assistant, Mary Switzer, who, as ruler over the Public Health Service, had discussed the subject with me back in July 1940. At that time she told me the medical men in Public Health Service were expressing alarm because of the exclusive control the Atabrine patent by the Farben-Sterling-Winthrop management. Three years later, when the alarm had been vindicated, Miss Switzer chose not to discuss the subject.

The National Research Council, which might be considered an official and, therefore, disinterested party to the Atabrine controversy, also refused to express an opinion or even to admit having one. Herr Goebbels himself could not have improved upon the way someone—perhaps Mr. Corcoran—enforced the *verboten* order on all public mention of how Winthrop had failed to make good.

As an aftermath of Vice President Henry Wallace's fights with Jesse Jones on the quinine shortage and with Leo Crowley on the Atabrine shortage Wallace was vindicated on both scores— and then was fired from his job as Chairman of the Board of Economic Warfare after the row between the Vice President and Jesse Jones resulted in the President being persuaded to turn the whole mess over to Leo Crowley in July 1943. Why Mr. Wallace, the official who was right on Atabrine was made the victim of Mr. Crowley the official who was wrong on Atabrine is one of those things yet to be explained.

The humiliating record shows Sterling-Winthrop executives, while boasting publicly of Atabrine as better than quinine, and of their huge production as saving the nation, were still entrenched behind the Farben patent and secretly refusing to permit others to utilize ample facilities for production and research, which

Winthrop lacked, to supply the quantities needed and to correct admitted defects in the formula.

The record likewise shows high government officials, charged with the duty to provide Atabrine to our armed forces, instead were secretly permitting this gross misuse of our patent law and defending Winthrop against all comers, while publicly they covered up the facts—and the disaster that resulted.

The horrors of war are usually remote to those who remain at home. However, to the soldier or sailor whose life may have hung in the balance there could be nothing remote or abstract in the story of Atabrine.

To those who may feel it difficult to appraise properly the significance of these facts about Atabrine it is suggested that they project themselves, in thought, to a hospital cot, or a foxhole, in the jungles of Asia or the South Pacific; racked with malaria and near death—as result of a wartime shortage of quinine or an insufficient supply of the only quinine substitute; which deficiency may have been caused by some one at the nation's capital who was aiding in the protection of alleged patent rights of I.G. Farben and its allies.

Perhaps, some day, as one result of the part played in the last war by Farben, and by Farben's allies, will come a demand for new definitions of the words "enemy" and "treason."

CHAPTER XII

Patent Medicines—And Freedom of the Press

the Council on Pharmacy and Chemistry of the American Medical
Association announced that it was going to enforce a rule which
provided that the Council should not "accept" products of a concern which was more largely engaged in selling patent medicines
than in distributing ethical preparations. The rule had existed
for many years, but had never been applied to the Winthrop, Alba,
Metz and Cook subsidiaries of Sterling—not even after the ghastly
Sulfathiazole affair. Yet no firm had as many nationally advertised
patent medicines as Sterling, and it may appear that no firm had
made more dangerous false advertising claims than they.

An interesting light on the attitude of this company appears
in its first report to the stockholders, after its purchase of the Bayer
company. This read, in part:

> Bayer aspirin was introduced throughout the United
> States by the medical fraternity, and it is the object of Ster-
> ling Products to popularize this product to the laity by means

of newspaper advertising and other mediums of publicity. Sterling Products is the largest advertiser in the world. We believe we know more about proprietary advertising than anyone else, and as far as aspirin is concerned, we know that the field has been merely scratched on the surface . . . . . We intend to develop Bayer aspirin not only in this country but all over the world . . . . . we estimate that the earnings of these two companies will be at least $2,000,000 per year, and we know that the future of the business is a bright one.

Mr. Weiss either underestimated his own capabilities or else he had not begun to realize how far he would go with Farben's help. In the next twenty years the gross profit was to increase to more than seven times that estimate. And in those two decades Sterling spent many millions of dollars to popularize the name Bayer, and to hold the price at a level which showed at least 1,000 percent spread between the cost of acetylsalicylic acid and the price that the consumer paid when he specified Bayer.

As the Sterling position grew stronger, fantastic advertising claims were made about the cure-all properties of Bayer aspirin. Salesmen for the company alleged that their employers had ample medical opinion to support their advertising, but somehow, those opinions were not broadcast with the identifications of the physicians who allegedly gave them.

Throughout this period, the *Journal of the American Medical Association,* and its Council on Pharmacy and Chemistry. were strangely silent. And the A. M. A.'s widely heralded reform campaign contended itself mainly with exposing little-known fake nostrums in which few of the public and none of the physicians could have had any possible interest. The fact that the Bayer claims went uncontradicted by the spokesmen for the medical profession was the strongest argument in Sterling's favor, at least in the minds of the public; and many professional men justified their own silence by that of the A. M. A.

It was in this period that purchasers of the tablets were handed the little tin box, or the bottle, enclosed in an envelope on which the utterly false claim, "Genuine Bayer Aspirin Does Not Harm The Heart" appeared in conspicuous lettering. This use of a false legend on an enclosure, or circular accompanying the package, was criminal misbranding under the Wiley law. And while Mr. Campbell of the Food and Drug Administration steadfastly refrained from taking any action to restrain Bayer, another maker of aspirin—a small concern in Little Rock, Ark., was taken into court in 1933 for precisely that offense—for claiming that his aspirin would not depress the heart.

The Bayer advertising was national advertising on a huge scale, and it served a double purpose; it sold enormous quantities of aspirin at a tremendous profit, and it served to legitimatize a huge subsidy to the press of the United States at a time when the friendship of the publishers was highly essential to the purpose of Farben. Such leading newspapers as *The New York Times* held their noses, and accepted the account.

The following are a few examples of the countless indecencies published as legitimate advertising by American publications:

Bayer Aspirin . . . . . quick complete relief—and no harm done . . . . . no effect on the heart; nothing in a Bayer tablet could hurt any one . . . . . it can head-off the pain altogether; even those pains many women have thought must be endured.

Hearst's Cosmopolitan, Jan. 1929.

The fastest possible relief . . . . . the sure safe way is to see that the name Bayer is . . . . . on any tablet that you take . . . . . carry in mind too that Genuine Bayer Aspirin Does Not Harm the Heart.

Collier's, Sept. 24, 1929.

Headaches come at the most inconvenient times . . . . . often it's the time of the month . . . . . why wait . . . . . Bayer Aspirin can't harm you because there is nothing harmful in it.

N. Y. Daily News, Nov. 11, 1930.

Sick headache . . . . . the modern woman feels a headache coming on . . . . . systematic pains . . . . . Bayer won't fail you and can't harm you. They don't depress the heart . . . . . and take enough to stop the pain.

N. Y. Journal, Nov. 5, 1931.

. They don't depress the heart and may be taken freely. That is medical opinion.

N. Y. Sun, Oct. 15, 1931.

Genuine Bayer Aspirin will not harm you. Your doctor will tell you it does not harm the heart.

Saturday Evening Post, Nov. 26, 1932.

Don't take chances with "cold killers" and nostrums . . . . . the quickest, safest, surest way . . . . . get the real Bayer Aspirin tablets.

Capper's Weekly, Dec. 24, 1932.

Quicker relief . . . . . the fastest, safe results, it is said, ever known to pain . . . . . Genuine Bayer Aspirin does not harm the heart.

McCall's, Nov. 1933.

Of course the Bayer advertising was not the only instance of false claims by Sterling; it was merely the most extensive and the most obvious. At the same time, because of its utter disregard for truth and legality, it appeared to be the most vulnerable point of attack upon Farben's American-drug front.

Accordingly, in 1929, I decided to force the matter to an issue. Sterling, I knew, was wide open under both the Federal Trade Commission Act, and state laws. My campaign got under way with an open letter to Dr. Fishbein, which included the following queries:

Why is it that in your "exposure" of fake influenza cures (*A. M. A. Journal,* Jan. 19, 1929, page 253) you failed to mention any of the products of the one large group of brands and trademarks under a single unified financial control, despite the fact that this group was among the most flagrant violators of all the canons of medical ethics in the advertising it published at that time?

Was this suppression because this same unified patent-medicine group, unbeknown to the rank and file of the medical profession, also controls about one out of every five retail pharmacies in the country along with a number of the largest and supposedly most ethical pharmaceutical manufacturers, whose constant advertising in the A. M. A. publications must be very profitable financially?

Will you or will you not list the brands, trademarks and company names of this gigantic monopolistic group or "corner" of patent and ethical medicines and pharmacies, and indicate which are financial supporters of the *A. M. A. Journal* and of *Hygeia* together with the extent of their existing control of the medicine industry and of its advertising expenditures?

As an ethical medical question, what is your opinion of patent and proprietary-medicine advertising which teaches materia medica, self-medication and home treatments by the legends on the bottles, and glowing advertisements in the lay and popular press?

Then in 1930, before a Senate Committee on the enforcement of the Wiley Food and Drugs Act, I took the opportunity afforded by a rebuttal statement to force the issue of the Bayer advertising into the official records of the Senate. One of my statements in these hearings was as follows:

> To those of your committee who may now say that I am going far afield from the enforcement of the Federal Food and Drugs law permit me to point out that a situation such as I have attempted to disclose has always two general motives . . . . . greed and power.
>
> So in this presentation I deem it my duty to point in one direction where your committee may, if it follows through, discover a part of the responsibility for the flooding of this country with impure drugs; and—far more important and menacing—a long arm reaching out in an attempt to control by devious ways not only our health but some of our vital resources for national defense and our channels of public information and editorial opinion.

I repeated this same statement several times over the air—in the fall of 1930, when for a few short weeks I was given broadcasting privileges by a small station owned by a brother of Bernard Baruch. Then one evening the engineer in charge of the

station greeted me with, "Better give 'em hell tonight, mister, this
is your last chance."

"How come?" I asked, "My time isn't up."

"Your time may not be," was the answer, "but the station's is."

"I just got my orders to tear 'er down, and down she comes
tomorrow."

So ended that! I might add here that when I asked permission
to speak on the subject over the National Broadcasting Company
chain, I was informed that it would not be ethical, and that the
management feared that what I had to say might alarm some of
its audience. There was much truth in that latter conclusion.

Not long after the 1930 Senate hearings appeared in print, and
my broadcasting had met its sudden demise, I wrote to the presi-
dents of all the state medical societies calling their attention to
the abominable character of the Bayer aspirin broadcasting and
advertising as:

> . . . . . absolutely contrary to the truth as regards legitimate
> medical opinion, and a distinct menace to the public health
> . . . . . I am writing you this letter to ask what the medical
> profession, and the organization of which you are the head,
> proposes to do about this.

For good measure, I added this postscript:

> . . . . . as I stated over the air last fall, the man who wrote
> this aspirin advertising, and the executives of Drug Inc., re-
> sponsible for it, ought to be in jail.

Copies of this letter were sent to various publishers; one went
to the late Louis Wiley, business manager of *The New York Times;*
and to my gratification Mr. Wiley replied promptly, as follows:

Dear Mr. Ambruster:

We acknowledge your letter of November 17th, and a
copy of your letter concerning the advertising of a medical
preparation.

The New York Times regularly takes up with various
scientific authorities any advertising which is offered to us.

We have recently been looking into this specific statement

concerning which you write. Originally the statement was made to us by more than one physician that this preparation did not depress the heart. Our physicians now inform us that in certain cardiac cases there may be a depressive effect. We have already taken up the matter with the advertiser.

Very truly yours

Louis Wiley.

And for a period the *Times* did not carry Bayer aspirin advertising. Then it backslid. I had several heated discussions with that paper's advertising censor, who described himself as a high churchman, although what that had to do with false advertising I did not entirely comprehend. He never appeared to get my point of view, and I confess I never got his.

However, immediately after receipt of Mr. Wiley's encouraging letter, I put the matter up to the Federal Trade Commission by sending them copies of the correspondence with Mr. Wiley, with a statement that I assumed the Commission would immediately institute proceedings to stop that kind of advertising. I also offered to submit additional data. My assumption of immediate action was incorrect. All that the Commission instituted, so far as Bayer was concerned, was two-and-a-half years of procrastination and evasion.

Meanwhile my letters to the state medical societies had brought a few responses. In one of them, a president of the Kansas Medical Society, Dr. L. F. Barney, assured me that he was wholly in accord with my reference to criminal advertising, and that due to such advertising, far too much aspirin was being taken.

Another state society president, Dr. Arthur S. Fort, of Atlanta, Ga., advised me that there were regularly organized agencies of the Government, and the American Medical Association, to handle such matters and that he would await their instructions before acting. Apparently these agencies instructed the good doctor to forget it.

In December 1931, I began needling the National Broadcasting Company stations that carried the Bayer Program, and, for good measure, threw in some pointed comments about Dr. Fishbein and Dr. Copeland. The latter at that time was on the air for Sterling's

Milk of Magnesia which was sold to the public as Phillips, the name of its original producer. My first letters to the stations concluded with the following:

> Won't you also advise me whether you are handling the N.B.C. hookup for the women in the week-day morning hours when that Senatorial medical faker, Royal S. Copeland, is handing out propaganda for this same Drug, Inc., concealed under the title "Health Clinics"?
>
> You are at liberty to read this letter over your station if you so desire.

Those stations that did not reply promptly to my first letter received a follow up which repeated my challenge to Drug, Inc., to produce a single reputable member of the medical profession who would publicly defend the allegations made on behalf of Bayer.

With the first of these letters the fun began in earnest, with the honors undoubtedly going to one Clarence G. Cosby of Station KWK, St. Louis, Mo., who headed his letter:

> Re Criminal Aspirin Broadcasting
>
> This station does not broadcast the Bayer aspirin account or Senatorial medical faker, Royal S. Copeland.

One other station, KGA, of Spokane, Wash., indicated that the matter had been taken up with NBC and, for the time being, Bayer advertising was not being released over that station.

Others, however, were critical or querulous of my intrusion, and my motive in the matter gave them more concern than the falsehoods they were sponsoring. Some of the replies were intriguing, and a few are worthy of brief note here:

> The Secretary of the Maine Medical Association (advises) that your claim as regards the ethics of aspirin advertising from a medical standpoint, do not hold in this territory at least. *Eastland Station, Portland, Me.*

> See nothing criminal about either the aspirin or the programs in which Copeland is featured. *WEBC, Superior, Wis.*

Suggest that you take the matter up with the proper medical authorities . . . . . Until you do something about what you plainly call a criminal situation, I doubt that I'll have time to conduct any more correspondence. *WDAY, Fargo, N. D.*

The Bayer's Aspirin program and Dr. Royal S. Copeland's Health Clinic program are very well received and we regard them as praiseworthy. *WJDX, Jackson, Miss.*

. . . . . interested to know just what your connection is which would make these programs so objectionable to you. *WKY, Oklahoma City, Okla.*

I cannot see anything in the credit lines of the Bayer's aspirin copy that could be considered harmful. *WMAQ, Chicago, Ill.*

We do not hesitate to accept any program which the N.B.C. send us . . . . . We feel that the complaint you make is their problem, not ours. *WRVA, Richmond, Va.*

I continued to badger the stations as long as any of them would reply. Only one answered more than two letters, and apparently all that any of them did, save those at St. Louis and Spokane, was to pass the buck to NBC or to Dr. Fishbein.

When the Crosley stations WLW and WSAI of Cincinnati demanded to know my identity and business connections I sent them the information, and added a suggestion that they notify NBC that they would discontinue broadcasting the Bayer program unless NBC and Drug, Inc., brought immediate criminal action against me for libel. That ended the correspondence with Crosley.

KOMO, of Seattle, Wash., sent me a copy of a letter signed by the executive secretary of the Public Health League of Washington which stated that from a purely health standpoint the Bayer advertising was not objectionable. My correspondence with the Public Health League brought no response except a rebuke for my reference to Dr. Fishbein which, they wrote, "seems entirely unjustifiable." Apparently, the members of the league were indifferent to positive proof of injury to the public health. But they went all out to defend the professional standing of the medical editor whose prolonged silence on the subject was the one chief reason why Sterling was able to avoid prosecution for the false and dangerous claims.

Another set of letters went to more publishers, and W. L. Chenery, Editor of *Collier's*, responded in one instance with the emphatic statement that *"Collier's* does not publish patent-medicine advertising." I wrote back asking how he classified Bayer aspirin. And that ended that.

Throughout this one-man campaign, governors and attorney generals were receiving my demands that they prosecute the Bayer company under their rigid state laws. The Governors usually stalled or referred the matter to their health officials. In not one instance was any action taken, but some amusing replies were received.

Governor Pinchot's Deputy Attorney General naïvely referred to the Bayer broadcasting as originating not in Pennsylvania but in New York, and wrote that he would be pleased to hear from me as to what action, if any, New York State had taken in connection with the alleged misrepresentation. My reply called attention to the fact that several NBC stations in Pennsylvania carried the Bayer advertising, and that newspapers circulated in his state did likewise.

The Governor of New York, Franklin D. Roosevelt, referred the Bayer hot potato to John J. Bennett, the State Attorney General. And Mr. Bennett, through a subordinate, advised me that his "unofficial answer" was that the matter was one for the local district attorneys.

Governor John G. Pollard of Virginia wrote me graciously if plaintively, that:

> It is a national question, and there is no legislation in Virginia that will allow us to deal with the question adequately.

I replied quoting chapter and verse of the Virginia statute which penalizes false advertising, and reminded the governor of the ancient and honorable doctrine of States Rights. No response.

The Indiana State Board of Health also had a good excuse; its secretary advised me that that Board "is not charged with the responsibility of enforcing any statute either specific or general on this subject."

Governor Albert C. Ritchie of Maryland, referred me to the State's Attorney at Baltimore, one Herbert P. O'Coner, who in 1939 was also to begin a long career as Governor. Mr. O'Coner advised me that no action condemning the Bayer advertising had been taken by either state or city medical organizations, and that:

> . . . . . if criminal action is to be taken it should be as a result of some action taken by the American Medical Association.

So here again the evidence of criminal advertising, which was broadcast to millions over the air, and circulated in millions of printed pages, was officially weighed in the balance against the silence of Dr. Fishbein; and as usual the silence won.

Finally, in April 1933, John A. Renoe, an able and earnest attorney for the Federal Trade Commission, paid me a visit, and informed me very frankly that more than sufficient evidence was available to sustain a complaint against Bayer, which he said would be filed very soon. Mr. Renoe evidently meant business, and I rejoiced—but too soon. Several weeks later I called at the New York office of the Federal Trade Commission and was advised that Mr. Renoe had been transferred to another "highly important" investigation. His successor on the Bayer case indicated that the subject bored him, and demanded to know what my motive was in persisting in the matter. The "highly important" investigation to which Mr. Renoe had been transferred I was later informed, concerned the possible injurious effect of the iodine content of seaweed, when used as cattle feed, upon the digestive processes of cows!

About that time a shakeup took place in the Federal Trade Commission. Former chairman W. E. Humphrey was booted out by the President, and a new Commissioner, former Congressman Ewin L. Davis of Tennessee, came in. Judge Davis was one of the very few members of the House of Representatives who had acknowledged receipt of my chart and proposed resolution and, as Chairman of the House Committee in charge of Radio legislation he proposed to do something about it.

He did what was probably the most useful thing a man of his high character could do; he accepted the appointment to the Federal Trade Commission, and, in 1934, forced through a complaint against Bayer, and compelled Sterling to accept a cease and desist order, without defense, and thus admit on the official record of the case that every single therapeutic claim they had made for the safety, and curative powers of Bayer Aspirin, was false, misleading, and illegal; and would not be repeated. The complaint also required that Bayer cease to claim that only Bayer was true aspirin, and that competitive brands were spurious.

However, Sterling did not give in immediately or graciously, and for some time the illegal advertising continued. It must have been impossible for the Sterling-Farben régime to believe that such an affront to its power and prestige could persist. Finally, one Sunday evening, my wife and I were listening to the radio to find out if Howard Claney would repeat his unctuous statement, "It cannot harm the heart." The program ended, and Mrs. Ambruster turned to me with, "Daddy, he didn't say it. You've actually done it at last!" But it was Judge Ewin L. Davis who had done it. For once Farben and Sterling had met their match.

The significance of this Bayer aspirin story, as it serves to illuminate the Farben pattern, is twofold; the criminal violations of the law were publicly committed over a long period of years and, as these facts reveal, hundreds of respectable citizens, many of them prominent, were involved directly or indirectly. Some of them knew that such advertising was dangerously false and illegal, yet would make no move to help put a stop to it. Call it fear, call it corruption, call it indifference—this long period of inaction by so many goes right to the crux of the pattern of Farben's intrusion on the affairs of the American people.

In March 1935, nine months after the Federal Trade Commission had started its proceedings against Bayer, and members of the Medical Society of New Jersey were publicly criticising the advestising policies of the *A. M. A. Journal,* the Council on Pharmacy and Chemistry issued its first report on the Commission's action, and Dr. Fishbein, in an editorial, made the first comment on Bayer aspirin that had appeared in the *Journal* since May 14, 1921, save for praise of Sterling advertising.

At this late date, the Council and Dr. Fishbein approved the action of the Federal Trade Commission, and summarized the voluminous medical data long available which proved the falsity and the danger to public health of the various Bayer claims. The final paragraph of the Council's 1935 report included the following:

> The indiscriminate use of Bayer aspirin, as urged in the advertising, is inimical to public and individual health, both directly and indirectly. Aspirin (acetylsalicylic acid) is potentially a dangerous drug and its unqualified use as a home remedy should be undertaken, originally in any case, under the guidance of the family physician, whose knowledge of the personal characteristics of the individual patient can alone render such use safe and advisable.

It is of course impossible even to estimate how many individuals in the United States were injured by the unwise use of aspirin in those years of silence on the part of the A. M. A. It is quite possible, however, to reach the very definite conclusion that that silence contributed in several ways to the consummation of Farben's plans for the present war.

After its squelching by the Federal Trade Commission, Sterling continued to advertise Bayer aspirin on a lavish scale, but did not repeat the forbidden claims. Its revised appeal rested upon the fact that the aspirin dissolved quickly in a glass of water; price reductions also received constant mention. The ads did not explain that the quick dissolving was due to the addition of cornstarch or some other harmless ingredient.

More recently Sterling started a new series of full-page advertisements depicting famous discoveries of serums and medical remedies (with which Sterling has no connection). Only the lower section of the page mentions Bayer—"The Famous Name in Aspirin." In view of the history of the company the choice of the word, "famous," seems an unfortunate one. Bayer would hardly appear a name to brag about—in the United States.

Finally resorting to claims, in radio advertising, that the druggists of America were sponsoring a national advertising campaign for "Bayer" aspirin, and that the price had "recently" been reduced to fifteen cents per dozen; the Federal Trade Commission again jumped on Sterling, in June 1946, charging that the drug-gists were not sponsoring and the price had been fifteen cents for years.

Then, shortly after this unfortunate incident Harvey M. Manss, Sterling's Vice President in charge of Bayer, was announced as the new Chairman of the Proprietary Association Committee on Advertising, to set up rules for decency in advertising copy.

The period of time required to induce action against Bayer, overlapped the span of existence of Drug, Inc., which had planned to continue its expansion and become the American counterpart of Farben as a drug and patent-medicine cartel. Among those tied in with Sterling in Drug, Inc., it will be recalled, was The Bristol Myers Company.

The Bristol Myers advertising presented a number of fine targets for the Federal Trade Commission sharpshooters. Much of it was so fat with absurdity and glamorous untruth that, when the Commission finally went to work on it, it was like shooting ducks in a barrel. Five of the best-known products of the firm were brought down with cease and desist orders; another has been shot at, but is still on the wing as this is written.

Those to feel the corrective action of the Commission's stop-lying orders were, Sal Hepatica, Ingram's Shave Cream, Ingram's Milkweed Cream, Minit-Rub and Vitalis. Action against the claims for Ipana Toothpaste was still pending over three years after it was started.

Early in 1931, before the start of the all-out fight on Bayer aspirin, Sterling had started an advertising campaign for its Phillips' Milk of Magnesia in which mothers were warned of children having been made ill by "bad" milk of magnesia. Therefore only Genuine Phillips' should be specified, etc. The resentment of competing manufacturers, and threats of retaliation, finally caused Sterling to withdraw this type of copy.

Some years later, Phillips started advertising two milk of magnesia cosmetic creams with the fantastic claim that they would overcome a disease called "acid skin" (which is non-existent). Again the Federal Trade Commission called a halt. And in 1946 another action was begun on claims for Phillips Milk of Magnesia facial creams.

One of the earliest Sterling remedies was Cascarets, long advertised as safe for children. The advertising, and the label, displayed claims that the preparation was essentially a harmless candy, and that physicians declare cascara (a botanical drug) an ideal laxative. However, it finally leaked out that a habit-forming coal-tar derivative, phenolphthalein, was being added to the pills without any change in the label or warning that cascarets were no longer harmless.

In 1933, various uncontested actions resulted in condemnation of these new-style Cascarets, and, two years later, criminal prosecution was begun (after complaints of lax-enforcement of the Wiley law). This was the first time that Sterling Products had ever been taken into court in a prosecution of this kind. However, it caused Sterling only slight inconvenience; their attorneys alleged that the complaint was so vague they could not answer the charges intelligently. A West Virginia judge appeared to agree with them, and dismissed the case. Why the government never amended the complaint so as to remove the alleged vagueness does not appear on the record.

Another patent medicine of a Sterling subsidiary on which the formula was changed, and which got into serious trouble, was Midol, sold originally by the General Drug Co. Midol was extensively advertised as a harmless remedy for the ills of women: "Midol is the discovery of specialists"; "Midol means complete comfort for women"; "No need to suffer, no need to be inactive"; "It is not a narcotic"; "It is safe," etc., etc. These statements were grossly false. The label did not say so, but Midol was a powerful compound containing aminopyrine (or amidopyrine).

In 1936 and 1937, Mr. Campbell seized shipments of Midol in several states, alleging that it was misbranded as a safe remedy for women. In all of these cases Sterling chose not to enter any denial of the accusations of dangerous fraud. As these proceedings were libels directed merely at this highly dangerous nostrum itself and not against the maker, the responsibility of the Sterling-General Drug people for it was never explored in a court action. Mr. Campbell chose not to prosecute.

Some interesting inside information about the Midol affair was uncovered in the material assembled from Sterling's files in preparation for the 1942 hearings before the Senate Patents Committee. A record of the minutes of a conference held at Leverkusen in 1935 between Dr. Weiss, his son, and Farben officials, stated that the 1934 turnover on Midol had been $629,000 with sales increasing in 1935.

> The amidopyrine scare has therefore not had any effect on this preparation, as its composition is not made known popularly.

The minutes went on to indicate that Midol was being sold in the Argentine as Evanol.

Another memorandum, which was represented as prepared in Mr. McClintock's office in 1936, referred to the fact that amidopyrine had been placed on the poison list in England. And, on September 2, 1937, according to a file copy, the Weiss Secretary wrote to Mr. McClintock:

> I have just received from Mr. Weiss your telegram of August 31st (re Midol seizures), on which he has made the following notation, for your attention: "this is serious; can you use your influence in Washington to get this settled"?

A strange request to make to one of the financial pillars of the Democratic National Committee which was appealing for the support of the feminine voters of the nation.

The upshot of the impasse on Midol, according to these records, was a determination to salvage the stock already made up by shipping it out of the United States. One memorandum indicated that Mr. McClintock would discuss with Mr. Wojahn, his export manager, the possibility of getting rid of the nasty stuff in the Argentine and Cuba. Another indicated that Argentine health authorities were already aware of the dangerous ingredient in Evanol, and objected to its sale; so the McClintock influence was again called for. This time McClintock was instructed by Weiss to

> . . . . . use every possible means to get pressure from Washington which will allow us to import these old Midol stocks into Argentine. Please keep me informed.

That kind of international team play might be called the Bad Neighbor policy of Sterling—under Farben direction.

And at the very time all this was going on, Sterling's Frank Blair made a speech about overseas drug markets before the Export Managers Club. Said Mr. Blair:

. . . . . a single racketeering concocter of a fake cure can bring discredit on the entire industry, and when the law catches up with him he frequently flees with speed to the export markets.

Which, coming from a Sterling executive, was about as neat a bit of irony as one could ask.

In 1937 the Federal Trade Commission also closed down on Midol, and Sterling was compelled to admit the falsity, and agree to discontinue all claims that Midol was a special medicine, or that it was recommended by specialists, or that it was safe. Those women readers who may have wondered what became of the old style Midol now know the story.

Among the well known remedies which many do not realize is owned by Sterling, Ironized Yeast ran afoul of the Food and Drug people in 1941 for misbranding claims that this preparation would add to the user's weight, vigor, charm, and other blessings. Notwithstanding this official rebuke Ironized Yeast was in trouble again in 1944 for press and radio claims that its vitamin content builds rich red blood and cures low spirits, jitters, and lack of energy. These allegations the Federal Trade Commission rudely denied as fiction.

And, curiously, a seizure of misbranded "Special" pills, and of "Formerly Madam Dean" pills, occurred on July 6, 1944, less than a week after Sterling had taken over Frederick Stearns & Co. of Detroit, a company which had been making both ethical and trademarked preparations. In this case the "Formerly Madam's" pills and the "Specials" lacked label warnings of dangers if used under certain conditions. However the new proprietors should not be blamed for these oversights; and this was not the first time that Stearns preparations had been in trouble with the pure drug laws.

Another huge group of home remedies was acquired by Sterling when it purchased the R. L. Watkins Company in 1934, and soon thereafter the advertising of Dr. Lyon's tooth powder, a

Watkins product, drew the fire of the Commission, and received a cease and desist order on the claim that it would correct acid mouth.

Watkins products taken to court in numerous actions for mis-branding or aduleration, or both; included Aspirol tablets, two Watkins headache and cold remedies; vitamin pills; cod liver oil tablets; and tonic for hogs and chickens. Quite a range.

Among other showpieces of this assortment of Sterling exhibits the parent company was caught in 1943 shipping adulterated senna, a U.S.P. product; and two of its other subsidiaries were in double trouble with both the Drug Administration and the Trade Commission. These were the Vita Ray Company which Sterling took over in 1938 and let go of in 1943; and the W. B. Caldwell Company which is one of the oldest Sterling possessions.

In 1941 Vita Ray Vitamin Cream, another vitamin product for which the label claimed power to produce soft, radiant smooth skin, was decreed misbranded under the Food, Drug & Cosmetic law; as was a Caldwell vitamin product labeled for pale underweight females. Despite these warnings the companies did not reform; so in 1942 and '43, the Commission ordered Sterling to stop ad-vertising that Vita Ray Vitamin Cream cured wrinkles and coarse pores, made its user radiantly happy, and that its discoverer was honored in the Hall of Science. The Commission also decreed, in abrupt legal language, that no more claims should be made that the pepsin in one of old Doc. Caldwell's compounds had any effect on its therapeutic qualities.

Before closing this grim and incredible tale of deceit and lying in advertising, mention might be made of a Standard Oil (N. J.) product called Mistol put out in different forms which have been in trouble with the Food and Drug Administration over a little matter of misbranding, and with the Federal Trade Commission for advertising which did not sufficiently warn prospective users that these nose drops were not safe for feeble infants nor for vari-ous types of adults.

It should be stated here that evidences of many more violations of the Food and Drugs Act are concealed in the secret files of the enforcement officials then ever become public in court proceed-ings. However, sufficient evidence is available in the cases which have been mentioned here to illustrate the indifference and contempt with which Farben's patent-medicine partners have regarded public health, the professions of pharmacy and medicine, and the governmental agencies charged with law enforcement.

In September 1934 a few weeks after the cease and desist order in the Bayer aspirin case was issued, Dr. Weiss announced Sterling's advertising plans for the following year. For Bayer aspirin these plans included 1200 newspapers, leading magazines, and radio programs on both national networks. Phillips' Milk of Magnesia; Dr. Caldwell's Syrup of Pepsin; General Drug's Midol; California Syrup of Figs; and Fletcher's Castoria were among the numerous subsidiary products for which advertising was then announced—to be placed in 3,500 newspapers, in magazines, in radio and in drug store display material.

Advertising expenditures of the Sterling group alone, can only be guessed at. In 1935 the total for twenty years was given as not less than 150 million dollars. In 1940, Sterling's radio bill alone was just under six million dollars. And in 1941 it was reported that its advertising in Latin America ran to about two million dollars.

We know the sales formula of the patent medicine industry: one third for production and distribution, one third for advertising, and one third for profit. Examine Sterling's 1942 financial statements: gross sales approximately $53,400,000, and gross profit (before taxes) approximately $16,000,000. The one-third-profit formula about checks, and it can be accepted that Sterling is one of the half-dozen largest advertisers in this country. We are confronted with staggering totals if we add to Sterling's the advertising expenditures of Farben's other industrial partners in the United States.

Here then, is a tremendous sum of money which conceivably might have been used to exert pressure on publishers to suppress or color news, and to modify editorial opinion. That the same procedure operates for radio stations has been made apparent.

In 1932, when Bristol Myers was a Farben affiliate through Drug Inc., its vice-president, Lee H. Bristol, was also president of the Association of National Advertisers, of which the Farben-Sterling affiliates were important members. The Association attempted to put the heat on publishers who were expecting to share the advertising budgets of its members by threatening to reduce their expenditures unless the publishers acceded to their wishes. Moreover, the threat was publicly made.

Pointed comment on this came from *Editor and Publisher*, leading journal of the newspaper fraternity, whose forceful editor at that time Arthur T. Robb, was always at his best when castigating any suggestion of censorship.

In an editorial on May 11, 1929, *Editor and Publisher* commented on conditions in the drug industry, and then declared:

> If a pharmaceutical trust can use its advertising appropriation as a screen to cloak the unlawful manufacture of preparations which aggravate rather than ease the pains of illness ..... The scandal involved makes the power trust's iniquities virtues by comparison.

More revealing was the radio debate between Secretary of the Interior Harold L. Ickes and Frank Gannett, in January 1939. The celebrated curmudgeon sustained his argument that the press was not free by the charge that the patent-medicine and cosmetic industries, through their advertising agencies, had directed the newspapers to kill the original Tugwell Food and Drug Bill.

A few days later the Philadelphia *Record*, suffering from an overdose of remorse, or from a desire to please Mr. Ickes, stated editorially that much he had said was true, adding:

> We are ready to confess that along with the rest of the newspapers we deserve criticism for the shameful part the press played under pressure from patent-medicine advertisers in fighting the so-called Tugwell Bill in 1933.

The accusation and the admission were clean cut enough to sustain our thesis that the German I.G. Farben, through Sterling was in a position to put pressure on the publishers of this country. Mr. Ickes, however, appeared to weaken his own case in this respect when he picked the Gannett newspapers and New York *World Telegram* of the Scripps-Howard chain as two of his targets.

It so happens that Mr. Chauncey F. Stout, publisher of the Plainfield, New Jersey, *Courier-News*, a Gannett paper, has opened his news columns time and again to my battle with Farben's affiliates when the story was being ruthlessly suppressed elsewhere. And no newspaper editor in America has been more willing to publish news and editorial expressions which have dealt severely with Farben and the Sterling patent-medicine group than Lee B. Wood, Executive Editor of the *World-Telegram,* while Thomas L. Stokes, as a Scripps-Howard feature writer, contributed by far the most powerful series of exposures on the Farben influence in official Washington of any writer in the country.

Nor did the *World-Telegram's* gentle and fair-minded premier columnist, the late Raymond Clapper, ever pull his punches in comment about Farben's lobby.

However as to publishers in general, and especially as to certain very conspicuous ones, I accept Mr. Ickes' accusation, and the *Record's* confession, that they all got kissed—and some kissed back.

On May 15, 1943, the *Journal of the American Medical Association* reported on another defective preparation, Fletcher's Castoria, put out by one of Sterling's companies, with the statement that:

> At the time *The Journal* goes to press there seem to have been three deaths in which physicians reporting the incidents feel that the toxicity of the product were responsible.

In this instance Dr. Fishbein's journal was much more prompt (the news was out already) in informing his professional readers of a medical calamity than he had been during the long period of silence while the Winthrop Sulfathiazole was causing death and injury. In this case it was a Sterling patent medicine that was in serious trouble, and that kind of stuff could not be advertised in the *Journal,* even under Dr. Fishbein's elastic code.

On May 3, 1943, announcements in the press had made public the fact that one of the oldest and best known of Sterling's patent medicines was in serious trouble. Fletcher's Castoria, that age-old remedy, advertised since the dawn of time as, "Babies Cry for It" had suddenly been found to make babies cry at it. And adults who tried a spoonful of the stuff very promptly lost their dinners. It was announced by an official Sterling statement that all outstanding Castoria in the United States, estimated at 3,000,000 bottles, was being recalled. Next day, advertisements appeared in all leading newspapers announcing that some of the supposedly gentle cathartic contained a foreign ingredient which caused nausea and vomiting, and as consumers could not tell the difference between the good and the bad, it was necessary to recover it all. Much mystery surrounded the incident; both the company and Commissioner Campbell announced that it had not been possible to determine the cause of the adulteration or the nature of the injurious ingredient.

Some years before, the label on the Castoria bottles indicated that its contents—"Recipe of Old Dr. Samuel Fletcher"—included Rochelle salts (potassium and sodium tartrate), in addition to bicarbonate of soda and various vegetable drugs and flavoring matter. However, it was advertised as a "Pure Vegetable Compound" for babies and children, and in later years the Rochelle salts were not mentioned on the bottle, although it was still labeled and advertised as, "Original Chas. H. Fletcher's Castoria."

The advertising, especially in the women's magazines, usually pictured a series of touching family incidents which ended with mother inserting a spoon in her smiling infant's mouth.

Sterling, with a blaze of publicity, proceeded to make a virtue of necessity, and the Food and Drug Commissioner joined in with a public statement praising that company for having gone to "unusual and very commendable lengths" in calling in the adulterated material (Each shipment of which was a criminal violation of the law). The Commissioner also stated:

> It is inevitable that instances of this kind will occur even in the best regulated plants.

If Mr. Campbell is correct about this, then it is no longer safe to take any medical preparation without testing it first. However, I can assure the former Food and Drug Commissioner, and so can a great many others, that his statement was untrue; because it is a complete and utter impossibility for an incident of this kind to occur in a "best regulated plant." If proper tests are made to check each step in the compounding of the product, such a defect would be detected before the product was bottled. And if sufficient controls are instituted on the finished product, it surely would be detected before shipment. No properly managed chemical plant or pharmaceutical plant is operated without both of these types of tests.

Mr. Campbell, in issuing this apology for Sterling, evidently forgot his comment on the adulterated Sulfathiazole—when he finally admitted that his belated investigation of the Sterling-Winthrop plant disclosed sufficient evidence of inadequacy of controls in the process by which the Sulfathiazole was manufactured, to warrant revocation of the Winthrop license to manufacture this product.

In excusing Sterling's Castoria offense as unavoidable, Mr. Campbell also appears to have forgotten the criminal prosecution which he caused to be instituted in 1940 against a chemical company for shipping tartar emetic, a poisonous substance, which a shipping clerk had labeled by mistake, "Tartaric Acid U. S. P.," a nonpoisonous substance. The distinction which Mr. Campbell appears to have made between the misbranded tartar emetic and the adulterated Castoria—with error the defense in each instance—indicated either an undue harshness in the one case or a strange gentleness, toward Sterling, in the other.

Mr. Campbell likewise must have forgotten that in 1941 he caused another brand of Castoria (Pitcher's) to be condemned in court for misbranding because the label created a false "impression" and the "active ingredients" were not properly listed.

However, this is somewhat aside from the story. More than a year before the discovery of the contaminated Castoria, Sterling had announced what it was pleased to call a national defense drive in Latin America, the purpose of which seems to have been to bring the war to a victorious conclusion by means of hair tonics and bellyache cures. Unhappily, though, it was our allies who got the nostrums instead of our enemies. Of which more later.

Because Castoria was sold extensively throughout Latin America, and because the blaze of publicity about recalling all Castoria made no mention of what had been exported, I determined to try and find out how much of the adulterated product had been inflicted upon our good neighbors to the south.

The replies from Government departments which might be supposed to have such information, State, Treasury, and Board of

Economic Warfare, were polite but highly uninformative. One paragraph, however, in a letter from the Coordinator of Inter-American Affairs, bears quoting:

> I am informed that a complete investigation has been made in connection with Fletcher's Castoria that has been exported to the other American republics. This investigation proved that none of the exported Castoria contained the unfortunate toxic ingredient.
>
> Thank you for calling this to our attention.
>
> Sincerely,
Harry W. Frantz
Acting Director
Press Division.

My reply was, in part, as follows:

> Statements issued by the Sterling Executives, and by Food and Drug Commissioner Walter G. Campbell, are to the effect that it had not been possible to determine the identity of the toxic ingredient in the Castoria which caused the trouble. Obviously if they have not been able to identify the ingredient which was added to the Castoria by some one then it is impossible for anyone to say that none of the exported product contained this toxic ingredient. Either they know what it is and how it got there, or they don't know anything.
>
> One of the Sterling Company's statements also said . . . . . "It is necessary to recover all *Fletcher's Castoria outstanding.*" "All" means everywhere.
>
> If you will be so kind as to advise me promptly of the identity of the individual who made the statement to you which your letter referred to, I am inclined to believe that I can be of further assistance to you in this fantastic affair.

And then, while waiting for further word from Mr. Frantz, the great mystery of the nauseous nostrum was abruptly solved. For seven weeks, according to the official Sterling statement, twenty Castoria chemists had worked on the strange case of the cathartic that had suddenly become an emetic, and at last had made known their findings—it was sugar and water. Under war-time conditions, the sugar content had been reduced, and the water; well, it seems that, "a chemical change—harmless in itself—occurred in the characteristics of the water used in making Castoria," and that this change, "in combination with the reduced sugar, increased the degree and rate of normal fermentation." And that was that.

Sterling announced that in future their Castoria carton would state that the product was "Laboratory Controlled" and would have a green band around it. The old carton stated that it was "Chemically Controlled." It had a yellow band around it. Great is science!

In theory, at least, all of Sterling's Latin American advertising had been subject to scrutiny and approval of Government officials. And in this connection it is of interest that among the Sterling documents which the Senate Patents Committee had available, and which presumably the Justice Department staff had access to in 1941, when the Sterling investigation was stopped, were a number which revealed that the sales agencies of the Farben-Sterling partnership in South America used the blackjacking technic of withholding advertising from newspapers which refused to be friendly to the Nazi cause.

Max Wojahn, head of Sterling's Bayer Export Department prior to the alleged house-cleaning, was a brother of one Kurt Wojahn, of Farben's South American staff, (as mentioned in Chapter v). In January 1938 Kurt Wojahn was informed by Farben that one of the Argentine newspapers, *La Razon*, which was friendly to the Nazis, was not getting its share of the Sterling advertising, and that an anti-German paper, "Critica," was getting much advertising. So Farben demanded of Sterling that this situation be corrected at once, saying:

> . . . . . for us Germans it is intolerable that this newspaper should be aided by being given such important advertising orders, while the pro-German newspapers either gets no orders or very modest ones.

Max Wojahn, according to these records, replied to this Farben complaint by stating that:

Naturally, we are quite inclined, everything else being equal, to give preferences in our advertising schedules to newspapers which are fair minded in their editorial policy.

The exhibits bearing upon the cooperative blackjacking of Latin American newspapers for propaganda purposes, included the report of a conference between Farben and Sterling officials at which Mr. Weiss is recorded as undertaking to issue whatever instruction might be necessary so that proper attention would be given to requests made by the German Government concerning Kurt Wojahn—as conveyed to Weiss by Farben's Counsel General, Mann. It was team work all right—Hitler to Farben to Weiss to McClintock to Wojahn—and smack went a blackjack on the pocketbook of an Anti-Nazi newspaper. Shall we believe that none of these smacks are ever directed at pocketbooks nearer home?

CHAPTER XIII

Good Neighbors, and Bad

GEHEIMRAT SCHMITZ,
Director von Schnitzler and Professor Herlein, who send their
best regards to Mr. Diebold and you, are very happy over
the valuable support and assistance that you have extended
to us.

With this expression of gratitude Dr. William E. Weiss, of
Sterling received the thanks of Farben's top leaders for defeating
the British blockade by supplying Sterling-made drugs to Farben's
outlets in Latin America where they could be sold as German
products.

The letter was written to Dr. Weiss by Dr. Wilhelm R. Mann,
the Farben director in charge of Bayer, on February 8, 1940, in
Florence, Italy, after an extended conference with Earl McClintock, head of Sterling's Latin American affairs, who had gone to
Italy to meet the Farben leaders to make a deal which would
protect their joint business dealings from injury by the war, and
from certain seizure as soon as the United States should enter it.

Other excerpts from these Farben war-time greetings to Sterling's Fuehrer are as follows:

254

Our conferences were held in the spirit of trust and friendship that you, dear Dr. Weiss, strove in such an understanding manner to create already in times of peace . . . . .

Your and our power will lead us to a solution which will not mean relinquishing our pre-war position.

I view the future with calm, confidence and trust, which will be influenced by you and our work, by our experience, by the strength of the knowledge of our collaboration . . . . . we are living today only to fulfill our duty to serve our Fatherland.

Mac (McClintock) will tell you the rest; he was, and is, a splendid interpreter of your thoughts and wishes, but also a true friend of our common interests . . . . .

May the time soon come when we can emerge from the darkness of these months into the light, and continue our activities!

Dear Dr. Weiss, my revered friend, I clasp your hand! In true and devoted friendship.

Always yours,
Wilh. R. Mann.

Several years previously when America was still being lulled to sleep by assurances that we could deal profitably with Hitler, and that war was an impossibility, Sterling's management had begun conferences with Farben's leaders about the dangers to their Latin American partnership that would arise when war began. In 1938, McClintock went to Europe to ask Farben to sign a document in blank by which, if need be, a transfer to Sterling of the Latin American inventories and machinery could be recorded. Negotiations continued at conferences in Europe and in New York, but when the war began the assets of Sterling and Farben were still hopelessly scrambled in various Latin American countries. Sterling's requests for a blanket assignment were refused, and Farben countered with proposals that new outlets be formed which ostensibly would be owned by Sterling but actually would be operated by Farben agents.

The most active and influential of the Farben pre-war agencies in Latin America were those which handled Bayer aspirin and similar drugs; where, as in the United States, with customers in every hamlet, and advertising before every eye, they created a huge machine, and an effective screen, for espionage and propaganda.

So, when the British blockade cut off Farben's exports to Latin America late in 1939, Sterling rushed into the breach and began shipping quantities of aspirin, Winthrop specialties and other drugs, in bulk, or in cartons and packages which closely resembled Farben's. The Farben agents frequently were not required to pay Sterling for this merchandise. When it was sold, the proceeds were retained—for Gestapo purposes.

Late in 1940 it became evident that the situation might lead to trouble because of Sterling's too direct dealing with German agents. So what appeared to be an entirely new set of branch houses, owned and operated exclusively by Sterling, was organized. The plan was to continue taking care of the Latin American business in Bayer aspirin and other Farben-Sterling preparations under cover of these new houses.

These Sterling storm cellars, known as Farma companies, were actually erected in seven Latin American countries during the first half of 1941, some of them after President Roosevelt's freezing orders of June 18, 1941, which tied up all German assets in this country. This order of course covered all such partnership arrangements as Sterling had with Farben. This was also the period of the Justice Department dragnet investigation into the relations of Sterling's executives with Farben (referred to in Chapter IX) which was halted by Attorney General Biddle.

Even up to the last moment, William E. Weiss apparently never gave up hope of inducing Farben to turn over the Latin American aspirin business (worth a million a year in profits) to Sterling, for the duration, on some basis that might block action by the United States Government. On August 14th the day before Sterling submitted its proposals to the Government to break its already outlawed agreements with Farben, Weiss sent a long cable begging his Frankfurt friends to consent. The Farben directorate replied tersely insisting on fulfillment of their partnership agreements.

The extent of the assistance which Sterling's executives had rendered Farben's agents, and were still arranging to give when threats of criminal indictments became a reality, was indicated in later statements that, subsequent to the consent degrees, the company destroyed more than 100,000,000 pieces of advertising and packaging prepared for its Farben Latin American brigade. The material destroyed carried Farben's trademarks such as Cafiaspirina, Bayer Aspirina, Instantina and Tonico Bayer, at a cost for printed matter alone of $100,000.

The total cost of Sterling's alleged housecleaning, including repackaging of huge stocks bearing Farben's trademarks, closing all of the old offices, and liquidating all of its branch tie-ups with Farben, and its 1941 Farma branches, was in excess of $450,000, according to a statement which Sterling's new Chairman E. S. Rogers, filed on February 10, 1942, with the Interdepartmental Committee of the Government. This was to prove that the face lifting operation on Sterling was not a mere relabeling, but a true reform and rebirth of Americanism.

Sterling and Farben had disposed of over a quarter million pounds of aspirin in Latin America in 1938, enough to produce over 300,000,000 five-grain tablets. But it also takes a tremendous number of Bayer Aspirin tablets to make a $100,000 bill for new cartons and circulars.

A vivid indictment of Sterling's part in the Farben-Nazi activities in Latin America was pronounced by former Assistant Attorney General Norman M. Littell after he was removed from office in December 1944, because of differences with Attorney General Francis Biddle on the Corcoran affair.

Mr. Littell's accusations, as they appeared in the Congressional Record were in part:

> In many cases the funds of this business were diverted from the German agents to spread German propaganda. Payments were made to I.G. Farben's agents in South America and supplies were sent to German agents in South America. The German Bayer Co. in Rio de Janeiro was accused of diverting funds to the German embassy; and Renata Kohler, head of the German Bayer Co. was accused in Brazil of being a Nazi Agent. A new branch of the Bayer Co. of New York

was organized in Venezuela in March 1941 and a German citizen was made the head of that branch. Many of the agents in South American countries were exposed as Gestapo agents, as abundant records in the State and the Department of Justice will show . . . . .

. . . . . every avenue of trade penetration was used for political propaganda, collection of strategic information about foreign countries, and efforts to suppress the development of strategic industries in areas which might be hostile to Germany. As an example, in 1934, I.G. Farbenindustrie and Sterling Products agreed to use their advertising as a political weapon and decided that notoriously anti-German newspapers should not receive any advertisements for Cafiaspirina or other products showing the Bayer cross . . . . .

These actions were carried out under the direction of William E. Weiss, President; Earl I. McClintock; A. H. Diebold, and other personnel, some of whom owed their positions to I.G. Farbenindustrie, which had sent them to this country.

A few months later, in June 1945, Assistant Secretary of State William L. Clayton brought out some of the State Departments secrets when he testified before Senator Kilgore's Sub-Committee about the Farben "safe havens" in foreign countries; where, he said, the facilities for another war were being hidden.

Among other exhibits which the Assistant Secretary introduced were several reports made to Farben by its Latin American agents as late in the war as July 1943. These contained references to the activities of the Farben sister firms in various South American countries, and the ease with which drug supplies were still made available to Farben's agents in certain countries, until things tightened up. Mr. Clayton then identified the sister firms as Farben's cartel associates, or former associates, in the United States.

And in the State Departments' famous Anti-Peron Blue Book issued in February 1946, stress was laid on the part played by Farben's Quimica Bayer and Anilinas Alemanas in furnishing financial support to the pro-Nazis of the Argentine, and in assisting in building up secret intelligence service on the political, social and economic life of the country.

Let it be stated that Sterling was not the only Farben affiliate in the United States which "helped out" Farben's Latin American agents after Winston Churchill locked them inside a ring of floating steel.

There was the old established dye stuff jobbing firm of Fezandie & Sperrle which took over, as a blind, the export of General Aniline dyes to Farben agents who were on the British and American blacklists; also Röhm & Haas as mentioned in Chapter IV, began taking care of the blockaded South American agents and promised faithfully to give them back to Farben when the war ended. Advance Solvents & Chemical Co., of New York, another Farben affiliate, joined in this war emergency relief of Farben's customers. And Standard Oil of New Jersey, faithful unto death, also continued to supply gasoline through its South American sales branch to Nazi airlines operating across the South Atlantic.

It is interesting to note that in arranging for General Aniline to take over Farben's South American business in the last months of 1939 after the war began, two executives who handled the matter were our old acquaintances E. K. Halbach, president of General Dyestuff, and Rudolph Hutz, vice-president of General Aniline.

It may be recalled that Halbach and Hutz were officials of the Badische and Bayer American fronts during the first World War, so they already knew just what to do and how to do it.

A Farben sub-manager in the Argentine, named Alfredo Moll made the arrangements for blinds or dummy houses there through which Fezandie & Sperrle, a New York Farben ally, shipped General Aniline dyes which ultimately reached Farben agents. It was a game of double dummy—one at each end—and Farben took all the tricks.

In November 1941, some one in General Aniline attempted to have Moll, who worked with Halbach, approved by the Treasury and State Departments as the company's representative in the Argentine. This was after Judge Mack had become president of General Aniline and Homer Cummings was its attorney. Every known Farben agency in Latin America was at that time on the State Department's official blacklist. Moll, who was well connected in the Argentine, is reported to have sold out his interest in Anilinas Alemanas, the Farben dyestuff subsidiary, and retired as its manager just before the company was blacklisted. As the Treasury agents caught up with the identity of the various dummy fronts set up by Moll for Fezandie & Sperrle, Moll would then arrange new ones. Finally some of the Treasury rough-neck squad cracked down and put Fezandie & Sperrle out of business. But Alfredo Moll retained his standing, or his stand-in, with the State Department—which, with characteristic blindness apparently continued not to disapprove of Farben's ex-manager.

Meanwhile the office of the Alien Property Custodian, after taking over General Aniline in 1942, is reported to have permitted Moll to act as its sales agent in the Argentine. In midsummer of 1943, Mr. Moll still had friends in high places; according to an official of the Alien Property Custodian's office it was not necessary to blacklist everyone just because he had dealings with Farben.

In supplying gasoline to the Fascist South American Lati and Condor Air Lines, Standard Oil alleged compulsion to do so under the terms of a binding contract, but according to one government official in testifying before the Truman Committee in April 1942, no such contract existed.

When, in October 1941, Standard Oil refused to comply with the State Department's request to desist, Assistant Secretary of State, A. A. Berle, Jr., announced that steps might be taken to put Standard's Brazil subsidiary on the blacklist. Mr. Berle, of sterner stuff than some of his colleagues, used the diplomatic "perhaps" but obviously meant "no." Blacklisting would have been a solar plexus smack on Standard's protestations of patriotism; still worse, it would have prevented Standard from supplying anything to its Brazil subsidiary, either for Nazi planes or for any other customers. The objectionable deliveries of gasoline ceased forthwith: call it voluntary compliance—or shotgun diplomacy, and divorce for cause.

According to other testimony before the Truman Committee in April 1942 by William La Varre, South American expert of the Commerce Department, the two Farben affiliates, Standard Oil and Sterling, were among the few American corporations that did not fully cooperate with Government agencies in eliminating Nazi agents in their operations in Latin America.

Late in November 1941, on the eve of Pearl Harbor, Attorney General Biddle described to a Congressional committee a manual of instructions for German spies which contained propaganda and espionage directions for both North and South America.

Significantly Mr. Biddle added that the Nazi organization in the United States worked ostensibly without a chief; through individuals who might not even know of the existence of other operators.

A few days later, on December 5, 1941, in a public address, Mr. Biddle protested the immense amount of propaganda coming into this country, some of it intended for distribution in Latin America, and demanded identification of "its source and financial backing . . . . . so that the public shall know and judge."

Official identification of the companies and individuals thus accused or suspected of propaganda and other subversive activities in the United States and Latin America, did not emerge. Rather did they tend to submerge under an unfortunate policy of inaction.

However some of the evidence which persistent inquiry made available is revealing—so it is now possible to comply with Mr. Biddle's request of December 5, 1941, "so that the public shall know and judge."

For example, in one of the frank protests by the British Minister of Economic Warfare in May 1941 he named William E. Weiss, and Earl I. McClintock, of Sterling, and described the activities directed by these gentlemen in South America as:

> Financial assistance (which) they have heretofore felt obliged to render to a country which is now unblushingly engaged in trying to make both hemispheres unsafe for democracy.

So, too, the press statement credited to Assistant Attorney General Thurman Arnold on September 25, 1941, relative to the Sterling consent decrees, contributed a ray of light on the subject with the comment about German control of drug outlets in South America: as "one of the most effective instruments of propaganda and German influence in this hemisphere."

When this 1941 statement was issued, Mr. Arnold had before him certain evidence pertaining to the subject which, on Mr. Corcoran's instructions, Mr. Arnold was not permitted to present to the Grand Jury. Lack of space makes it impossible to do more than outline such material here. It is voluminous.

The Treasury report, already referred to, which was originally prepared for an Inter-American Conference to discuss Latin American problems in June 1942, indicated the official conclusion that the "personal fealty" or "close personal relationships" of individuals involved in the I.G. Farben business tie-ups had aided the latter:

> To finance propaganda, sabotage, and other subversive activities in the United States and other areas (Latin America) of strategic importance to this country . . . . .

As an example let us examine the 1933 message sent to Max Wojahn, the Sterling-Bayer manager of its exports to South America from the Farben Board of Directors, dated March 29, in which employes of Farben in foreign countries were told to hold their noses and refrain from objecting to the indecencies practiced by the New Order in Germany, and

> . . . . . immediately upon receipt of this letter to contribute to the spread of information as to the actual facts in a manner in which you . . . . . consider best adapted to the conditions in your country and to the editors of influential papers, or by circulars to physicians and customers; and particularly to stress that part of our letter which states that in all the lying tales of horror *that is not one word of truth* (italics underlined in original document).

Instructions of this character came to the Sterling organization in Latin American companies in accordance with the original agreements with Farben, which provided that German Bayer, or I.G. Dyes, should suprvise and share various expenses, including Latin American advertising and propaganda. Out of that beginning had come mutual ownership by Farben and Sterling of a lengthy string of branch houses and sub-agencies in Latin America, also other agencies owned solely by Sterling or Farben.

The stake for which Farben played in Latin America, assisted by its tie-ups with huge corporate entities in the States, was the ultimate control of both continents. And, unbelievable as they may appear, there are proofs that Farben affiliates in the United States, directed by native-born American citizens, actually took care of a large share of Farben's expense for these subversive activities. Let it be read with shame that this continued even after the United States by Lend Lease and other actions, had allied itself definitely against the Nazis.

The fact that much of the evidence of how such activities were financed by Americans seems to have been pigeonholed in the files of the State, Justice, Treasury and Commerce Departments, may appear to be as bad, or worse, than the treachery thus immunized.

In Colombia, the country nearest to the defenses of Panama, Farben branches had as advisers with excuse for frequent visits two distinguished "American" citizens who were closest to the top Farben leaders—Deitrich Schmitz, as director of Colombia's Anilinas Alemanas; and Walter Duisberg, as "visiting" director of Colombia's Quimica Bayer. Both of these ersatz "Americans" made frequent business trips to Colombia—as the day approached when the possible destruction of the Panama Canal might mean the destruction of liberty on both continents.

According to the Treasury report referred to, Farben placed assistant business managers in its branches in eight Latin American countries who knew nothing about the business but were there solely for political purposes and for espionage and sabotage.

While these Farben activities, directed at the security of the American continents, were taking place in Latin America, a barrage of high-class pacificist propaganda was laid down by the Farben directed Board of Trade for German-American Commerce. This propaganda, circulated in the most influential circles of American industry, finance and politics, included such appeals as the following excerpts from the German-American Commerce Bulletin of March 1941:

And what about Germany's trade with the Latin American countries? Germany has not the slightest intention of destroying American trade with Latin America. Her trade with

the Spanish American Republics has never and never will
constitute a threat to the U. S. A. . . . . . Therefore a side-by-
side rather than a counterplay of German and American interests in South America is not only desirable but inevitable.

In these days when the military conflict is still the immediate
issue, Germany already thinks in terms of a peace . . . . . which
offers unlimited opportunities for the restoration of the old
as well as the development of many new ways for mutually
beneficial trade . . . . .

Having thus disposed of all menace to the United States by
appeal to the commercial instincts of American business leaders
and politicians, the editorial concluded with this tender of appreciation for the efforts of the Farben cartel partners:

There is still a sufficient number of influential people in the
United States who have a realistic understanding of present
events, and therefore demand that America preserve her independence and freedom of action for her own sake. This
course includes the maintenance of peaceful relations with
the German people.

As Farben's Dr. Mann wrote to Sterling's influential Dr. Weiss
in the letter cited at the start of this Chapter: I view the future
with confidence . . . . . influenced by . . . . . the knowledge of our
collaboration.

The high talent of Sterling during the 1940–41 period of pinch-
hitting for Farben in Latin America, among others included
David Corcoran (brother of Thomas) in charge of the Sidney
Ross Company, export subsidiary with its numerous Latin American branches which prior to that time had been distributing only
such Sterling patent medicines as Fletcher's Castoria, Phillips'
Milk of Magnesia, and Cascarets; in which Farben presumably
had no direct interest.

Weiss (who died in 1942) and Diebold, both were forced off
the Sterling Board in December 1941, as result of the agreement
on which the consent decrees were based. Of the others involved
in guiding Sterling during the period of continued cooperation
with Farben in Latin America, and in the United States, Messrs.

Rogers, McClintock, James Hill, Jr., G. S. Hills and George C. Haigh continued in the saddle.

In December 1941 shortly after Pearl Harbor, Sterling blithely announced in the press that it was beginning an economic war against German domination of Central and South America with the purpose of strengthening American defense efforts throughout all parts of the Western Hemisphere.

This economic war was inaugurated in Mexico City with large scale advertising by press and radio and a parade of pretty Señoritas handing out samples of Sterling's Bayer Aspirin which had been renamed Majoral in Latin America; and a procession of trucks carrying enlarged photographs of Sterling Radio stars heard on Mexican broadcasting stations.

In addition to Majoral the Mexican campaign included other Sterling trademarked remedies such as Phillips' Milk of Magnesia, Ross Pills, Adams Tablets, Glostora and Fletcher's Castoria.

As this "national defense" drive to push Sterling's widely advertised preparations in the Southern Hemisphere got under way, the methods of the old time pitch artists were revived and refined, with the use of sound trucks, free moving pictures, and, in one instance a modernized show boat which chugged its way up to river towns in the Republic of Colombia—the advertising of patent medicines being blended in with moving pictures and messages on the blessings of hemispheric solidarity.

Another novelty in the sale of such products was introduced by Sterling's when "bullboards" were used instead of "billboards" as outdoor advertising of its product Majoral, the name being painted on the sides of the bulls that went to their doom in view of shouting thousands in Latin American bullfight arenas.

And in Mexico City it was reported that a parrot was being trained to shout Majoral, but either the word or the remedy was too much for the bird, or perhaps it was not a pro-Farben member of the feathered family, as this psychological warfare stunt failed to materialize.

According to reports, more than 10,000,000 free samples of Majoral were given away and more than one million dollars was expended during the first twelve months in advertising this new aspirin trademark in the press while another million was spent advertising other Sterling preparations; along with several hundred radio shows from Latin America's leading broadcasting stations. The fleet of autos and trucks equipped with sound equipment and motion picture projectors for propaganda concerts and shows increased to nearly two hundred and the Majoral drive was proclaimed as the biggest American promotional job ever undertaken in Latin American history.

As one of the conditions, or Sterling promises, which led up to the Sterling consent decrees in 1941, all employes of Sterling in the United States and in South America were carefully scrutinized, and supposedly those with pro-Nazi affiliations were removed. That some were discharged, and a few in the United States interned, has been stated, but the list has always been an official—and a Sterling—secret.

However, an unfortunate incident occurred in 1943, when the F.B.I. arrested a Spanish Count named Cassina at the export offices of Sterling in Newark, New Jersey, where he was being trained to become a field agent in Brazil. The company stating that this man had been employed in good faith by Sterling on the basis of high recommendations. On December 20, 1943, Cassina pleaded guilty to a charge of failing to register with the State Department as an agent of the Nazi Government, and was sentenced to a term in jail to be followed by deportation. He had been sent to America in November 1940 by Gestapo agents who expected him to furnish information to Germany through letters to his father in Spain.

An example of the official attitude of the State and Treasury Departments and the Board of Economic Warfare was a refusal by those agencies to comment in writing on two peculiar radio broadcasts delivered by Earl I. McClintock, over Station WMCA in June and July 1942. In these radio addresses the former financial aid of the Democratic National Committee told his listeners that he had just returned from South America, then explained at some length why a certain well-informed Chilean believed that his country should not declare war on the Axis.

These broadcasts were delivered at a time when the United States Government was making desperate efforts to induce both Chile and the Argentine to join the other American nations by breaking with the Axis. Such remarks made so publicly by a man reputed to have high official connections caused much indignant comment in Washington, especially among members of the staffs of those agencies engaged in promoting friendly relations with our neighbors to the South.

So, in a visit to the State Department, I asked several questions of one member of the staff who appeared to be informed:

"Did the State Department know that McClintock intended to make those remarks about Chile?" "No," was the reply.

"Did the State Department approve of them after they were delivered?" "No," was the reply.

"What did the State Department do about it?" "We told McClintock we did not approve of it," was the reply.

"What else did the State Department do about it?" "Nothing," was the reply.

Mr. McClintock, vice-president and director of Sterling, subject to the continued approval by the United States Government, continued to hold his job. And Edward J. Noble, former director of Drug, Inc., who had made that broadcasting possible, recently had purchased station WMCA (with the reputed assistance of Tommy Corcoran); also subject to the approval of a Government agency, the Federal Communications Commission, the very Commission which for several years had declined all suggestions that Farben's influence over broadcasting chains required investigation and action.

Attorney General Biddle was heard later to complain to Congress that he had a headache because that body had not defined more accurately the meaning of the word "subversive." Examination of the McClintock broadcast and of the conditions existing when it was delivered, along with a glance through various statutes relating to such matters, might have afforded the Attorney General greater relief from his official headache than could a trunkful of Sterling's Bayer aspirin. The best cure for headache is to eradicate the cause.

Possibly there is no better illustration of official hush-hush policy than the war-time reluctance of the State Department to reveal voluminous reports in its possession regarding the activities of I. G. Farben and the latter's agents in various parts of the world, especially those in North and South America. This reluctance to mention Farben as a factor in Germany's domestic and foreign activities was apparent in the State Department's 1943 Red Book on Peace and War which disclosed Germany's step-by-step rearming; and in its 1943 White Book on National Socialism which revealed details of the Nazis' domestic and foreign organizations. In neither of these publications was the name Farben, or of Farben's leaders and allies, even mentioned. The files of the State Department, it is reported, tell a different story.

It may not be fair to refer to our State Department as Sees All, Knows All, and Does Nothing, but the unhappy fact remains that in the record of Secretary Hull's staff there appeared few if any public statements on the subject of Farben.

However, the State Department did respond with one opinion regarding the distribution and advertising of such patent medicines as Castoria in Latin America. Advertising Castoria in leading Latin American papers as the laxative which "is meant for children," containing "no substance which harms," good neighbor Sterling had been begging the mothers of those babies never to make the "serious mistake" of giving their children any laxative but Castoria.

One Bernard Meltzer, State Department Acting Chief of Foreign Funds Control, advised that investigation of such matters could not be undertaken, and that:

> Neither the (State) Department nor any other agency of this Government has taken any measures which may be construed as approving all . . . . . activities, including advertising, of Sterling Products, Inc.

Which pronouncement appears to be a somewhat comprehensive denial of responsibility for matters which related to our wartime good-neighbor policy, as well as for one of the conditions of the 1941 Sterling consent decrees.

CHAPTER XIV

Again, Espionage and Sabotage

A"... STRUCTURE
of espionage," which made "weekly and monthly reports to
Germany . . . . . They were soldiers in the army of Germany."

So said Francis P. Garvan, Alien Property Custodian, in 1919,
when denouncing certain American agents of I.G. Dyes.

An . . . . . instrument so aptly devised for espionage purposes. Persons were carried on the payroll of the General
Aniline and Film Corporation who were unknown in the
company. There was a constant traffic in German agents who
would be employed by General Aniline and Film Corporation
for a few months and then moved on to other fields.

So said Henry Morgenthau, Jr., Secretary of the Treasury, in
1942, when denouncing certain of the successors of I.G. Dyes (including some of the same individuals who had been involved in
Mr. Garvan's charges).

The part played by Bayer's Schweitzer and other I.G. Dyes
agents as saboteurs in World War I need not be repeated. Over
two decades later another Government official, who like Garvan,

had spent months digging beneath the surface of the activities of the dye trust agents in this country before and during World War II made precisely the same charges which Garvan, in his attempts to induce senatorial action, had first made years previously.

This later official indictment of Farben's espionage and saboteurs in a Treasury report of investigations made in 1941 and 1942, said in part:

> In the twenty-year period between 1919 and 1939 German interests succeeded in organizing within the United States another industrial and commercial network centered in the chemical field . . . . . It is unnecessary to point out that these business enterprises constituted a base of operations to carry out Axis plans to control production, to hold markets in this Hemisphere, to support fifth column movements, and to mold our postwar economy according to Axis plans . . . . . This problem with which we are now faced is more difficult than, although somewhat similar to, the problem faced by us in 1917. The background is vastly different from that which existed in 1917.

The report went on to say that:

> Certain individuals who occupied a dominant place in business enterprises owed all of their success to their business contacts in the past with . . . . . I.G. Farben.

Also that it was regarded as "naïve in the light of Axis practices" to believe that Farben relied only upon the services of those who were actually citizens of Axis countries.

This Treasury report, in discussing the Farben practice of sending spies and agents to become citizens of this country (see Chapter v) stated that it had been found necessary to dismiss one hundred American citizens from General Aniline and Film Corp., including five key executives, three of whom received salaries in excess of $50,000 a year; also that it had been necessary to liquidate the General Aniline patent law firm, composed of W. H. Hutz, son of the only original Bayer's Rudolph Hutz (bobbing up again), and another attorney named H. M. Joslin.

The Secretary of the Treasury, according to the report, had the power to define as a national of Germany any person determined to have acted directly or indirectly for the benefit of, or under the direction of, Germany. To the reader of this story it may appear that this power has not been utilized as fully as might be.

The report described how the payroll of this American front for the German dye trust in World War II, as in World War I, was being utilized by Farben's spy bureaus. Under these conditions any past connection with Farben by a General Aniline employe appeared to be considered, by the Treasury, as cause for immediate dismissal.

Among the pre-war activities of the Agfa-Ansco Division of General Aniline & Film are reported (by others, not this Treasury document) to have been demonstrations of its photographic and blueprint apparatus and materials, conducted ostensibly for the edification of our army and navy authorities. It is said that these tests included the taking of stills and moving pictures, and the reproduction of drawings and documents, of what may have been regarded as "top secrets" of the limited national defense preparations which were permitted by a stupid Congress prior to the outbreak of combat war in Europe.

Complacent Government officials who permitted these generous tokens of Agfa-Ansco patriotism may have felt suitably compensated with copies of the films and photoprints thus supplied, gratis, for their use. And we may safely assume that Max Ilgner, in Berlin, was also gratified to see such movies and pictures of American defense plans as may have reached him through these channels.

When it came to weeding out the undesirables in Sterling the Treasury firing squad was unable to apply its formula and the report states that the removal of some forty-two persons on the payroll (for relations with Farben) was merely suggested. The suggestion evidently went to the Justice Department—and Mr. Corcoran.

If it may appear difficult to understand why such discrimination would be tolerated it should be understood that the German dye trust had immeasurably improved its technic over that employed in World War I both in espionage and sabotage, and for the protection of the more important of its agents. This was especially true in the case of Sterling's Bayer.

During the months following Pearl Harbor, when the attempted housecleaning of the Sterling-Bayer-Winthrop organization at Rensselaer, New York, got under way, considerable excitement prevailed in that town and at Albany, across the Hudson River, where many of the personnel of the Sterling companies resided.

The head of a beauty parlor which was patronized by ladies of the Winthrop-Bayer families was reputedly put on the F.B.I. payroll, and feared for her life while thus serving her country in checking on subversive utterances of some of the lovely patrons whose husbands' loyalty to this country was under observation.

One of the Winthrop scientific staff who was removed from his duties and locked up on Ellis Island was Wolfgang Schnellbach, mentioned in Chapter v, who, it developed, had charge of "testing" the 400,000 adulterated Sulfathiazole tablets shipped out in 1940 which caused so much death and injury before the Winthrop management warned the public of this danger.

At Ellis Island, Mr. Schnellbach protested vehemently that the catastrophe was not his fault—that his superiors refused to permit him to make proper tests on the tablets.

Months before the United States entered the war in December 1941, there was available to the Congress testimony direct from the Gestapo relating to Farben's espionage and sabotage activities in this country and Latin America. This information was publicly presented to the Dies Committee on un-American Activities in May 1941 by the celebrated Richard Krebs, who wrote "Out of the Night," under the pen name of Jan Valtin.

Mr. Krebs, as a former Gestapo agent, testified at length from personal knowledge regarding the part played by the German dye trust in the organization of Nazi propaganda, espionage and sabotage in this hemisphere.

Naming Hamburg-American Line offices, and the Zapp Transocean News Service as mere appendages of the Gestapo, Krebs told how business houses in the United States employed Gestapo agents themselves and also placed these agents in other concerns which were not pro-German. The Gestapo, said Krebs, had its

"Industrial Reports Department" with special schools for training Germans, or Americans of German origin, to go to America as mechanics, engineers, and draftsmen, also as newspaper men and teachers—for work in vital industrial and cultural establishments of North and South America.

According to the witness, the Gestapo regarded any country where it operated as a "hostile country" with which "war" began the moment one of its agents crossed the border. (The country would learn in good time that "war" was going on.) In addition to inducing propaganda which might retain a semblance of legality, the purpose of the Gestapo, and especially of its Farben spies, was revealed by Mr. Krebs to be:

> . . . . . to obtain information about our security (defense) program, and to produce choke points, or to sabotage our war efforts." (We may recall that Francis Garvan had said the same thing in 1919, and that Henry Morgenthau repeated it in 1942.)

Mr. Krebs was specific when he stated:

> The I.G. Farbenindustrie, I know from personal experience, was already in 1934 completely in the hands of the Gestapo. They went so far as to have their own Gestapo prison on the factory grounds of their large works at Leuna, and . . . . . began, particularly after Hitler's ascent to power, to branch out in the foreign field through subsidiary factories . . . . . It is the greatest poison gas industry in the world, concentrated under the title of I.G. Farbenindustrie . . . . .

During World War II there may have been fewer instances than in World War I of destruction of ships and munition plants by explosive bombs but the new technic did largely delay, and in some instances may have prevented, building the ships and the plants.

Possibly readers may perceive little difference in results between the "sabotage" that destroys, with bombs, a munition plant, after it is built; and the "sabotage" that prevents, by what Harry Truman called treason, the utilization of an improved process or the building of a new munition plant.

In August 1942 during the closing days of the Bone Committee hearings the word "sabotage" rang out in the Committee room while Standard Oil's Frank Howard was attempting to explain why a Farben-Standard patent restricting tie-up forbade Standard from using an advantageous process for making synthetic nitrogen and ammonia.

Irritated at cross-examination of the committee counsel, which brought out an admission that Standard did not appeal to the United States Government to do something about the matter until August 1941, Mr. Howard exclaimed:

> The sabotage you speak of, Mr. Fath, was simply a blanket refusal on the part of the German Government to do any business at all in America . . . . . You are arguing that we should have disregarded the limitations that . . . . . existed on our rights. I might tell you that if we felt it was necessary, and important in the national defense, we certainly would have done it; but at the moment we apparently did not think it was necessary to do anything different from what we had.

As indicative of the significance of the use of the word "sabotage" in that connection it may be pointed out that when Mr. Howard gave this testimony the "limitations" on Standard's rights had already been adjudicated as criminal violations of our laws; and the "moments" when Standard did not find it necessary to act extended until August 1941, within a few short months of our entrance in combat war, the importance to our national defense being that synthetic nitrogen was vital in our production of military explosives.

Just as this kind of "sabotage" went on before and during the war, it may also occur to readers of this chapter that in some of the law enforcement problems to be mentioned later another type of "sabotage"—of government—may be observed.

Another incident of the Standard-Farben partnership which should properly be classified as "sabotage" had to do with that other vital military need, toluol. Back in 1920 appeal was made by the United States Navy authorities to the Senate that we should not again be caught short of toluol for TNT as we had been in World War I. But the Senate, and every one else in authority, apparently forgot that warning; so we were again short of this all-important military requirement because, among other reasons, of restriction imposed by Farben upon the use of a new process for producing synthetic toluol which was developed by Standard from the germ of one of the Farben patents on the hydrogenation of oil. Although the process was developed long before the war, Standard's Frank Howard appeared to believe that even after the war began Farben still controlled its use because it did not relate directly to the oil industry. So Standard, in May 1940, turned down requests for the synthetic toluol which the Trojan Powder Co., required for a War Department contract.

Large scale production of this product was delayed by Standard out of deference to Farben until 1941, long after the need for immense quantities of synthetic toluol had become pressing. In World War I toluol was needed mainly for TNT. In World War II its use for TNT was tremendously increased because of the larger use of military explosives, and also because of further enormous requirements of toluol for production of butadiene, an essential infredient for synthetic rubber, and for high-test aviation gasoline.

But Standard feared that Farben might object to the use of this process—and sue for damages after Farben had won the war.

In 1944 the United States was still short of high-test aviation gasoline and Buna rubber.

Instances of this later variety of sabotage have been indicated and it may be that here is the place to include an excerpt from the "Act (of April 20, 1918) to punish the wilful injury or destruction of war material . . . . . and for other purposes," which was amended on Nov. 30, 1940 and includes this addition to the original law:

> Sec. 5. That whoever, with intent to injure, interfere with, or obstruct the national defense of the United States, shall wilfully injure or destroy, or shall attempt to so injure or destroy, any national defense material . . . . . shall, upon conviction thereof, be fined not more than $10,000.00 or imprisoned not more than ten years, or both.

However it was not the above statute but the antitrust laws which were invoked—oh, how gently—in such cases of Farben's

Industrial espionage and sabotage, as were taken to court after Thurman Arnold finally got his Irish up and went gunning for the dye trust American fronts.

General Aniline and Film is amply discussed elsewhere in this story. This Treasury report of 1942 also described the seizure of Farben-owned Chemnyco, Inc., which was incorporated in 1931 as successor of the United States and Transatlantic Service Corp., Inc., a high sounding title that had succeeded a group called the Committee on Political Economics in 1930. Max Ilgner was its organizer.

Wilfrid Greif, a Farben director and also one of the top men in American I.G. Chemical Corp., originally held stock control of Chemnyco and he was succeeded in 1935 by our old acquaintance D. A. Schmitz.

William vom Rath, another of the sons of Farben was a part-time holder of Chemnyco stock and his pal Walter Duisberg included this organization among his multitudinous duties as Farben's chief trouble shooter in its American hideouts.

Among the notables who served as directors of Chemnyco were Dr. Karl Hochswender, who was also active in Farben's magnesium set-up; Carl B. Peters, vice-president of Synthetic Nitrogen, and its one-time president (of whom more later); and the late William Paul Pickhardt, son of one of the Kuttroff & Pickhardt founders who started as an office boy in that Badische-Farben hideout, became its president and, before he died in 1941 had also served as an American-born figurehead for Farben in many of its hideouts.

Mr. Pickhardt was also president of Chemnyco but its real head was Rudolph Ilgner. Each of these four Chemnyco directors, as told elsewhere, was indicted one or more times—and never punished save for the picayune $1,000 fine paid by Ilgner for burning Chemnyco secret files.

Nominally a wholly American-organized and owned corporation, Chemnyco started out with a yearly subsidy from Farben of $84,000 which annual retainer by 1938 had increased to $240,000.

However it was not restricted to this generous budget outlay, the Chemnyco management being authorized to incur any additional or "special" expenses which were considered "necessary or expedient." This blank check arrangement indicated that Uncle Hermann and brother Max had great confidence in Rudolph Ilgner—or else they thought that this might be a convenient method of denying responsibility for expenditures which later could be embarrassing to the Farben high command at Frankfurt.

In addition to its stated income and special expenses, Chemnyco also handled enormous sums while acting as a receiving or collection agency for funds due Farben from various partnership and patent license agreements in America.

Among the services which Chemnyco was obligated to perform was to "facilitate" the activities of such individuals that Farben chose to send to this country—including their introduction to our top level notables, when such contacts were deemed essential to the "accomplishment of the purpose of their visit."

The details of these services as outlined in the agreement may appear sinister in view of some of the activities which have been uncovered.

The Chemnyco staff undertook to make reports and act for Farben on governmental matters, including the recovery of property which had been seized by the Alien Property Custodian during the first World War, or to induce compensation (from the United States Treasury) for same. They also conducted negotiations and liaison relations with American corporations; acted as blind holders of American securities, prying into the affairs of such concerns, and reporting on scientific developments.

Chemnyco was forbidden to do one thing—it was specifically provided that it had no authority to do anything which American courts could construe as the "doing of business" by Farben inside of the United States. Thus its status as a false front was established in pseudo-legal language. However, Joseph J. O'Connell, Jr., head of the raiding squad of Treasury Secretary Henry Morgenthau, Jr., disregarded this camouflage and on December 11, 1941, the day on which Germany declared war, seized Chemnyco as a Farben property.

A great mass of Chemnyco's secret records were burned by order of Rudolph Ilgner after the F.B.I. came to examine them in July 1939, as told elsewhere, but those which have been uncovered reveal in part the comprehensive character of Chemnyco espionage on industrial developments, especially as they related to war-making potentials. The Chemnyco pre-war reports to Farben dealt with such things as progress of the research in atomic fission, synthetic rubber tires, duPont's Nylon invention, manganese and magnesium resources and the annual production of the coke ovens of America.

While the war in Europe was in progress there were compiled, under dates in June, 1941, long lists of reports on research and developments in Standard Oil (N. J.) laboratories and producing plants.

Ostensibly occupied wholly with the handling of patent application licenses and matters of this sort, Chemnyco practised espionage on the secrets of American industry, with results which were of tremendous value to Farben's preparations for war in Germany and for crippling and obstructing preparations for war in America. By its great number of industrial contacts permitting correspondence. reports, and inspection visits which produced up-to-the-minute information of scientific and industrial progress here, Chemnyco was enabled to transmit secret intelligence to Max Ilgner's spy bureau at Berlin. This included confidential data which could not possibly be obtained by the conventional methods of secret agents. As a friendly patent holding company Chemnyco readily obtained the desired data at little cost and no risk, through exploitation of its industrial and commercial contacts. Tons of this material; process secrets, blueprints and national defense plans, were thus transmitted to Farben.

An example of this pre-war espionage of a vicious type in spying upon American synthetic rubber research was revealed before the Bone Patents Committee of the Senate on May 20, 1943. This espionage was directed at development work on rubber substitutes which had been conducted for some years by Dow and Goodyear; both companies had expended large sums and made good progress in this field; Dow already was marketing a rubber substitute which was acceptable for some purposes.

According to testimony given before the Bone Committee by Professor R. M. Hunter, of the Justice Department's Antitrust Division, a request was made by Dow and Goodyear for licenses to utilize the Buna synthetic patents, about which it will be recalled (from Chapter IV) Farben kept Standard guessing for many years as a bait for the lopsided exchange of processes between them, and finally refused point blank, for military reasons, to supply the know how. Dow and Goodyear got a runaround instead of a license to make Buna. An act was staged by Standard and I.G. Farben for the rubber companies, while they were kidded into believing that licenses might be forthcoming.

And documentary evidence was also presented to the Committee showing that Chemnyco, as Farben's patent agent, reported to headquarters on June 3, 1937, that:

> We thought it expedient to conduct the negotiations in such a way that we would continue to observe and become acquainted with Dow's and Goodyear's experiments.

Posing as patent license negotiators on this vital munitions product, Rudolph Ilgner's Chemnyco spies were pillaging results of this invaluable research work done by Americans for secret transmittal to Max Ilgner's espionage bureau in Berlin.

During the summer of 1945, after Germany was occupied and some of Farben's staff were in custody, Dr. Oscar Loehr of the Farben staff at Frankfurt recalled that particular report from Chemnyco on synthetic rubber snooping, and admitted frankly that this Farben front in the United States did "conduct industrial espionage for I.G."

A general conclusion recorded by Dr. Loehr during one of his examinations is to the point:

> Question: So I.G. was able to suppress completely the synthetic rubber production in the United States, was able to use an American company, Standard Oil, to protect I.G.'s patents in case of war between the United States and Germany, and in that way I.G. itself undermined the military potential of the United States, and I.G. itself was able to carry on industrial espionage in the United States using its representatives, its participations and its agreements with American firms, to carry on economic warfare against the United States. Is that true?

Answer: These are the conclusions which seem to disclose that I.G. impaired the military strength of the United States Yes.

Likewise informative are excerpts from interoffice reports between Farben's offices and government officials in 1940, when the Germans thought that the war was already won, and that the United States would stay out of it.

One report, dated August 8, 1940, praises Chemnyco's services:

Extensive information which we receive continuously from the Chemnyco . . . . . is indispensable for our observations of the American conditions especially with a view to the technical development . . . . . Moreover this material is, since the beginning of the war, an important source of information for governmental, economical and military offices. Also in view of the later revival of trade with America, these informations are of importance to us.

Another communication indicates prewar knowledge by officials of the United States Government of precisely what Chemnyco was up to. This report, dated July 20, 1940, states:

We would not fail to mention that the Chemnyco was several times examined by the Authorities in the U. S. A. on its work and its connections with the I.G. and we would like to point out the confidential character of the above mentioned fact.

Some day, it may be hoped, these pre-war "examinations of Chemnyco" by officials of our own government will also be brought to light, and the identity revealed of those so complacent "authorities" who did not act when the character of Chemnyco's espionage was uncovered, especially after destruction of its secret files in 1939. Perhaps those prewar investigators of ours are among the men who expressed such shocked surprise when, after we entered the war, some of the truth about Farben's allegedly secret activities inside the United States came out in Congressional hearings (before these were choked off).

Chemnyco had its headquarters at 551 5th Avenue in New York, and during the prewar period there was also located at that address the Chemical Marketing Company, another hideout of a Farben affiliate, the Deutsche Gold-und-Silberscheide Anstalt-a-g. This American front was incorporated in 1935 as the Frank von Kroop Company, changed its name to Chemical Marketing in 1937, and was headed by a German chemist, Dr. Ferdinand A. Kertess. That individual came to the United States in 1923 and commuted regularly back to Germany without becoming an American citizen until 1938, by which time he had prospered in many varieties of activities and was established in a sumptuous suburban estate in Westchester County, New York.

Dr. Kertess won what appears to have been the exclusive honor of being the only one of Farben's ersatz citizens to be lodged in jail in the United States. The crime for which he and his company were indicted in four different actions on November 6, 1942, was violation of the Trading with The Enemy Act, for which the defendants were convicted in July, 1943. The court fined them $14,000 and also awarded Dr. Kertess six years in jail, where, supposedly, he now languishes.

Farben's connection does not appear in the record of these cases but its war plants undoubtedly were in dire need of the rare metals shipped by Kertess, such as palladium, rhodium and iridium, all invaluable in the production of war munitions and implements. Dr. Kertess made use of a woman courier to smuggle the precious metals out of this country to Germany via a circuitous route first to the Canal Zone, then to Colombia and Chile in South America, and overseas to Italy by plane.

This criminal agent appears to have been deeply involved in many varieties of subversive activities. He was known as the power behind the scenes in the Board of Trade for German-American Commerce, Farben's hideout for Nazi propaganda agencies, which is discussed in the next chapter. According to statements which he made to the Dies Committee in 1940, his Chemical Marketing Company had acquired the Maywood Chemical Company of Maywood, New Jersey, to manufacture a "specialty," which he did not identify. The Maywood company was the long established narcotic producer of cocain from coca leaves and kola nuts. Also the maker of the syrup known as "Merchandise No. 5," which is used in well-known beverages, and around which revolved one of the most bitterly contested court cases in the early years of Harvey Wiley's Pure Food and Drug Law.

Why Dr. Kertess should have acquired a large plant for the production of narcotics has not been revealed. He was also on close terms with the American I.G. Chemical people and was active after the war broke out in shipping chemicals to Farben's South American agents, whose supplies had been cut off by the British blockade. His company likewise served as an alleged American assignee of German patents, in a vain attempt to prevent their seizure after the war started.

Among his other public-spirited activities, Dr. Kertess took a leading part in promoting an organization called the American Foreign Trade Association which, according to a letter written in August, 1939, to Germany about it, was promoting a friendly attitude towards Germany among members of Congress by the employment of lobbyists at $50 per day, plus expenses for "secretaries."

This reference to the use of money by the phony Kertess organization to influence members of Congress as World War II was beginning, may be a reminder of the statement made on the floor of the House of Representatives on September 31, 1917, by Tom Heflin of Alabama, then a Congressman, when it was revealed that German Ambassador von Bernstorff, prior to our entry into the first world war, had cabled the Kaiser's government at Berlin for:

> . . . . . authority to pay out . . . . . $50.000 in order, as on former occasions, to influence Congress, thru the organization you know of, which can perhaps prevent war.

Tom Heflin, later to become famous as a firebrand in the Senate, asked for investigation of those members of the House and Senate who had acted in a suspicious manner by their pro-German speeches, resolutions or bills, and demanded their expulsion if found guilty of being influenced by the mysterious organization referred to by von Bernstorff.

Having placed this challenge to his colleagues on the record Mr. Heflin followed up with some even more crude remarks in the press about "lady spies" and a gambling room in Washington where "peace-at-any-price" members of Congress were extraordinarily lucky at cards.

The only result of these 1917 charges was a rebuke to Congressman Heflin. Demands for investigation of similar legislative misconduct before and during World War II were likewise ignored.

On May 4, 1939, four months before the German army crossed the Polish border, Dr. Kertess cabled one of his friends in Frankfurt that he was "together with friends, ready for war." Shortly after this he engaged a New York newspaperman, James E. Edmunds, for espionage work, which he termed "research," and for which Mr. Edmunds was paid some $1,500 by Chemical Marketing.

In justice to Mr. Edmunds, it should be stated that his activities in reality constituted counter-espionage of a very clever character, and were conducted under the directions of the F.B.I. and British and French Intelligence officials, to whom he reported as soon as he realized the character of the "research" he was to do. Originally engaged by a representative of the Japanese News Agency Domei, who paid him handsomely, Edmunds became suspicious and reported to the authorities. These suspicions became a certainty when the Jap, Mr. T. Sato, sent him to Dr. Kertess, and the latter in turn asked him to contact one Dr. Herbert Gross, described as a German agent, who was operating a news agency in New York as a front. Gross wanted information about American war plants, British and French ships sailing from the United States and Canada, and other espionage matters. Mr. Edmunds accordingly traveled to Halifax, Nova Scotia, on his pretended spying, hoping to contact the Kertess-Gross agent across the border, and supplied his treacherous paymasters with much false data which was gotten up for him by the American and British authorities. He had some difficulty in securing from Dr. Gross the additional funds which the latter promised him, but appeal to Dr. Kertess always caused such financial troubles to be adjusted. The latter assured Edmunds that he was personally delivering the data thus secured to the German Naval Attache at Washington. Gross also asked Edmunds to bribe employees of Pan-

American Airways to supply information about British defenses at Bermuda, and the establishment of a convoy base there, with reports on its shipping.

Finally, according to Edmunds' sworn statements, Dr. Kertess solicited his aid in getting shipments of chemicals through the British blockade. On the record, Dr. Kertess appears to have been a most important cog in Farben's domestic espionage machine. But Mr. Edmunds made a monkey out of this Farben agent with his counter-espionage fairy stories.

Our old acquaintance, Dr. Eugene R. Pickrell, the Metz handyman and Farben lobbyist, reappears in the picture as receiving an annual stipend of $6,000 from Chemnyco on an arrangement that was made in 1931, by which Dr. Pickrell represented Farben's interests in a legal capacity. Unhappily for Dr. Pickrell, the freezing order issued by President Roosevelt in June, 1941, appears to have interfered with the delivery of the Pickrell meal ticket in the customary manner, and Farben accordingly cabled its good friends Röhm & Haas, of Philadelphia, to please arrange a special license from the Treasury so that Chemnyco could pay Pickrell out of funds which the Philadelphia firm owed to Farben, for which Chemnyco acted as collector.

Mr. Morgenthau unkindly said "nothing doing," so Mr. Pickrell, who is not easily discouraged, made another try after the Alien Property Custodian had taken possession of funds due Farben from Röhm & Haas. In 1943 Dr. Pickrell put in a claim to the Custodian for the $4,500 still unpaid on his 1941 salary for serving Farben in his native land. Again Dr. Pickrell lost out. The Custodian's Vested Property Committee decided that the Pickrell "evidential burden has not been sustained."

Dr. Pickrell, like Dr. Kertess, appears again in the next chapter as an important figure in Farben's propaganda hideout.

Among other duties Chemnyco and its predecessors also agreed to prepare, publish and circulate in America any advertising or other publicity which Farben might request. Chemnyco had no publication of its own. Here obviously was where the joint direction by Rudolph Ilgner of both Chemnyco and the German-American Board of Trade became so useful. The latter's monthly Bulletin circulated among the cream of American industry, commerce and finance, as the organ of a group of top ranking public spirited companies and individuals. Farben thus possessed an agency to wield influence in business circles and on high Governmental policies which far exceeded that of all the rest of the blatant pro-Nazi publications representing the Bund and other groups of the less respectable levels of American society.

So Rudolph Ilgner's powers as Chairman of the Board of Trade executive committee fitted in splendidly with those which he exercised as head of Chemnyco.

Which activities his brother Max, head of Farben's world-wide spy bureau in Berlin, was to admit (after his capture in 1944) "might" have violated the United States security statutes. They did. But Rudolph, by then raising chickens in Connecticut, should worry.

CHAPTER XV

Propaganda for Wall Street and Washington

"EVERY AMERICAN businessman should endorse what James S. Kemper, President of the United States Chamber of Commerce said in a statement issued on May 18th: "The primary concern of American business today is that our country will not become involved in any foreign war. Business is not looking for the advantage of war profits and definitely is opposed to sending American boys and young men to fight on foreign soil!"

The pacifist views of Mr. Kemper, who was elevated to preeminence among business men and politicians by his title as President of the U. S. Chamber of Commerce, were thus extolled in the Bulletin of the Board of Trade for German-American Commerce for June 1940, during that tragic period of the war when Germany's ultimate victory appeared inevitable—providing a craven America could be persuaded to keep out of it, disarmed spiritually and physically, and thus he destined to stand alone in a final hour of German triumph.

After the death of Wendell Willkie, on October 8th, 1944, it was revealed that when the Republican National Committee was being reorganized, he aided in assembling data which was published regarding the isolationist record of James S. Kemper, who had been appointed financial chairman for the Dewey campaign. He was designated to handle the task of securing contributions from those business men and industrialists who believed that their best chance for a peace-time set-up satisfactory to their purposes would be by a Republican victory in that November election.

It would appear that Mr. Willkie, in examining Mr. Kemper's record, did not grasp the full significance of the use which had been made of the Kemper doctrines by the organization which had so praised his appeal to American industrial leaders that America must keep out of the war.

This organization was the supposedly respectable Board of Trade for German-American Commerce, the New York offices of which were finally raided and closed in December 1941, when the secretary and editor, Dr. Albert Degener, was interned and later shipped back to his native Germany.

Mr. Kemper's full statement as it appeared in the June, 1940, Bulletin, followed the usual isolationist line but was slanted to the viewpoint of businessmen by enlarging on the inevitable increase in our national debt and heavy taxes should we become involved in the war. It demanded that "we must be realistic and not emotional" by refusing to fight Germany. Insofar as the European war was concerned, profits rather than patriotism appeared the important thing for businessmen to consider.

That this kind of an appeal in the name of the United States Chamber of Commerce should have appeared in such a publication, and at such a time, is ominous. Probably neither Mr. Kemper, nor many of the respectable American business companies which belonged to the Board of Trade ever took the trouble to find out that this organization was registered with the State Department as a representative of foreign principals, the names of which included German I.G. Farben and other German industrial and financial enterprises which were tied into that huge war machine. However, these gentlemen could have discovered that many of its American members were affiliates or subsidiaries of I.G. Farben, and that its executive officers were employees of, or dominated by, I.G. Farben.

The German-American Board of Trade as a source of pro-Nazi propaganda was immune until after we entered the war because of the apparent respectability and high position of some of its members. A fact which escaped Mr. Willkie and those who dug into Mr. Kemper's record is that ample evidence was available that this allegedly legitimate organization of businessmen engaged in import and export with Germany appears in reality to have been just another one of the "Tarnung" or false fronts of German I.G. Farben, set up in this country by its predecessors of the Dye Cartel and directed by its employes under cover of the names of respectable American companies which either did not realize its real purpose or which, for benefits received, were willing to act as stooges for the mighty I.G. Cartel.

Chief organizer of the German-American Board of Trade, in 1924, was the notorious Herman Metz, who has already been revealed as one of the most obnoxious American agents of the Dye Cartel for a quarter of a century, a professed Democrat who in 1919 switched his political and financial support to the Republican Ohio gang and its weakling, Warren Harding, for President. Metz, as its first president, announced that the purpose of the German-American Board of Trade was to find proper outlets for American products in Germany and to divert German imports in this country to channels where they would not conflict with American industries. To Metz it was to be a commercial "love thy neighbor" affair. (Love thy German neighbor—forget the war.)

In 1934, when Metz passed to his reward, he was still president of the Board of Trade and by that time, according to evidence revealed before the Congressional Committee on un-American Activities, some of the board's officers and members were busily engaged in spreading the Nazi brand of sweetness and light (kill thy non-Ayran neighbor) in the United States.

When legislation for return of enemy properties was pending in Congress in the 1920's, the German-American Board of Trade vehemently denounced all those who opposed this proposal with insistent demands that "American honor would be stained" unless all German properties we had seized were handed back.

Again in the late 1930's it was the Farben Board of Trade that led the assaults on Washington, first in protest to the Treasury Department for imposing countervailing duties on German imports; and, after the war began, to the State Department for not breaking the British blockade.

These Board of Trade gentry, from the time that it was organized, included a considerable number of those who during World War I had been engaged in similar subversive activities, in close cooperation with the American representatives of the German Dye Cartel of that earlier period. Herman Metz merely had the stage scenery repainted for the new false front—the actors and the action were frequently the same as before and during the first World War.

When officers and directors of the German-American Board of Trade wrote to or appeared before Cabinet officials and Congressional Committees, they had behind them a list of representative American corporations which appeared untainted by Nazi influence. They disguised and kept well in the background the I.G. Farben controlling influence.

It was James S. Martin of the War Division of the Justice Department, who later was to try to undue some of the post-war mess created by Farben's friends in Germany—who finally realized the true significance of the German-American Board of Trade as the headquarters where Metz and Ilgner had brought together the old crowd of Dye Trust pals of World War I with those newly added to Farben's Tarnung. And these important figures, when associated with other influential personages who were untainted by Nazi ties, were then able to flaunt their high place in public banquets and thus launch materialistic propaganda aimed at the cream of America's social and political economy.

In the fateful year of 1939 the Honorary President of the German-American Board of Trade was the late Julius P. Mayer, American-born top man of the Hamburg-American Steamship Lines in the United States for many years, the same Mr. Mayer who, during World War I, was closely associated with that notorious German spy, the American Bayer Company's Dr. Hugo Schweitzer; with the Kaiser's pay-off man, Dr. Heinrich Albert, and all the rest of the gang of German agents who made the Hamburg-American offices headquarters for propaganda, espionage, and sabotage during the war period until the United States Government finally raided it and sent some of its personnel to jail.

Among Mr. Mayer's other World War I associates in the conduct of the earlier "Keep Us Out of the War" campaign, was none other than the still-celebrated Edward A. Rumely, who in April 1946, was to win an acquittal after two trials on an indictment for refusal to show a Congressional Committee the names of contributors to his more recent activities.

It was an executive secretary of the Committee for Constitutional Government, in which Mr. Frank Gannett was a prominent participant, that Mr. Rumely crossed swords with Congressional Committees in 1938 and 1944 for refusing to reveal the identity of those who put up the funds used by his new organization; much of which, before the war began, was violently isolationist and anti-war. Mr. Rumely, being held in contempt by Congress for his refusal to tell all, finally went free by grace of a second trial jury, despite his earlier record as an ex-convict.

It will be recalled that during the earlier war Rumely conspired with Bayer's Schweitzer to purchase the New York *Evening Mail* with secret German funds, and after the war served a jail term for these subversive activities. As was elsewhere shown he also came within the Sterling-Farben orbit in 1929.

Mr. Mayer's training during the first war, which qualified him to become the honorary head of the Board of Trade in preparation for the next war, included membership in the fake German University League, a propaganda agency financed largely by the American Bayer Company through H. C. Seebohm, Bayer's secretary; with Dr. Schweitzer as a trustee, and all of the other important Bayer officers (including those who were indicted and interned) among its members.

It was the president of this German University League, Dr. Edmund von Mach, who in February 1917, bombarded members of Congress with impudently worded pamphlets and letters attacking President Wilson's request for a declaration of war on Germany.

President of the German-American Board of Trade in 1939 until he died on February 20th of that year, was Herbert A. Johnson, whose ostensible business was that of handling publicity for the Leipzig Trade Fair (of Germany) in the United States. Mr. Johnson's death occasioned a noteworthy tribute in the next issue of the Bulletin, which featured cables and letters of condolence received from Dr. Max Ilgner of Berlin (Head of Farben's Secret Intelligence Bureau); attendance at the funeral of representatives of Farben's Chemnyco, Inc., and beautiful flower arrangements bearing the card of I.G. Farbenindustrie a.-g. of Frankfurt, Germany. (A long distance to say it with flowers.)

However the actual director of the Board of Trade after Herman Metz died appears to have been the chairman of its executive committee, Rudolph Ilgner, brother of Max and head of Chemnyco, whose job there was described in the last chapter and discussed elsewhere. Rudolph Ilgner was indicted on the day Germany invaded Poland, for destroying evidence in the files of Chemnyco which a federal grand jury had demanded. This indictment was kept a secret from the public for a long time after it was handed down, but Mr. Ilgner and Farben knew about it, and in November 1939 the Board of Trade, with expressions of deep regret and praises for his invaluable services, accepted Mr. Ilgner's resignation as chairman of its executive committee. Perhaps the vote of thanks had special reference to Mr. Ilgner's criminal destruction of records which would have exposed some of the treasonable activities which were being conducted through the offices of Chemnyco and other Farben affiliates in the United States; or perhaps the Board's directors merely wished to pay tribute to their chairman for having arranged an elaborate reception and dinner at the Deutsche Verein in New York City in honor of Captain Fritz Weidemann who had just arrived in this country to become Consul General for Nazi Germany by order of Adolph Hitler, and who had acted, a few months before, as the official escort of former President Herbert Hoover during the latter's grand inspection tour of Nazi Germany in 1938 (of which more later). This Ilgner-Weidemann dinner took place some months before Captain Weidemann was exposed as Pacific Coast head of Nazi espionage and was ordered to get out—and stay out—of the United States.

The Farben-Ilgner executive body of the German-American Board of Trade included Ernst Schmitz, director of the German Railroad Information Service; J. Schroeder and C. J. Berk of the

Nazi combined Hamburg-American and North German Lloyd Steamship Company and other notables. Mr. Schmitz's Information Services, financed by the Nazi government, had included engaging the public relations firm of Carl Byoir and Associates for $6,000 per month, presumably to give council to Americans how to become German tourists. The ubiquitous George Sylvester Viereck, editor of the German Library of Information "Facts on Review" was also on the Byoir payroll at $1,750 per month, plus many more thousands from other sources, helping to edit a propaganda sheet called the *German-American Bulletin*—for the guidance of the prospective tourists. Mr. Schmitz also tied in with the notorious Manfred Zapp, the Casanova head of the Nazi handout agency Transocean News Service, until the latter was interned and indicted in 1941; Transocean, according to information found in Zapp's files, was owned among others by I.G. Farben's Robert Bosch, and the Hamburg-American Lines.

On November 30, 1939, according to a letter written by Mr. Schmitz, that member of the Board of Trade's directorate wrote inviting Zapp to attend a meeting at the Schmitz apartment in New York of a "number of people of the Intelligence Service of the Rome-Berlin Axis." This invitation gives some indication of the kind of people included in the management of the Metz-Ilgner-Farben Board of Trade. Mr. Schmitz, like Mr. Mayer, had World War I training in pro-German, anti-war activities; he was then an editor of the Ridder family's *Staatz-Zeitung*, which attained notoriety during the first war and, while preparations for the next war were under way, heaped editorial ridicule on the heads of those who saw the slightest impropriety in I.G. Farben's penetration into American munition industries.

Mr. Schroeder, who had been with Hamburg-American for thirty years, was vice-president of the Board of Trade in 1939 as well as director and member of its executive committee; Schroeder, along with his North German Lloyd colleague, C. J. Berk, also aided in Viereck's editorial labors. Among the Hamburg-American propaganda activities during the second world war, as during the first one, was the transportation to this country of tons and tons of printed matter of the most vicious character such as Ivy Lee, Farben's American hired press agent, once described as "books and pamphlets, and newspaper clippings and documents, world without end."

Incidentally it was the Hamburg-American-North German Lloyd, and the German Railroad Information Office which relayed from the Hitler government the funds through which Heinz Spanknoebel (until he was indicted and skipped) had financed the original gutter publication of the Nazis in this country *Das Neues Deutschland* (The New Germany). The Board of Trade's Mr. Schroeder saw to it that this alleged newspaper he was helping to finance had plenty of readers—in 1932 he sent a letter to each Hamburg-American employe instructing them to join the Friends of New Germany. The ships of these German lines, including the *Bremen* and *Europa*, when docked in New York between trips, were thrown open to the Bund and other Nazi groups, for meetings and banquets in full uniform. The Hamburg-American did yeoman service in the inside job of softening up America for World War II—just as it did for World War I.

Officers of the Board of Trade who were not members of the select Ilgner committee included Dr. Degener, already mentioned, and Heinrich Freytag its Treasurer, who was also an employe of the German Embassy at Washington. Dr. Degener, according to evidence said to have been seized and suppressed by the McCormack Committee in 1934, contributed large sums to Nazi organizations in America. Degener started a red hot campaign against the anti-Nazi boycotts when they began in 1933; he threatened publicly that the boycott would cost this country's businessmen their most profitable customers in Germany, and the interest on over two billion dollars of American investments in the Fatherland. Degener was particularly bitter at New York City's LaGuardia for advocating the boycott; he denounced the pugnacious Little Flower for endangering what he termed the "peaceful relations" between the United States and Germany.

One of the directors of the Board of Trade in 1939 when the war began was our old friend Dr. Eugene R. Pickrell. This ubiquitous gentleman, still on Farben's payroll as revealed in the preceding chapter, was now listed as a customs attorney, his office was across the hall from the Trade Board at 10 East 40th Street, New York City; and he made another trip to Washington on December 1, 1939 with Dr. Robert Reiner then president of the Trade Board, to protest bitterly to Secretary Hull against the British embargo on exports from Germany. These Farben Board of Trade protests in 1939, after Germany had gone to war, at interference with the rights of American citizens to engage in trade with Germany, were framed in almost the same words as those made by the Dye Cartel's Herman Metz to Secretary Bryan, and to President Wilson himself in 1915 about the British blockade in Germany's first world war. History repeats.

Carl Schreiner, of the Pilot Insurance Company of New York, was also a director of the German-American Board of Trade in 1939. Back in World War I days Schreiner had achieved notoriety through mention as an alien enemy in a Justice Department report on what was called the German Insurance Pools conspiracy, the purpose of the pool being to fight the British boycott and black-list by the creation of dummy insurance companies. The Justice report indicated that the German Dye Trust's American Bayer and Cassella outfits were involved in this insurance monkey business.

Another 1939 director of the Farben Trade Board whose name recalls World War I was George W. Simon, listed as vice-president of the Heyden Chemical Company. Back in 1915, Mr. Simon was chief chemist for the Heyden concern when Dr. Hugo Schweitzer put over his phenol deal on Tom Edison with the assistance of Simon's father-in-law, Richard Kny. It was Heyden, it may be recalled, who purchased the surplus Edison phenol and used it in making drugs in order to prevent its conversion into munitions for use against Germany.

Active in the behind-the-scenes affairs of the German-American Board of Trade until the end was Dr. Kertess, whose jail term and espionage escapades appear in the previous chapter. To be always available, Dr. Kertess moved his offices to the same building as those of the Trade Board and his colleague, Dr. Pickrell, and as a supporter of Nazi propaganda, in 1939, helped to found the notorious American Fellowship Forum, whose *"Today's Challenge"* was edited by George Sylvester Viereck (before he was jailed), and whose National Director was Dr. Friedrich Ernst Auhagen, former instructor at Columbia University, who was also jailed for failure to register as a German agent, and, when he got out, was promptly interned as an enemy alien, and his citizenship revoked.

Dr. Kertess protested to the Dies Committee in 1941 that he took no active part in organizing the Forum, but it developed that he paid the rent for its offices on West Forty-Second Street, New York, out of his personal funds. The vice-president of his Chemical Marketing Company, Richard Koch, was one of its founders, and when Dr. Auhagen retired as Director, Dr. Kertess became one of the holders of the registered title of the Forum.

Until he got into difficulties with the law, Dr. Kertess devoted much time and talent to arranging a grandiose plan for what he called the "Organization of German Industry in America after the War." This peace-time absorption of American industry was to be managed by none other than the Board of Trade for German-American Commerce—with Dr. Kertess and other representatives of I.G. Farben as Directors.

A 1939 director of the German-American Board of Trade who had an exemplary record as an American-born citizen and who engaged in pronounced isolationist propaganda, was James D. Mooney, World War I veteran, Lieutenant-Commander, U. S. N. R., and vice-president of General Motors Corporation. One of Mr. Mooney's anti-war contributions was an appeal on the subject which was introduced into the Congressional Record by Democratic Senator E. C. Johnson of Colorado, reprinted and distributed as a pamphlet and then published in amplified form in the Saturday Evening Post, August 3, 1940, under the title "War or Peace in America."

In that article Mr. Mooney described the horrors of war and Germany's defense of her own position. He criticized our attempt to aid England as futile, and insisted that the influence of the United States should be directed toward saving England a further beating by using our strength in the situation to compel a peace with Germany.

As a native-born American, Mr. Mooney was in strange company among some of the German nationals of the Board of Trade. According to Who's Who of 1940–41 Mr. Mooney was awarded the "Order of Merit of the German Eagle." Apparently some one in the Fatherland liked his brand of Americanism.

In the *Bulletin* of the Board of Trade for October, 1940, General Motors' Mr. Mooney was quoted as saying, with reference to our possible entrance into the war:

"On the day was is declared, we can kiss democracy good-bye."

When Mr. Ilgner threw a banquet it was a sumptuous affair, with big names on the seating list overshadowing the identity and purposes of those in the background. For a grand luncheon which he gave in the name of the German-American Board of Trade on May 27, 1937, to honor His Excellency Dr. Hans Heinrich Dieckhoff, the German Ambassador, parts of the seating list read like a directory of representatives of Farben hideouts and affiliates in this country.

One table seated I.G. Farben's distinguished Director Dr. Wilhelm Ferdinand Kalle, along with Sterling's president, A. H. Diebold; General Dyestuff's E. K. Halbach; Synthetic Nitrogen's A. L. Mullaly; W. P. Pickhardt of the old Badische agency; and Dr. E. R. Pickrell, the Metz handyman. With these close pals of Farben sat E. H. Meili, vice-president of the J. Henry Schroder Banking Corporation, of New York and London, lending a high note of Anglo-American financial approval to that group, and Ferdinand Andreas, Prince of Liechtenstein, added a touch of royalty.

Another table was graced by Rudolph Ilgner himself; Dr. K. Hochswender, of Magnesium Development and Chemnyco and D. A. Schmitz, of General Aniline. Among other Farben affiliates American Bemberg Company was represented by director H. W. Springorum; Fezandie & Sperrle by Oscar E. Sperrle."

Scattered through the seating arrangements were George Sylvester Viereck and Fritz Kuhn (this was some time before these two were convicted and locked up), also another celebrated pair, Dr. F. E. Auhagen and Dr. A. Degener (this was also before that couple were picked up by the F.B.I.).

Two other notables who graced this gathering were Dr. Herbert Gross who hired an American spy for Dr. Kertess, as revealed in the previous chapter; and Col. Ed. Emerson, notorious as a German agent during both world wars. Theodore Dinkelacker and Willy Luedtke, national leaders of the Bund, were also present. It was what might be called a "mixed" gathering.

On the dais with the guest of honor and Board of Trade officers sat James D. Mooney of General Motors; Editor Victor F. Ridder; F. W. La Frentz, president of the American Surety Corp.; Col. Sosthenes Behn, of the International Telephone & Telegraph, and other notables. It surely appeared to be a representative peace-time gathering of influential American citizenship.

When its connections are noted it may be more readily understood that this Farben organized and directed Trade Board was so respectable or so powerful, even after its offices had been raided and closed in December 1941, that its name was conspicuously missing from the long list of propaganda agencies, espionage hideouts and subversive organizations which was published as defendants or participants in four blanket indictments handed down in the District of Columbia in 1941–'42 and '43, out of which George Sylvester Viereck drew one conviction in 1942, which was reversed by the Supreme Court, and one in 1943, which put him back in jail.

The Trade Board's subversive activities were largely ignored by the Dies Committee when the latter partially uncovered many of the less important pro-Nazi propaganda agencies in the United States, and by the Truman and Bone Senate Committees when they partially lifted the lid on other Farben-American hideouts. It remained for hard-hitting James S. Martin, Chief of the Justice Department Economic Warfare squad to bring out some of the background facts and pre-war activities of the Board of Trade in testifying before Senator Kilgore's Sub-Committee on War Mobilization in September 1944.

Ample evidence has been revealed in Chapter II and elsewhere in this story that the German I.G. through Bayer and other American fronts engaged in propaganda, espionage and sabotage prior to and during World War I. The Ivy Lee advisory service engaged by Farben as discussed in Chapter x revealed how that agency of the dye trust continued its propaganda activities in anticipation of World War II.

In considering much of the evidence relating to appeals for pacificism, isolation and disarmament, it is frequently difficult to distinguish criminal propaganda from the protest which arises in the idealism of thousands of patriotic citizens whose normal, sincere hatred of war formed the nucleus of much of the pre-war sentiment which has divided public opinion in the United States on our mythical isolation.

To step away from the domestic scene for the moment, we might consider the "Union of Democratic Control" of London which, in 1932, published an expose of what its authors described as the secret "Bloody International" or munitions combination, which included I.G. Farben and was accused of continually conspiring to cause wars in order to reap profits from the resulting demand for battleships, guns and munitions.

This pamphlet advocated abolition of private manufacture of arms and munitions to insure world peace by disarmament. This was the same thesis which allegedly motivated the United States Senate Munitions Committee in 1934 when it uncovered the hold that Farben had already secured on our national defense industries—and then did nothing about it except to aid in weakening our own security.

Evidently the idealistic English group was not directly inspired by Farben; actually that doctrine of disarmament thus preached was an integral part of the pattern of propaganda of the German dye trust in the period before we entered World War I, and again in the period before we entered World War II.

When we examine the activities of many of the peace groups in the United States during the last pre-war period, it must be admitted that thousands of those men and women were sincerely patriotic citizens who would be quick to rebuke the suggestion that their detestation of war was induced even indirectly by foreign propaganda.

One such group was World Peaceways Inc., of New York City, the letterhead of which carried the names of many distinguished citizens. This organization advertised its demands for peace by picturing the fact that women and children would be killed in the next war. On June 26, 1941, it issued an appeal for funds, copy of which was handed to me, with a message entitled "A Referendum on War." Accompanying that World Peaceways circular letter was a single page entitled "Sorry to Bother You," on which a wistful-looking youth asked you to talk over his plea to:

Be a little careful, willya, about whether you send me to
war or not. I mean, I'd hate to have you send me over to
fight and maybe die . . . . . and then find out you'd made a
mistake *again,* etc.

Underneath was the demand:

Keep America from making mistakes with her boys' lives.
Write to the President today. Issued by World Peaceways,
Inc. 103 Park Ave., New York.

This appeal was sent out a few short weeks before the near
tragedy in the Congress of the United States, on August 12, 1941,
when the addition of just one more negative vote would have destroyed the training of our new Army.

The vast majority of members of World Peaceways, and of
its contributors, who would bitterly resent an intimation that
I.G. Farben or any of its friends had anything to do with this
organization, may be equally indignant to have it appear that
an elaborate radio program which was staged in the name of
World Peaceways some years previously was paid for by a pharmaceutical house which enjoyed close relations with Farben affiliates in the United States, and the head of which was reported
to have approached Farben officials at Berlin with the intention
of offering the latter a participation in the business of this company in the United States.

After Pearl Harbor, contributions were again solicited by World
Peaceways in letters stating that funds were needed to enable
it to resume advertising—to educate leadership for the next peace.

Other expressions of this same type of idealism were found
in numerous articles and books published in America during that
critical period when it seemed at times that the people of the
United States, and its government, would never start to arm, or
take a stand until too late to do so—except alone.

One such book was "War, Peace & Change" by John Foster
Dulles, published in 1939, a very studious pre-war volume which
indicated the author's conclusion that quarantine, non-recogni-
tion and sanctions were not solutions for problems of aggression
by "dynamic" nations such as Germany, Italy and Japan.

Mr. Dulles appeared to praise the peoples of these countries and to believe that they should not be confused with adventurers, soldiers of fortune or criminals, who might be "safely" repressed.

The arguments and the peaceful desires of Mr. Dulles as thus expressed were no doubt welcome to the peace-at-any-price idealists of this country during that tragic period. It may also appear that they were equally welcome to those who in Germany were guiding the behind-the-scenes preparations for war.

Thus the great value for Farben of the propaganda agencies controlled or guided from within the membership of the German American Board of Trade was the fact that among its members were honorable American companies and individuals whose commercial relations with Germany were legitimate and of long standing. For this reason the Trade Board for a long time was looked upon as above suspicion and as it spoke for business—big business at that—it was not subjected to that kind of public suspicion and distrust which was attached to groups like the Bund in the minds of many citizens during the decade before the entry of the United States into World War II. When on June 16, 1941 the United States Government struck its first real blow at Nazi propaganda and subversive activities in this country, the three organizations which were ordered to close up with the twenty-four German consulates for "Activities of improper and unwarranted character" were the German Railroad Information Office; German Library of Information, and Transocean News Service—as three of the principal Nazi propaganda agencies in this country. All of these were tied in with the I.G. Farben-directed German-American Board of Trade as a clearing house for information, and a safe refuge until then for their personnel. But the Board stayed open until after Pearl Harbor.

When President Harry S Truman, in December 1945, stated that the American people were responsible for what happened at Pearl Harbor as much as were our military forces, it might appear that our Chief Executive overlooked several highly important factors which are brought to light in this book, and especially in this chapter. Granted that the spiritual disarmament of the American people was due in part to the genuine idealism and pacificism of many honorable citizens, the fact remains that much of that idealism had a materialistic background, and much of this was induced, directly or indirectly, by the top level propaganda created and broadcast among our most influential circles to which I. G. Farben was able to appeal through the highly respectable Board of Trade for German-American Commerce. The President, in that blanket indictment of American public opinion, overlooked what is perhaps the more important aspects of Farben's secret weapon—of influence at the top levels of industry, finance, and politics—which made it impossible for those who not only saw what was coming, but wanted something done about it, to be heard.

Regardless of how the President's remarks may be taken, the excuse may be offered that when the *Bulletin* of the subversive agency parading as a Board of Trade publicized the isolationist views of Republican Finance Chairman James S. Kemper it meant no more than when the opinions of other prominent American citizens were likewise broadcast in this or any other publication. It is thus interesting to examine the contents of an issue of the German-American Commerce Bulletin which appeared in March 1941, somewhat later than that containing Mr. Kemper's appeal. Many of the articles and editorials in this issue were emphatic pro-Nazi, anti-war propaganda appealing to the "business as usual" and appeasement sentiments of its readers. Various Farben officials and Farben's war-time accomplishments, making Germany now invulnerable, received mention in sketches and news articles. Included were pleas for appeasement of Germany and isolation for this country by pacificist advocates like General Robert E. Wood, National Chairman of the America First Committee, and Dr. Edward Lodge Curran, who stated that current "war mongering propaganda" ignored the fact that we had fought two wars with Great Britain in our history. A New York *Daily News* article, also bitterly anti-British, was reprinted, and the leading article, entitled "German-Americans in the World War," by Frederick Franklin Schrader, compared the hostility to German nationals in the United States during World War I, to current harrowing reports of racial persecutions by the Nazis in Germany. A description of Mr. Schrader as a well known author of historical works failed to mention other activities, such as associate editorship of the *Fatherland* propaganda journal published during World

War I, by our old friend George Sylvester Viereck; and during the present war again assisting the Viereck literary efforts as editor of *Facts in Review,* for the German Library of Information. According to Congressional records, Schrader was also for a time editor of *Deutscher Weckruf und Beobachter,* official organ of the German-American Bund, which, it need not be said, circulated among citizens of much lower levels of society than those of the highly refined industrialist readers of the Board of Trade *Bulletin.*

In such select company there was also published in this same issue of the *Bulletin* an urgent appeal to its readers to read a book entitled "Shall We Send Our Youth to War," which was described as a "a plea . . . . . that the United States should stay out of the war." This book, which appears to have escaped the notice of the literary reviewers of this country, recited from the personal experiences of its author the "unparalleled famine and pestilence" which resulted from World War I. A few of the significant passages in the book may be quoted here:

> Amid the afterglow of glory and legend we forget the filth, the stench, the death of the trenches. We forget the dumb grief of mothers, wives and children. We forget the unending blight cast upon the world by the sacrifice of the flower of every race.
>
> We may need to go to war again. But that war should be on this hemisphere alone and in defense of our firesides or our honor.
>
> We should hold that the basis of international relations should not be force, but should be law and free agreement. The first thing required is vigorous, definite statement from all who have responsibility, both publicly and privately, that we are not going to war with anybody in Europe unless they attack the Western Hemisphere. The second thing is not to sit in this game of power politics. These are the American policies that will make sure that we do not send our youth to Europe to War.

The author of this book also stated that prior to World War I he had lived with the "invisible forces which moved its causes," that he knew Europe intimately, "not as tourist but as a part of my workaday life," and that in 1938 he had spent "some months in Europe with unique opportunity to discuss its problems with the leaders of fourteen nations." On the cover of this book is a picture of a soldiers' cemetery, row after row of little white crosses; with quotations from the book, and a blunt request:

> If you want the United States to keep out of war, here is a book to send to your friends, to your Representatives, to all people who have power, directly or indirectly, to sway public and legislative opinion.

Neither *The New York Times* nor the *Herald Tribune* book review sections ever mentioned this book, and according to the *Book Review Digest*, no other literary publication gave it any notice. That honor was reserved for the *Bulletin* of the German American Board of Trade, which urged its purchase and also announced its author to have been Herbert Hoover, former President of the United States and Elder Statesman of the Republican party who strangely enough was to be elevated an *expert emeritus* on post-war problems of world famine by President Truman.

In reply to my inquiry, Mr. Thomas R. Coward, of Coward, McCann, Inc., advised that the book was contracted for with the personal representative of Mr. Hoover, and that insofar as he knew, no one connected with the German-American Commerce *Bulletin* had anything to do with it.

This statement may be accepted as entirely sincere as would be the protestations from thousands of Mr. Hoover's followers that his sentiments did credit to him and were shared by many others.

The fact remains that the German-American Commerce *Bulletin* appears to have been the only publication in which mention of this book appeared. And that *Bulletin* was the official organ of the Board of Trade for German-American Commerce, Inc., the organization started by Herman Metz, in 1924; registered with the State Department as the agent of a foreign principal; and directed, in 1939, by Rudolph Ilgner, head of Chemnyco, the patent-holding and espionage outfit maintained by Farben in the United States. And Mr. Hoover's guide in Europe in 1938 during his "unique opportunity to discuss its problems" was Captain Fritz

Weidemann. The position occupied in the public mind by our only living ex-President, a highly educated man of long experience in international affairs, gave dignity and impressiveness to his demands that we keep our sons out of the war—unless—and until—the invasion of the American continents should begin. (This could only have occurred after Hitler had conquered Europe, and had landed in the Argentine, or Panama, or Long Island.)

So Mr. Kemper, again the National Committee Treasurer, was still in good Republican company.

CHAPTER XVI

Counter-Propaganda & the Lobby

IT IS A SAD thing to find men so money mad as to be willing to betray their country and their families for just a few more dollars.

Thus Francis Patrick Garvan, in a speech before the American Institute of Chemists, summed up his feelings about those Americans who had helped his life long enemy reestablish itself in the United States.

For Garvan, until the day of his death in 1937, was the implacable foe of the German dye trust—a tireless crusader who never gave up trying to warn his countrymen of the industrial Trojan Horse of the Germans had deposited on these shores.

One of Garvan's greatest triumphs was the 1926 decision of the Supreme Court which decreed that:

The purpose of the Trading with the Enemy Act was not only to weaken enemy countries by depriving their supporters of their property . . . . . but also to promote production in the United States of things useful for the effective prosecution of the war.

Aside from the importance of that decision in preventing the immediate destruction of our new organic-chemical industry by returning the seized patents to the Germans, it is of tremendous significance to many phases of this story.

Garvan made good use of this decision in meeting the many German-inspired attacks made upon him, and to further his work as director of the Chemical Foundation. The Foundation distributed millions of pieces of educational literature; books, periodicals and pamphlets, and for many years was the strongest single force in America in pointing out the importance of organic chemistry to national security.

The fact that Francis Garvan, who had wealth, power, and prestige to support his efforts, was ineffectual in curbing the encroachments of the German industrialists, makes more understandable my own many failures to break through the Farben defenses. And perhaps it should be explained here that despite the suggestion of mutual friends that Garvan and I should work together, we never did. So I fought my own fight, in my own way.

From the very beginning, the only organized support I received was of an indirect character from groups of physicians and pharmacists, mainly in New Jersey. In just one instance was financial assistance given me by one of these groups—and stark tragedy was in the aftermath of that contribution. After the recent war began, I did, however, receive very welcome cooperation from a propaganda organization which started when Hitler came to power, the Non-Sectarian Anti-Nazi League.

Founded by the late Samuel Untermyer in the early 1930's, the League began a boycott against the Nazis which included allies of Farben in the United States, and imports of Farben products.

In Philadelphia, at one of its early mass meetings in 1934, the League was addressed by a local attorney named Francis Biddle, who demanded action, "in the only effective way that Mr. Hitler can understand—the economic boycott, sustained, aggressive and unrelenting." "Words become pallid," said Mr. Biddle, "a little absurd in the face of Nazi actions. We too must act."

Seven years later it was the same Francis Biddle who as Attorney General substituted the "pallid words" of consent decrees for criminal prosecution, "sustained, aggressive and unrelenting." And, when the Anti-Nazi League wrote to the Attorney General about one of those polite consent decrees, the reply, by his executive assistant, the James Allen of Chapter IX, indicated that the Attorney General considered Sterling to be of great value to the nation in its war with Farben's empire.

While the bellicose views of Mr. Biddle have softened with the passing of time, those of the Anti-Nazi League as directed by Professor James H. Sheldon never wavered, and its *Bulletin* distributed much valuable data regarding the danger of Farben, and the necessity of boycotting the products of such firms as Sterling, Winthrop, and General Dyestuff.

In May 1941 after the failure of my efforts to induce Assistant Attorney General Arnold to tackle the Farben lobby (Chapter IX) I turned my attack back on the Senate with an appeal to its Majority Leader, Alben W. Barkley. My letter, in part, follows:

> I say that the lobby is now and has been since I first exposed it, the spearhead of the German plan of pacifism, isolation and to stop us from arming, or from using the arms we have.
>
> Some of the lobby members identified on my 1931 chart are still on the job among your members, others have joined the lobby in recent years.
>
> The vindication of my forecast and warning ten years ago gives me the right and the duty to insist that the Senate must act now to destroy this lobby as a vicious and dangerous branch of the Hitler fifth column. Should any member of the Senate oppose such action now, ask him what he is trying to cover up.

Senator Barkley thanked me profusely, promised to give my request his consideration—and then retired to a hospital to recuperate.

In agreement with me that the Farben lobby at Washington constituted the spearhead of Farben's subversive activities and of immunity for its allies, the Anti-Nazi League then joined in the attack, and began its own systematic effort to induce action.

The Justice Department, Secretary of State Hull, and Secretary of the Treasury Morgenthau were among those appealed to by the League, unsuccessfully.

One letter from the League, in July 1941, went to the Hon. Walter F. George of Georgia, then Chairman of the Senate Foreign Relations Committee. It referred to the activities of Farben affiliates in the United States and Latin America, and to the well-organized lobby at Washington by which "Congress is being improperly influenced." Therefore, wrote the League:

> For the sake of the integrity of American industry, and for the sake of national defense during the present critical time, we respectfully urge you to investigate this lobby.

About that same time I also sent a letter to Senator George asking for an investigation of the Farben Lobby. The Senator's replies to these two separate requests for similar action were somewhat odd. He told the League that he thought the Judiciary Committee or the Justice Department should make any investigation of that character, and that he understood the latter was so doing. He told me that he was referring my request to the Dies Committee. Thus the Senator covered up on our lobby investigations demands, but he played fair, he called his shots and gave each peanut shell a name: Dies, Judiciary, and Justice. He must have forgotten there was a dead letter office. The latter would have served equally well.

The League continued, as I did, to hammer away for investigation of the Farben lobby but it was no use. The lobby did not choose to be investigated, and even after war was declared on the United States, all such appeals fell upon deaf ears.

While world war II was under way there appeared on the national scene a new organization which was called, aptly enough, "The Society for the Prevention of World War III." Many well known public figures were identified with this group and it has done yeoman work in publicizing the menace that is Farben, and in denouncing the plot to revive this threat to future world peace.

In October 1941, on the theory that my 1931 diagrammatic chart had by then been sufficiently confirmed as to Farben's control

f our national-defense industries, I sent a reprint of the chart
o each member of the Senate and House with another urgent
demand that my long-standing appeal for investigation of the
obby be granted. In that letter I said, in part:

> I suggest also that no one of you hazard the opinion that
> I merely guessed at the facts on my 1931 chart. Obviously
> I had to know such facts to state them and not be jailed for
> criminal libel.
>
> Moreover that 1931 chart is now, in 1941, the irrefutable
> proof which Messrs. William E. Weiss, Earl I. McClintock,
> et al. cannot meet when they plead that they did not even
> suspect, years ago, just what were the subversive activities
> which their German associates were directing them to con-
> duct. If I knew these facts in 1931 then they knew them even
> before 1931. They are not that dumb.

Again, silence in the halls of Congress.

Later, I submitted to the Justice Department and to the Truman
and Bone Committees of the Senate another appeal entitled "Tender of Proof" which outlined some of the evidence that supported
the allegations on the chart. I again informed the Justice Department and the Senators that the significance of this chart was the
obvious fact that its circulation, a decade previously, constituted
irrefutable proof that those same facts must have been suspected
or known by the American industrial and financial leaders who
negotiated with Farben.

In September 1941, Senator Connally, of Texas, who had succeeded Senator George as Chairman of the Senate Foreign Relations Committee, advised me that the Department of Justice was
already investigating the lobby, so there was no need for his
committee to do so. Then began one of the finest examples of the
runaround that I have observed in a long experience with officials who are afraid to say "yes" and hate to say "no."

Accepting Senator Connally's information as authoritative, I
wrote Attorney General Biddle how happy I was to learn that
he was at last investigating the Farben lobby, and would he please
let me help. This was in the period when Tom Stokes and a few

others were panning the daylights out of the Corcoran-Biddle
weasel-worded consent decrees. Mr. Biddle, after due consideration, referred my letter to his subordinate, Mr. Arnold. Mr. Arnold,
with his tongue in his cheek, referred me to his subordinate Mr.
Sam S. Isseks, Harvard classmate of Mr. Corcoran, who had done
the spade work at the funeral of the Sterling investigation. Mr.
Isseks, after a brief interview, referred me to his subordinate Mr.
Robert Wohlforth, ace investigator of the Antitrust Division, and
former chief sleuth for several Senate Committees.

Mr. Wohlforth, whom I had never previously encountered, as
he had not been in on the current Farben mess, happily turned
out to be too straightforward and forthright to play clown, no
matter who ran the circus. After checking up to get his facts
straight, Wohlforth gave me the first definite and clean-cut statement I had received from any public official in fifteen years of
effort to get action on the lobby. Wohlforth's reply, condensed,
was a courteous but firm "No." There was no lobby investigation
in progress and there could be no lobby investigation started without orders. So that was that.

To complete the record I sent out some letters headed Re:
Lobby Employed by German I.G. Farben-Sterling Products, et al.
These letters were as follows:

> Dear Mr. Wohlforth:
>
> Referring to conference with you on the 23rd instant re-
> garding the above subject, to discuss which I was referred
> to you by Mr. S. S. Isseks, I regretted very much your in-
> structions that no investigation would be made of the lobby
> employed by the German I.G. Farben-Sterling group.
>
> Under these conditions it would have been useless for
> you to have considered the information which I was pre-
> pared to present relating to this lobby but I do feel obliged
> to express to you my deep appreciation for your courtesy
> and forthright attitude.

> Dear Mr. Isseks:
>
> Referring to conference had with you on the 3rd. inst.
> regarding the above subject I regret to inform you that Mr.

Robert Wohlforth of your staff, with whom you instructed me to discuss this matter has informed me that no investigation would be made of the lobby employed by the German I.G. Farben-Sterling group.

Dear Mr. Arnold:

Referring to your letter to me dated the 26th ultimo, regarding the above subject I regret to inform you that Mr. S. S. Isseks of the New York staff, with whom you instructed me to discuss this matter has caused me to be informed that no investigation would be made of the lobby employed by the German I.G. Farben-Sterling group.

Dear Mr. Biddle:

Referring to my letter to you dated the 15th ultimo, regarding the above subject I regret to inform you that Hon. Thurman Arnold, Assistant Attorney General, to whom you referred my letter has caused me to be informed that no investigation would be made of the lobby employed by the German I.G. Farben-Sterling group.

Dear Mr. Chairman Connally:

Referring to letter dated the 4th ultimo, regarding the above subject, in which I was advised that you considered action by the committee unwise because the Department of Justice was making an investigation of this matter. I regret to advise you that Hon. Francis Biddle, Attorney General, has caused me to be informed that no investigation would be made of the lobby employed by the German I.G. Farben-Sterling group.

The Dies Committee also has indicated to me that it has no intention of making such an investigation so it would appear that some one deliberately misinformed you on this subject.

In view of the above I again request that you bring to the attention of your committee my letter to yourself of August 12 and the copy of my letter of July 18 to your predecessor

Senator George, also my open letter to the Congress dated October 6, all requesting investigation of this lobby.

Respectfully,

H. W. Ambruster

The pressure of events, or something, deterred the Senator from replying.

CHAPTER XVII

Alibis and Excuses

FRANK A. HOWARD,
who conducted so many of the negotiations with Farben, wrote
his Standard Oil colleague E. J. Sadler, on February 6, 1940, that
Germany's policy for fifteen years had been the exporting of
patent rights, "resulting from their learning that, if they did not
. . . . . secure their exploitation abroad by appropriate deals, un-
licensed competition would pirate the new processes, leaving
the originators neither an export market nor anything to sell in
the way of patent rights or technique."

This comment illustrates the absurdity of the alibi that our
industrialists entered into illegal agreements with Farben because
they were farsighted and, had they not done so, the United States
would not have derived the great benefits from the Farben patents
covering dyes, drugs, explosives, magnesium alloys, rayon, synthetic rubber, plastics, etc.

These disingenuous sophistries have been broadcast most as-
siduously by Farben's American cohorts since the exposure of
the character of their agreements, and the resulting injury to our
national defense.

Possibly the most widely publicized of these excuses was the so-called official press release already discussed in Chapter IX which was prepared by Tommy Corcoran and issued over the signature of Attorney General Biddle. This remarkable apology for a convicted corporation contains these words:

> Under this agreement (with Farben) many new and important discoveries in the pharmaceutical field were disclosed to Winthrop Chemical, thus making them available to the United States.

Another bit of excuse propaganda is found in one of the pamphlets distributed in 1942 by Standard Oil, quoting allegations made by its president, W. S. Farish:

> . . . . . whether (or not) the several contracts made with I.G. did or did not fall within the borders set by the patent statutes or the Sherman Act, they did inure greatly to the advance of American industry and, more than any one thing, have made possible our present war activities in aviation gasoline, toluol and explosives, and in synthetic rubber itself.

However, it is apparent that Farben's United States patents would have been valueless to the Germans had not agreements for their use—legal or illegal—been made with our industrialists. Otherwise, the patents could only have served as a means of preventing manufacture; and as such they would have constituted so glaring a repetition of German cartel practices prior to World War I that the inevitable result would have been a change in our patent laws.

On the other hand, should Farben have refrained from taking out patents in this country, its new processes would have been available to our industries here as rapidly as they were revealed— when the patents were issued in Germany, and published.

Farben's leaders knew all this, their American partners knew it, and the Government knew it. Nevertheless, the illegal unions were made and consummated. The Justice Department and the Congress twiddled its thumbs, and when our so-innocent industrialists asked for the know-how on some of the more important German patents they were told that it was "withheld for military reasons."

One appeal to public opinion issued by duPont on January 6, 1944, in part, was as follows:

> Surely it cannot be the policy of the Department of Justice to attempt to prevent the continuance . . . . . of such immensely beneficial arrangements which have been a common practice in American industry.

This plea referred to the announcement that another antitrust action had been filed involving duPont; in this instance with the British Imperial Chemical Industries and the duPont subsidiary, Remington Arms, also named as defendants.

This statement was cleverly phrased; it contained allegations that the agreements had never been concealed and that

> . . . . . copies have been in the possession of Governmental agencies for approximately 10 years.

All this was unquestionably true. The same statement was repeated in duPont's next annual report, but what may appear to have been an unfortunate omission, in each instance, was any mention of the fact that some of the restrictive agreements referred to in this antitrust action involved not only the British I. C. I. but also included tie-ups and financial partnerships with I.G. Farben subsidiaries making and distributing both commercial and military explosives.

It was by repetitious publicity of this character that duPont escaped much of the press criticism that was heaped upon some of the others who were not involved in as many court actions for conspiring with Farben as was this oldest and largest of American munition makers.

DuPont's public relations, since 1936, were handled by Herbert Hoover's former White House Secretary, the late Theodore G. Joslin, until he died in April 1944. Mr. Joslin knew his way around Washington and Newspaper Row. His public relations department contributed numerous terse press handouts, and, along with duPont's elaborate radio program, "Cavalcade of America" contributed effectively to the appeasement of public opinion.

This publicity featured denials that duPont "ever has been a party to any cartel arrangement, using the term in its usually accepted sense," or that the company ever had "any connection with the German company (Farben) of a nature detrimental to the United States." These denials may be considered merely as expressions of opinion—with the duPont definitions of the words *cartel* and *detrimental* still at issue.

However one of the duPont radio pleas incurred an official rebuke from the Federal Communications Commission, which, in a report issued in March 1946, criticized that company as using "its commercial advertising period" to "explain one side of a controversial issue."

The comments which were thus criticized were sandwiched in with interesting references to "Better Things for Better Living Through Chemistry" in a broadcast in January, 1944, during a period in which some hostile press comments were appearing relating to court actions which involved Farben's ties with duPont. The broadcast was a vigorous protest that the duPont agreements with I. C. I. had been of great benefit to the American people and to the war effort.

Also naming numerous products which, it was admitted, duPont chemists had improved but which "came originally from abroad."

Again Farben was not named although vague references were made to continental European companies, and mention of synthetic nitrogen and ammonia, plastics, rayon, dyes and cellophane may have caused listeners to believe that many vital products which in reality had been made in this country since the days of the first world war were actually the result of the benevolences which I. C. I. and the unnamed European companies had contributed to America during the recent pre-war period.

There was a defiant note of challenge in these duPont statements which ignored any suggestion that the benefits thus alleged could have been secured equally well without any questionable tie-ups with I.G. Farben. And little was said about those instances where, as will be revealed in the next chapter, the duPont company pleaded *nolo contendere,* or agreed to a consent decree in cases involving Farben tie-ups.

From across the Atlantic, Lord Harry McGowan, chairman of I. C. I. made several contributions to a friendly duPont press, with statements cabled through the press associations which termed such charges against his company "iniquitous." The noble lord declared that the cooperation between I. C. I. and duPont had been beneficial to both the United States and Britain, and formed a good pattern for post-war international agreements.

In debate in the English House of Lords, both Lord McGowan, and Lord Melchett, another I. C. I. director, on occasion shouted defiance at the United States Department of Justice regarding the numerous instances in which I. C. I. was accused with duPont of tie-ups with Farben. Lord McGowan ridiculed as innuendo the news items which had appeared in the American press indicating improprieties in any such relationships. He boasted that I. C. I. "is not indicted" for any breach of American law (which was hardly accurate) and had not "done anything to be ashamed of," (which, being a lord, may have been true). Finally he announced that it would be time enough for the House of Lords to ponder the matter of Farben when and if Parliament should enact legislation against such relations.

Undoubtedly the news and editorial comment in the American press which stressed duPont's relations with our British allies, the I. C. I., rather than the tie-ups with the German enemy, I.G. Farben, tended to soften public opinion towards duPont. That company's greatest triumph in public relations belongs in the next chapter.

In 1941, when Sterling began getting hostile criticism in the press, a public-relations firm with special training to correct just such unfortunate situations was engaged.

Baldwin, Beech, & Mermey, of New York City, was given the task—a happy choice, as this was the outfit which had been selling the public the idea that a rejuvenated McKesson & Robbins, under many of the same old directors, was rid of all taint and odor of the fraud and criminal activities of its erstwhile guiding spirit, Donald (Musica) Coster.

A glance at the earlier record of the firm of Baldwin, Beech, & Mermey indicates that its qualifications for the job were also well founded on experience which Mr. William Baldwin and Mr. Maurice Mermey had when they were retained in the late 20's to sweeten publicity in favor of a low tariff on sugar imports from Cuba. In this case the sweetening came from the Hershey Co., the Coca Cola Co., and an organization known as the American Bottlers Association.

According to testimony given by Messrs. Baldwin and Mermey before the Caraway Lobby Committee in 1930, some rather weird methods were utilized in order to induce favorable publicity, called "legitimate news," some of which might indicate animosity in Cuba towards the United States. Commenting on the evidence, Senator Robinson accused Baldwin and Mermey of:

> Arranging to have cartoons published in these Latin-American newspapers, inflaming the sentiment against the United States. (Farben would have liked that as much as the sugar people.)

So on the record, Baldwin, Beech & Mermey was well qualified to inject some sweetness and light into the sourness of the Sterling reputation. Its task was not an easy one, and, unhappily, news items continued to come out of Washington which were reminders of the close personal relations between the Sterling executives and the leaders of Farben.

However, the agile press agents got to work and Sterling soon got some publicity which paid unqualified tribute to its reformation and to its executive personnel, especially Messrs. McClintock, Rogers, and James Hill, Jr., who represented the old regime as well as the new.

Two New York publications which gave space to favorable mention of Sterling (in February 1942) were *The American Business Survey*, a sheet devoted to articles praising various companies and individuals, and *Printers Ink*, long established organ of the advertising and publishing business.

The articles in both of these publications praised the new Sterling set up. *Printers Ink* also praised its past and, rather oddly, appeared to credit Sterling with having secured for the medical profession such remedies as Salvarsan, Novocain and Luminal, all of which, it may be recalled, were introduced in the United States long before Sterling supposedly had any tie-ups with the Germans. *American Business Survey* talked about the "Monr Doctrine puissant" and "cultural coordination" between the Unitea

States and Latin Americans induced by Sterling's anti-German drug drive. It was pretty bad.

Reprints from both of these publications were distributed gratis, and with apparent liberality, but as none of the dodgers were handed to me, I called at the office of *The American Business Survey* to secure a copy. Only one individual was visible in the office—a zealous gent who wanted to quote me prices on lots of a hundred or more. I got my copy, thanked him, and left. A few weeks later the Federal Trade Commission lit on the interesting "Survey" publication as a fake.

Another disingenuous publicity stunt by which Sterling attempted to live down its Farben relations was the free distribution through druggists and doctors of thousands of copies of a booklet entitled "Footprints of the Trojan Horse," which was originally published as a warning against fifth-column activities in the United States. This time it was handed out in the name of "The Bayer Company, Inc., makers of Bayer Aspirin." It was a strange book for Sterling to circulate in the year 1942.

When the adverse publicity of 1941 got under way, the trade and industrial press did everything in its power to convince the public that Sterling, Standard Oil, and other Farben affiliates had done nothing wrong in making tie-ups with the Germans, and that in any event the results had been beneficial to the United States. This was merely following the line of indirect apology that for many years had been held to in such journals as *Chemical and Metallurgical Engineering*, the McGraw Hill publication long accepted as authoritative in the industries.

For example, back in May 1929, this publication had lauded the formation of the American I.G. Chemical Corp., and belittled its critics as hysterical. Again, in April 1942 its editorial made the preposterous accusation that it was Thurman Arnold's prosecution of Farben affiliates that had obstructed our national defense supplies of magnesium, Buna rubber, and other strategic materials.

In normal news channels Sterling fared a bit better than Standard Oil, possibly because it escaped the Truman and Bone Committee inquiries. These inquiries went sufficiently deep into Standard's relations with Farben to cause its president, at that time, the late W. S. Farish, to attempt a public defense before both committees. Much of Mr. Farish's testimony was devoted to denials of the accusations that Standard had delayed synthetic rubber production in this country. This allegation, he stated before the Truman Committee, "has not a shadow of foundation." However, Mr. Farish appeared unable to explain, even to his own satisfaction, the long delay in getting the Buna program started. "I don't know what has caused the delay" he said at one point.

In the ensuing discussion of the delayed rubber program, Senator Connally, old Texas colleague of Mr. Farish, contributed this gem of official explanation and foresight:

> We were hopeful that we wouldn't lose the Dutch East Indies and hopeful that we wouldn't lose Malaya . . . . . Whoever, if any one, did it (caused the delay) was probably acting through motives they thought were wise and good motives.

Before the Bone Committee, Mr. Farish assumed an aggressive attitude and denounced the case which had been presented against Standard as "one sided." Senator Bone retorted hotly that he was fed up with that kind of defense from big outfits like Standard.

When Mr. Farish alleged that Standard's relationship with Farben was severed by the so-called Hague agreement in 1939, he was forced to admit that there was still in existence a carry-over understanding subject to later adjustment (which means, of course, after the war). Mr. Farish then started to enlarge upon the thesis that "All of you know now of the enormous advantages to the public of our contracts with I.G. Farben."

Challenged on this one by Mr. Creekmore Fath, Mr. Farish replied plaintively, "We are human beings. In 1927 we could not foresee 1942."

So it was made to appear that the master minds running the world's largest industrial organization, with agents in every country, never even suspected that a war was in the making.

As examples of the enormous advantages to America that had been brought about by the Farben partnership agreements, Mr. Farish listed the original process for producing 100 percent octane gasoline; the method of making synthetic toluol, the basic ingredient of TNT; and Paratone, an improvement in lubricating oils for planes, tanks and ships.

These generous tokens of Farben's esteem sounded good to some of the Senators—until three of Mr. Farish's assistants gave their testimony. It then appeared that the products named by Standard's president had been perfected not by Farben, but by Standard Oil's own research men.

An item of rather unfavorable publicity also developed when Professor Hunter, of the Justice Department, told the Bone Committee that five Standard officials had made deliberate misstatements. Some of the discussion that followed was so heated that it was expunged from the record.

Standard's efforts before the Senate Committees to excuse or vindicate its relations with Farben were supplemented with numerous press releases and circulars—the latter distributed from filling stations and at employes' meetings. Informal talks before gatherings of all kinds were also in order.

Robert Haslam, elected vice-president of Standard Oil and in charge of public relations, contributed vigorous articles and letters to the press defending his company's relations with Farben against what he termed sensational, unsubstantiated charges which painted a false and distorted picture.

One Haslam article, which appeared in the *Petroleum Times* of London, England, on December 25, 1943, struck fire in an unexpected quarter—no other than the headquarters of Farben at Frankfurt, Germany (although this effect was not known in the United States until the war ended). Mr. Haslam alleged in this article that secrets brought to America from Germany had turned into mighty weapons against Germany. He then mentioned the same three developments which had been cited by Mr. Farish before the Bone Committee; high octane gasoline; toluol; and Paratone as having been secured from Farben. Apparently he did not remember that he was one of the three Standard scientists who, to the Senate Committee, had indicated opinions that Standard, rather than Farben, had actually developed these processes.

Mr. Haslam's article likewise indicated that America got Buna rubber from Farben.

It did not take long for the Haslam alibi to get through to Germany, whereupon Farben's chief counsel, Dr. August von Knieriem, put his own experts to work picking flaws in the Haslam thesis—with counter-claims that it was Farben and not Standard, that had all the best of it in the pre-war horse trading.

Many valuable contributions, said the Farben boys, were received as result of their contracts with the Americans—including lead-tetra-ethyl (gasoline); polymerization; improved lubricants; and finally, that it was through friendly relations with Standard that Farben had purchased large reserve stocks of aviation gasoline and lubricating oils for the German government just before the war.

As for Iso-octane, said the Farben experts, Standards research men had recognized that long before they had any knowledge of the Farben process—and it was Farben that got the best of the exchange of ideas on that item. And regarding toluol, the report went on, Mr. Haslam's talk of a miracle was all bunk. According to the Frankfurt technicians, Standard did not use Farben's process as it already had all the toluol methods it needed.

On Oppanol, or Paratone, again it was Standard's improvements that helped Farben. The retort on Buna rubber was emphatic—Farben didn't give Standard anything important to war economy, and whatever may have been revealed in the patents America could have procured without any agreements—as enemy patents in war time.

Altogether, the Farben boys appeared to have shot Mr. Haslam's alibi and that of Mr. Farish full of holes. It will be recalled, too, that in Chapter XIV, Farben's Dr. Loehr admitted that his company had undermined the military potential of the United States through its connections with Standard.

However, the Haslam-Farish versions had wide circulation in the United States, and the Farben retorts did not. The result of Standard's publicity was a lessening of criticism.

Other things, however, may have contributed. It was stated by Walter Winchell that in May 1942 a news broadcaster for CBS had been effectively silenced on the Truman and Bone Committees exposés. This man had included in the script of his broadcast mention of the accusations that Standard intended to resume ties with Farben when the war ended. The CBS censor killed the item

and, it was reported, told the radio newsmen to "go easy on
Standard, you know we carry plenty of their business."

Harry S Truman, while still a Senator, paralleled that revealing
incident with a public accusation that Standard, with huge government contracts, was advertising at taxpayer's expense to coun-
teract the fact that its tie-ups with Farben had materially retarded
the development of synthetic rubber in America.

The 1942 and 1943 stockholder's meetings of Standard at Flem-
ington, N. J., were the occasions of spirited defense speeches by its
executives. At both of these meetings a committee of minority
stockholders, ably led by one William Floyd, II, and his attorney,
Amos S. Basel, proposed queries and resolutions which appeared
to embarrass mightily the Standard defenders.

At the 1942 meeting Messrs. Floyd and Basel attempted in vain
to put through a resolution requiring the Standard executives to
answer "fully and adequately" the Senate Committee accusations.
At the 1943 and 1944 meetings they tried again, unsuccessfully,
to get Standard on record that it would not resume cartel relations
with I.G. Farben after the war, unless the Government should
desire it to do so.

At the 1943 meeting President Ralph Gallagher, who had succeeded to that office at the death of Mr. Farish, made the fantastic
assertion that Standard "never had any cartel agreement with I.G.
Farben." He then declined to reply to a question as to whether
or not the Farben contracts would come into existence again when
the war was over.

Senator Kilgore, on the morning of the 1944 meeting, issued a
statement at Washington calling attention to Standard's reluctance
to make any commitment on post-war cartels. At the meeting Mr.
Basel, raising his voice above the uproar which arose whenever he
pressed the Standard-Farben issue, quoted the substance of the
Kilgore remarks. Whereupon Mr. Haslam, his ire aroused, demanded that Mr. Basel read the entire statement. "I will," replied
the speaker, "if these people will keep quiet." The claque, for
once, subsided.

James Gerard, Ambassador to Germany in the first World War
and financier of the Democratic National Committee, defended
Standard's leaders at all of these meetings. In 1942 Gerard quoted

Leviticus about the priest and the goat. In 1943 Mr. Gerard's contribution was of more serious import. Said he:

> I can assure you that some of us who are thinking over what is to happen after the war are contemplating universal cartels, and it may be that our own government will tell or even order our management to join some international cartel.

At the 1943 Standard Oil meeting, approval was voted to a proposal of the directors to transfer permanently to the United States all of the Buna rubber patents. There were, of course, certain provisions, but it was good publicity, only a comparatively few people knew that under the terms of the 1942 consent decrees Standard had already been forced to throw open its Buna patents, and that the Alien Property Custodian had already seized title to all of the Farben United States patents which allegedly had been transferred to Standard—after the war started.

While I did not attend the 1943 meeting, I did go to the one in 1942—as proxy for a stockholder, and asked just one question:

> Mr. Farish, would you or the other officers of the company desire to state to this meeting the date when you first became convinced or suspicious that the activities of the German I.G. Farben in its relationship to Standard Oil of New Jersey were hostile to the national security of the United States?

Mr. Farish, after some quibbling, declined to reply. "I don't think the question is proper," he said.

So this challenge, which must go pretty close to the root of the matter, remains unanswered by Standard. Neither does it appear that the executives of duPont, Alcoa, Sterling, or any of the other Farben affiliates have ever stated the date when they first suspected that Farben's intentions might be hostile to the national security of their country. And yet this might seem to be a fair question—one which any man would desire to answer.

No Sacrifice on the Altar
of Moloch

DON'T THINK THAT
you need prove how great the United States is by throwing
it sacrifices. That was all right for the hideous God Moloch,
but it would be intolerable if you or any . . . . . (group)
thought that they could add to the majesty and dignity of the
United States by proving its power through an injustice.

This moving appeal came near the close of a solemn address
which, on June 20, 1945, in impressive surroundings at Newark,
New Jersey, was listened to in respectful silence by a group of
representative citizens, flanked by men high in official, industrial,
and other circles important in the affairs of this nation.

Leading up to his magniloquence about the Old Testament's
God of War and Vice, the speaker had said:

It would be a hideous, a monstrous, an unconscionable
thing, if any of the rights of these defendants which I have
outlined to you were neglected by you, or if any one of them
should be sacrificed to the might and power of the Govern-

325

ment just to prove the Government's right and power. The Government of the United States asks no sacrifice of anybody to prove its might and greatness. The United States of America proceeds with majestic instancy towards that goal which has been marked for it by God Almighty, and it does not require any fictitious or factitious accretions to its greatness. It proceeds along the path of justice and will not deviate from that path so long as it fulfills the will and intent of the Divine Creator who brought this country into being for its own unmeasurably wise purpose.

Thus did this modern Solomon picture to six men and six women in a jury box, the sacrificial blood of innocent victims staining the altar of that wicked God of the Ammonites, as a warning of the abomination that might be their verdict, should it be induced, mistakenly, by too great love for their native land—or grief for the blood of their own sons and daughters sacrificed on a less high altar, erected by one of those named in the conspiracy to be judged by that jury, I.G. Farben, of Frankfurt-am-Main.

Having been instructed also that the Government of the United States was entitled to a just verdict, the jury retired and ten hours later brought in a verdict of NOT GUILTY for the two corporations and six individuals whose fate, for those ten hours, had been in their hands.

I.G. Farben was not technically on trial in that case, having been accused merely as a co-conspirator, of conspiring with duPont and Röhm & Haas of Philadelphia, with eight of their officers, as defendants; along with two other co-conspirators, Imperial Chemical Industries of England and Röhm & Haas of Darmstadt, Germany.

As discussed heretofore in Chapter VI those named were accused of having entered into agreements to fix prices and restrain production and distribution of acrylic, or plastic, glass-like products, in violation of the Sherman Anti-Trust Law.

One mystifying aspect of the trial was the dismissal of Counts 2 and 3 of the indictment on motion of Walter R. Hutchinson, Special Assistant to Attorney General Francis Biddle, who represented the Government. This left only Count 1 of the indictment at issue and confined the case to charges of violation of Section 1 of the Sherman Act, forbidding conspiracies in restraint of trade. Whereas Counts 2 and 3 alleged also violations of Section 2 of the Sherman Act which forbids monopoly or attempt to monopolize. (It might be noted here that no explanation has been forthcoming of this apparent free gift to the defendants of immunity without trial under the specific charges in Counts 2 and 3. However it is known that Mr. Hutchinson, who had just returned to the Justice Department from army duty overseas, was ill, and in no condition to have tried this case.)

The Court, in its charge to the jury made certain the omission was understood and that:

> The second section, relating to monopoly, has been abandoned by the Government . . . . . so that there remains for your consideration only the first count which is violation of Section 1 of the Sherman Act.

The Court then made this astounding misstatement of the language and scope of Section 1 of the Sherman Act, as follows:

> Performance of an overt act to effectuate the object of the conspiracy is necessary to bring the combination within the ambit of the statute, because a conspiracy of itself, a combination of itself, is not denounced by the statute unless there be something done to effectuate its purpose.

This weird dictum being absolutely incorrect we may wonder how and why the Judge came to so inform the jury.

The Court also appeared anxious that the jury be not led astray regarding the significance of a letter introduced by the Government and quoted a small part of this letter, which was from Mr. Haas of Philadelphia, U. S. A., to Dr. Röhm of Darmstadt, Germany, in 1936, about consultation on prices, as follows:

> A matter like this cannot be put into the contract because it would be against the law.

Strangely, the Court did not feel called upon to quote the next sentence of that same letter, which was as follows:

We have to rely on our verbal assurance and our experiences with duPont during the last fifteen years has proven that they can be relied upon to live up to an arrangement of this kind.

Noticeable in the trial were the harmonious relations which prevailed between opposing counsel during the six weeks which were required to present the voluminous evidence to the jury. This love fest, so different from the cat and dog courtroom fights which frequently occur among counsel in a case of this type, caused the Judge to pay tribute to the "eminent fairness which has been exhibited by counsel for the defense and counsel for the Government." Said the Court:

I'll pay my tribute to counsel because it has made the work of the Court so much easier . . . . .

One of the distinguished members of the bar whose nice courtroom manners were thus complimented by the Judge, was the well-known attorney, Bruce Bromley, whose forensic snarls and sneers are famous.

The Philadelphia Röhm & Haas, with its admittedly close ties to the Darmstadt firm and to I.G. Farben, was represented by Mr. Bromley, whose New York and Washington law firm of Cravath, Swaine and Moore (formerly Cravath, de Gersdorff, Swaine and Wood), had also represented Farbwerke Hoechst of Farben in several peculiar cases in the New York District Court against one of Herman Metz's companies, during the same period when Farben (as discussed in Chapter II) was paying Metz other large sums of money to turn over his drug and dye interests in this country to Sterling and General Aniline.

It also may be of interest here to note that a few weeks later, on September 11, 1945, Hoyt A. Moore, Esq., of this same Cravath firm, was indicted by a Federal Grand Jury at Scranton, Pennsylvania, with former Federal Judge Albert W. Johnson and others on charges of conspiring to obstruct justice and defraud the United States Government. Judge Johnson resigned to avoid impeachment and the House Judiciary Committee in February 1946

turned in a report castigating the "corrupt connivance" of Mr.
Moore and pointed out that the Cravath firm had charged over
$125,000 for its services.

Later the indictment of Hoyt Moore was dismissed by the Court
on his plea at the Bar based upon the statute of limitations, because the acts of which he was accused were all performed "more
than three years prior to the date said indictment was found."

The Judge who tried the duPont–Röhm & Haas case in 1945
was the same jurist who had sealed the original indictment in
August 1942, from public knowledge, during the period when
five members of Senator Bone's Patents Committee were voting to
forbid further investigations and hearings on the Farben tie-ups.
This jurist was none other than Hon. Thomas F. Meaney, whose
nomination for the bench in 1942 provoked a bitter fight in the
United States Senate. During the final debate in the Senate it was
the late W. Warren Barbour of New Jersey who stated the issue as:

> . . . . . Like Caesar's wife a Federal judge should be above
> suspicion . . . . . Mr. Meaney cannot escape always being
> viewed as a pawn of Mayor Hague.

And, the aged Senator George W. Norris, in one of his last im-
passioned appeals denounced the Hague organization as a contemptible, crooked, bipartisan machine, and the nominee as "one
of his tools," whom Hague "is trying to put on the bench." Said
the Senator "The confirmation of Meaney would be like putting
Hague on the bench."

When the six men and six women brought in their verdict of
not guilty in the trial of the duPont-Röhm & Haas-Farben tie-ups
there came to an end the first, and as this is being written, the
only case, in which American corporations and some of their
officers, have been tried before a jury for alleged criminal conspiracy with I.G. Farben. And, under our system of American
jurisprudence, the record of acquittal stands—that these corporations and these men were not guilty of any unlawful act in having
made the agreements with Farben and with each other, or in
doing any of the acts alleged as unlawful by the Government.

Nothing can better illustrate than this trial the failure of the enforcement of the antitrust laws to impose either punishment for past associations with Farben or warning against future renewals of such affiliations.

When the duPont-Röhm & Haas-Farben trial ended in so complete a fiasco for the Government and established so complete a vindication for Farben's partners, press statements appeared immediately credited to representatives of duPont in which the Government's accusations were belittled with the allegation that "when the time came to produce supporting evidence in court, the prosecution was unable to do so."

Thus a battle was fought, or staged, and lost in a New Jersey courtroom, against Farben, in those hectic weeks of May and June 1945, immediately after the armies and government of Germany lost their last battle, to surrender ignominiously and unconditionally—and simultaneously the plot to revive Farben's Cartel structure emerged, as announced in Washington by Senator Kilgore on June 21st, the day after the jury in Judge Meaney's court officially recorded the lawfulness of the duPont-Röhm & Haas-Farben alliance.

In this case the result was at least a clear cut acquittal of the defendants. In some of the cases to follow the results, where there have been any and the lack of results in others, are so vague and indefinite that sabotage of government may not seem an unfit term to apply.

We must go back to the direction of the Anti-Trust Division by Robert H. Jackson, for the initiation of the first Anti-Trust case in which was involved a tie-up with I.G. Farben, or rather with one of its international cartel alliances. This case was filed in 1937, against the Aluminum Company of America (Alcoa), its disowned Canadian offspring or counterpart, Aluminium Limited, and twenty-three subsidiaries, along with thirty-nine individual officers and others accused of unlawful monopoly in the production and distribution of aluminum.

In this case Aluminium Ltd. was accused of direct participation in the international aluminum cartel with Vereinigte Aluminium Werke of Bitterfeld, Germany. one of the I.G. Farben affiliates.

The lower court in 1940 having found no unlawful monopoly existed, this judgment was reversed on March 13, 1945, by the

Court of Appeals which ruled that Alcoa was in fact a monopoly—and then returned the case to the lower court for further proceedings.

The participation of Farben's German affiliate in the international cartel received little attention in this celebrated case, but it is timely here to reveal that in aluminum, as in so many of our other important war materials, Farben had succeeded in a participation in restrictive cartel tie-ups reaching into this continent. The initial action involving Farben brought by the Anti-Trust Division under Mr. Arnold was that against Rudolph Ilgner for destroying Chemnyco records which was described in Chapter v. The Chemnyco records sought and destroyed had been demanded by a grand jury for the antitrust investigation of nitrogen and ammonia fertilizer materials which resulted in five blanket indictments; two of these named as defendants Farben's Synthetic Nitrogen Products Corporation, and its executives, including one Carl B. Peters as vice-president, along with numerous other Farben affiliates in the United States, Europe and South America; the affiliates as either defendants or co-conspirators. Mr. Peters is given special mention here because he makes a dramatic reappearance in a later chapter.

The American I.G., also Farben, and the International Nitrogen Cartel of London, which Farben organized to control and restrict the world's nitrogen production, were among those listed as co-conspirators.

The several conspiracies which the Antitrust Division thus attempted to attack and which included the misuse of patent licenses, were those by which Farben, careful not to appear reaching for control of nitrogen and ammonia as military products, attained its purpose by restricting world production of these vital materials through tie-ups in the fertilizer industries.

However, these indictments, mysteriously sealed by the Court and hidden from the public for months after the grand jury acted, then all petered out. In June 1941, about the time when Attorney General Robert Jackson was kicked upstairs to the Supreme Court, Mr. Arnold backed down—or was sat upon—and his assistants began filing, in batches of a dozen or more, *Nolle Prosequi* entries which dismissed over one hundred charges against defendants in

these cases. Thus were wiped out all criminal cases on the Farben conspiracy to fix prices and restrict production of synthetic
nitrogen and ammonia.

The public heard little of these cases, and in 1941 and 1942
while the war was well under way, three civil complaints and
consent decrees were filed covering these fertilizer materials. In
these the Farben subsidiary, Synthetic Nitrogen Products, also
Imperial Chemical Industries, duPont and Allied Chemical and
Dye, with their leading officers, promised in profound legal language to refrain from doing in the future those acts of conspiracy
which, in the same breath, they denied having done in the past.
No trial, no publicity, no penalties; as the war-time answer to
a Farben conspiracy which had restricted production of those
keystones of chemical munitions in the pre-war era, nitrogen and
ammonia. Carl B. Peters was also named in one complaint and
decree involving Synthetic Nitrogen Products, which concern was
listed among the co-conspirators in the other two civil cases.

Mr. Arnold's next indictments against Farben conspirators were
three filed on January 30, 1941, covering conspiracy in restricting
production of magnesium metal and alloys through patent and
process finagling, as described in Chapter IV. These knocked
around until April 15, 1942, while a softening-up process was
going on inside the Justice Department. Then all of the defendants
except Farben and its two German directors, pleaded *nolo contendere* (which means "Oh, well, what if we did?") and paid fines
of $25,000 each, for Alcoa, Dow and American Magnesium;
$20,000 for Magnesium Development (half owned by Farben);
$15,000 for General Aniline (also owned by Farben); and $5,000
each for six of the corporation officials who were indicted. Of the
latter Farben's Karl Hochswender, president of Magnesium Development and of Chemnyco, had his fine graciously returned.

Meanwhile Farben, with Hermann Schmitz, its president, and
Gustav Pistor, one of its directors, have never been tried and undoubtedly consider this whole affair a joke. Messrs. Schmitz and
Pistor were busy in Berlin or Frankfurt a/Main making Farben's
munitions and directing Farben's war against the United States.
How they must have sneered when they heard the bargain price
of $140,000, less the $5,000 discount, that was charged by the

Yankee Court as total penalties for the injury to national defense caused by a woefully insufficient magnesium production when war broke out.

Next antitrust cases relating to Farben were the nominal fines and consent decrees involving Sterling and its affiliates which have already been described in Chapter VIII and elsewhere. It will be recalled that the fines in these cases totaled $26,000. However if the attorney's fees were over a quarter of a million dollars, as it was rumored in the Justice Department, then it might seem that the bargain between the parties on which the consent decrees were based included pre-arranged penalties for Sterling of around $300,000—of which the United States Treasury was to receive $26,000, and some one else was to get the balance.

Even though these consent decrees may have cost Sterling several hundred thousand dollars in huge fees exacted by Mr. Corcoran plus not so huge fines exacted by the Court, yet this whole transaction may be said to have shown a nice net profit for Sterling. Because when the decrees were arranged it appears that there was due to Farben, from Sterling-Bayer under the profit-sharing agreements, the tidy sum of $544,000, which amount Sterling was permitted to retain in its own pockets.

As events proceeded it may appear that as a result of the alleged abrogation of the Farben agreements Sterling's profits were increased by a sum of well on to $1,000,000 annually, this being the share of the booty which prior to the consent decrees had gone to I.G. Farben. The United States Treasury appears as the real loser of these millions because the Treasury had already frozen all Farben funds, and after the Alien-Property Custodian began seizing Farben's belongings (some of them) in 1942, these Sterling profits due Farben would have gone to the Custodian's bank account. If it were not for those consent decrees which Mr. Corcoran induced his Sterling clients and his friend Mr. Biddle— to consent to.

That Sterling appreciated the advantage of this war opportunity to retain these profits is shown by the fact that this company actually went into the Canadian courts in 1944 with a plea to set aside contracts in the Dominion between its subsidiary, the Bayer Company Limited, and Farben's Bayer. However, the

Canadian High Court ruled that the monies owed by Sterling's Canadian Bayer to Farben's German Bayer must continue to be paid to the Canadian Alien Property Custodian.

Another peculiar feature of these Sterling-Bayer-Winthrop-Farben criminal actions and civil consent decrees of 1941, is that although all agreements between Sterling and Farben were supposed to have been abrogated, this does not appear to be true. We need only to examine the records of the Securities and Exchange Commission to discover two other agreements with Farben entered into by Sterling's British subsidiary, Bayer Products Company Ltd., and its Canadian subsidiary Bayer Company Ltd. It was the latter of these two agreements which Sterling attempted to cancel in 1944 so as not to keep on paying the Canadian Alien Property Custodian.

These two British and Canadian agreements were, as late as May 1945, officially hidden from public inspection by the Securities and Exchange Commission where they were on file. In a letter dated January 31, 1945, the Securities and Exchange Commission denied inspection of these agreements on the allegation that they had been filed with the Commission by Sterling in 1936 with a stock registration along with two other Farben contracts, with request from some unidentified person that they all should be kept secret. The Commission also refused to exhibit the request for this secrecy.

However, on May 17, 1945, I was notified to appear to testify before a Senate Committee on a bill to require that all restrictive foreign trade agreements be registered before some Federal Agency; and by a strange coincidence the Securities and Exchange Commission decided on the same day that the still secret Sterling-Farben agreements could properly be made public "without objection by the Sterling Company," said the letter.

When we recall how painfully shocked and surprised so many public officials appeared to be after the Justice Department officially discovered illegal agreements made years before with Farben—and we then discover that at least some of them had been filed with an important official agency but on a pledge to hide them as trade secrets, we begin to wonder what kind of hocus pocus our Government really is.

And when one department of Government publicly brands an entire group of these Farben tie-ups as illegal from the days when they were entered into, and a court so decrees in both criminal and civil actions, while another branch of the Government still keeps some of them hidden as lawful trade secrets, then it becomes a burlesque of government. And by the same token we may accept this as a typical illustration of the pattern of I.G. Farben's activities within the fabric of this nation before the war, during the war, and as now revealed after the combat war has ended.

Another anti-trust action involving cartel tie-ups between Sterling-Winthrop and I.G. Farben, as set forth in Chapter III may be mentioned here to refute the idea that the 1941 consent decrees constituted a complete divorce between Sterling and Farben.

In February 1944, the Anti-Trust Division intervened in a patent infringement case in Illinois in which the Wisconsin Alumni Research Foundation was prosecuting another company for allegedly violating the Vitamin D patents. The Government brought counter-charges of violation of the Sherman Act against Wisconsin Alumni and some sixteen of its licensees which were marketing Vitamin D in medicinal or food products. These included Winthrop; duPont; The Quaker Oats Company; Standard Brands Inc.; The Borden Co.; Parke Davis & Co.; E. R. Squibb & Sons; Abbott Laboratories and others. The intervention by the Government caused the court to enjoin Wisconsin Alumni from further restrictive activities and the Vitamin D patents were thrown open to the public. However, the injunctive decree did not mention the 1928 cartel agreement with Farben covering these patents.

War had been declared only a few days before the next batch of Farben cases was ground out by the anti-trust boys with the able assistance of Joe O'Connell's Treasury raiders; this crop being three multiple indictments against General Aniline and Film, General Dyestuff and I.G. Farben, along with numerous individual members of Farben's royal families and exiled employes. These cases have already been well discussed in earlier chapters.

However there are several mysterious aspects of these three cases, which are still as this is written, postponed and untried and also disparaged as unnecessary in certain official circles.

It may be recalled that I.G. Farben itself as well as its stooges, false fronts and errand boys, is a defendant in two of these cases. In the other it is merely called a co-conspirator. Farben did not answer "here," or "not guilty," in January 1944 when the others appeared to plead. Nobody would admit knowing who was Farben's official or legal representative in this country. So the summons was marked "Unable to Find." Then after an unsuccessful attempt to pin that honor on Mr. Hochswender of Chemnyco, the court on February 28, 1942, announced the appointment of William M. Wherry, Esq., as Special Master to determine the identity of Farben's agent in the United States.

Unfortunately, the court appears still uninformed. More than four years later, as of May 16, 1946, Mr. Wherry had never had a copy of the order served on him, so he never was officially started on this ardous task. What became of the order the records do not show.

After reading some of the chapters of this book the court and the Justice Department might be able to make several good guesses as to the identity of Farben's representatives in this country, especially as appearances for I.G. Farben were finally entered on the records of the Magnesium indictments by a well known New York law firm which came forward as Farben's legal representative in those cases.

The local address of the chief villain still being an official mystery, and the General Aniline-General Dyestuff properties firmly in the custody of the Alien Property Custodian after being allegedly deloused of all Farben taint, a strange conflict inside the Government got under way with reports of urgent pleas from the Custodian's office that the cases be abandoned. (In which event the basic contracts with I.G. Farben would remain in effect, and a resumption of those ties after the war would be expedited.)

In one of these cases a demurrer was filed in the names of Farben itself and its two subsidiaries and several officers, including the celebrated overseas Schmitz brother team, Hermann and Dietrich. This demurrer presented the topsy-turvy spectacle of the Alien Property Custodian of the United States, who now controlled General Aniline, asking the Court to throw out as false, preposterous and unwarranted, indictments which had been handed down by a Grand Jury at the request of the Attorney General of the United States.

Claims were made that the relationship of Farben and General Aniline being that of parent and offspring, it was silly to allege that they conspired by merely being nice to each other. One of those who filed this demurrer was the same Dietrich A. Schmitz, who back in 1938 gave his solemn oath before the Securities and Exchange Commission that he did not know who owned General Aniline (then American I.G.). Evidently Dietrich, by 1944, had discovered the surprising fact that its parent was big brother Harmann's I.G. Farben.

The attorneys representing the Alien Property Custodian's management of General Aniline and Dietrich Schmitz had still another reason why the case should be tossed into the wastebasket, arguing that it could not be against public policy for Farben to keep foreign chemicals out of the United States by private arrangement, because Congress did the same thing with the Tariff Act.

These arguments were successfully met by Herbert A. Berman, Chief of the Patents and Cartel Section of the Anti-Trust Division, whose brilliant handling of such work was recognized as one of the bright spots in the Justice Department, until he finally resigned in disgust early in 1946. The Court threw out this demurrer on November 6, 1944, and a few days later in another branch of the same court all three of the indictments against D. A. Schmitz were dismissed. (As already discussed in Chapter v.)

So these three cases, in some respects the most important involving Farben and its huge American false fronts, remained untried while the war went on—so as not to interfere with its conduct and, a year after the war was over, were still untried—because one branch of the Government did not want another branch to enforce the law. If Farben's Schmitz, looking ahead before the war had planned it this way, could he have done it better?

Another indictment accusing General Aniline and General Dyestuff of conspiracy in the dye industry was filed in the New Jersey District Court on May 14, 1942; but in this instance Farben (local address still unknown) was named only as a co-conspirator. Those indicted included duPont; Allied Chemical and Dye; and American Cyanamid; also Farben affiliates the American Ciba, Sandoz and Geigy. Some twenty officers of the corporate defendants, including Ernest K. Halbach and two of his Farben pals were also indicted in this case.

The alleged conspiracy included world-wide restrictions in the manufacture, distribution, import and export of dyestuffs, stemming out of the international cartel set-up in 1928 in which co-conspirator Farben was the dominant influence. A long list of other co-conspirators included the Swiss Ciba, Sandoz, and Geigy companies with Cincinnati Chemical Works, their jointly owned American concern; Imperial Chemical Industries and its Canadian subsidiary; the French Kuhlmann; Japan's Mitsui; and duPont-I. C. I. branches in Brazil and the Argentine. In this case antitrust spread its largest net and landed speckled fish of many varieties and many nations. All had been gathered in Farben's net of the world's dye industry.

When Secretary of War Stimson and Attorney General Biddle agreed to postpone the trial until it would not interfere with war production, one Justice Department official was quoted as saying sourly, "First they hurt the war effort by their restrictive practices, and then if caught they use the war effort as an excuse to avoid prosecution." A tug of war went on under cover whether to compromise, dismiss or forget this case. Finally compromise won. In April 1946, after Tom Clark had become Attorney General, the indictments were completely dismissed as to eleven of the defendants, including General Dyestuff's celebrated Halbach, and were partially dismissed as to four of the corporations and eight of the other individuals named. At the same time pleas of *nolo contendere* (which is equivalent to guilty) were entered and the Justice Department notified the court that under these circumstances it would not be in the public interest to stage a trial. No decree was entered by the court, so the contracts were not officially abrogated.

The fines totaled $111,000 including four of $15,000 to duPont, Allied Chemical and Dye, General Aniline, and General Dyestuff. For the last two the procedure required the transfer of a fictitious bookkeeping item of $30,000 from one of Uncle Sam's pockets which the Alien Property Custodian used to another where the

Attorney General's winnings are deposited. And Farben's agents who ran General Aniline and General Dyestuff went scot free, save for the American-born Rudolf Lenz, General Dyestuff vice-president, who was clipped for $5,000 fine on two counts. However Mr. Lenz (as revealed in Chapter v) was one of those paid off for his title to General Dyestuff stock in 1945. He got $47,200 for his share, so perhaps this fine did not make him feel too badly.

We come now to the long delayed action against Standard Oil (N. J.) regarding which numerous threats of indictments had been heard prior to March 25, 1942, when a criminal information, a civil complaint in equity, and a consent decree were all filed on the same day involving Standard, six of its subsidiaries (in several of which Farben had an interest) and, in both criminal and civil actions, three of its executives, Messrs. Teagle, Farish and Howard. Four of Standard's lesser officers were also named in the civil action.

The accusation in both the criminal and civil complaints was conspiracy by Standard, its subsidiaries and its officers, with I.G. Farben and others, in entering into and consummating restrictive partnership agreements, as were outlined in Chapter iv. For appearances' sake Farben was named as a co-conspirator in both actions. Not being a defendant Farben need not consider itself bound by these Court actions. For each of the ten defendants in the criminal actions there were pleas of *nolo contendere* and a modest fine of $5,000. Thus the total payoff for the ten defendants was a mere $50,000 and, without admitting that the criminal acts had been done for which the fines were paid, another nice set of promises not to so act in the future were listed in the final judgement.

If the reader thinks that these $5,000 bargain-day penalties were not commensurate with the offense charged, it may be stated here that just such an opinion was held very emphatically by some members of the Justice Department who had been sweating it out in preparation of this case. Some of them had demanded that multiple criminal indictments should be sought with fines totaling $1,000,000.

It was claimed as justification for the lack of punitive features in the outcome of this case that all of the patents in which Farben was involved, including those concerning Buna rubber, would be released by the consent decree royalty free to all comers for the duration of the war and six months afterward.

However the Alien Property Custodian also signed the consent decree, having a few hours previously asserted the Government claim to all of the Farben patents, to which Standard alleged they had acquired title through various Farben contracts, including the so-called Hague agreement. All these agreements now were declared by the court to have been unlawful when entered into. What the Judge's injunction did not say was that the decree was an attempt to lock the stable door long after the horses, and the harness and the hay, were gone.

Among the many subsections of this consent decree were provisions regarding undiminished rights of Standard to patents, trademarks, and shares of stock, which inhibitions may appear strangely gentle when it is considered that the decree was predicated upon charges and tacit admissions, of criminal acts by the defendants.

Later the purposes or results of some of the ambiguities inserted in this decree were to become apparent. The court proceedings may appear to have been neither punishment, parole, nor pardon. Rather they resembled absolution, or a rain check for a repeat performance—after the stormy weather of war should end.

As an aftermath of this case, and of the seizure by the Custodian of some 2,500 Farben patents and Farben or jointly-owned shares of stock, Standard began an intensive campaign of propaganda and excuses as described elsewhere, leading up to a court action in July 1944, which denounced the Alien Property Custodian for seizing patents and other property involved in the Farben agreements.

Taking advantage of the ambiguities in the consent decrees and relying upon the transfer of title by the so-called Hague memorandum which Standard's Dr. Howard and Farben's Dr. Ringer negotiated after the war began, Standard asserted that the Custodian was actually obligated to disgorge all the seized patents and property.

This came to trial without a jury on May 21, 1945, in New York

Federal Court before Judge Charles E. Wyzanski, Jr., a bitterly fought contest between aged John W. Davis, former presidential candidate, as attorney for Standard, and a very able Assistant to the Attorney General, Philip W. Amram, for the Government.

Judge Wyzanski dealt an almost fatal blow to the Custodian's defense at the start of the trial by holding in effect that it did not make a mite of difference whether the Farben patent titles had passed to Standard by unlawful contracts. This decision, with which some may not agree, was hailed with great relish by the Standard officials and lawyers grouped around Mr. Davis.

However, Standard was not to have things all its own way. Frank Howard, by his evasive, forgetful, and contradictory testimony made what appeared to be most important contribution to proving Mr. Amram's contention that the so-called Hague agreement was a fake and a fraud.

A surprise witness for the Government added a dramatic touch to the trial when Farben's director and Chief Counsel, Dr. August von Knieriem, was flown overseas in custody in an Army bomber. This Farben star witness on June 23rd testified in precise stilted English—after clicking his heels, bowing to the Court, and explaining that he needed no translator. His testimony was in conflict with that of Standard's Mr. Howard.

Among the interesting documents identified by von Knieriem were original letters taken from Farben's files at Frankfurt, proving conclusively that Farben officials had been in continuous contact with the Oberkommando der Wehrmacht and high officials of the Nazi Government before and during the signing of the Hague agreement. It was evident from some of this correspondence that the transfer of title to Standard, after the war began, was purely a matter of expediency for the purpose of preventing if possible, their seizure as enemy property when the United States became involved in the war.

Said one letter written by Farben to Nazi Defense Headquarters on September 16, 1939:

> German interests would not be jeopardized by the transfer . . . . . Moreover we would be able to resume at any time without hindrance the relationship existing now.

Said another dated October 5th.

> By this transfer . . . . . the patents in German possession
> will be removed from possible enemy seizure.

> We consider it right to transfer the patents to an American
> holder who is in friendly relations to us and of whom we
> know that in the future, as well, he will cooperate with us
> on a friendly basis.

The Nazi Generals and Ministers replied O. K. to these naïve
proclamations of Farben's intentions to pull another fast one on
the stupid Yankee Government—with the friendly cooperation of
Standard's Dr. Howard and his associates. "I do not raise objections" wrote one. More careful, another Nazi official instructed
Farben not to give Standard "inventions and experience data designated as 'secret' by the Wehrmacht." Such letters were marked
at the top "Secret" "To be kept . . . . . under lock and key."
But General Dwight D. Eisenhower's boys had rudely busted
all the locks and brought both the letters and their custodian over
the ocean to a Yankee court room.

After studying the voluminous testimony and exhibits, Judge
Wyzanski on November 7, 1945, handed down a lengthy "Findings
of Fact and Conclusions of Law," along with an opinion which,
so to speak, split the Farben patent hairs into two groups, giving
back to Standard everything which they had prior to the attack
upon Poland in 1939, and permitting the Custodian to keep all
those which Standard had pretended to acquire at or after the
Hague conference in September 1939.

> The so-called Hague memo was false and incomplete.
> Said the Court, "The falsity was of a type to mislead public
> authorities."

Again he said:

> The so-called Hague Memorandum was neither an accu-
> rate summary of the past dealing . . . . . nor a complete or
> faithful representation of the agreements made at the Hague.
> . . . . . scrutiny of many documents and of the oral testi-
> mony of Mr. Howard . . . . . reveals that the real agreement

was . . . . . subject however to an obligation to reconvey at the end of World War II or on demand of I.G.

These findings of the Court were in decided conflict with Mr. Howard's testimony that there was no understanding "implied or expressed that these patents would be returned to Farben after the war."

Judge Wyzanski in a series of judicial reprobations directed at the fabrications in the testimony of Standard's star witness left no doubt as to what he termed "the general impression as to his credibility which Mr. Howard made upon the court."

Among the features of Mr. Howard's allegations under oath of which the court indicated disapproval were the latter's findings that the witness had failed to keep copies of various important letters, and notes of all that was said at the Hague conference, also that Mr. Howard's recollection was faulty on matters which the Court believed he should have recalled readily.

This part of the Findings of Fact may appear as a painfully polite (it might be termed Courtly) way to record the fact that the Judge did not believe Frank Howard spoke the truth when under oath.

Regardless of Standard's motives in slipping its neck into Farben's noose during the pre-war period, the record now stands in this decision that after the war began Standard made a fake agreement with Farben for the safe keeping of Farben's patents and other rights, with the purpose of returning said property to Farben and resuming the partnership when the war ended.

The decision evidently gave complete satisfaction to neither Standard nor the Government, and rumors of contemplated appeals by both sides were heard, while additional proceedings were required in order to decide which of the 2,500 patents should go to which party under the decision. When legal hairs are split into 2,500 pieces, the job of sorting them out becomes tedious.

Another item, the metal molybdenum, important as an alloy for steel, was brought into the cartel picture by antitrust bloodhounds in August 1942 with a complaint and consent decree which named the sales subsidiaries of the Anaconda and Kennecott Copper Companies, Greene Cananea Copper, the Climax Molybdenum Co., and Molybdenum Corp. of America, as having conspired among themselves and with others unnamed in foreign countries, to divide up world markets, fix prices and quotas for this metal or its concentrates.

Among those with whom the American molybdenum companies and Greene Cananea had international contracts were I.G. Farben and other European concerns, but Farben and the others were not named in the complaint, nor in the consent decree filed a few days later. The uproar about Farben was then at its height; in the Senate the Truman Committee had quietly diverted its attention to other matters, and the squelching of Senator Bone's investigation was being consummated. Behind the scenes every particle of influence and pressure the Farben lobby possessed was being applied to hush the talk. So it may be that it was feared that defendants might refuse to consent to a consent decree without a court fight unless the name of Farben was omitted from the record. In the decree the usual "we never done it—and we will not do it again" was duly entered and the curtain was rung down on this particular scene of the Farben comedy with only a hint that one of the blind alleys shown led to the Big House at Frankfurt.

During the latter part of 1942, unseen hands firmly forced down the lid on further attacks on Farben's partners. Senator Bone by now had been forced to call off his fight. Thurman Arnold was about to quit, and the rapid succession of Farben indictments and complaints ceased for almost a year.

Then in June 1943 antitrust again went into action against Farben with a lengthy indictment of National Lead Company, Titan Company and duPont, along with four of their officers, for having engaged in a world-wide cartel conspiracy with I.G. Farben and some twenty other foreign companies to restrain the production and distribution of titanium and titanium compounds. These pigments for the manufacture of paints, rubber, glass, paper and other articles are important in peace and are strategic war materials. National Lead and a co-conspirator, Titan Co. A/S of Norway, were accused of having started the conspiracy as far back as 1920, and the others of joining in it from time to time since that year. I.G. Farben entered the cartel in 1927, with control of most of Europe, also of Japan and China. Imperial Chemical Industries, and Canadian Industries, the latter jointly owned by I. C. I. and duPont, were among the co-conspirators.

Trial of this indictment being postponed for the duration (and not having occurred as this is written), a civil complaint, which called for neither fine nor imprisonment was filed, on June 24, 1944, covering the same titanium cartel conspiracy and the same defendants and co-conspirators that were listed in the criminal case, including Farben.

After trial of this civil complaint without a jury, Judge Simon H. Rifkind's decision found National Lead and duPont guilty of conspiracy with I.G. Farben and others. However, the final decree in this case was criticized rather caustically by the Antitrust Division in an appeal to the higher court. In effect, the appeal complained that even though Judge Rifkind found the defendants guilty, the punishment or remedy as proposed was insufficient. The defendants also appealed.

One of the law firm of Cravath, Swaine and Moore representing duPont proposed to Judge Rifkind that it could not be a lawful function of the courts to rule that an American company should renounce the advantages which had been gained by its competitors through membership in an international cartel. The Court squelched this impudent suggestion that duPont should not be penalized, with the comment that "perhaps the answer is that duPont having discovered the conspiracy should have asked the Attorney General to break it up."

Thus Judge Rifkind gave an apt answer to the alibi that so many poor innocent American industrial leaders were really compelled to join Farben's cartels—and thus help Farben hamstring our war industries.

Another cartel civil complaint on January 6, 1944, involved duPont, Imperial Chemical Industries of England and New York, and duPont-controlled Remington Arms, as defendants, along with five of their executives. Named as co-conspirators were two German makers of explosives controlled by Farben, and other companies jointly owned by duPont and I. C. I. in Canada and Latin America. Farben also had an interest in some of the latter.

While this complaint was mainly directed at cartel agreements covering explosives, as described in Chapter IV, it also covered the widest range of chemical products of any of the preceding anti-trust actions in a series of comprehensive tie-ups between duPont and I. C. I. In substance the complaint alleged that the program of I. C. I. and duPont enabled the former to enter into numerous agreements with European chemical manufacturers for world cartelization of the chemical industry. Thus it was charged that a gigantic Anglo-American pool had been formed of the most important chemical products for peace and for war, from acids to alkalis, from solvents to synthetics and were tied together—with other lines stretching out from I. C. I. or duPont to Farben. As this is written the case is still untried. Perhaps it never will be—or perhaps another consent decree will result.

Next to feel the threat of court restraint for being in a tie-up involving Farben were a group of thirteen of the leading alkali manufacturers of the United States, two export associations and the I. C. I. of England, also the latter's New York subsidiary. These were named as defendants in a civil action filed in New York in March 1944 for allegedly misusing the Webb Pomerene Export Trade Act to take part in foreign cartel alliances. The conspiracy, it was alleged, unlawfully divided up the world markets for alkalis. Farben was named as co-conspirator (as usual) along with Solvay Process (owned by Allied Chemical and Dye), its Belgium namesake Solvay et Cie, and the German-owned American Potash & Chemical Co., which had been in the hands of the Alien Property Custodian since 1942. This was the first such suit involving the export act, and the defendants made an unsuccessful appeal to the Supreme Court to have the case dismissed without trial. Having failed to secure relief they waited trial. They are still waiting.

Another civil complaint filed on May 1, 1944 against the Diamond Match Company, six other American match makers, and three British, two Swedish and one Canadian companies who were accused of world-wide cartel conspiracy to restrict competition in matches. This stemmed out of the original American match trust of 1880 and included after World War I a peace treaty with Sweden's notorious international swindler and suicide, Ivar Krueger.

International Match, a holding company, Krueger's bankrupt

company, Krueger & Toll, and Krueger himself, although dead
were named as co-conspirators. In this case the dead were to
tell tales—if they would kindly wake up.

Farben came into this picture through an arrangement made by
one of its predecessor companies for the restriction of production
in the United States of chlorate of potash, a very important ingredient in match making, and in war munitions.

American production of this war material had been discontinued
and the plants scrapped when World War II began. This experience precisely duplicated the fix this country was in when German
imports of chlorate of potash were cut off during World War I.

On April 9, 1946, co-conspirator Ivar Krueger not being present, a consent decree dissolved the cartel and also forbade suppression of what is known as the everlasting match which can be
struck thousands of times—so they say.

A year was to pass before another alleged Farben anti-trust
plot was hauled into Court, after mysterious delays inside the
Government. On May 16, 1946, the International Nickel Company
of Canada and its wholly-owned namesake, both located in New
York, with three of their officers, were named as defendants in a
civil action accusing them of cartel price fixing alliance with Farben, and illegitimate aid to German re-armament.

Why action on this alleged conspiracy with Farben had been
delayed has not been explained as a tight situation on nickel had
long been a matter of common knowledge and consideration inside the Justice Department. Perhaps the delay may have been
influenced by the fact that among the directors of International
Nickel was none other than that celebrated Republican statesman
and adviser of high Democratic officials, John Foster Dulles, of
the law firm of Sullivan and Cromwell. This is not to suggest that
Mr. Dulles would have interceded for one of his companies with
the Justice Department; rather it is possible that someone inside
the Government may have believed that it would be poor taste
publicly to hold up to scorn a company of which Mr. Dulles was
a director—and I.G. Farben a partner. It will be interesting to
follow this case to its conclusion—should there ever be one.

The sixteen groups of prosecutions summarized above, which
include thirty separate court cases, do not comprise all such ac-

tions which involve some tie to Farben. But they are sufficient to reveal the utter lack of appropriate punishment which has resulted in the belated efforts of the Government of the United States to utilize our anti-trust laws for chastising Farben and its associates for injuries done to our national security.

Statistics may be unreliable in appraising matters of this kind but it is of interest that in the fifteen cases which were based on criminal indictments the penalties provided by statute, which might have been inflicted on the corporate and individual defendants should they have been found guilty, would total almost four million dollars in fines and, for the corporation executives indicted, over four hundred years in jail.

What actually resulted were fines totaling $323,000 and no jail terms whatever.

Perhaps it would be more fair to omit the one criminal case which resulted in acquittal of the defendants; even then the possible penalties in the other fourteen would be over three and one-half million dollars along with almost four hundred years in jail.

In the fifteen civil actions, four were consent decrees which followed fines imposed in criminal actions; and in eight others the Government also won complete or partial victories. But in the civil actions no penalties were possible under the law.

It is worthy of note that more than half of the criminal indictments have never been tried. And the fact that so many of them have been dismissed without trial leads to an inescapable conclusion that either those indictments should not have been sought in the first place—or else each of them should have been submitted to a jury long before this.

I.G. Farben, indicted five times, and with its German subsidiaries, named twenty four times as co-conspirators, has never yet been tried. However its American subsidiaries General Aniline and Film, and General Dyestuff have each pleaded *Nolo Contendere*, or Guilty, in at least one criminal case, as have each of Farben's leading American associates, including Allied Chemical & Dye; Aluminum Company of America; American Cyanamid Co.; duPont; Standard Oil; and Sterling-Winthrop-Bayer. The fact remains that the only criminal anti-trust action involving Farben to reach a jury resulted in a verdict of not guilty.

This much must be said for the small band of junior attorneys in the Anti-trust Division who under the leadership of Herbert Berman, dug out the facts and prepared most of these cases involving Farben.

The existence of most of these Farben tie-ups was not a secret, as has been shown elsewhere in this story, but it required this belated official recognition of their illegality and menace to our national defense, to awaken public indignation and provide the facts on which three Senate Committees could act.

These committees, headed by Senators Truman, Bone and Kilgore, which began their hearings in 1941, 1942, 1943, could have made very little headway without the great mass of evidential documents provided by anti-trust, some portions of which were thus made public before the committees were choked off.

Public access to this data appears as the only tangible result from the drag hunt so bravely started by antitrust when the war in Europe was getting under way.

Behind America's Iron Curtain

"CONFIDENTIALLY,
it stinks," said Senator LaFollette. It was April 24, 1942, more
than four months after Pearl Harbor. The Wisconsin Senator was
expressing his opinion before the Senate Patents Committee of
the failure of the Justice Department to punish the affiliates of
I.G. Farben who conspired to obstruct production of defense
materials, and its neglect to require full disclosures of the know-
how of the patented processes thus obstructed.

Thurman Arnold, Assistant Attorney General, had been making
a half-hearted defense of the consent decrees in the Standard and
Alcoa-Dow cases, as having been the best which the department
could obtain *under the circumstances.*

However, it was apparent from Mr. Arnold's testimony on this
occasion, and previously before the Truman Committee, that he
did not wish to make public exactly what circumstances, or whose
intercession had caused the Justice Department to give in to the
offenders after ample evidence had been uncovered for criminal
prosecution for conspiracy and interference with the war effort.
Mr. Arnold admitted that he had been faced with a "take it or

leave it" attitude in dealing with the Farben affiliates and that when he "took it" he agreed to fines, which he considered inadequate punishment, and to terms in civil consent decrees which he conceded did not properly supply the know-how on the patents which had served as pass keys in the illegal tie-ups with Farben.

While Mr. Arnold was before the Patents Committee he had ample opportunity to reveal to the Senate and the public the reasons, and the influence which caused him to consent to what amounted substantially to immunity for those who had conspired with Farben to obstruct our preparations for war. Mr. Arnold, however, chose not to volunteer such information, and the Senators who were questioning him chose not to press the questions that would have compelled him to do so. Senator LaFollette contented himself with his jibe at the odor of the situation, and Senator Bone with comments that anyone who had withheld technical knowledge and vital necessities from his country at such a time "was not decent" and "has no business in this country."

Mr. Arnold, in testifying later before the Bone Committee and elsewhere made no secret of the fact that he was not in accord with the postponement of the other prosecutions which he had instituted against Farben affiliates in plastics and other munitions industries. Nevertheless he had meekly consented to them on the ground that it would interfere with the pursuance of the war to prosecute those accused of conspiring to obstruct our preparations for the war.

It was not mere rumor in Washington that Thurman Arnold resigned as anti-trust chief in March 1943 because of dissatisfaction (honest rage might better describe it) with what seems to have been pseudo-legal sabotage of his efforts to eradicate Farben's industrial sabotage of this nation.

Be that as it may, when the appointment was tendered him, the chunky frame of the Assistant Attorney General bounced ungracefully down the steps of the Justice building, and found dignified repose a few blocks away in the U. S. Court of Appeals of the District of Columbia—where, as Mr. Justice Arnold, he could at least write his own decisions. No obstructions were placed upon Mr. Arnold's departure. The Senate held no hearing on the confirmation of his appointment. "My friends didn't require a hearing," he told me at the time, "and my enemies were only too anxious to get me out of the Justice Department."

Mr. Arnold is honored for the things that he started out to do, rather than criticized for the things he did not do; and his admirers regret that he did not state in public the conclusions which he expressed so fluently in private about why his efforts had failed so dismally to put the fear of God into Farben, and its American accomplices behind bars.

As the reader may by now have concluded, always it has been largely this official policy of "hush hush" that has made Farben's subversive activities possible. After the war began and revelations of those activities began to come out, it then helped provide immunity for the individuals involved.

On Feb. 11, 1942, when these very facts were tumbling out, when public indignation was mounting and Washington was seething with rumor about efforts being made to protect certain individuals who were involved with Farben, the following letter was received by the Speaker of the House of Representatives:

Office of the Attorney General
Washington, D. C.

Honorable Sam Rayburn,
The Speaker,
House of Representatives,
Washington, D. C.
My dear Mr. Speaker:

I desire to call your attention to the advisability of a law to protect the contents of secret or confidential Government records and documents from unlawful disclosure.

Under existing law, it is an offense unlawfully to conceal, remove or destroy any record, paper, or document deposited with any public officer of the United States (U. S. Code, Title 18, Sec. 254). It is likewise an offense for any person who has custody of any record or document to conceal, remove or destroy it (U. S. Code, Title 18, Sec. 235). There is no prohibition, however, against furnishing copies of or divulging the contents of secret or confidential files or documents. It would be advisable in the best interest of the public business, and particularly in the interest of national defense and internal security, to make it a criminal offense to disclose confidential Government information without authority to do so.

Accordingly, I recommend that enactment of legislation to make it a criminal offense for anyone without authority to divulge the contents of secret or confidential Government documents.

A proposed bill to effectuate this purpose is enclosed herewith.

I have been informed by the Director of the Bureau of the Budget that there is no objection to the presentation of this proposed legislation to the Congress.

Sincerely yours,

Francis Biddle,

Attorney General

Provisions in the proposed bill which Mr. Biddle's letter transmitted caused the Chairman of the Senate Judiciary Committee to state that, "It is more or less a censorship bill . . . . . We will have hearings."

Attorney General Biddle appeared before a sub-committee of the Senate Committee on February 24, and denied that the bill would be a curb on the freedom of the press, but he conceded that its censorship powers might be utilized by officials who desired to escape criticism for their acts.

Kenneth G. Crawford, then Washington bureau chief of the newspaper *PM* and chairman of the censorship committee of the Washington Newspaper Guild, testified that the bill, if enacted, would empower a bureaucrat to stamp as "confidential" documents relating to a scandal in his department and thus prevent all publicity.

On February 28, 1942, I addressed to the Chairman of both the Senate and House Judiciary Committees a protest on the bill's provisions and requested that I be permitted to testify against it. My letter said in part:

There is something very fishy about the way this so-called official war secrets bill has been trotted out just at this time, when it is no secret in Washington that those influences which were spending time and money without limit to retard our entrance into combat war prior to Dec. 9, have since then merely gone underground with their treasonable efforts to hamstring our war effort and to protect their spokesmen from punishment.

I suggest that your committee should plumb to its muddy depths the origin of this bill. When you find out who actually conceived the infant, and uncover who induced its adoption by the amiable Mr. Biddle, I suggest that you may also uncover certain subversive individuals or groups who still appear able to obtain a mysterious immunity from investigation and prosecution, an immunity which constitutes a distinct menace to our national unity and to our national defense.

This bill . . . . . is not merely an attack upon the freedom of the press, it is also an attack upon the freedom of any American citizen who may hereafter join in a demand that our long-delayed effort to preserve our future liberties must be purged of individuals whose past records prove them unworthy of trust in this crisis.

This bill, if passed, would make it a criminal offense for me to offer to state to your committee, under oath, my knowledge of corrupt protection of subversive agencies from inside government departments. This bill would make it a crime punishable by jail for me to reveal the fact that members of Mr. Biddle's own staff have already threatened to resign because they have been ordered to discontinue investigation of influential subversive individuals, and that some of these men have been threatened with reprisals because of having revealed these protests.

It would also attempt to make it a crime for any public official to resign, and publicly protest because of protection and immunity which criminal or subversive individuals may be receiving while we are engaged in war.

I trust that your committee will permit me to testify before it to support the above with greater detail. It may be obvious that the writer, a private citizen who possesses neither political nor any other kind of influence, may not make such statements as above unless he is either prepared to prove them or to go to jail. Mr. Biddle would very properly order me locked up tomorrow if what I have said here is either untrue or unjustified, or is impelled by unpatriotic motives.

The chairman did not reply, but able and upright Senator Warren R. Austin advised me that he had added my name to the list of witnesses to be called. In acknowledging receipt of the Senator's letter on March 9, 1943, I outlined the testimony I intended to present if called before the committee as:

A summary of the numerous alleged official secrets which I have encountered in recent years . . . . . regarding each of which I have already demanded investigation and action. And in each instance there has been indicated a secret power and influence to provide official secrecy and immunity.

Although many of these cases involve what might be termed ordinary crimes and criminals, there are certain of them which also involve subversive and fifth-column activities, and in nearly every instance the secret immunity granted is related directly or indirectly to the activities of individuals acting as agents, representatives, or attorneys receiving compensation from, or under direction of, either a foreign political organization or a domestic organization subsidized by a foreign corporation or government.

I suggest that there is no use whatsoever in passing any more laws about protecting official secrets for national defense as long as every Tom, Dick and Harry who has a friend or an accomplice planted in some government department can walk in and see what he wants, or can phone and have it brought to his side door.

I think that it is a matter of plain common sense, for our urgent self-protection in this crisis, that the first thing the Congress should do is to identify and demand prosecution of these official-secret fixers, including the author of the original bill as presented. The least that should be done is to run these rats out of the nation's capitol, and keep them out until the war is won.

Chairman Hatton Sumners of the House Judiciary Committee wrote me that if hearings on the bill were held I would be advised. That was the last I heard about that official-secrets bill; it died in Committee when the 77th Congress ended, and was not reintroduced in the 78th.

However its significance appears in the source and time of its inception. The failure of this bill, with its threat to officials who might talk, did not, however, end the profound silence by Government officials on matters relating to Farben and its affiliates— a silence which extended to matters of public record.

In March 1943, I sent to the office of Earl G. Harrison, then Justice Department Commissioner of Immigration and Naturalization, a lengthy list of individuals involved in the activities of I.G. Farben. This list included executives and employes of Sterling, Winthrop, Bayer, and Alba, who had been removed as undesirable; and other American citizens who had been indicted or kicked out of General Aniline, General Dyestuff, Agfa Ansco, Magnesium Development, Synthetic Nitrogen, Chemnyco and other of Farben's ersatz American fronts. My request for information about the internment, de-naturalization or deportation of these Farben stooges was met with the response that the Immigration and Naturalization office was forbidden to discuss the subject. Also, that no copy of the regulations on which that refusal was based could be supplied.

Addressing Assistant Attorney General Wendell Berge, then in charge of the Criminal Division, I requested:

> Which if any of the 53 individuals named on my list have ne-naturalization or other court proceedings pending, which involve the revoking of their citizenship?
>
> Which if any of those named has been interned?
>
> Which if any has had any other type of criminal proceedings instituted against them?
>
> If no such proceedings are now completed or pending, what is the reason why people who have been engaged in subversive and other criminal activities are not being prosecuted?

Receiving no reply I wrote again asking why those individuals on my list who had been involved in activities inimical to our national defense had not been indicted and prosecuted under the conspiracy statute for interfering with the functions of the government. My letter continued, in part, as follows:

> I have asked this question of the Justice Department more than once in the past and I have been advised more than once in conversations with members of the staff (who had sought my assistance in this Farben mess) that they agreed with me that such prosecutions—for conspiracy to obstruct the functions of the government—offered the most effective way to proceed against certain individuals because it obviated the necessity of utilizing any of the statutes relating directly to subversive acts . . . . .
>
> Why are men of this stripe immune? Is it because of their political influence?

The only reply to either of these letters was advice that the Assistant Attorney General was not permitted to reply to my queries. The reasons for not prosecuting Farben criminals were "deemed confidential."

The lack of action under the conspiracy statute against two decades of pre-war plotting could have been justified if the anti-trust actions against Farben's accomplices had resulted in heavy penalties of fine and imprisonment. But not one of these offenders has gone to jail, and many of the most conspicuous among them have been immunized from prosecution with the official excuse that to try them would interfere with the prosecution of the war.

We may ponder how it could have interfered with the prosecution of the war to lock up these indicted gentlemen from Germany, at least for the duration? Or why such matters have been none of the public's business? Or why not try them after the war?

It should be noted that in numerous other cases naturalized German nationals of little or no importance have been rightfully stripped of citizenship on the circumstantial evidence that they must have had mental reservations when they took the oath of allegiance to the United States—and then joined a German-American Bund. As compared with the subversive activities in which some of these immunized Farben gentry have taken part as members of our higher cartels, membership in some guttersnipe Bund is indeed small potatoes.

A special War Policies Unit of the Justice Department took over enforcement of the statute requiring the registration of foreign agents when this was transferred from the State Department in 1942. Publication of lists of all those registered as alien agents was then discontinued.

My request for information as to what prosecutions had been instituted against agents of Farben or of Farben's affiliates for failing to register brought the response that no such proceedings had ever been instituted against any such Farben agents.

I then supplied the War Policies Unit with a list of individuals, lobbyists, lawyers and law firms, which included some of Farben's most important agents, and requested advice as to whether any or all of those named were registered as agents of foreign principals. The response indicated that the only one of those listed had ever been registered as an agent of I.G. Farben. He was our friend Rudolf Ilgner, the Farben employe who, as told elsewhere, pleaded guilty in 1941 to destroying files and records of Chemnyco, Inc., and got off with a token fine of $1,000 instead of a jail sentence.

The official reason given by the Justice Department as to why none of the others listed by me were required to register was that their activities were regarded as "non-political" and confined to "bona fide trade and commerce." This seems a rather strange reason for not requiring the registration of individuals who are known to have been involved in criminal conspiracies, and in subversive activities here and in Latin America—activities which in some instances at least the courts have held did not constitute bona fide trade and commerce.

According to House Majority Leader, John W. McCormack, the Foreign Agents Registration Act was the most important legislation of its kind to pass in the last fifty years, and was enacted as result of efforts of the 1934 Committee of which Mr. McCormack was chairman. This was the committee that publicly exposed some of the Farben-Nazi propaganda of super press agent Ivy Lee and others, but locked and sealed other evidence secured.

When, in July 1945, Tom C. Clark succeeded Francis Biddle as Attorney General it was stated that the latter's antitrust policies would be continued (which might have meant more than was intended). Later Mr. Clark announced publicly that there would be "strict enforcement . . . . . but no witch hunting," and following this the new Attorney General was quoted as stating that civil actions were sufficient in cases where "a certain industry practice, operated openly for years, is a violation of Sherman Act . . . . . it does not seem fair under such circumstances to institute criminal prosecutions."

On the basis of the long-standing history of the Farben tie-ups in this country, and the fact once denied, but now proven, that most of these illegal partnerships were common knowledge, this pronouncement from the new head of the Department of Justice did not offer much encouragement to those of the staff who really wanted to put some of Farben's criminal associates behind bars. Subsequent to these indications of a soft post-war enforcement policy, several Anti-Trust resignations, long deferred under the Biddle regime, were handed in. What was aptly described by Mr. Clark himself as a "political anti-trust system" was now in order.

The hush-hush policy on Farben and its affiliates has not been confined to the Justice Department. Ominous when considered in their relation to events to come are some of the matters involving the office of The Alien Property Custodian.

Leo T. Crowley, shortly after he qualified as Custodian in March 1942, informed the Senate Patents Committee of his intention to seize all enemy-owned patents which had been assigned to American holders when such patents had placed restrictions upon American industries, and particularly those which might impede war production.

Despite this gratifying declaration, it was not long before members of the Custodian's staff were at loggerheads with officials of other departments because of the gentle treatment of the Farben-Sterling-General Aniline-Winthrop-owned patents. The Secretary of the Treasury announced his right to define as a foreign national any person, even an American citizen, who was found by the Treasury to have been acting directly or indirectly for the benefit of, or under the direction of, an enemy country.

From these two pronouncements it would appear that it had

been the intention of both the Secretary of the Treasury and the Custodian to seize the Farben patents held by such companies as Sterling, whose agreements were illegal conspiracies. Such patents would be seized under the precise language of the 1926 Supreme Court decision (referred to in Chapter xvi).

On the basis of fact and of law the only explanation for the refusal to seize the property and patents of the Sterling-Winthrop-Bayer-Alba group may well be found in the reports that certain of Mr. Crowley's staff failed to agree with their chief's policies, and got away with it while he was otherwise engaged.

It so happens that the same member of the Custodian's staff who first advised me that there was no intention to break the Winthrop-Atabrine monopoly also pronounced the fantastic conclusion that there was no intention to seize any property which had German ties or control in cases where the possibility existed that the former owners might recover the property by court action after the war ended.

Another member of the Custodian's staff when asked what pledge of continued American ownership was being exacted from those to whom seized properties were sold, replied by asking what was the use of such a pledge in view of the fact that after the war was over the Germans could come over again and buy back any property they had a mind to. (Just as they did after World War I.)

Later it developed that the Custodian's office had not adopted the rules for the sale of seized properties that were in effect in the first World War, and which required a very real pledge of permanent American control with penalties for violation. So it seemed that in this war, properties controlled by Farben or by Farben's allies need not always be seized, and if seized and later sold, all such foolishness as pledges of permanent American control might be dispensed with.

The rules finally adopted when sales of seized property got under way, required the purchaser to state that he was an American citizen or a foreign national who had complied with all regulations; also that no one ever connected with the office of Alien Property Custodian had any interest in the bid, and that no agreement with respect to the purchase had been made with an undisclosed principal or with anyone on the Government's blacklist.

On April, 1945, these regulations were apparently waived when the Alien Property Custodian sold the Farben-General Aniline-owned 50 percent of Winthrop Chemical for some $9,500,000 to Sterling, of which company Earl McClintock, a former attorney in the office of the Alien Property Custodian in the first World War, was a director and vice-president.

Sterling was required to deposit the purchased Winthrop stock with the Custodian in a ten-year voting trust to ensure that until 1955 it would not get back into Farben's clutches, as the Bayer Company did after World War I despite Sterling's promise not to permit this. Unless of course the Alien Property Custodian should decide to release the voting trust—or Farben's Swiss I.G. Chemie should upset the whole apple cart by getting back title to General Aniline through a phony act of Congress or a phony judicial decision.

Great uncertainty has been manifest as to the administration and ultimate disposition by the Custodian's office of the General Aniline and Film Corp. after that very valuable property was taken over from the Treasury by Mr. Crowley in March, 1942.

Little official information was forthcoming about the affairs of the company save that the Custodian's office was operating it as trustee for the foreign-held (Farben) shares, to which the Custodian had taken title.

However, early in 1943 reports appeared in the press that another new board of directors for General Aniline was to be appointed, several of them being directors or business affiliates of Standard Gas & Electric Co., of which Mr. Crowley, in his spare time, was the $50,000 (or was it $75,000?) a year president and chairman. Then came an announcement that the Custodian proposed to sell at public auction some of the more important properties seized, including General Aniline. This was followed by a statement that the announcement had been an unfortunate error.

Finally a new board for General Aniline was appointed, mainly of men having no experience in the dyestuff, photographic, or other chemical industries.

Tom Stokes, in the Scripps-Howard newspapers, took his usual jab at the situation with the remark that Mr. Crowley was a triple-job man with two government titles and one in private industry. Stokes then added—a hasty reminder of what happened during the Harding Administration:

> The office of Alien Property Custodian is considered here to be extremely important. This same office was investigated after the first World War with some unpleasant results.

In July, 1943, when Mr. Crowley received a fourth job as head of the Office of Economic Warfare, replacing Vice-President Wallace, it was reported that he would take a leave of absence from his public-utility presidency, but for the time being would retain his other government titles. However, he still held on to his Standard Gas jobs and salary.

It appears a proper comment to make that in the Custodian's office, as in other agencies dealing with Farben and its affiliates, there existed a vaguely defined line-up—of those who wanted to be gentle with Farben and with Farben's friends as opposed to those who wanted to turn on the heat. And between those two extremes the play-safe brigade moved whichever way the wind blew.

Regardless of the power of the lobby in peacetime, it is almost unbelievable that such a condition could exist when the United States was actually at war. On the record, however, nothing relating to Farben is unbelievable.

In March 1944, when Mr. Crowley stepped out as Alien Property Custodian to devote more time to his expanding duties as the President's Foreign Economic Administrator, and his assistant, one James E. Markham, who was also a salaried director of Standard Gas & Electric, stepped in to succeed him as Custodian, it was reported on reliable authority that another man who was recognized as much better qualified through long experience had actually been decided upon to succeed Mr. Crowley until outside intervention at the White House caused the appointment of Mr. Markham.

The situation regarding General Aniline and General Dyestuffs continued with conflicting reports that they would or would not be sold, and with no change in what might be termed the strange clemency toward former important employes under the Farben regime.

Not only Mr. Halbach, as previously mentioned, remained on the payroll of General Dyestuffs at a very fancy annual stipend, but two of the others who recovered sizable sums for their stock in General Dyestuffs were still listed in the Directory of Directors for 1944 as executives: R. Lenz, as Vice-President, and A. T. Wingender, as Treasurer.

These were all among the group described by Mr. Markham in his December, 1944, affidavit before the General Dyestuff stock suits were compromised, as having acted "in behalf and for the benefit of I.G. Farbenindustrie, a national of an enemy country, Germany," and as having held that stock as part of the "complicated threads of a conspiracy extending over many years and involving persons in many different countries."

The Alien Property Custodian seized more than 44,000 foreign patents, some 32,000 enemy owned, mostly German. Licenses, free save for a $15 fee, were granted to all comers on several thousand of these patents but a difficulty about the free grants was a reservation by the Custodian of a right to revoke any license—which provision hardly encouraged heavy investment to operate under such patents.

However, the numerous General Aniline patents, also enemy owned, were not included in the $15 free license offer, despite the recommendations of the President's Committee on Foreign Economic Policy, which was approved by him, that these General Aniline patents should be licensed like the others, free to all comers.

Request made to the Custodian long after the war ended for information about these licenses was referred to General Aniline; whereupon Mr. George W. Burpee, its president by designation of the Custodian, was emphatic in declining to consider granting any free licenses and his company patent counsel advised that the title to all of these Farben patents might still be clouded by the claims of I.G. Chemie, Farben's Swiss hideout, to ownership of General Aniline itself.

Meanwhile the distinguished patent attorney, William H. Davis, under retainer from General Aniline, protested publicly that it would be most unwise to open up these patents to all comers because that "futile method" had failed after the last war whereas:

> . . . . . the situation would have been quite different if the American patents had held by a strong competitive organization in this country, able and willing to enforce the German patents against them.

This illogical thesis of Mr. Davis disregards the historical fact that after the last war the thousands of seized German dye trust patents which were turned over to Francis Garvan's Chemical Foundation for licensing to American firms did not get back into German control, whereas those which were sold to what Mr. Davis might describe as "two strong competitive organizations," Sterling and Grasselli, and which appeared "able and willing to enforce the German patents against them," did exactly the opposite.

As will be recalled, some of these drug patents and all of the dye patents were later handed over to the partial or complete ownership of General Aniline-Farben-American I.G.

Mr. Davis must have been hard pressed for an argument when he made his plea for exclusive retention of the Farben patents by General Aniline, the management of which apparently still fears, or believes, that Farben's fake Swiss title may some day restore Farben's control of this enemy property. In the words of the poet, whatever there is concealed in this patents woodpile, the odor is suspiciously like some of those of the 1920's when Frank Garvan was being called names for not turning all of the dye trust patents over to one or two *strong* organizations—like General Aniline.

Perhaps nothing could better illustrate the peculiar attitude of the Alien Property Custodian's office than an incident in 1945 when request was made to inspect some thirty-seven claims which had been filed with the Custodian demanding return of various items which had been seized. These claims had been listed merely by number and name of claimant in the annual reports of the Custodian, and it was stated in the 1944 report that full publicity was given to all activities of the "Vested Property Claims Committee" by which the justice of all such claims was decided, and that "the records of the committee are also open to the public."

Despite this, the official secretary of the office of the Custodian refused to permit inspection of these records until after vigorous protest, and even then inspection of only one out of the thirty-seven was reluctantly permitted. The balance was kept under lock and key on the mumbo-jumbo explanation that the attorney for the Custodian still had them and therefore they were not public records.

The real point of this incident may be found in the fact that substantially all of these particular claims had been filed by individuals or corporations who had been either accused, convicted of or who had pleaded guilty to violating the laws of this country in their relations with I.G. Farben. Several were convicted criminals.

Press criticism of Mr. Crowley's conduct of his various positions, especially that of Alien Property Custodian, appeared from time to time. These were usually based on the conclusion that he held too many titles, official and private, and had too many duties to do justice to all of them, or that his relations with Victor Emanuel (to whom he owed his large salary from Standard Gas and Electric) were incompatible with his official duties.

Perhaps the best way to permit the reader to consider the fairness of these criticisms, and without any reflection upon the good faith and patriotism of Mr. Crowley, or of Mr. Emanuel, would be to refer directly to the records of the Securities and Exchange Commission of January 19, 1943 when that official agency issued its Findings and Opinion that certain private banking firms were affiliates of Standard Power and its affiliate Standard Gas and Electric, and therefore there could not be the "arms length" trading between them that the Public Utility Holding Company Act required in certain transactions.

Among the firms involved in this opinion were Schroder, Rockefeller & Co., Inc., an affiliate of the J. Henry Schroder bank of New York and London; and Emanuel & Co., of New York, in which Mr. Victor Emanuel was a partner.

In a voluminous statement of the ramifications of control of the Standard Companies, and of the reorganizations of Standard Gas under the Bankruptcy Act, the Commission discussed the—

". . . . . close relationship between Emanuel and the Schroder interests" and concluded that "The Schroder interests in London and New York have worked with Emanuel in acquiring and maintaining a dominant position in Standard affairs."

The findings also showed that Leo T. Crowley replaced Emanuel as Chairman of the Board of Standard Gas in 1939 when Emanuel became Chairman of its finance committee, also that James G. Markham was then elected a director of Standard Gas.

Just for good measure it might be added here that the celebrated Cravath law firm appeared in the Securities and Exchange Commission case referred to as counsel for one of the banking firms who were found to be too close for "arms length" dealings with Mr. Emanuel's Standard Gas and Electric.

That Mr. Crowley should be obligated to Mr. Emanuel and the J. Henry Schroder bank for the high salary he received during his tenure of public office (for which he is said to have refused compensation) may appear unusual and, insofar as is recalled such a situation had been seldom, if ever, duplicated at Washington.

An aspect of this which has provoked comment is the fact that the J. Henry Schroder bank acted as financial agent for the Nazi Government just prior to the start of the war and also was reported to be a financial backer for one of the firms in Farben's international nitrogen cartel: also the London Schroder had close business and family ties with the notorious General Kurt von Schroeder, of the Stein Bank of Cologne, Germany, that particular member of the Schroeder clan having been one of the strongest financial links between Hitler and his Farben industrial backers.

By another coincidence, Sullivan & Cromwell, the law firm of John Foster Dulles (advisor to Mr. Crowley as Custodian and Counsel for General Dyestuffs stock claimants), is also reported to be counsel for the Schroder bank; and Allen W. Dulles, brother of John Foster and a member of that law firm, likewise is one of the directors of the J. Henry Schroder bank.

It may be stated possibly in extenuation of Mr. Crowley's too numerous duties, that he has not been the only man holding high place in official Washington who appears to be under rather definite obligations to Mr. Victor Emanuel—while at the same time wielding very considerable official powers.

Among others reputed to be indebted to Mr. Emanuel for various private directorships is the former hotel manager George Edward Allen who, while drawing approximately $50,000 a year from numerous corporations and acting as a "public relations man" for private interests had been holding down various Government jobs including a desk in the White House.

Mr. Allen was appointed by President Truman to be a Director of the Reconstruction Finance Corporation with the chairmanship in prospect. He was confirmed by the Senate on February 18, 1946, after a bitter debate in which Mr. Allen was accused of knowing nothing about banking by his own testimony, and of having been made a director of numerous corporations through his friend Victor Emanuel and the latter's friend, Alien Property Custodian James Markham.

These directorships included the General Aniline and Film Corporation and the Hugo Stinnes Corporation, both controlled by the Custodian. Unfavorable newspaper criticism of some of Mr. Allen's activities, by PM's omniscient I. F. Stone, which were read into the Senate record caused Senator Bilbo to praise Mr. Allen's family as Mississippi's best, and Senator Scott Lucas to defend Mr. Allen vigorously. This Illinois statesman in 1942, as member of the Senate Patents committee, had voted to halt Senator Bone's investigation of the I.G. Farben tie-ups, and in 1946 he was chairman of the committee on contingent expenses which voted to cut off the funds for Senator Kilgore's investigations of the conspiracy to revive of I.G. Farben.

Said Senator Lucas in denouncing the critics of Mr. Allen:

> Who is going to pay any attention to . . . . . speculation as to the influence which George Allen might have upon some one in Washington with respect to I.G. Farbenindustrie.

So Mr. Allen then became director of the Government's multi-billion dollar lending agency.

This is not to imply that Victor Emanuel or the Schroders wielded improper influence upon any Government official.

Unhappily, many leading financiers and industrialists in this country, patriotic and wise according to their lights, who have not been directly involved with Farben, have seen no wrong in the part played by Farben before and during the war, or in a revival of Farben's world cartel system after the war. These beliefs and this policy not being the officially announced creed of the United States, it may be regarded merely as a matter of judgment (similar to the issue raised by Justice Jackson against Justice Black), as to whether the two men who, as Alien Property Custodian, have had the direction of General Aniline, General Dyestuffs, and other Farben properties, should be so friendly to Mr. Emanuel and the Schroder banking influences. And it may be of no significance that Mr. Emanuel and several of his associates have been appointed by them to the Board of Directors of these seized enemy properties, which, vastly increased in size and financial strength, are still holding intact the patents received from Farben and refuse to throw them open to all comers with the excuse that the legal ownership of General Aniline & Film is still claimed by Farben's Swiss I.G. Chemie. The latter now disguised under the so innocent name "Society of International Industrial and Commerce Participation."

Investigation of the conduct of the office of the Alien Property Custodian under Mr. Crowley, and under Mr. Markham, has been threatened more than once, and in one instance actually started.

The Federal Deposit Insurance Corporation under Mr. Crowley also has been criticized severely, once back in 1942, when a resolution was proposed in the House of Representatives to investigate the F. D. I. C. because of heavy advances made to bankrupt banks in Jersey City, the baliwick of New Jersey's Democratic Boss Mayor Hague. Other complaints have been registered because Mr. Crowley's F. D. I. C. attempted to collect huge sums for alleged liquidating expenses from officers of banks which had paid off 100 percent of the bank's obligations after having been ordered closed for unexplained reasons.

Finally, in July 1945, a Senatorial investigation was begun after severe criticism of the handling of the American Bosch Company by the Alien Property Custodian (this being a repetition of the seizure of the predecessor of this company during World War I).

A Senate sub-committee conducted a fact-finding expedition into Alien Property Custodian affairs but refused to make public its findings when request was made to the committee for same.

One important key to the situation in the Custodian's office was supplied in an interview with members of the staff in October 1942, when I had been officially requested to supply certain information relating to Farben. In the hectic conference which followed, I finally mentioned with some skepticism that part which Mr. Corcoran was reported to be taking in the affairs of the Alien Property Custodian. This comment met with an immediate challenge. However, other members of the staff were anything but enthusiastic about Mr. Corcoran's cooperation.

Meanwhile the nearest approach to investigating the Farben lobby or Mr. Corcoran developed late in 1941, when Senator Carl A. Hatch introduced a bill to restrain former government employes from receiving fees for such lobbying activities for two years after leaving office. This bill caused some talk—and died in committee. The lobby did not approve.

Then came the Truman Committee lobby hearings in December 1941 (Chapter IX) at which Mr. Corcoran declined to talk about his Sterling-Farben activities and fees, and was informed that he would be recalled later to tell the committee all about it. Mr. Corcoran was not recalled and he did not return. After a number of unsuccessful efforts to induce this committee to permit me to testify before it, I sent its chief counsel, Hugh A. Fulton, in April 1943, a reminder of the committee's intention to recall Mr. Corcoran, and asked whether the reappearance of the Sterling consent-decree expert had been required.

Mr. Fulton's reply was a bit childish; he requested a memorandum on the subject (I had already sent the committee a dozen or more memoranda and letters relating to Mr. Corcoran), and also made the strange allegation that:

> The Committee does not have the facilities for complying with private requests, such as yours, for analysis of material in the committee files.

Conceding freely the great value of work which the Truman

Committee and its counsel Mr. Fulton may have done on many other matters relating to the war, this Committee apparently lost interest in the Farben tie-ups in the United States after its partial exposé of the Standard Oil arrangements on Buna rubber and other products. It was Senator Bone's Patents Committee that later did attempt to explore all of the Farben tie-ups—until halted, allegedly through the efforts of Mr. Corcoran.

In view of Mr. Fulton's effort to twist the plain meaning of my letter and his refusal to explain why Mr. Corcoran had not been required to reveal his activities relating to the Farben-Sterling drug tie-ups, it may be proper for me to recall that Mr. Fulton's legal experience prior to entering government service was gained as a junior attorney with the New York and Washington law firm of Cravath, de Gersdorff, Swaine and Wood, now Cravath, Swaine & Moore, which firm, and its predecessors, as discussed in Chapter xviii for many years had been the legal representative of Farben's German Hoechst and Farben affiliates in America.

Mr. Fulton may also recall that in 1939, after he had become executive assistant to John Cahill, United States Attorney of New York (who was later attorney for Sterling), when I called upon him to discover if possible what his official attitude might be with regard to the investigation of the drug industry, he made a vituperative attack upon a visitor whose assistance in those matters had already been solicited and acknowledged by the Justice Department.

This attack came after Mr. Fulton had stated to me that because of his former connection with the Cravath law firm in cases involving the drug industry, he would take no part in the official investigation of that industry then getting under way.

However the controversy about Tommy Corcoran's influence with Mr. Biddle and others in the Justice Department was not to die completely because of the refusal of the Truman Committee's counsel to act on its Chairman's earlier announcement that Mr. Corcoran was to return and explain things. The entire humiliating record was revived and considerable new light was thrown upon it when Assistant Attorney General Norman M. Littell began airing his side of his row with Mr. Biddle in December 1944 about the Corcoran influence. And after Mr. Biddle attempted to reply to the Littell charges, the latter let loose a blast which was so strong that the Senate Committee on National Defense (of which Mr. Fulton had been counsel) now headed by Senator James M. Mead, of New York, refused to make it public.

But on January 22, 1944, Republican Representative Lawrence H. Smith, of Wisconsin, to his everlasting credit, courageously rose to the occasion by inserting the Littell statement in the Congressional Record, along with his own accusations and a resolution demanding an investigation of the conduct of Biddle as Attorney General with special reference to the influence exerted by Mr. Corcoran in the Sterling case.

The Littell statement started with the indictment that the settlement of the Sterling case "marks the lowest point in the history of the Department of Justice since the Harding Administration."

After summarizing the history of Sterling and its subservience to Farben and the Nazi Government, also Sterling's subversive activities in Latin America (as discussed in Chapter XIII), Mr. Littell turned his guns on the record of the Sterling case when Mr. Biddle became Acting Attorney General and traced, step by step, the actions of Thomas Corcoran in "defeating the indictment of the companies and individuals involved."

> "Corcoran," said Littell, "was engaged in a race with time to (1) stop the investigation before it reached such a conclusive stage and (2) get the cases filed on a civil basis with consent decrees merely restraining further violation of the Anti-Trust Laws, and above all things (3) prevent the presentation of the evidence to a grand jury."

Mr. Littell also stated that the anti-trust staff working on the Sterling case were apprehensive because Corcoran was in and out of the Justice Department and it was also known that he was working hard to secure Mr. Biddle's appointment as Attorney General and "Biddle was then to urge Tommy's appointment as Solicitor General, which he later did but without success."

In a time table of events leading up to its final disposition Mr. Littell, with his prestige and knowledge as recently one of the highest officers of the Justice Department, confirmed in substance and in fact the statements and reports heard back in 1941 (as told in Chapter IX) about how Tommy Corcoran rode rough-shod through the Department with Mr. Biddle's approval.

This Littell blast also placed new light on certain aspects of the matter, including the hiring by Earl McClintock and William E. Weiss, of David Corcoran, brother of Tommy, to be an executive of Sterling's subsidiaries which handled Latin-American business in the Farben partnership. This engagement of a brother of the court favorite took place in the early 1930's when Tommy Corcoran was the White House piano player and legislative deviser.

Other aspects of the case which Mr. Littell revealed were: that Sam S. Isseks, friend and classmate of Tommy Corcoran, was moved mysteriously into charge of the Sterling case over the heads of those handling the investigations. that anti-trust violations had been clear, but far more sinister facts appeared on the record because Sterling in its subservience to Farben had in fact become an agent of Nazi Germany, carrying out policies aimed at the security of the United States; that some of the Justice staff believed not only anti-trust indictments were justified but also indictments for criminal conspiracy (against the Government of the United States) under Section 88, Title 18, providing fines of $10,000 and two years imprisonment; that while the battle was going on inside the Justice Department Mr. Biddle was merely Acting Attorney General, until August 24, 1941, when his nomination for the office was announced, events then moving rapidly as it thus became clear he would have authority to act. So on September 4th the Senate confirmed the appointment and the next day the notorious consent decrees and nominal fines were announced. And finally the fact that in the meantime the new Attorney General had ordered the Justice Department staff to stop the Sterling investigation and mark the case closed (with no indictments), after some thirty thousand documents had been assembled revealing as conclusively as any case in the history of the Justice Department the means employed by Farben, in World War II as in World War I, to serve the purposes of the German Government in the Western Hemisphere.

Following his timetable, Mr. Littell attacked Mr. Biddle's crude attempt to defend his conduct at another Senate Committee meeting. He denounced as false several of the Attorney General's statements, especially an assertion that the only conference Biddle had had with Corcoran was in October 1941, after the consent decrees were filed. This, commented Mr. Littell, was obviously untrue, as the pressure prior to September 5, 1941, because of the interference of Tommy Corcoran was so great that resignations were threatened within the staff of the department.

As one commentator put it, Tommy Corcoran hung his hat in the Attorney General's office during this period.

Other allegations by Mr. Biddle which drew the fire of his former assistant were that Biddle had asked for maximum fines in the Sterling case and that jail sentences were never imposed in any anti-trust actions.

The "maximum fines" said Mr. Littell, were assessed not after action of a grand jury but upon an information which "by no means includes all of the acts or refers to all of the evidence in the Department of Justice."

"And, furthermore," Mr. Littell declared, "Mr. Biddle's statement (regarding prison sentences) is untrue" as in some 184 other anti-trust criminal cases tried, 786 months of prison had been imposed.

Mr. Littell also expressed his own opinion, as a prosecutor, that many other laws might have been invoked against the Sterling conspirators, including those Federal Statutes dealing with trading with the enemy, espionage, and interference with our foreign relations, also that actions under the law requiring registration of agents of foreign principals might have been invoked because that law affects any:

. . . . . . attorney for. or any other person, who receives compensation from, or is under the direction of . . . . . a foreign business, a foreign political organization, or a domestic organization subsidized directly or indirectly in whole or in part by any of the above.

A grand jury, said Mr. Littell, might well have reached the conclusion that Tommy Corcoran as well as executives of Sterling fitted into the above definitions of terms prescribed by the Attorney General as foreign agents.

Finally, Mr. Littell dismissed as unfounded allegations by the Attorney General that the action by the Justice Department had purged Sterling of German influence.

Taken all in all, Mr. Littell's accusations were so specific and so forcefully presented that immediate challenge and reply might have been expected from Mr. Biddle, Mr. Corcoran, and Sterling. But no reply in public was forthcoming. Nor was reply ever made to the charges of Representative Smith, which included statements that Sterling supplied the Nazi Government with funds in 1938; that Sterling had had fake offices and secret hideouts in New York and New Jersey where funds could be diverted to pay for German propaganda and Gestapo agents, and that the Sterling officials "were concerned not with the protection of American interests, but with advancing the interests of our common enemy."

Along with the resolution introduced by Representative Smith was a second demand along the same lines which was proposed by Representative Jerry Voorhis of California. The latter, who has earned a name for himself similar to that of the late Senator Norris for sincere, forthright action regardless of who may be involved, also introduced a resolution demanding investigation of the allegations of undue or improper influence upon officials of the Justice Department and the truth or falsity of the charges made by Mr. Littell.

Coming from Representative Voorhis, who was a strong supporter of the Roosevelt Administration, his resolution, to some, appeared of even greater significance than that of Republican Representative Smith. And Mr. Voorhis had already paid tribute to Mr. Littell on November 30, 1944, and had demanded an investigation of the situation in an earlier speech in the House at the time when Biddle had induced the President to remove Mr. Littell for alleged insubordination, but before the latter's counter-accusations had been made public.

Both the Smith and the Voorhis resolutions were referred to

the Rules Committee, which promptly sat upon them, and, almost a year and a half later was still withholding action which would permit the Congress to take a vote on whether to investigate Mr. Biddle, or Mr. Corcoran, or the Sterling case settlement.

One voice was raised in public, feebly, to defend Corcoran and Sterling. Thurman Arnold from his dignified retreat in the Court of Appeals was reported to have indicated publicly that his opinion as expressed in September 1941, after the Sterling decrees had been filed, remained unchanged. This reference to the weird press release issued from Mr. Biddle's office in the name of Mr. Arnold on September 25, 1941, may not appear to be much of a reply to the Littell charges, in view of the inaccuracies (noted in Chapter ix) in this earlier makeshift exoneration issued over the Arnold name.

Aside from its startling revelations, the greater significance of the battle between Biddle and Littell appears to be in the familiar pattern; that charges of so specific a character could have been made during war-time on the floor of the House against one of the highest officials of the Government, involving collusive immunity for those accused of collaboration with I.G. Farben and the Nazis—and thereafter, while the war went on into peace, the charges remained hushed, and the immunity continued.

During my war-period efforts to bring about an investigation of matters relating to I.G. Farben, Dr. J. B. Matthews, celebrated researcher for the Dies Committee explained to me in August, 1942, that such an undertaking would be difficult because the committee had no investigators competent to make such an inquiry. Furthermore, Dr. Matthews, with asides from R. E. Stripling, the Dies chief investigator, lectured me on the thesis that I should distinguish between the commercial and political significance of international agreements, such as Standard Oil had with Farben. This argument may well indicate the competency of the Dies investigational staff.

Another example of Congressional war-time silence on matters relating to Farben was the squelching in October 1942, of one of the most robust two-fisted members of the lower house, Representative John M. Coffee. Mr. Coffee, in a fiery speech, did not mince words in describing an attempted sabotage of the war effort by Farben allies, but his resolution to explore the matter was then buried in the trash basket of the House Rules Committee.

Other incidents of hush and immunity will be related, but those mentioned should suffice to show how soon the pattern of hidden protection for Farben's allies which prevailed during the long pre-war years had actually begun to reappear, after the brief period of partial exposé and abortive prosecutions which followed Pearl Harbor.

Perhaps the most disturbing aspect of this renewed defiance of the integrity of a Nation's war-time mobilization was in the Congress of the United States, where no member of either house, with ample knowledge of these facts, was permitted to stand up and hold the floor in protest until his colleagues and the Nation should have been compelled to listen, and to act.

Even in the Senate, with its unlimited debate and its high powers, no such voice was raised.

This aspect of the Farben pattern has never been described more concisely than it was in a public address delivered by Supreme Court Justice Robert H. Jackson, in June 1941, shortly before he retired as Attorney General of the United States. Mr. Jackson appealed for assistance to defeat what he defined as the

> . . . . . pattern of a premilitary and nonmilitary invasion of business, finance, labor, public opinion and political organizations . . . . . alien-directed and financed propaganda against the policy of our Government . . . . . at Congressional hearings . . . . . in court . . . . . against investigational officials and agencies, prosecution policies, and law enforcement itself.

It was just at this time that pressure was being brought to bear upon members of the Attorney General's staff to relax their efforts in several investigations and prosecutions which Mr. Jackson had ordered into Farben's long-standing illegal tie-ups and subversive activities in the United States. As Attorney General, Mr. Jackson had given Thurman Arnold the green light to get tough and clean out the Farben framework. In view of what occurred thereafter, it is unfortunate that Mr. Justice Jackson did not remain as Attorney General until the last vestige of the Farben pattern should have been rooted out and eradicated in this country, in anticipation of a similar clean-up by America's Prosecutor Jackson in Europe.

CHAPTER XX

Plans for Peace—In Time of War

I. G. FARBEN,
unlike the governments and the armies of Germany, never surrenders and never dies. Win, lose, or draw, the pattern of Farben goes on. When the first World War ended, Farben turned abruptly from the production of munitions no longer needed by a defeated army to rebuilding its international framework in preparation for the next attempt at world conquest. Again, this tenacity of purpose and flexibility of pattern are clearly discernible in the events which developed so speedily in those hectic weeks following the surrender of Germany on May 6, 1945.

An important phase of this pattern of eternal life and perpetual war is found in numerous carry-over agreements or understandings already referred to between Farben and certain of its affiliates in the United States, all of which provided for, or promised, resumption of pre-war arrangements when the war should end.

Aside from written agreements are the verbal understandings such as that described in Chapter II in the 1914 letter from the German Hoechst to Herman Metz:

Our entire relationship is really a confidential relationship and it will be and must, without agreements, so continue in the future as in the past.

A similar relationship may be observed in a report of the duPont Foreign Relations Department, dated February 9, 1940, in which reference was made to various current agreements with Farben relating to nylon and plastics, and to an arrangement made to return to Farben certain funds advanced to purchase shares in Duperial, the duPont-I. C. I. dye subsidiary in South America. The British I. C. I. had objected to Farben's purchase of the shares, so duPont was arranging to repay the money. The report went on to say:

> The duPont Company informed I.G.. that they intended to use their good offices after the war to have the I.G. participation (in Duperial) restored.

Senator Bone was indignant at this and other evidence of an intended resumption of "business as usual" with Farben after the war. Said the Senator:

> Everything that has been revealed so far . . . . . on the relationship between these big private outfits indicates clearly that as soon as this bloody war is over the gentlemen are going to get their feet under the table and restore their antebellum status as soon as that can be accomplished . . . . . I am wondering if the high officials of this government are aware of the fact that these gentlemen, who have parcelled out this world, have intended to make such adjustments of this property after the war. That is a picture which should be very clearly presented to Congress, and Congress should have something to say about it. I am disposed to think that it will.

Senator Bone was mistaken. Congress had nothing to say about it.

On one other occasion before his Committee closed up shop, Senator Bone warned of the future, saying:

> You recall how we were caught up after the last war? We took over a lot of German patents in the pharmaceutical

and chemical fields and our business entrepreneurs proceeded
to fix things so that they were given back to the Germans . . . . .
through finagling devices . . . . . After this war, unless we are
wiser or smarter than I think we may be, we will probably
find that the block of patents that the Alien Property Custodian has will ultimately find their way back into the hands
of smooth German operators, and we will go through this
same wretched process again, in spite of the fact that there
may be a million of our boys who have paid the price with
their blood and broken bodies.

As the events of the war progressed favorably, confusion increased at home and a new voice was raised in opposition to a
future renewal of international cartels in general and that of
Standard Oil-Farben in particular.

On July 26, 1943, Vice-President Henry A. Wallace, smarting
at having been removed as head of the Board of Economic Warfare, delivered a political comeback speech in Detroit in which
he took a slap at cartels; a few weeks later, in Chicago, on September 11, he became more specific, referring to the "creators of
secret supergovernments."

Prior to the Chicago address the Vice-President had received
a mass of data on the subject from William Floyd II, Chairman
of the Standard Oil Minority Stockholders Committee. His attack
was so specific that the following day Standard's president, R. W.
Gallagher, replied defending his company's tie-up with Farben
and bitterly criticizing the Vice-President for the attack. In passing
Mr. Gallagher mentioned his own opposition to cartels and a few
days later, Standard's pugnacious public relations pacifier, Robert
T. Haslam. permitted Sylvia Porter to quote him in the *New York
Post* that the dispute between Mr. Wallace and Mr. Gallagher
was all an unfortunate mistake because Standard was already
in agreement with the Vice-President.

Next, Assistant Attorney General Wendell Berge, now returned
to anti-trust as its chief, called Messrs. Gallagher and Wallace
into conference and it appeared that a semblance of harmony
was restored; both parties seemed to oppose international cartel
agreements (with Farben) unless such agreements were to be

registered with the State or Justice Department. This quaint reservation hardly indicated much hope of action which would do away with cartels as such in the future, or to eradicate I.G. Farben and its pattern for all time as the primary essential for an enduring peace in the post-war era. A week later Mr. Berge published an article in the *New York Times Magazine* entitled "Can We End Monopoly," in which he first admitted that for the last forty years, "emotional promises to enforce the Sherman Act" by both political parties resulted in elected officials who "with equal consistency did nothing about it."

Despite this painful admission, Mr. Berge also naïvely asserted that during the present war "the spirit of the anti-trust laws has not only been preserved, but much of the effect as well." Perhaps the new anti-trust enforcement official was thinking of the adage, "the spirit is willing but the flesh is weak."

Mr. Berge also paid unconscious tribute to the official Farben policies of hush-hush and immunity by saying that:

> The full story of our unintentional industrial contribution to the German war effort . . . . . has not been told . . . . .

He finally concluded that

> . . . . . enforcement of the anti-trust laws . . . . . is being pressed as vigorously now as available manpower permits.

It was hardly an optimistic forecast.

It may appear that the outspoken opposition of Henry Wallace to cartels in general and to Farben in particular was not the least important of the reasons which cost him the renomination as Vice-President. The truth regarding President Roosevelt's health was even then known, or at least suspected, by the inner councils of his party leaders. They chose his successor.

The foregoing brings this story, for a brief space, to France and North Africa, through which, when the Nazi doom became visible, the leaders of I.G. Farben established a bridgehead of escape to a financial bomb shelter in Algiers. It was then reported that certain Vichy French financial collaborators, hoping to salvage some of the Nazi loot by aiding in its concealment, had joined hands with Farben in a scheme to transfer the huge funds Farben had accumulated by absorbing four of the largest chemical and dye industries in France, to North African banks, where they might remain safe regardless of who won final victory in Europe.

The United States appeared in this picture with the landing of its troops in North Africa in October 1942. Then, while thousands of American youths were dying—to end what Farben had started —there came the disquieting rumor that the on-the-spot representative of the State Department of the United States was in accord with the obviously German-inspired proposal to freeze the financial *status quo* in North Africa.

Here the same old pattern reappeared, hazily perhaps, but nonetheless the outline of a *modus operandi* of survival—a bridgehead out of the war zone of beaten Germany by which Farben could emerge as a going concern, financially strong and ready to resume business.

Meanwhile there appeared on the stage the obscure figure of Fritz Thyssen, whose steel trust had been tied in with Farben since 1927. Thyssen, in a true-confession story, "I Paid Hitler," whined, repented his error, and proclaimed that the one way to insure the next peace would be for "men of good will" to reestablish the new Germany as a corporate state.

So Thyssen emerged at a propitious moment as a leader who might induce the thoughtful citizens of the Fatherland to throw out the vile Hitler and join hands with the Allies in a plan which would save Germany's industries and industrialists, and create a reformed Reich and a peaceful world.

After the landing of the Allies in France and as the war speeded toward its inevitable end, discussions of how best to handle a defeated Germany centered around German industry in general— and I.G. Farben in particular.

So the struggle beneath the surface of official Washington continued, between those who favored Farben survival and those who did not.

While the late Commander-in-Chief was under stern compulsion to devote time and energy to global war, the greatest of all time, he was forced to rely upon subordinates and upon Congress to defeat and destroy the pattern of Farben. And it may appear that already certain of those underlings and their legislative colleagues fell in step one by one, and blindly took places assigned to them in the nooks and crannies of a new Farben framework as it was to be revised to fit the new peace.

Let it be said here, again, that there is no force which can restrain or turn such men from folly save only the lash of public indignation aroused by revelation of facts now hushed.

They are not stupid men who reach through all the barriers of war or peace to seduce other men who are stupid to new betrayals —with specious arguments of a better, normal world, or potent draughts of suggestion, of power to come. The dispute raged— should professors, politicians or plutocratic leaders of industry direct the war and build the peace. As to which of these Farben does not care. Its pattern has always found places for all three and can do so again.

For one more moment go back—go back—to Bayer's Schweitzer telling Ambassador von Bernstorff in 1916 not to worry about the future as it would be easy to choose a President with the "right politics" to respond favorably to a post-war comeback of I.G. Dyes in the United States. So does history repeat.

Or go back again, not so far, to the aged Gerard still politically powerful, in June 1943, defending Standard refusal to abolish all ties with Farben because:

> Some of those who are thinking what is to happen after the war, are contemplating universal cartels.

Officially there could be no doubt that President Roosevelt favored a hard peace for Germany and the most vigorous handling of Farben. On September 8, 1944, Mr. Roosevelt made this clear in a letter to Secretary of State Hull, which he made public and in which he said:

> The history of the use of the I.G. Farben trust by the Nazi reads like a detective story. Defeat of the Nazi armies will have to be followed by the eradication of those weapons of economic warfare . . . . .

Prior to this blast by the President it was reported that the soft-peace sentiments of certain members of the European Advisory Commission had produced a proposed handbook of directions for officers of the Allied Military Government (A. M. G.) which so favored a survival of the I.G. Farben set-up that Secretary of the Treasury Henry Morgenthau, Jr. hit the ceiling, protested to the President and, as a result, was summoned to the second Quebec conference which was held by the President and Prime Minister Churchill in September 1944.

The so-called Morgenthau Plan was then revealed, calling for the elimination of German chemical and metallurgical industries and the conversion of that nation largely to an agricultural economy with no peacetime industries save those which could not contribute to a future war.

Mr. Roosevelt and Mr. Churchill initialed and approved a memorandum which outlined this plan and which concluded with:

> The program for eliminating the war-making industries in the Ruhr and the Saar is looking forward to converting Germany into a country primarily agricultural and pastoral in character. The Prime Minister and The President were in agreement upon this program.

When the Morgenthau Plan was made public the storm broke over his head, and the same barrage of epithets was aimed in his direction that had previously been hurled at England's leading advocate of a hard peace, Lord Vansittart.

President Roosevelt thereupon, in December 1944, through United States Ambassador John G. Winant in London, outlined to the Allies his demand for a complete and ruthless abolition of German war industries, but as this outline allowed for some survival of chemical industries for civilian requirements, it appeared less severe than the Morgenthau plan.

At Yalta, in February, 1945, Mr. Roosevelt, with Churchill and Stalin, stepped back a bit more from a program of total elimination of Farben by declaring merely an "inflexible purpose" to "eliminate or control all German industry that could be used for military production."

This was to be the last official pronouncement of policy on this subject by President Roosevelt. Those who were closest to him believed that he never wavered from his determination that

As for Germany, that tragic nation . . . . . we and our Allies are entirely agreed that . . . . . we shall not leave them a single element of military power or potential military power.

However in April, after Harry S. Truman became President, there was issued and then withheld from public knowledge, a Joint Chiefs-of-Staff order (J. C. S. 1067) instructing General Eisenhower for the governing of occupied Germany. This order required basic objectives "to the full extent necessary to achieve the industrial disarmament of Germany." It prohibited all research laboratories save those necessary to the protection of the public health, and stipulated abolition of all "laboratories and related institutions whose work has been connected with the building of the German War Machine." Also it forbade all research that would in any way contribute to Germany's future war potential.

These vigorous directives were softened however by a later reference to the "pending final Allied agreement on reparation, and on control or elimination of German industries that can be used for war production . . . . ."

The Potsdam Agreement, arrived at in July and August by Prime Minister Attlee of England, Marshal Stalin of Russia, and President Truman, followed closely the earlier directives "to eliminate Germany's war potential" by control and restriction of industry "to Germany's approved postwar peacetime needs" and ordered that:

> In organizing the German economy primary emphasis shall be given to the development of agriculture and peaceful domestic industries.

On July 5, 1945, under instructions contained in J. C. S. 1067, the U.S. Military Government in Germany (O.M.G.U.S.) promulgated General Order No. 2, which directed seizure of Farben for the purpose of making its plants available for reparations, and for destruction of all Farben arms or munitions of war or of any ingredients for same, which are not generally used in industries permitted in Germany.

Special Order No. 1, of the same date, appointed a control officer for Farben to prevent the production by and rehabilitation of these plants except as might be specifically determined in accordance with objectives of United States.

However, within a few weeks of the promulgation of this order Brigadier General William H. Draper, formerly of the New York banking house of Dillon, Read & Co. (which floated the thirty million dollar bond issue of Vereinigte Stahlwerke, Fritz Thyssen's Steel Trust, in the United States) was reported in a published dispatch from Berlin to have declared that a considerable portion of Germany's pre-war industry must remain if Germany was to survive. General Draper was chief adviser to General Eisenhower on German industry.

This apparent defiance of official military orders appeared strange, but no more so than the address delivered by the Honorable John J. McCloy before the Academy of Political Science in New York City on November 8th. Mr. McCloy, who had just resigned as Assistant Secretary of War, argued that Germany could never be made into an exclusively agricultural or pastoral society. He belittled the capacity of the enemy's remaining industrial plants and indicated that their plants should be put to work as soon as possible to pay for food that was to be imported. Concluded Mr. McCloy, "For a long time to come there is no justifiable fear that Germany's war potential is being rebuilt."

The Assistant Secretary of War, until 1940, was a member of the law firm of Cravath, de Gersdorff, Swaine & Wood, which firm as mentioned in earlier Chapters had been representing I.G. Farben or its affiliates in the United States. It may appear to be a coincidence that Mr. McCloy should have turned up in the War Department in 1941, in a position in which he could speak with authority on such matters as handling the destruction of that mainstay of Germany's war potential—I.G. Farben. The coincidence may also be recorded here that other members of the Cravath law firm also held responsible places in the War Department, including Alfred McCormack, and Howard C. Peterson, as assistants to the Secretary. Another former member of this firm, Col. Richard A. Wilmer, was commissioned after the war began and had to do with such problems.

One fact is apparent—General Dwight D. Eisenhower was definitely not in accord with those who favored softness. While on a visit to Washington on October 20, 1945, the General publicly demanded the complete dissolution of I.G. Farben in order to assure future world peace. That this was his intention may not be doubted. But the General of the Armies in Europe, with all his powers as a combat soldier, did not make policy and did not select many of the men who were sent to Germany by the State and War Departments and the F. E. A.

The retreat from the official policy of eliminating I.G. Farben continued with a statement by Secretary of State James F. Byrnes, in December 1945, in which he announced that German administrative agencies should be set up to control foreign trade and industry, and that German industrial production should be permitted to increase, and German exports permitted to finance necessary imports.

In August of that same year President Truman had been persuaded to send the well-meaning former war censor, Byron Price, to Germany to survey conditions. Mr. Price's report, while highly informative, ignored completely the lessons of Farben's quick emergency after the first World War by stating that . . . . .

> There certainly is not the slightest evidence that Germany can become, within the forseeable future, sufficiently strong to permit diversions of production for German war purposes.

In the Halls of Congress, Senators and Representatives were bombarded by the forgive-and-forget brigade and the advocates of immmediate restoration of German industry—so that the dear little baby Nazis would not starve.

Some of this special pleading was sincere idealism, and some of it arrant hypocrisy all too similiar to the brazen demands for the restoration of the German dye trust after the first World War. History repeats.

One very informative speech, which indicated the under cover struggle in official circles on the future of I.G. Farben, was delivered in the Senate on January 29, 1946 by Nebraska's distinguished funeral director, Republican Senator Kenneth S. Wherry. This mortician-turned-statesman referred to the

> Bitter rivalry between Mr. Morgenthau's henchmen in the Treasury Department and representatives in the War and State Department . . . . . as far back as 1942;

and stated that:

> Mr. Morgenthau finally won his battle . . . . . and forced the incorporation of his plan into the new infamous document J. C. S. 1067 despite the repeated warnings . . . . . of Mr. Stimson and of many high officials in the State Department.

Unfortunately, the speech was received with acclaim by all too many members of the Senate of the United States.

As illustrative of the non-partisan pattern of all such legislative propaganda, Senator James Oliver Eastland, Democrat colleague of Bilbo from Mississippi, contributed a fine appeal to passion and illogic on December 4, 1945, in a lengthy diatribe against Secretary Morgenthau for wanting to eliminate German war industry—and at Russian soldiers for, allegedly, raping German maidens.

In associating these two varieties of injury to the German people as a single great humanitarian issue, the Senator propounded this disingenious query:

> Why blur the easily defined distinction between peacetime industry and wartime industry? . . . . . to de-industrialize German is not necessary to render Germans powerless again to wage war. We are concerned instead with the great issue of humanitarianism.

However, it remained for that great Republican statesman from Indiana, the Honorable Homer E. Capehart, to win the Senatorial humanitarianism sweepstakes with an outburst on February 5, 1946, in which he denounced Mr. Morgenthau and the advocates of his plan, rather than the Nazis, as responsible for mass starvation of the German people and the deliberate destruction of the German state. Accusing them of "burning with an all-consuming determination to wreak their vengeance," the Senator stormed at his colleagues that their "technique of hate" had earned for Mr. Morgenthau, and Colonel Bernard Bernstein, the titles of "American Himmlers."

The thesis that the eradication of Farben's war potential was all wrong because people were starving in Germany was also found in a November 1945 report of a House of Representatives Committee on post-war planning, of which another Mississippi statesman, William M. Colmer, was chairman. This report stressed the pre-war dependence of other European countries (Farben's victims) on Germany's industry. Ignoring the obvious fact that chemical and metallurgical industries could operate just as efficiently for peace if moved out of Germany into adjoining countries where the lust for world conquest does not exist, Representative Colmer's report naïvely proclaimed that to strip Germany of its ordinary industries would injure industrial production in other countries (those ravaged by Germany) and also would impose a heavy burden on the United States or widespread starvation and dangerous conditions all over Europe.

Over the air and in the press the pleas to save Farben were heard in a great variety of argument. Among the gems of radio propaganda against the Morgenthau plan was the conclusion expressed by Saul K. Padover, biographer of emperors and former college professor, who is credited with effective work in the Army's Psychological Warfare Division. Professor Padover in a World Peaceways broadcast on December 16, 1945, ended his plea that we must re-make the German mind (he admitted that this would take decades) with a caution that there was an element of danger should we punish I.G. Farben or destroy its plants. "Destroying factories will achieve nothing" concluded the Professor.

Then he left in a hurry to return to his official duties in Germany. Months later, after Professor Padover had re-examined the stealthy resuscitation of the German industrial war potential in the guise of a peace-time economy, he changed his views. On September 9, 1946 in the newspaper *PM* the Professor expounded ably on the necessity to deprive the Reich of its industrial might in order, as he said, to turn it into "a giant without weapons, and consequently not to be feared."

However, as will appear later, the Professor's recognition of the menace of the Farben war potential did not appear until after our Secretary of State had taken one more step away from the Roosevelt program of destruction for all time of the real menace to future peace.

Meanwhile Raymond Moley, the kiss-and-tell hero of early New Deal days who had openly advocated a new era of German industrial cartelization to be directed by Americans, broadcast his conclusion that already the Morgenthau plan was gone, and that Farben, "one of the most unusual and important organizations in the world," need not be destroyed as it could be properly *controlled*, now that Americans had taken over.

Among the columnists, Dorothy Thompson, strangely changed from her earlier attitude, was probably the most vociferous and certainly the most hysterical opponent of Franklin Roosevelt's announced determination to eradicate the industrial war potential of I.G. Farben.

As justifying her attacks on "de-industrialism," as she called it, Miss Thompson made the point that "Only a limited number of industrialists helped Hitler in any way to come to power," and stated that her criticisms were based upon:

> Unswerving allegiance to the principles of democracy, the rarely practiced ethics of Christendom, the long range interests of America, and an unflagging defense of humanism.

Sylvia Porter, brilliant rival of Miss Thompson, replied in her column in the *New York Post* that the fundamental issue was to so direct Germany's post-war economy that she would never again be able to threaten world peace. Summed up Miss Porter on August 6, 1945:

> The Nazi party didn't make Hitler. Germany's industrialists made him and made his invasion possible.

And Farben's friends did not have it all their own way in the United States Senate. In June 1945 a few weeks after the surrender, Democratic Senator Harley M. Kilgore returned from an early postwar trip to occupied Germany with the announcement that he had uncovered proof of the plot to revive I.G. Farben and other German war industries, and that German industrial leaders were already preparing for the next world war.

Senator Kilgore, made Chairman of the Sub-Committee on War

Mobilization of the Senate Military Affairs Committee in 1943, had done excellent work in uncovering and recording evidence of Farben's prewar criminal conspiracies in the country and had also explored some aspects of the cartel problem in general.

In fact, Senator Kilgore became the first member of the Congress to express written approval of my own earlier efforts to expose the influences which were protecting the Farben prewar conspiracy when he wrote me in February 1944 that:

> If Congress had only investigated this (Farben) lobby in 1931 as you recommended, we should have had a more healthy realism about Germany and cartels rather than the realism of war.

On June 22, 1945 Senator Kilgore called the Honorable Bernard M. Baruch as a witness, and the latter, to his everlasting credit and to the dismay of many of his Wall Street friends, delivered a most devastating blast at Germany's industrial war potential which, he demanded, must be smashed for all time. Bluntly he described Farben's industrialists:

> War is their chief business . . . . . and always has been . . . . . Her war-making potential must be eliminated; many of her plants shifted east and west to friendly countries; all other heavy industry destroyed . . . . .

The elder statesman's testimony constituted a substantial approval of Secretary Morgenthau's proposals and as such went further than the Yalta agreement of the three heads of state. Over and over Mr. Baruch denounced the German industrial leaders as equally guilty of murder as were the Nazis.

> "German industry is a war industry," he said. "You cannot industrialize Germany and keep her from being a war agency."

Other witnesses who followed Mr. Baruch before the Kilgore Committee included Assistant Secretary of State William L. Clayton, who testified regarding evidence uncovered in Germany of the grandiose plot engaged in by I.G. Farben and other war industries in concealing their capital assets and technicians in "safe havens," as he termed them, in foreign countries in order to prepare for the next war.

Perhaps the most important testimony presented to the committee, in its significance as regards the postwar administrative policy on I.G. Farben, was a lengthy program outlined by Leo T. Crowley who, at the time, was still wielding his great powers and influence behind the scenes as Foreign Economic Administrator. In the outline of his program of economic and industrial disarmament Mr. Crowley indulged in a series of contradictory allegations and proposals which, facing both ways, would appear to be merely aimless double-talk if it were not for its more serious aspects. Mr. Crowley's thesis at the start very ably pointed out that:

> It was not the amount of military material which Germany was able to save from destruction by the Allies nor the handful of military material which Germany was able to manufacture . . . . . during the years which immediately followed the defeat of 1918. . . . . Rather it was the fact that Germany retained intact a vast aggregate of economic and industrial war potential and was able to continue to experiment, plan and prosecute its development in terms of future war production that was important . . . . ." and "that later enabled the German nation to organize itself completely and entirely for war . . . . .

The above appears to be an extremely well expressed recognition by Mr. Crowley of German's real war potential. However, in concluding, Mr. Crowley openly advocated another era of control instead of eradication, saying that "economic security from future German aggression must," among other things, "recognize the differences between a powerful war economy and a healthy peace-time economy" and "be achieved by . . . . . affirmative industrial and economic controls as a first step."

Among the gems in this list of "musts" relating to the control but not the elimination of Germany's war potential were requirements that the control ". . . . . be possessed of a maximum of administrative feasibility and simplicity. Complicated and detailed controls may be practical during the period of occupation. . . . . Be simple and understandable for the common people of the world. . . . ."

With gibberish of this sort emanating from one of the highest ranking administrators in Washington, is it any wonder that minor O. M. G. officials who wanted to do a job were discouraged and ineffective.

It is appropriate to recite here statements of necessity for the disarmament of Germany which are set forth in the summary of the final program prepared under Mr. Crowley's direction and made public some months after his statement before the Kilgore Committee.

One of these necessities is stated to be that "The achievement of security from future German aggression should be the primary and controlling element in our foreign policy toward Germany."

Another admits the inadequacy of any program which merely stops the direct production of arms and munitions and states:

> Military potential in a total war is a combination of modern industrial, scientific, and institutional components of such a nature as to make them equally useful for war or civilian productions.

Having thus ably stated the necessity to eliminate completely I.G. Farben and its allied metallurgical industries, the Crowley program and its appendix in some 660 closely printed pages of figures and discussion then recommends the continued operations of these same industries with the trained management and scientific research which must accompany them—all this to be "controlled" for an indefinite period. In other words a substantial repetition, step by step, of the control of German industry instituted by the Allies after the first World War which fumbled and foozled until it was abandoned, while the men of Farben went right along with their plans for the next war.

With respect to Mr. Crowley's contradictory recommendations on German industry it is only fair to state that Henry H. Fowler, Director of the Enemy Branch of the F. E. A., who did much of the work on the problems, also presented numerous exhibits to the Kilgore Committee on June 26, 1945 which were notable contributions to the unmasking of Farben's war potential.

Having contributed his final compendium of governmental policy which related to the survival of I.G. Farben, Mr. Crowley retired from his numerous and onerous government jobs to his duties as president and chairman of the Standard Gas & Electric Company and other public utilities in which he held office. However, criticism of Mr. Crowley did not cease with the end of his governmental duties, as the Federal Power Commission on June 18, 1946, issued an order forbidding him to continue as chairman of one electric light company and director in two other utilities, giving neglect of his duties as the reason for thus ousting him.

CHAPTER XXI

Another Farben Peace

SENATOR KILGORE
in October, 1945, publicly expressed his concern at reports that high officials were planning a revival of I.G. Farben's export trade instead of dismantling its facilities.

In December, after his committee had assembled and made public voluminous records extracted from the I.G. Farben files in Germany which proved its war guilt beyond question, the Senator called as a witness Col. Bernard Bernstein, formerly Treasury Counsel, who, as Director of the Division of Investigation of Cartels and External Assets in the O. M. G., had recently returned to the United States, having been sent back, according to report, because he was too insistent in his efforts to uncover the part Farben played in the war and in searching for the accomplices through whom its assets were still hidden.

Colonel Bernstein, in a lengthy statement prepared from original documents with meticulous care, brought out the startling fact that 87 percent of Farben's industrial war machine was ready to operate, and instead of being destroyed as required by the Yalta and Potsdam Agreements, was actually being put back into operation. His testimony showed conclusively that the German war machine could not have functioned without Farben, and that Dr. Carl Krauch, pre-war Nazi Chief of Germany's entire chemical industry, and chairman of Farben's board of directors, along with the other Farben leaders, had long known of the Nazi plan of aggression. The witness expressed the hope that the criminal role played by Farben's officials would result in their indictment and conviction as war criminals. Vain Hope.

Shortly after this, Col. Bernstein resigned from the Government service. His successor in the O. M. G. set-up in Germany, Russell A. Nixon, a former member of the Harvard faculty, let loose a blast in Berlin, saying that Farben's high officials who had been arrested were being released, their plants were not being destroyed, and the uncovering of their hidden assets abroad was being hindered by State Department officials.

So Mr. Nixon was also returned to the United States and he, too, gave his testimony before the Kilgore Committee.

Mr. Nixon was now out of the Government service and was free of official restraints. He minced no words in stating that O. M. G. officials directly engaged in carrying out Order No. 2 of July 5. 1945, were deliberately violating it, and that the I.G. Farben war potential was being actually rebuilt and reintegrated instead of being destroyed. Among high points of Mr. Nixon's testimony were detailed charges that: no I.G. Farben plants had been destroyed, those widely heralded as having been blown up were in reality government-owned plants. No law to destroy cartels in Germany had been promulgated and no policy existed in this respect. Farben officials and employes who had been arrested had then been released from custody—in some cases were actually assisting in the activities of the O. M. G. The instructions for a complete mobilization of Farben's external assets had not been carried out.

Farben's stock had gone up and up on the Munich and Frankfurt Stock Exchanges (from 68 to 142½) because the German people on the spot knew what was going on.

The State Department and the British Foreign Office had acted together in preventing the seizure of Farben's foreign assets.

Possibly the most significant item in Mr. Nixon's story was his statement that Farben's re-growth followed closely the expectations which had been expressed by the notorious Max Ilgner, in a letter discovered by the O. M. G., which Ilgner wrote in 1944 to several of his associates and in which this Farben foreign-espionage head confidently advised his pals to stick together because he, Ilgner, could assure them that the American authorities would eventually came to their rescue and permit I.G. Farben to resume business as usual.

Mr. Nixon not only minced no words in denouncing the official malpractice by which every order to destroy Farben was being aborted, but named some of those individuals in the O. M. G. set-up in Germany whom he believed to be responsible for this ghastly repetition of the sabotage of Allied control of this same German dye trust in the years following World War I.

Among those Mr. Nixon indicated had taken the attitude that the Morgenthau plan was hysterical or impracticable were Ambassador Robert D. Murphy, representing the State Department; General William H. Draper, Director of the Economics Division; Col. E. G. Pillsbury, control officer; Major Petroff, former attorney for General Motors; Laird Bell, Chicago attorney who had been outspoken in his disagreement with Potsdam and J. C. S. 1067; and Col. Joe Starnes, former member of the noxious Dies Committee of the House of Representatives who, when defeated for reelection, was rewarded with a commission in the Army and as a member of the O. M. G. urged that the de-Nazification order should be ignored and German industry should be started.

Mr. Nixon went into some detail regarding the peculiar actions of Col. Carl B. Peters, former president of Synthetic Nitrogen Products, director of Chemnyco, and an official of the Advance Solvents Corporation, all Farben subsidiaries, who was quietly removed from Germany for engaging in numerous relations with high I.G. Farben officials.

Col. Peters, Swiss-born American citizen and a Major in ordnance during World War I, was active in the chemical industry and took a leading part in Farben's false front set-ups in the United States. Then in 1939 he was indicted in two of the synthetic nitrogen ammonia cases which were kept secret from the public and later were mysteriously *nolle prossed.* And on September 5, 1941 he was defendant in the civil complaint and consent decree involving the same conspiracy with Farben to restrain synthetic nitrogen production. Colonel Peters reentered the Army and was sent to Germany originally by Mr. Crowley's Foreign Economic Administration, coming to grief as Mr. Nixon stated, when United States Counter-Intelligence decided that his relations with Farben personages were improper and indicated that he looked forward to renewed inter connections between Farben and American interests.

Readers may ponder at this typical example of the familiar pattern, of the way a man who served Farben purposes during the pre-war period in its American fronts and was thus personally involved in court actions for conspiracy against this country, should then have been commissioned in the Army and sent by Mr. Crowley to help carry out the destruction—or control—of I.G. Farben's war machine in Germany.

While Senator Kilgore was making a direct attack upon the Farben conspiracy, one other robust member of the Senate, the Hon. Joseph O'Mahoney, Wyoming Democrat, had been approaching some aspects of the Farben mess by indirection with an insistent demand that the Government of the United States take a forthright position on the total abolishment of all international cartels—particularly those by which Farben had disarmed this nation and its other victims.

In May, 1945, Senator O'Mahoney held public hearings before Senate Committees which were considering cartel legislation, and his first two witnesses, Attorney General Francis Biddle and Assistant Attorney General Wendell Berge, distinguished themselves by expressing conclusions that executives of the corporations who signed and carried out the illegal tie-ups with Farben were innocent of any attempt to injure the national security and did not present any moral problem in so doing.

This gratuitous effort to apply a coat of official whitewash to men whose acts had contributed to obstructing the national defense, was more remarkable in view of Mr. Biddle's admission that some of those same individuals were parties to carry-over agreements through which the illegal agreements were already being resumed. And Mr. Berge's friends and admirers were chagrined when he ignored official records to the contrary, and expressed the absurd opinion that the United States Government had "no knowledge" of Standard Oil's partnership agreements with Farben during the thirteen-year pre-war period. Out of my own high admiration for Wendell Berge let it be said that whoever induced him to put such statements into a public record was not a real friend of this kindly gentleman.

Leaders of the oil industry also appeared, including Orville Harden, vice-president of Standard Oil of New Jersey, and other executives of that company—each to express, quaintly, their bitter opposition to cartels. They each appeared at first to hate these infamous arrangements. Then the words *nevertheless, however,* and *but* would creep in, in a way which indicated that just possibly the speakers were afraid that perhaps we could not afford to be too harsh in future about such tie-ups with foreign companies. The oil magnates put on a good show.

On the last day of these hearings Senator O'Mahoney called on me, as an authority on cartels and I.G. Farben, and thus made it possible to put into a Senate record a few of the pertinent facts (which now may be found in this book) about the vicious political influence by which I.G. Farben during the pre-war era had so profoundly molded opinion and policy inside Germany and also in other countries, including the United States.

I utilized this opportunity to refute the earlier allegations of Messrs. Biddle and Berge that none of their so-called innocent American industrial cartelists knew that the national security was involved in their partnerships with Farben, and that the United States Government was not informed about these illegal agreements until after Germany began the war. The documentary proofs which I cited to disprove the Biddle-Berge allegations were received in painful silence, especially those which clearly indicated that the political influence of I.G. Farben might have been responsible for the innocuous results of flabby Anti-Trust Law enforcement against those whose tie-ups with Farben did weaken our national security.

It was merely a coincidence, but surely a pleasant one, that Mr. Biddle resigned from his position as Attorney General the day after my testimony recorded some of the weird results of his tenure of that office. However, rumor had it that he had been slated to go ever since former Assistant Attorney General Norman Littell forced into the record some of the proofs relating to Mr. Biddle's relations with Thomas Corcoran.

How and why Francis Biddle under these circumstances later wound up as the United States member of the Nuremberg Court by appointment of President Truman remains a mystery on which the readers of this record may well ponder.

As the aftermath of having thus placed on a record of the Senate for the first time evidence that the political influence of I.G. Farben had been reaching inside the Government of the United States, the printing of the record of these hearings was held up for months, while parts of my testimony were suppressed.

However, it developed that the Wyoming Senator was unwilling that political influence of I.G. Farben should prevent his colleagues in the Senate, and the public, from reading testimony on that same political influence of I.G. Farben which had been recorded before his Committee. Thus, in the final printing of these hearings, there appeared a reproduction of my 1931 Chart or Flow Sheet (described in Chapter VII) showing I.G. Farben's control in that early pre-war era, of our munitions industries, its influence on our press and our government. Thanks to the courage of Joe O'Mahoney, this proof that it was then known what Farben had planned for ten years later, became a public record fourteen years after it had been sent to members of the Congress.

On December 12, 1945, after Colonel Bernstein's public testimony, Senator Kilgore, in an off-the-record conversation with me, expressed his indignation at incidents which I related as illustrations of Farben's influence in security immunity for some of its Amercan stooges. I was then advised that I would be called back to Washington as a witness before the Kilgore Committee. Instead, a letter from the Senator advised me that the public hearings were discontinued and would I kindly send him a written statement to be printed with the Committee's other testimony?

On December 21, 1945, a few days after our private conversation on Farben's political influence, Senator Kilgore issued a ringing public statement dealing with this same subject of influence. And in restrained but unmistakably critical language the Senator discussed the conduct of affairs in occupied Germany with this query:

For what private and selfish ends are our national security and the security of our allies placed in jeopardy?

He became more specific as he continued:

The attitude of these military government officials is an out-growth of their connections with industrial and financial enterprises whcih had close pre-war ties with the Nazis.

His statement also named some of the same O. M. G. officials mentioned in the Nixon testimony, but unfortunately Senator Kilgore did not bring out clearly the basic issue of Farben's continued political influence inside government at Washington, where obviously the real resonsibility lay for putting into the O. M. G. men who would deliberately sabotage the orders issued by General Eisenhower to smash I.G. Farben. These men did not appoint themselves to office.

As one way to remedy the silence on this issue I included in the statement which the Senator had requested for his Committee's hearings some of the ample proofs available that the most dangerous aspect of the German war potential was the political influence of Farben inside the Government of the United States. Incidents, a few of the many in this book, were recited.

My medicine was too strong for Senator Kilgore—the heat was on for what he had already put into the record. My statement was returned with advice that it could not be published because: "It is not the policy of the Sub-Committee to make charges against individuals . . . . ." (which was a rather peculiar allegation in view of the charges against members of the O. M. G., and many others made in the Kilgore Committee Hearings). Tactfully, the Senator's letter added:

"I am not questioning your veracity."

Friends of the Senator then complained to me that I was causing him embarrassment. Be that as it may, his probe of I.G. Farben had already caused such dismay and resentment that no appeasement policy would suffice and the Kilgore Committee's investigations were marked for the same end as those of the Bone Committee.

Following Mr. Nixon's testimony in February, it was announced that witnesses from the State Department would appear before the Kilgore Committee to refute the Nixon charges. But no such witnesses appeared. Instead, the Audit and Contingent Expenses of the Senate reached out to strangle Senator Kilgore's brave effort to defeat the Farben revival plot, by cutting the appropriation for his Sub-Committee to a fraction of the sum required.

This is not to imply that this action, by the Senators involved, was not motivated by a desire for economy or was influenced by the I.G. Farben lobby.

While the tug-of-war was going on in the United States Senate between the save-Farben and smash-Farben teams, important contributions were made by those two valiant battlers, Representatives Voorhis of California and Coffee of Washington. Among the several forceful speeches by Mr. Voorhis touching on the I.G. Farben tie-ups in the United States was that delivered on May 21, 1945, in support of his House Concurrent Resolution 55, which demanded that the Government prevent the economic financial or technical resources of Germany from rebuilding the future war potential of the enemy in any other nation, and to prevent any citizens or corporations of the United States taking any action "through cartel agreements or otherwise" which would contribute to the rebuilding of that future war potential.

Again on July 20, 1945, Mr. Voorhis complained bitterly that:

> Some of the very people who hold top positions in the American Control Commission in Germany are men who either in the past or at this very moment are officials of American companies who had . . . . . connections with some of the very German companies which the Senate (Kilgore) Committee has warned about . . . . .

Mr. Voorhis also put his finger on the issue by saying that:

> To select men with connections of this sort and to pass over the thousands of other American businessmen whose companies never had any such connections is, to put the matter very mildly indeed, a mistake which may have the most serious consequences for the future peace of the world.

Representative Coffee also has a long and notable record of well-documented and forthright attacks upon the cartel as an institution and I.G. Farben tie-ups in particular. On October 4, 1945, while Colonel Bernstein's battle against the sabotage of the directives to destroy Farben was at its height in Germany, Mr. Coffee delivered in the House a blasting attack upon I.G. Farben political influence in which he paid me the honor of referring to my own efforts, citing among other things my exposé of the way the Geneva Economic Conference in 1927 was influenced by Farben's Dr. Lammers.* Mr. Coffee then put into the record his own views on the way Farben influenced both international and our own domestic affairs, including the following:

> We have all, I think, felt the impact of such influence here at Washington, at times like these, when investigation and legislation which may affect any cartel activities is under discussion, or pending. Then it is that some visitor—in plain language some lobbyist—attempts his persuasions with quaint sophistries, or more subtle argument. Now what essential difference can anyone point out between the lobbyist—or fixer—exerting pressure here at Washington or in Europe in our reconstruction set-up, in 1945, for cartel survival; and Farben's Dr. Lammers at Geneva in 1927 successfully persuading that international assembly not to act against the cartel.
>
> In the light of events since then, which are known to all of us, it may be admitted that should the Geneva Economic Conference in 1927 have protested at the evils of the cartel, and had it even raised the lid a fraction of an inch to peer within the Pandora's Box of I.G. Farben. then those beastly, tragic human ills, which later were loosed from that casket of evil and death, might not have brought us, now, to a war and a victory so dearly won with the blood of American youth. In 1927 I.G. Farben's leaders had to prevent action by the League, so Farben's distinguished Dr. Lammers was on the spot to do so.
>
> Who shall dare to say that some other Dr. Lammers, dis-

* In monograph, The Cartel, published in the Encyclopedia Americana, 1945.

guised in sheep's clothing as a learned technical adviser, or in
the raiment of an apostle of democracy and peace, has not
been around Washington to advise anyone so credulous as
to listen to him; or is not among those who at this very time
are in Europe to help decide on the spot what to do about
saving German industries, or what punishment, if any, shall
be meted out to guilty German industrialists.

The eloquent Representative summed up his conclusions with:

. . . . . the one great national and international issue which
the cartel presents to us at this time, and which we must face
before it is too late, is that of the cartel's political influence,
as we see it now revealed in preparation for this war, and as
it must be met if its impact upon the next peace is to be immunized. We have won the war in Europe and in Asia, but are
we doing those things which must be done if we are to win
the peace, while the friends and allies of I.G. also plan and
connive in secret to reconstruct their private cartel super-
state? Remember, too, that much of the propaganda which
clandestinely attempts to foment discord among the Allies in
this war and in this peace has its origin and its motivation
among the adherents of another era of world cartelization.

These references to the influence which might effect what punishment, if any, shall be meted out to guilty German industrialists
are a reminder that up to the time this is written there appears no
record of the indictment or the punishment of any officer or employe of I.G. Farben, in Europe, save for the gentle protective
custody in which some of them have been held, until they were
released by influences exerted upon subordinate officials in the
O. M. G.

As one of the few columnists who wield an objective pen and cite
names and facts on the I. G. Farben problem, Tom Stokes followed
up Jerry Voorhis' exposé in the House with a series on the same
subject, of the official folly of putting men in the O. M. G. in Germany to eradicate Farben who were officers of American Companies tied in with I.G. Farben and in some instances under indictment for such offenses.

The Nazi conspirators, and in particular the industrialists among them, embarked upon a huge rearmament program and set out to produce and develop huge quantities of materials of war, and to create a powerful military potential . . . . .

Dr. Schmitz, indicted in the United States in 1941, remained untried for those offenses; and at Nuremberg he was not even indicted with other and lesser criminals.

In view of the record thus summarized it is not surprising that on May 1, 1946, former Secretary of the Treasury Henry Morgenthau, Jr., broadcast a denunciation of the State Department policies on elimination of Germany's war potential, with careful analysis which included this positive statement:

We have failed to de-industrialize Germany.

The speaker then reflected the views of many others by saying:

It is still not clear to me whether Mr. Byrnes intends to scrap the Allied program of Quebec, Yalta and Potsdam . . . . . If it is Mr. Byrnes' intention to scrap the Potsdam pact and allow Germany to remain industrially powerful, then I prophesy that we are simply repeating the fatal mistakes of Versailles, and laying the foundation for World War III.

Mr. Morgenthau's query to Secretary Byrnes was a voice crying in the wilderness of synthetic public clamor which demanded the survival of German industry—of Farben. This appeal was disguised in a confusion of many voices, of hysterical pleas for a starving Germany and fears of a Russian menace.

In July 1946, Russia's Molotov had made an obvious public bid for the favor of an unrepentant Germany. Then late in August Lieutenant General Lucius D. Clay, Deputy Military Governor of the American Zone in Germany, contributed what may appear as the first of a series of answers to Mr. Morgenthau's query. As reported, General Clay's statement included inaccurate and rather naïve allegations that Germany no longer had any physical war potential of her own and could only be a threat if some other power with the industrial wherewithal used her as a mercenary.

One of those identified by Stokes in his column of May 26, 1945, was Col. Frederick Pope, who had been with the Office of War Mobilization before being selected as Chairman of the F. E. A. Committee on Chemicals which prepared that section of Mr. Crowley's Program for German and Industrial Disarmament (already mentioned).

Without questioning Mr. Pope's high standing as an industrial engineer, or the good faith of his recommendations relating to the peacetime control rather than the destruction of Farben's production of war chemicals, Mr. Stokes pointed out that Mr. Pope was a director or official of more than one of I.G. Farben's American affiliates.

These have included Mr. Pope's directorship of the American Cyanamid Company (fined $10,000 in April, 1946, for conspiring with I. G. Farben) and of the Southern Alkali Co. (defendant in action filed in 1944 for conspiracy with Farben in the alkali industry) and prior to 1939 Mr. Pope was also closely associated with the Farben subsidiary Synthetic Nitrogen Products Co., along with Col. Carl Peters, which company's record has also been presented.

The press in general, as has been mentioned in earlier chapters, continued its customary reluctance to publish all of the real truth which came out of Germany.

As the struggle inside of the O. M. G. proceeded, between those like Bernstein and Nixon who wanted to be harsh, as ordered, with Farben, and those opposed, there were increasing protests from news correspondents stationed in our occupied zone in Germany that either direct censorship or indirect pressure was making it difficult to send back home the real facts on what was going on behind the scenes. Correspondents of even the conservative *New York Times* joining in these protests justify a belief that they were well grounded. It remains fortunate that Messrs. Bernstein and Nixon, when they returned to the United States, resisted such efforts to silence them as we may be quite sure were made.

This may be the appropriate place to cite that dramatic incident which took place in the courtroom in New York on June 6, 1945, when, as told in Chapter xviii, Farben's chief Counsel, Dr. August von Knieriem, flown from Frankfurt, in custody in a military plane, was produced as a surprise witness by Philip Amram, Assistant Attorney General, and testified regarding the celebrated fake agreement made by Standard Oil of New Jersey with Farben at The Hague in September, 1939, after Germany had invaded Poland.

Dr. von Knieriem produced from the Farben files a signed copy of the so-called Hague agreement which he identified as his own original, and on its margin in his own handwriting there were numerous notations made at the time to explain the various clauses in the agreement. One of these conclusions recorded by Farben's chief legal adviser in 1939, when the Farben leaders' vision of world conquest held no possibility of the tragic revelations in 1945, was a short pungent phrase in German which, translated, shouted out the fraud and the confident expectation of a future renewal of the mesalliance between Farben and Standard. The words were "Post-War Camouflage."

We may well ask how much of the contemptible double talk and worse relating to Farben which has been uncovered comes within lawyer von Knieriem's definition of camouflage to deceive the Government and the people of the United States.

James S. Martin, previously mentioned in Chapter xv, succeeded Mr. Nixon as control officer for I.G. Farben in the American Military Government for Germany. After he had appealed for the establishment of another tribunal to try the guilty industrialists, Mr. Martin was permitted to organize a unit to be devoted specifically to the de-cartelization of Farben and its affiliates. However, the efforts of this group to eliminate Germany's industrial war potential appeared to be restricted to surveillance and control of the so-called peacetime economy, which, since Potsdam, the higher ups had found so conveniently elastic and expandable.

Meanwhile, as the trial of Nazi leaders at Nuremberg proceeded, many Americans sought in vain for some sign that punishment would be inflicted upon the Farben leaders who were in the custody of the American authorities. The criminal acts of these men had again been established by countless original documents uncovered in their own files, as not only responsible for Hitler and Hitler's armed might and the weakening of Germany's victim

countries, but also as directly involved in some o[f the] deeds of the Nazi regime.

These included such acts of criminal depravit[y as par]ticipation in the Nazi slave labor practices which h[ave been] "in the blackest periods of the slave trade," by whic[h Farben] plants had been manned with forced labor of haples[s victims,] manufacturing and knowingly supplying the deadly [poison] used to murder millions of helpless humans in the death [chambers] at Auschwitz (Oswiecim); and, after these mass murde[rs, the] conversion into fertilizer of the ashes remaining from th[e cremavation] tion of the corpses.

It so happens that ample evidence of all these unbel[ievable] practices was produced at the trial and recorded in the[official] judgment of the Nuremberg Tribunal.

With relation to this evidence of depravity, it may be [men]tioned that Georg von Schnitzler, called by some the No. 2 Far[ben] criminal, admitted to our O. M. G. officials long before the Nure[m]berg trials began that he, and other Farben directors, had know[n] that poison gases manufactured in a Farben plant were being used to murder human beings in the Nazi concentration camps, and did nothing about it—save to continue the supply.

However, at Nuremberg all this evidence was not related to the guilt of Farben's leaders—they were not on trial. The senile Krupp was the only one indicted who was publicly identified as an industrialist (with side-door ties to Farben). He was not even tried.

And, as the trial dragged on, the slimy Schacht, close associate of Farben, and involved in Farben's pre-Hitler preparations for war, but usually referred to as a mere financier, boasted complacently that he would not be convicted.

To some it may have seemed strange indeed that there were no Farben figures in the Nuremberg dock, especially in view of earlier insistence of United States Prosecutor Robert H. Jackson that some of them should be. The indictment, where it dealt with certain vital aspects of aggressive war—for which Hermann Schmitz and his associates obviously were responsible—included the following:

A week later, on September 6, 1946, Secretary of State Byrnes made his counter-bid for the friendship of the prostrate nation in a broadcast at Stuttgart, in which he threw overboard all pretence of implementation of the plan to eliminate Farben's war potential—which the Potsdam conference had decreed.

In double talk decrying the oversight that no allowance had been made in fixing levels of industry for reparations and a self-supported Germany, Mr. Byrnes assured his listeners of a balanced industrial economy to be controlled by trained inspectors, and an export-import program out of which reparations (and industrial profits) might come.

Described in the press as America's bidding against Russia for German favor, columnist Edgar Ansel Mowrer aptly called it Byrnes' plan "to fight fire with fire," while expressing the vain hope that "we come through unharmed."

And Upton Close complacently termed it "a cardinal principle of democracy," and "a reminder to the Reich that we recognize the right of every nation to govern itself."

The Secretary of State then returned to the Paris Peace Conference and his bi-partisan foreign policy which, whatever else it may or may not be, does have the unqualified approval of that good friend of Standard Oil's late Mr. Farish, Democratic Senator Tom Connally, and the learned legal adviser of Farben's Mr. Halbach, Republican statesman John Foster Dulles.

President Truman, nudged rather violently on foreign relations by the man he had displaced as Vice-President, then publicly indicated his full support of the policies of the Secretary of State.

With another swift turn of the wheel, one more completed design in the pattern of things to come was unfolded when, on September 30, 1946, the Nuremberg Tribunal handed down its verdict convicting the Nazi riffraff and military gangsters, but acquitting both Franz von Papen and Hjalmar Horace Greeley Schacht. Subsequently mysterious press reports intimated that Francis Biddle, as American Judge, had voted to convict Schacht. However, Mr. Biddle declined to say how he voted. The Judgment states "The Tribunal finds Schacht not guilty . . ." Of the four Judges, American, British, French and Russian, only the last dissented.

The dissent of Russia's Judge J. I. Nikitchenko appears as an understatement when he declared that:

Schacht's leading part in the preparation and execution of a common criminal plan is proved.

In the light of damning facts, showing the involvement of Schacht, which were recited in the verdict itself, he was obviously guilty on Counts 1 and 2 of the indictment, of:

. . . . . participation in a common plan or conspiracy to commit crimes against peace . . . . . in the planning, initiation or waging of a war of agression.

But after reciting the evidence of Schacht's guilt the judges who wrote the weasel-worded acquittal then accepted the Schacht alibi that he "didn't know" that the rearmament for which he and his Farben associates were responsible was intended for aggressive war. The naïve judges who concocted this decision attempted to justify the Schacht innocence on his plea that "when he discovered the Nazis were rearming for aggressive purposes he attempted to slow down the speed of rearmaments."

So this close associate of Dr. Hermann Schmitz and other directors of Farben and Vereinigte Stahlwerke, who sat with him on the board of the Reichsbank, went free on that moth-eaten alibi of Farben's allies: "I didn't know," despite a showing of guilt which included substantially each of the various offenses that can be proved against Dr. Schmitz and the rest of the Farben brood—if and when these gentry are tried.

So out of Nuremberg has now emerged the judicial dictum and high precedent behind which immunity for the leaders of Farben may be made secure.

Disheartened, Robert Jackson (who five years earlier, as Attorney General, had complained of the "pattern" of non-military invasion which interfered with "law enforcement itself"), was quoted as agreeing fully with the Russian dissent. "I'd rather see any man but Schacht get off," said the American prosecutor, and "the further prosecutions of industrialists . . . . . which have been planned, will have to be studied from the text of the opinion."

What he might have said was that it now had become an almost

futile task either to indict or to try the Farben criminals. Unless
an outraged public opinion—when the truth is revealed—will smash
down the pattern of immunity which has protected war criminals
of two world wars.

With his acquittal, many of Schacht's close friends outside Germany, industrialists, financiers and politicians, breathed in relief
from the fear that had been haunting them; fear that the vengeful
tongue, of a Schacht, if convicted, would have spilled the beans; a
fear now abated because stupid men on a high bench had been
persuaded to say that Schacht's guilt had not been "established
beyond a reasonable doubt."

A verdict so bad that it outraged many of the German people
themselves may give rise to the query whether the Nuremberg
trial was arranged to provide a judicial warning of the hangman's
noose to gangsters who may plan aggressive war in future; or to
provide judicial safe havens for respectable criminals who created
the gangsters thus condemned—a crowning example of the un-
written law of the Farben jungle.

Following quickly on the heels of the Schacht fiasco was the
announcement of an official economic mission to study the possibility of advancing United States Government funds to German
industry to implement its controlled peace-time economy by a
revival of the German import-export trade. This mission was
headed by George Allen, as director of the Reconstruction
Finance Corporation, and Howard C. Peterson, Jr., as assistant
Secretary of War.

Time will reveal whether any Farben plants or Farben affiliates
now in dire need of financial aid will be judged as deserving it
by Mr. Allen, friend of Victor Emanuel, and director of Farben's
General Aniline; or by Mr. Peterson, former member of the Cravath
law firm which represented Farben, and official successor of that
other ex-Cravath firm lawyer, John J. McCloy.

Then came a significant resignation at Nuremberg. Abraham
Pomerantz, distinguished American attorney and Prosecutor of
the industrial war criminals (who had asked me to serve as his
advisor on I.G. Farben) quit the job in protest at the calibre of
the Judges designated to try these cases.

Other reports, not confirmed, indicated that Dr. Herman Abs, one of the most powerful of Farben's directors, had been immunized in the British Zone, where he was acting as adviser to the English officials; and that Fritz Thyssen, safe in his pleasant quarters on the Island of Capri, was also immune from prosecution.

Meanwhile Schacht announced that he had a plan to solve "Germany's economic problems." Thyssen had already produced his plan for a German corporate state in his true-confessions book. And surely the Geheimrat Hermann Schmitz, with the help of nephew Max Ilgner and of Georg von Schnitzler, could supply a plan—if not convicted.

Schacht-Thyssen-Schmitz—what a team that would be to rebuild German's peace time economy, and direct it jointly with a select group of Anglo-American industrialists, financed with American taxpayer's funds!

The foregoing constitutes a small part of the record, and of the proofs available that the conspiracy to save the Farben war criminals from punishment, to revive the Farben structure, and to renew the Farben carry-over tie-ups, here and elsewhere, is proceeding on schedule.

Just as Max Ilgner told his criminal associates in 1944 that it would be, this plot is proceeding in the pattern of another false peacetime tragedy which, in reality, is another intermission for rebuilding of a superstate and another era of secret preparation for World War III.

That the same influence which reaches into high places to make a treason's peace is also active in promoting friction among the victorious Allies of World War II may be in some respects the most dangerous manifestation of that cancer in the vital organs of government.

That Great Britain under Attlee, as under Churchill, has favored a soft peace for Farben and has changed little from its prewar dependence upon cartel trade restrictions, and that Moscow has severely criticized the Anglo-American policy of hard talk and soft action regarding Farben has been apparent in many news items coming from London, from Berlin and from Moscow.

This book is not the place for appraisal of the post-war relations between the United States and Great Britain on one side and Russia on the other, nor to comment on the manners and tactics of Moscow or the pin prickings and vacillations of Washington.

It is, however, within the purposes of this book to point out that ample proofs have been recorded here of many aspects of the pattern of I.G. Farben which show a purpose always to divide and conquer, and that this pattern very definitely traces its slimy threads into the sabotage of the eradication of I.G. Farben's war potential by the same influences inside the Government at Washington which have been pressing our foreign policies and our stand in the United Nations away from a possible rapprochement with Russia.

The arguments heard that the recrudescence of Germany's armed might by a revival of Farben's industrial war potential may be desirable to provide a buffer, or a threat, to Russian expansion (call it imperialism, or demand for security as you will) appear as cockeyed and as vicious as would be a demand for the reorganization of Max Ilgner's spy ring in South America in order to help us protect the Panama Canal.

Readers of this book may perceive emerging now the shadow of the Frankenstein's monster rebuilt—by folly, or by treason— no less alive in now socialistic Britain than in capitalistic United States. This creature may introduce that culmination of final world conquest for which Farben's leaders have already planned and made possible two World Wars.

Of what avail a victory at arms, with its ghastly sacrifice of sweat, and blood, and tears; of youth destroyed, or warped, or wrecked—if out of it shall come another peace of Farben's pattern, a peace disguised this time as a union of nations to rule by force, by the atomic bomb, if you will, with men of Farben's choice to make up that super-state?

If that shall be the sacrifice and the victory and the profit, then this ghastly price will have been paid merely to yield our own destinies, and those of all the world, to the tender mercies of a supreme corporate state guided by men of Farben's choice; a union of nations, as a super-world-government, which, call it by what name you will, in reality will be the consummation of the world conquest planned by faceless Farben figures to be consummated by Farben's faithless dupes.

Democracy at its worst – and at its best

THIS, THEN, IS THE PATTERN
*of Farben, as it has appeared and re-appeared before and during
two world wars—and as that same pattern has already re-appeared
in the peace.*

*This story has been cut in length and cut again, in order to
bring it within the covers of this book. For lack of space many
facts which should be told have been omitted here. But those
which are presented are sufficient to show that the people of this
nation must clean their own house of Farben before hoping to
instruct other peoples of the world how to eradicate for all time
this obstacle to an enduring peace.*

*The accusation of muckraking which will be made has its own
reply in the fact that those who claim to be accused by this story
may not again plead ignorance of the facts presented here, facts
which bear so vital a relation to the peace which is to come.*

There will be those who will allege that Pan-Germanism and

*the Teuton lust for world conquest were conceived and thrived
many centuries before the era of modern warfare and the German
dye cartels. I reply that since the age of modern war began all
of the so-called military groups of Germany, including the Prus-
sians and the Junkers, would have been helpless without the munitions supplied by Farben; nor have those groups ever had any
important influence inside the United States save that created
through Farben's pattern of conspiracy—as revealed in this story.*

*It is not necessary to conclude that some of those named here
were knaves and some were fools, nor does the author so assert.
And, just so, it must not be assumed that any individual, merely
because his name appears in this story, is accused by the author
of guilty acts or of guilty purposes.*

*We may disregard all issues of intent, and on the sole issue of
intelligence the reader is entitled to say whether leadership by
men who thus did Farben's bidding must be rejected now, so that
the pattern of Farben may be uprooted. Otherwise we will again
be led astray by Farben's guile—even before the grass grows green
or the tears are dry upon the graves of those who have died and
are dying now for the blind stupidity of those who would reject
the lessons of World War I, and again of World War II.*

*Grant that it be not treason, grant that it be not greed, it re-
mains that unforgivable folly because of which men and women
of America—who hate war because they love liberty—have thrust
the bodies of sons and brothers, of husbands and fathers, twice in
one generation before the war machine conceived by German
science, in the hands of Farben outlaws, while Democracy's leaders sat shamelessly silent and now cry out "We did not know."
I say that these leaders did know. I say that the facts assembled
in this story should prove to all that those things which the German dye trust planned to do, and then did with the assistance of
key men in its framework in the United States, had long been
revealed as in an open book to those in high places who cared to
listen or to examine the record. I say that those facts have been
known from the days of the dying Wilson Administration by lead-*

ers of high and low degree of all three branches of our Federal Government and by leaders in industry, in finance, and in public opinion.

Somehow, the public has been kept in ignorance. A purpose of this book is to rectify that wrong. I say that the immunity which these men of Farben's pattern have enjoyed—and which still endures—shall not prevail unless these facts remain concealed. These facts must be made known now, this pattern must be recognized NOW, if final disaster is to be averted.

To those who may protest that I overdraw my canvas I say that the youth of this generation have had this war to fight because they and many of their elders were not permitted to learn in time the facts told here. Is this to happen again while they—those who have come back—move on from youth and their sons in turn shall have another war to fight because the spawn of I.G. Farben again shall make a mockery of those two keystones of human liberty, free speech and free press?

I say that those two phrases are futile, senseless words so long as they are subject not to statute, but to secret fiat or corrupt subservience. I say here that much of the responsibility for the tragic era of two senseless, wicked wars is upon those who for any reason have refrained from revealing such facts and their meaning to the people of this nation. Perhaps that era came to a close when fortune and enduring faith at the end of a long and dreary path has finally resulted in this publication of the story of that pattern which survives in war and endures in peace.

This is the story of democracy at its worst. The fact of its telling here without restraint of censor, and despite opposition from high places—is democracy at its best.

FINIS

APPENDIX

Those names listed below have been identified from official sources as companies located in the United States which, at some time during the period between the two world wars, had financial relations, patent agreements or other alliances involving direct or indirect ties with I.G. Farben.

Many of those named here are not mentioned elsewhere in the book. The list has been compiled solely to illustrate the width and depth of I.G. Farben's penetration in American industry. Identification here, as was stated at the end of Chapter iv, does not imply impropriety or illegality in relations with I.G. Farben by the company thus named.

In those companies marked with asterisk (*) Farben is reported to have had a controlling financial interest, or relations approximating control. In those marked with dagger (†) Farben is reported to have had a limited or minority financial interest.

Abbott Laboratories
Acetol Products Co.
* Advance Solvents & Chemical Corp.
* Agfa Ansco Corp.
* Agfa Photo Products Co.
* Agfa Raw Film Co.
* Alba Pharmaceutical Co.
Allied Chemical & Dye Corp.
Aluminum Company of America
American Active Carbon Co.
American Bemberg Corporation
American Cyanamid Co.
American Enka Corporation
American Glanstoff Corporation

* American I.G. Chemical Corporation
* American Magnesium Corporation
American Potash & Chemical Corporation
American Solvent Recovery Corporation
American Window Glass Company
American Zirconium Company
Anaconda Sales Company
Anglo Chilean Nitrate Corporation (N. Y.)
* Ansco Photo Products, Inc.

* Antidolor Company
Atlantic Refining Co.
Ayerst, McKenna & Harrison (U. S.) Ltd.

Baker & Co.
The Barrett Co.
Barnsdall Corporation
Bayer Company, Inc.
Bayer-Semesan Co.
Bell and Howell Co.
Bernuthe Lambecke Co.
Berst-Forster-Dixfield Co.
* Board of Trade for German American Commerce, Inc.
Bohn Aluminum & Brass Co.
Borden Company
Bradley & Baker
Bristol Myers Co.

Calco Chemical Company
California Alkali Export Association, Inc.
Carbide & Carbon Chemicals Corporation
Carnation Co.
Carter Oil Co.
Casein Company of America
L. D. Caulk Company
* Central Dyestuff & Chemical Co.
Central Scientific Company
* Chemical Marketing Co.
* Chemnyco, Inc.
Chilean Nitrate and Iodine Sales Corporation
Chilean Nitrate Sales Corporation (N. Y.)
Chipman Chemical Engineering Co.
Church & Dwight Co., Inc.
Ciba Company, Inc.

Cincinnati Chemical Works
Cities Service Co.
Climax Molybdenum Co.
Columbia Chemical Co.
Commercial Pigments Co.
* Consolidated Color & Chemical Co.
Continental Oil Company
Cook-Waite Laboratories

R. B. Davis Company
Davis Emergency Equipment Company
Diamond Alkali Company
Diamond Match Company
Dow Chemical Company
Drug, Inc.
Dry Milk Company
duPont Cellophane Company
† E. I. duPont de Nemours Co.

Eastman Kodak Company
Ellis Flotation Corporation
Ellis-Foster Company
Ethyl Gasoline Corporation

Federal Match Co.
Ferrocart Corporation of America
* Fezandie & Sperrle
Firestone Rubber Company
Fitchburg Yarn Company
Fleischmann Company
Ford Motor Co.
Freyn Engineering Company

Gasoline Products Company
Geigy Company, Inc.
* General Aniline & Film Corp.
* General Aniline Works, Inc.
General Chemical Company

General Drug Co.
° General Dyestuff Corporation
General Electric Company
General Mills, Inc.
General Motors Corporation
General Motors Research Cor-
poration
General Tire and Rubber Co.
Glidden Company
Goodyear Tire and Rubber Co.
William Gordon Corporation
Grasselli Chemical Company
° Grasselli Dyestuff Corporation
Greene Cananea Copper Com-
pany
Gulf Oil Corporation of Penn.
Gulf Refining Company
Hercules Powder Co.
Hoffmann-LaRoche, Inc.
Hooker Electrochemical Com-
pany
Household Products, Inc.
° Hutz & Joslin (law firm)
† Hydro Carbon Synthesis Cor-
poration
Hydro Engineering and Chem-
ical Company
Hydro Patents Co.

Imperial Chemical Industries
(N. Y.) Ltd.
Indiana Condensed Milk Com-
pany
Interchemical Company
International Catalytic Oil Proc-
esses Company
International Hydro Patents
Company
International Match Company
International Nickel Company

Interstate Chemical Company
of Rhode Island

° Jasco, Inc.

M. W. Kellogg Company
Kennecott Sales Corporation
Kerr Dental Manufacturing
Company
Koppers Company
Koppers Construction Company
Krebs Pigment and Color Cor-
poration
° Kuttroff Pickhardt and Com-
pany

Lautaro Nitrate Company, Ltd.
Lever Bros.
Life Savers, Inc.
Louis K. Liggett Company
Lion Match Co.
Loose-Wiles Biscuit Company

° Magnesium Development Cor-
poration
° Marion Company
Mathieson Alkali Works (Inc.)
Mead Johnson & Company
Wm. S. Merrell Company
Metal & Thermit Co.
° H. A. Metz Company
° Metz Laboratories
Mid Continent Petroleum Cor-
poration
Molybdenum Corporation of
America
Monsanto Chemical Company

National Aniline & Chemical
Company
National City Company

National Distillers Corporation
National Distillers Products Company
National Lead Company
Nestles Milk Products Company
New Jersey Zinc Company
New York Match Company, Inc.
Niagara Alkali Company
North American Rayon Corporation

Ohio Match Company
Okonite Company
Oldbury Electro-Chemical Company
Owl Drug Co.
° Ozalid Corporation
° Ozaphane Corporation of America

Pacific Alkali Co.
Parke Davis & Company
Penn-Chlor, Inc.
Pennsylvania Salt Manufacturing Company
Pet Milk Company
Phillips Petroleum Company
Pittsburg Plate Glass Company
° Plaskon Company, Inc.
Polymerization Processes Corporation
Proctor and Gamble Company
Pure Oil Company

Remington Arms Company, Inc.
Richfield Oil Company of California
Röhm & Haas Company, Inc.

Sandoz Chemical Works, Inc.
Selden Company

Semet-Solvay Company
Shawinigan Chemicals, Ltd.
Shell Chemical Co.
Shell Development Corporation
Shell Union Oil Company
Sinclair Refining Company
Skelly Oil Company
Socony-Vacuum Oil Company
Solvay Process Company
L. Sonneborn & Sons, Inc.
Southern Alkali Corporation
E. R. Squibb & Sons
Standard Alcohol Company
Standard Brands, Inc.
Standard Catalytic Company
† Standard I. G. Company
† Standard Oil of California
Standard Oil Development Company
† Standard Oil Co. of Indiana
Standard Oil Co. of Louisiana
† Standard Oil Co. (New Jersey)
Standard Oil Co. of New Jersey
Standard Oil Co. of New York
Standard Oil Co. of Ohio
Standard Oil Co. of Texas
Stauffer Chemical Company
† Sterling Products, Inc. (Now Sterling Drug, Inc.)
° Synthetic Nitrogen Corp.
Synthetic Patents Co., Inc.

Texaco Development Corporation
Texas Company
Three-in-One Oil Company
Titan Company, Inc.
Titanium Pigment Company, Inc.
Transamerican Match Company

Uniform Chemical Products, Inc.

Union Oil Company of California

Union Carbide and Carbon Corporation

United Drug Company

United States Alkali Export Association, Inc.

° United States & Transatlantic Service Corporation

United States Rubber Company

Universal Match Corporation

Universal Oil Products Company

Urbain Corporation

Vacuum Oil Company

Vegex, Inc.

Vernon-Benshoff Company

Vernon-Morner Company

Vick Chemical Company

Virginia Chemical Company

Viscose Company

Visking Corporation

Vulcan Match Company

West End Chemical Company

Westvaco Chlorine Products Corporation

West Virginia Match Corporation

° Winthrop Chemical Corporation

Wisconsin Alumni Research Foundation, Inc.

Wyandotte Chemical Company

INDEX

(Names of firms listed in the Appendix which do not appear in the text are not included in the Index.)